STATE AND DIPLOMACY IN EARLY MODERN JAPAN:

Asia in the Development of the
Tokugawa Bakufu

Studies of the East Asian Institute,
Columbia University

The East Asian Institute is Columbia University's
center for research, education, and publication on
modern East Asia. The Studies of the East Asian Institute were inaugurated in 1961 to bring to a wider
public the results of significant new research on
China, Japan, and Korea.

RONALD P. TOBY

State and Diplomacy in Early Modern Japan

Asia in the Development of the Tokugawa Bakufu

STANFORD UNIVERSITY PRESS
STANFORD, CALIFORNIA

© 1984, Preface © 1991 by the Board of Trustees of the
Leland Stanford Junior University
Stanford University Press
Stanford, California
Original edition published by Princeton University Press in 1984
Original printing of Stanford edition 1991

Printed in the United States of America

cloth ISBN 0-8047-1951-9
paper ISBN 0-8047-1952-7
LC 91-65279

Last figure below indicates year of this printing:

00 99 98 97 96 95 94 93 92 91

*For my parents
and in memory of
Herschel Webb*

CONTENTS

ABBREVIATIONS USED IN THE NOTES

CTT	*Chōsen tsūkō taiki.*
CWS	*Chosŏn wangjo sillok.*
GBTS	Kondō Morishige, *Gaiban tsūsho.*
HCO	*Honpō Chōsen ōfukusho.*
KKS	*Kaikō sōsai.*
NKSK	Nakamura Hidetaka, *Nissen kankei shi no kenkyū.*

IN THE last century and a half Japan has metamorphosed, in its own estimation, from the moral superior of a decadent China first to technological follower of a more advanced West, then to leader and liberator of Asia. After a postwar reprise as student of the West, in the late 1980s she found or fancied herself the "Japan as Number 1" envisioned in Ezra Vogel's prescient phrase, one many Japanese were quite happy to adopt. With every change, Japanese discovered or invented a new-found past appropriate to each newly felt present. Yet throughout the century following the Meiji Restoration, Japanese were at pains to discredit the Tokugawa past as the dead-weight tradition that had shackled their energies and condemned them to a backseat position in the political and economic order of the emergent modern world.

For most writing in the past century, the master narrative of the past has been based on an assumption of Western primacy, which, whether modeled in Spencerian, Marxian, or Weberian terms, accepted a post-Darwinian notion of social, economic, and political development. National development was often measured by the yardsticks of industrialism, capitalism, and imperialism, or socialism. Even though these were originally conceived as Western benchmarks, still, each was used to measure Japan.

By these yardsticks, among the tragic errors of the old order, few loomed larger than the decisions the Japanese state seemed to have implemented in the 1630s to cut Japan off from foreign diplomatic, commercial, and even cultural relations with other countries. This so-called "seclusion policy" (*sakoku seisaku*)—which suppressed Christianity and expelled Portuguese traders, confined Dutch traders to virtual imprisonment in Nagasaki, and was said to have prohibited Japanese from all travel abroad—allegedly nipped in the bud a flowering Japanese overseas expansionism that might have rivaled the Dutch, English, or Iberian seaborne empires and created a string of Japanese trading colonies from Nagasaki to Siam. Continued intercourse with the West, moreover, would have meant that Japan maintained complete access to the most advanced scientific, industrial, and strategic developments in Europe, and might even have fostered an enduring Japanese scientific and industrial revolution. Japan, which was by and large the technological peer of Europe in the sixteenth century, would not have "fallen behind" the West in centuries of self-imposed seclusion.

If "seclusion" explained Japan's lag behind the West, it also helped explain Japan's continued position as "follower," technologically and industrially, economically and politically. In the post-restoration era, indeed until the Pacific War, this view also fostered irredentist dreams of "reconquest" of continental territories, such as Korea, held only in mythic memory; it provided a salve for national pride, wounded by a second rank status that could be blamed on the wrongheaded choices of national leaders now long dead.

After the Pacific War, in the 1950s and 1960s, Western historians and other social scientists were interested not so much to explain the lag, but rather to understand how it was that Japan had succeeded in "followership" so thoroughly that she, alone (at the time) among non-Western peoples, had managed to "modernize." What was there in the hothouse, "world-within-walls" atmosphere of Tokugawa Japan that fostered Japan's superior followership? Why did "Confucian" Japan succeed, and maintain national independence, while China and Korea—both "more Confucian" than Japan—lost all or much national sovereignty, and failed to modernize? What lessons could be found in the Japanese case that might be applied in the managed modernization of other, slower followers?

In the longer term, this meant finding in the Tokugawa past—a hermetically sealed, hence entirely indigenous, past—

Japan's secrets of successful followership. In the rationalization of rural social relations, for example, T. C. Smith found the "agrarian origins of modern Japan"; in "education in Tokugawa Japan" R. P. Dore found higher rates of literacy and more widespread mass education than in any other premodern society except, perhaps, a few in the West; in "Tokugawa religion," specifically the heterodox eighteenth- and nineteenth-century Shingaku movement popular among the urban commercial classes, Robert Bellah found an analog to the Protestant ethic that might (implicitly) explain the successful spirit of post-Meiji Japanese capitalism.

But if Japan was a follower in industrialism and modernity, it is a leader in postindustrialism and postmodernity; indeed, some would argue that non-narrative, nonlinear discourses were already evident in Japan as early as the eighteenth century. Certainly since the mid-1970s, with the American defeat in Vietnam and the loss of transatlantic primacy; the surge of Japan into economic and industrial prominence, first in steel and shipbuilding, then autos, then postindustrially in ceramics, biotechnology, computers, and robotics, Japan and the West have *both* come to question the assumption that Japan is follower and the West leader. Japanese industrialists and cabinet ministers have come to mock the West, especially the United States, as declining societies. In increasingly vocal terms, they vaunt Japan as the world's most advanced "information society." And as more foreign leaders in government, industry, and scholarship now parade to Japan, seeking loans, advice, and technology, narratives that explain Japan's outstanding qualities in followership have lost their power to convince. Japan now requires heroic narratives of leadership, primacy, authority, and self-sufficiency.

The study reissued here is similarly part of a larger discourse resituating the Japanese past and rendering it a more credible preamble to the present as currently constructed. It extracts Japan from a discourse of seclusion, marginality, truncated development, and followership, and places it at the center of a narrative of self-determined construction of her own destiny.

When first conceived in the mid to late-1970s, this study rejected as inadequate the Eurocentric assumptions of earlier studies, particularly with regard to the relationship of Japan to a larger regional and global frame, which had minimized the significance of Japan's position in the East Asian region, the better to lament her rejection of a Eurocentric order offered by the early century of European contact, 1540–1640.

The model proposed here, by contrast, is one of active, autonomous Japanese relations with the world abroad, one that places Japan at the *center* of the world as Japanese conceived it, rather than at the margins of a China-centered world or beyond the periphery of a Eurocentric one. This book argues, indeed, that Japan's was not a cowering, passively isolationist stance, as the term *sakoku* implies, but a positive, constructive one, one that sought actively to reconstitute Japanese relations with the international environment in ways that advanced both international and domestic goals. Similarly, the active search for information about the external world, examined here as what might be termed "national security intelligence," is irreconcilable with the vision of an isolated, late-developing, follower Japan. But, like the active state-sponsored program of international commercial and technological intelligence I discussed in subsequent publications (which was tied to the development of eighteenth-century domestic import-substitution industries), the picture presented here resonates profoundly with the information past envisioned by Moriya and is therefore well-suited to the information age present of Japanese imagination.

When first proposed in scholarly presentations in both Japan and North America in the mid-1970s, the notion of a proactive Japan in seventeenth-century regional and international affairs was greeted with some skepticism. The notion that Japan's intent in the seventeenth century was the positive construction of an orderly relationship with the outside world, one that also enhanced domestic sovereignty and security and enabled the state to regulate a desired foreign trade rather than to flee the importunings of foreign traders at the closed doors of a reluctant Japan, challenged too much of the received vision. It could not be linked in a continuous narrative with a closed society, economy, culture, and polity. Nor could it be comfortably linked with visions of the nineteenth century that were essential to both Japanese and Western notions of their respective selves: The parade of eager Europeans, from Laxman and Rezanov, Willem II and Biddle, who all failed in the attempt, to the finally triumphant Perry, envoy of an American Manifest Destiny to span the Pacific, required a Japan that had been closed if the narrative were to cast these Westerners as opening it.

Narratives of the mid-nineteenth century endgame of early modern Japan, predicated on closure and passivity, could not be preceded by a narrative of opening and activity. Nor could *sakoku* and *uchi-soto* (inside-outside) explanations of Japan's ineptitude in dealing with foreigners, foreign relations, and the foreign proceed from such a narrative. For the conclusions offered here to be accepted would require a major reworking of the grand narrative tying present-day Japan to its early modern past. In an age that still saw the Japanese present as one of followership, of marginality vis-à-vis a transatlantic-centered world order, and of a poor and narrow resource-deprived country, a self-image still dominant in Japan in the mid to late 1970s, that narrative gap was difficult to bridge.

But in the post-Vietnam age of relative American decline and Japanese resurgence, both Japanese and the rest of the world have reconstituted their images of each other. As the world discovered the Pacific Rim and as Reaganomics consumed the American surplus and Japan replaced the United States as the world's leading creditor, Japanese and non-Japanese alike began seriously to consider the possibility of a sort of Japanese centrality in world affairs. After the fall of Saigon American power waned while the rising financial and industrial might of Japan came more sharply into focus. It was clear neither to me nor to others at the time, but I now realize that it was this process of re-centering Japan in the grand narrative of post-Vietnam history as much as any analytical acuity, and surely more than any conscious prescience, on my part that led me to propound an early modern narrative in which Japan asserted a centrality for itself in the East Asian world order.

In place of seclusion, I offered a set of "maritime prohibitions" (*kaikin*), attempts to regulate ingress and egress, both by Japanese and by foreigners; in place of isolation, I offered a native assertiveness, deduced from the discourse of Tokugawa Japan itself, that claimed to place Japan at the center of a regional and international world order. However little recognition this notion of Japan as Central Kingdom received from others abroad—very little indeed, unlike Chinese pretensions to being the Central Kingdom—the notion of Japanese centrality was critical to both the establishment and the maintenance of domestic legitimacy, and it was a major theme in the constructions of Japanese identity that would determine both the domestic politics of the Tokugawa downfall and the international politics of Japanese imperialism and expansion.

Japanese scholars had suggested even before the 1970s that the notion of *sakoku* was both anachronistic and fundamentally misleading; that the construction and perpetuation of domestic legitimacy were inextricably linked to the positive structures of Japanese intraregional and international relationships established in the first half of the seventeenth century. Yet these arguments, adumbrated in part by Nishijima Sadao, Tanaka Takeo, and others, never received the attention their originality and importance warranted—largely, I would argue, because they were ahead of their time; because Japan's then–present past still had a future, to which it was the required narrative prelude.

Now, however, the position argued here, of Japanese pretensions to centrality, of autonomously determined structures of intraregional and extraregional relations linked to domestic structures of social and cultural relations, politics, and ideology, and of an information-hungry Japan actively seeking to find and acquire—if not to disseminate—information deemed important to state, society, or economy, has an appeal to a present that seems ready to retrofit itself with a more suitable activist and internationalist past. The notion of a Japan actively constructing itself as the Central Kingdom while promulgating the active set of border regulations referred to above as maritime prohibitions, has recently been elevated by younger Japanese scholars, drawing largely on the work in this volume and that of Tanaka and Nishijima, to the level of a "Japan-centered world order cum maritime prohibitions system" (*kaikin/Nihon-gata ka'i chitsujo*) in one historian's formulation, and this model has acquired sufficient persuasive power that it has itself been attacked by those more comfortable with, or invested in, narratives of closure and falling behind the West.

Added to this debate has been a vigorous contestation of the very nature of Japanese boundaries in the medieval and early modern periods, especially in the work of Kuroda Hideo and Murai Shōsuke. This is particularly welcome, for it will be seen in the following pages that I take the boundaries of Japan in the Edo period as less clearly settled than many scholars have heretofore believed. Kuroda, Murai, and others consider the malleability and permeability of the very notion of boundary in premodern Japanese discourse; their work and my own challenge us once more not to take modern, post-Congress of Vienna (or United Nations) conceptions of boundary or sovereignty as applicable to early modern Japan.

The appearance of a Japanese edition of *State and Diplomacy* (*Kinsei Nihon no kokka keisei to gaikō*, Sōbunsha, 1990) has provoked further debate on this score. After the sort of painstaking reconsideration forced on one by reviewing a translation line by line, I continue to have confidence in the interpretation I propose here; yet I am not entirely comfortable with the transformation of the interpretations advanced here into a rigid model, especially one predicated on a Japan-centered world *order*. For in work I have done since the appearance of the first edition, I have come to distinguish more clearly between an immanent order and the ideological assertion of such an order, which is what characterized the discourse of Tokugawa-period Japan.

I had hoped that it was clear in my presentation that the

order I proposed had only discursive, rather than empirical, reality; that Japanese read their own behavior, and that of others, as representing that ideal order. But the reification of that order that has occurred in some subsequent scholarship has potentially disturbing ideological implications. So, too, does the transformation of gradations of ill-defined, even disputed, sovereignty and territoriality into clear boundaries, and of zones of indefinition, such as Ezo and Ryukyu (today's Hokkaido and Okinawa), into unambiguously Japanese territory. The status of Ryukyu, a vassal of both Japan and China, was so amorphously conceived that an eighteenth-century playwright, Chikamatsu Monzaemon, could wonder, "Where lies that country? Is it China's territory, or Japan's?" That question was not settled until 1879, and had to be resettled in 1972. And as Gorbachev's April 1991 visit to Tokyo painfully reminded Japanese, Japan's northern boundary is still unsettled.

In the years since *State and Diplomacy* first appeared, it is on these areas of gradation that I have focused my attention, examining representations of the foreign in the popular expressive culture of early modern Japan and the uses of those representations to constitute the identity and the bounds of Japan itself. In these contested representations of a sort of national self and other, however, the clear demarcation of precise boundaries to early modern Japan, either internal or external, seems increasingly problematic. Within, the claims of disdained minorities to descent from ancestor deities from abroad, the presence of large communities of potters descended from Korean captives, and the occasional adoption of Ainu clothing by fisherfolk in northeastern Japan, all subverted any notion of an impermeable barrier excluding the alien from Japan. And without, mythic claims to sovereignty over Korea, as well as pretensions that even China came as tributary to Japan, expanded Japan beyond those clear boundaries one expects of an island country, and authorized dreams of reconquest of "lost" territories abroad.

If those dreams were briefly realized in the prewar Japanese empire, it was but an affirmation of the power of representation ultimately to translate itself into programmatic action. Other dreams, other notions of Japanese selfhood, dominated in the first four postwar decades notions of late development and followership that had held sway in early Meiji as well. It is not my contention that these dreams are mutually exclusive, that one must lead to aggression and expansion, the other to docility and introversion, in an inevitable dialectical process. Rather, they have been symbiotic, sustaining and constraining each other. Yet both the expansive and the reclusive self-images have their bases in readings and rereadings of the relationships Japan crafted with the worlds beyond its shores in earlier times.

One is tempted to suggest a cyclical rhythm in Japanese history, between periods of relative introversion, and those of greater expansiveness—even expansionism—and involvement. Secluded pasts were convincing, even convenient, in a Japan that was catching up, unsure of its place, its role. Japanese may not yet, or ever, speak with a single, certain voice about their roles, but an age whose slogans are *jōhōka, kokusaika,* and *gurobarizēshon* (informationization, internationalization, and globalization), calls forth new visions of the Japanese past.

R.P.T.

Champaign, Illinois
April 1991

FOR MOST of the century and more since the end of the Tokugawa period (1600-1867) scholars and laymen alike have dealt with the history of that era in a curiously compartmentalized fashion. There is the "history of the Tokugawa state," or the "history of the Tokugawa economy," or, again, the "history of the Tokugawa 'seclusion,' " (by which is meant foreign relations). These, alongside histories of Tokugawa culture, society, and the like, have had separate adherents, formed into separate schools, and until quite recently there has been little traffic from one compartment to another.

This compartmentalization has been most thorough in the study of Japan's external relations in the early modern period, and that for clear reasons. During an interlude of national disunity in the sixteenth century, Japan's external relations were in utter disarray, due as much to the absence of any viable central authority in Japan that might bring order to foreign contacts as to the intrusion of the early European colonial powers into the region. The Europeans were ignorant of the traditional norms of international behavior in East Asia, and not particularly interested in abiding by them. These elements combined, in an era of nearly constant domestic warfare and political fluidity, with what appear to have been rapid urbanization, social mobility, and economic change, to stimulate an interlude of ninety years of unprecedented freedom for "private persons" and regional lords to engage in foreign trade and private diplomacy more untrammeled than in any other period of the Japanese past.

Beginning in the fifteen-eighties, however, as Toyotomi Hideyoshi and then Tokugawa Ieyasu began to articulate a new mode of central authority over all of Japan, the emergent state was compelled to bring order not only to the geographical entity called "Japan," but to the media and modes of Japan's relations with the outside world. However, the form which this "order" took was an increasingly more selective, narrower range of channels through which Japan related to the outside world, a narrower range of Japanese persons and institutions which were directly active in external relations, and a narrower range of foreign entities with whom Japan chose to permit relations. In 1575 there were, for all practical purposes, no restrictions whatever upon either entry to or exit from Japan, save the free-market restrictions of expense and technology. By 1640 all but a few Japanese had been prohibited on pain of death from going abroad; Portuguese and Spaniards—indeed all "Christians" (meaning Roman Catholics)—had been denied access to Japan; and incoming European and "Chinese" (a term which to the Japanese of the time might include overseas Chinese from Southeast Asia, Indonesia, and the Philippines) traffic was restricted to the single port of Nagasaki in the northwest corner of Kyushu.

This narrowing of channels also connoted, however, a greater coherence in the foreign relations of the post-1640 period than had been characteristic of relations before the process of national unification began. A new entity had been created in that process, the centralized feudal monarchy of the Tokugawa state, and that new national state, representing "Japan" to the rest of the world, converted the diplomatic chaos of the earlier age into an ordered expression of national power. Once the new state was established, all external contact, whether diplomatic, commercial, or strategic, could be conducted *only* by, or under the authority of, the Tokugawa government at Edo. At Nagasaki, incoming foreigners were under the watchful eye of the shogun's own representatives, the Nagasaki magistrate's office; the dealings of private parties—Japanese merchants—with those foreigners were also conducted under the magistrate's supervision. Those who engaged in outbound foreign relations, the daimyos of Tsushima, Satsuma, and Matsumae, did so at the ways calculated to aid in legitimating the new dynasty and the new political order that they were creating. I had also concluded that the foreign policy strategy of the early Tokugawa shoguns served in later decades and centuries to define the Japanese conception of the structure of international order, and of Japan's relationship to that order.

Economic historians as well were beginning to notice that the scale of Tokugawa foreign trade, even after the "accomplishment of isolation" in 1640, was too large not to be of significance to the Tokugawa economy, and indeed the entire East Asian economy as a whole. As early as 1949 John W. Hall had noted that the early Ch'ing currency was heavily dependent on imports of Japanese copper, and in 1953 Iwao Seiichi published a quantitative analysis of Japanese trade with China in the seventeenth century based on records from the Dutch, Chinese, and Japanese in Nagasaki that showed, for example, that average copper exports in the last quarter of the seventeenth century exceeded five million pounds annually, with a peak export in 1698 of over 13,000,000 pounds!

It remained only for someone to make explicit the links between the scale and content of the trade and the national economy of Japan itself, and this connection was made first from an unexpected quarter. Trade with Korea, though it had always been recognized to exist in the Tokugawa period, had been universally regarded as so small in scale that it was of no significance in the overall trade picture of the seventeenth century. Even Nakamura Hidetaka, the leading student of the history of Japanese-Korean relations, took this view. But in the middle and late 1970s, Tashiro Kazui demonstrated through analysis of the records of Tsushima han, the monopoly trader with Korea, that trade with Korea was a major factor in Japan's overall external trade in the seventeenth century, perhaps surpassing the Nagasaki silk trade in volume in peak years, and further showed that the silver exported to Korea in the late years of the seventeenth century to settle the trade accounts amounted to fully eight percent of the new silver coinage minted in Japan in those years.

Tsushima's trading profits in peak years were sufficient, in fact, to feed the entire population of Osaka, at current rice prices. Professor Tashiro was dealing only with the Korean trade, and yet she showed that that trade was sufficient by itself to be a factor in the economy of Tokugawa Japan as a whole.

More recently, Robert Innes has tied the economic development of western Japan in the post-1640 period more clearly to the growth in foreign trade, which was, after all, concentrated in the western provinces. Innes also suggests that both the mining industry and the silk-growing industry developed in ways that were inextricably connected to the development of foreign trade in the Tokugawa period. Certainly, a large part of the populations of Nagasaki, Tsushima and Kagoshima, Osaka and Kyoto, and several of the coastal towns along the Inland Sea, were dependent for their livelihoods on the foreign trade of Japan. Hayami Akira has found, moreover, that in the eighteenth century it was a rare village within migrant-labor range of Kyoto that had no one from the village off working in the Kyoto silk industry, an industry that relied heavily on imported silk for its raw materials until well into the century. If the fate of the mining industry as well was as intimately tied to foreign trade as logic and Innes' study suggest, then several hundred thousand people in late-seventeenth-century Japan drew their livelihoods in whole or in part from foreign trade. Seen in this light, it is clear that recent scholarship renders unacceptable the isolation of external relations from the mainstream of Tokugawa history.

This study focuses on early Tokugawa Japan's political and strategic relationship to the East Asian region, and attempts to show, through these elements of Japanese external relations, that foreign relations, and indeed, the maintenance of foreign relations, were important to the development of the Tokugawa state and were perceived as important by the leaders of that state well into its second century of existence. In dealing with diplomacy and security I am dealing with two of three interdependent elements of Japan's external relations; a study of the third element—trade—would require a separate book as long as this one, and Tashiro, Innes, and others have already proceeded quite far with studies of Tokugawa trade that complement the present endeavor.

I have pursued this task by starting with an introductory chapter that sets the field of Tokugawa external relations in the context of its own historiographical development, for I am challenging longstanding conceptions about the character of the Tokugawa period, and an understanding of the origin and development of those conceptions is essential background. Since this introductory chapter was written, Leonard Blussé's excellent historiographical essay, "Japanese Historiography and European Sources," has appeared, to which the reader is referred for a fuller treatment. Chapter II is an essentially narrative account of the normalization of Japan's relations with the neighboring countries of East Asia in the wake of the first centrally-directed war of external aggression in Japan's history: the invasions of Korea, 1592-1598. Although the main corpus of this work is more analytical than narrative, this chapter is essential to set the context for what follows. Much of the structure of Japanese relations with not only Korea, but China and other nations as well, was conditioned by the experience of this war. Moreover, it was in the resolution of this diplomatic crisis that Tokugawa Ieyasu emerged as a leader in diplomacy, even before his victory at Sekigahara.

The following three chapters, which constitute the heart of this work, analyze Tokugawa foreign relations up to 1715 in three different, interrelated ways, in each instance tying Tokugawa diplomatic behavior to the structure of politics and polity in the domestic realm as well. Chapter III presents the argument that in the first half-century of Tokugawa rule, the bakufu made conscious use of diplomacy—both of relationships it wished to maintain and strengthen, and those it wished to limit—as a propaganda medium to help to construct a legitimating order for the new shogunal dynasty. The conduct of diplomacy served to elevate the shogun to a new status within the Japanese polity, to locate him within that polity with greater clarity, and to clothe him in an aura of legitimacy more complete and more independent than had been possible for any earlier dynasty of shoguns.

The seventeenth century was also an age of severe civil and international strife in East Asia, an era when Japan felt uniquely vulnerable militarily to the turmoil surrounding her. In Chapter IV I examine the Japanese response to the maelstrom of international and civil war in East Asia into the ninth decade of the seventeenth century, both to understand the Japanese perception of security and the strategic relationship of the archipelagic state to its continental and maritime environment, and to demonstrate, by the shogunate's responses and level of continuing interest, the high degree of interaction that continued to take place between domestic Japan and the international environment.

Finally, the restructuring of the international strategic environment brought about by the final Ch'ing reunification of China in 1683 helped to alter the perception of China, and of the entire structure of international space that had until the eve of the Tokugawa period been defined by reference to China. Therefore, in Chapter V I proceed to an inquiry into the way in which the relationship that the bakufu had forged to the external world—especially, but not exclusively the diplomatic order, but the non–diplomatic order as well—was instrumental in the construction of a new self-referential perception of international order, a fundamentally altered perception that redefined Japan's place in the world, no longer in terms of the Chinese "other," but in terms of the Japanese "self." Tokugawa diplomacy, in tandem with the Confucianization of the Japanese intellectual tradition which occurred in the seventeenth century, created a new ideological conception of "self" and "other" which would help to carry Japan through the Western challenge of the nineteenth century.

ARCHIVES AND SOURCES

A word is in order about sources. Most of the time required to research this study was spent examining manuscript sources in a number of archives scattered in a semicircle from Tokyo to Seoul. Although Western students of Tokugawa period foreign relations have exploited archival materials in the past, these have for the most part been confined to European-language documents in Dutch, Portuguese, Jesuit, or other Western archives. I confess at times to have doubted myself for becoming involved in reading worm-eaten letters from nearly four centuries ago that Japanese laymen assured me, "even we can't read," especially when the corpus of printed and published primary documents is itself quite large. Indeed, at the outset it was my intention to work only from published sources.

However, the process of deciphering manuscript documents, and the sense of intimacy that they gave me with my principal actors, to say nothing of the information gained from the manuscripts that could not be gleaned from the published corpus, significantly advanced my understanding of my subject. And nothing can replace the excitement, after days of sweating, sorting through uncatalogued archives in Seoul, of finding that letter from the shogun's minister in Edo to the daimyo of Tsushima that provided the link of human consciousness and causation joining together events in Edo, in Nagasaki, in Tsushima, Pusan, Seoul, and Fukien, making of these events an integrative process demonstrating the organic connection of "isolated" Japan to the development of the entire East Asian region.

This study has taken more years to complete than I had imagined at the outset, and no small part of that time I have spent learning to read these manuscripts, ferreting them out of attics as well as libraries, and reading them—not always with joy, but usually with the excitement of the gradual mastery of a new skill. Had I foresworn these dusty friends and nemeses, this study would surely have been completed sooner. Just as surely, it would have been less satisfying. Not merely is this so for the uneasy conquest of a new and sometimes difficult technique, nor simply for the information gained and the insights it stimulated. The slow process of learning, finding, and reading these manuscripts forced upon this study a pace more realistic than that usually dictated by the demand to finish rapidly; it allowed materials and ideas to filter through my mind, to percolate, and to brew themselves into an understanding that would not have been possible one, two, or three years ago, and for that I am grateful.

ROMANIZATION, NAMES, AND DATES

A study such as this one, concerned as it is with peoples, events, and documents in several East Asian countries, as well as with the activities of Europeans of several different nationalities active in East Asia, inevitably raises a number of problems in the identification of people and places not native to the Roman alphabet, and in the dating of events and sources using a multiplicity of calendars. I have attempted to be reasonably consistent in the choices I have made and shall attempt here to be reasonably clear about what those choices were.

Romanization: Japanese words, names, and titles are spelled in the modified Hepburn system as employed in *Kenkyusha's New Japanese-English Dictionary*, fourth edition (1974), except that I have eliminated macrons from place names and common terms that appear in standard English dictionaries: "Tokyo," "Osaka," "shogun," etc. Names and terms appearing in quotations from contemporary European sources retain their original spellings.

Korean words are romanized in the McCune-Reischauer system, as presented in "The Romanization of the Korean Language, Based on its Phonetic Structure," by G. M. McCune and E. O. Reischauer, *Trans. Korea Branch, Royal Asiatic Society*, vol. XXXIX (1939), except for "Seoul," which has become standard English usage.

Chinese words and names are romanized according to the modified Wade-Giles system used in *Mathew's Chinese-English Dictionary* (rev. American ed., 1944), except for place names like "Peking" and "Fukien," for which the more widely recognized postal spelling is employed.

Names: Japanese, Korean, Okinawan, and Chinese names uniformly appear in their original order, with the family name preceding the given name. The only exceptions to this practice are in quotations, or in citations of Western-language works where the author's name appears in Western order.

Japanese of the noble and warrior classes used a sometimes confusing portfolio of lineage, family, and personal names, official titles, courtesy titles, and informal names to identify themselves and each other, depending on the situation, or upon the stage of their lives. To avoid a Tolstoian proliferation of names, however, I have chosen clarity over absolute fidelity, and have generally used only one name for any individual. Thus, although Sō Yoshinari, the daimyo of Tsushima from 1615 to 1657, had three other given names besides Yoshinari, and several different titles, signed his diplomatic correspondence with Korea as "Taira no Yoshinari" and his letters to the bakufu's councillors in Edo as "Sō Tsushima no kami" (Governor Sō of Tsushima), he will be uniformly identified as Sō Yoshinari.

Pronunciation of Japanese names is frequently not apparent from the characters with which the name is written, is often idiosyncratic, and may change over time as the person's tastes, or the fashion of the day, change. Sō Yoshinari, for example, could as well be "Yoshishige" if his family genealogy gave us no other clues, just as his father "Yoshitoshi" is erroneously identified in several works as "Yoshitomo." A modern scholar who has written numerous important studies of the history of Japanese-Korean relations indicated in his prewar publications that his name should be read "Nakamura Eikō," but now indicates that he prefers to have his name read "Nakamura Hidetaka."

Whenever possible I have verified pronunciations in standard reference works, genealogies, or phonetic glosses. Where the sources conflict, I have used the source that I judged most authoritative; in the absence of sources I have used my best judgment. This is a problem on which Japanese scholars are frequently of no help. Since they can simply write the Chinese characters for a name in their texts, they need not choose a pronunciation; the Western writer must choose. For a full discussion of the problems involved in reading Japanese names, see Herschel Webb and Marleigh Ryan, *Research in Japanese Sources: A Guide* (Columbia University Press, 1965), ch. 4.

Official titles present another knotty problem. I have sought to avoid overburdening the text with untranslated terms and have been guided in translating by the work of earlier scholars, especially Conrad Totman, *Politics in the Tokugawa Bakufu, 1600-1843* (Harvard University Press, 1967), for Japanese titles, and Edward Willett Wagner, *The Literati Purges: Political Conflict in Early Yi Korea* (Harvard University Press, 1974), for Korean titles.

Dates and calendars: The peoples with whom I am concerned in this study used a half-dozen different calendars and calendrical systems. Japan, Korea, China, and the countries of Southeast Asia all used lunar-solar calendars based on the Chinese calendrical system, but these were frequently at variance with one another: The Japanese and Chinese years corresponding to 1639 both started on 3 February 1639 of the Gregorian calendar, but in Japan this was a leap year, and ended on (N.S.) 21 February 1640, while in China it was an ordinary (i.e., twelve-month) year, ending on 22 January, and 1640 was a leap year. Dutch records were dated in the Gregorian calendar from 1582 onward, as were Portuguese and Spanish records, while the English continued to use the Julian (O.S.) calendar until 1752. The Julian calendar was ten days behind the Gregorian calendar when the latter was proclaimed in 1582, and had fallen eleven days behind by 1700.

Especially in view of the significance borne by choices of calendar for the substance of this study (see Chapter III), I have chosen to convert all dates to a single system, the Gregorian, which favors neither Japan, Korea, nor China, and have given the original dates of events or other records either in parentheses or in the notes, when appropriate. There are two exceptions to this practice. Dating of entries in the diary of Richard Cocks are preserved in their original O.S. dating.

Some events or documents that I have used can be dated only to a lunar month in the Japanese, Korean, or Chinese calendar; these are dated by lunar month and the corresponding Western year, with the native year in parentheses, where I have deemed it necessary: thus, "fourth lunar month of 1629 (Kan'ei 6)." When letters do not specify the day of the month, I have given the date as follows: "Kan'ei 6/4/X." The Japanese, Chinese, and Korean lunar calendars adjust to the solar year by adding an intercalary month once each three years or so, according to standard calendrical formulae. I have indicated these intercalary months by the prefix "i." Thus, Kan'ei 16/ill/26, the 26th day of the intercalary eleventh month of 1639, corresponds to 19 January 1640. An intercalary month *follows* the ordinary month of the same number. In converting dates, I have relied on *Shintei zōho Sansei sōran* (Kamakura: Geirinsha, 1973).

ACKNOWLEDGMENTS

However long or hard I worked on this project, my efforts would have borne little fruit without the inspiration, guidance, and financial support that I have received over many years, and from many sources. While none of them is responsible for this book's shortcomings—for those I take sole responsibility—they have all contributed to whatever success it may achieve. To them I am sincerely grateful.

Financial support for this study has come from the National Defense Foreign Language Fellowship program; the Mrs. Giles Whiting Foundation and the Fulbright Doctoral Fellowship program, which allowed me to spend two and a half years in Japan doing research; the Japan Foundation and the Junior Fellowship program of the East Asian Institute, Columbia University, which supported a year of writing on my return from Japan in 1976-1977. The Center for Japanese Studies at the University of California, Berkeley, provided a grant that made possible a valuable visit there in the spring term of 1980; and the Center for Asian Studies of the University of Illinois released me from teaching duties for that semester, so that I was free to travel to libraries, to do research, and to write without interruption. Grants from the Center for Asian Studies, the Center for International Comparative Studies, and the Research Board at the University of Illinois at Urbana-Champaign made possible a return visit to Japan and Korea in the summer of 1980, when greater experience and training enabled me to find substantial materials in the archives of Tokyo and Izuhara that I could not recognize as valuable with the ill-formed tools that I took there on my first visit to Tsushima in 1974. A later grant from the Research Board paid for typing and word-processor time for the final manuscript, and for cartography and photography for the maps and illustrations.

Portions of Chapter III have appeared elsewhere in earlier versions, in Japanese as "Shoki Tokugawa gaikō ni okeru 'sakoku' no ichizuke," in *Atarashii Edo jidai no shizō o motomete* (Tōyō Keizai Shinpōsha, 1977), and in somewhat less abbreviated form as "Reopening the Question of *Sakoku*: Diplomacy in the Legitimation of the Tokugawa Bakufu," in the *Journal of Japanese Studies*, 3.2 (Summer 1977). The publishers have graciously granted permission to use that material in this book. I am also indebted to several archives, libraries, religious institutions, and private collectors for permission to include photographs of materials in their possession as illustrations and jacket art. I gratefully acknowledge the kindness of the Kōbe Shiritsu Nanban Bijutsukan, now part of the Kōbe Shiritsu Bijutsukan; the Kokuritsu Rekishi Minzoku Hakubutsukan, Sakura City; the Kuksa P'yŏnch'an Wiwŏnhoe (National History Compilation Committee), Seoul; Mita Jōhō Center, Keio University, Tokyo; Rinnōji, Nikko; the Sō Collection, Banshōin, Izuhara, Tsushima; the Spencer Collection, New York Public Library; and the Tōkyō Kankoku Kenkyūin; Tōshōgū, Nikko.

I am especially grateful to the many people in the United States, Japan, and Korea who have given generously of their time, wisdom, and encouragement over the years that I have been engaged in this study. The plan for the project first emerged from work that I did in seminars with Herschel Webb and Gari Ledyard at Columbia University. They both helped to form my understanding of the histories of Japan and Korea, and of the techniques of research and the arcana of language; they also guided the project through its presentation as a doctoral thesis. In Japan in 1974-1976, Professor Kanai Madoka's sponsorship enabled me to work in unaccustomed comfort in an office at the Historiographical Institute, Tokyo University, and to roam freely through the Institute's vast holdings of unpublished archival materials. Across town at Keio University, Professors Hayami Akira and Tashiro Kazui, then a doctoral candidate at Chuo University, arranged access to the Sō Archives in the Keio University Library. Both also gave unstintingly of their time, energy, and ideas, instructing me in the reading of Tokugawa period manuscripts and teaching me the paths through uncharted, sometimes uncatalogued, archives. Their boundless intellectual generosity and their willingness to share hours in discussion helped me immeasurably to test my perceptions and interpretations, and ultimately to refine my argument. I also want to thank Professors Katō Eichi, Tanaka Takeo, Yamamoto Takeo, and Yi Wŏnsik for their many helpful comments and suggestions. In Izuhara, Mr. Tsunoe Atsurō, custodian of the Sō Archives, was generous with access to the wonderful storehouse of materials under his care. Professor Yi Hyŏnjong, now Director of the National History Compilation Committee, graciously arranged access to the Committee's holdings of Sō archival materials.

Several other teachers, colleagues, and friends have read earlier drafts of the book, or of particular chapters, and have made valuable suggestions that have led to many improvements in structure, argument, and style. At Columbia University, Gerald L. Curtis, James W. Morley, and H. Paul Varley; at the University of California, Berkeley, Frederic E. Wakeman, Jr., and at the University of Illinois, Lloyd Eastman, Patricia Ebrey, David Goodman, Frederic Jaher, Thomas

Kreuger, and William Widenor read and commented on all or part of the manuscript, as have Dr. JaHyun Kim Haboush; William Hauser, University of Rochester; and John E. Willis, Jr., University of Southern California. Lynn Struve, of Indiana University, provided valuable advice on the geography of early Ch'ing China. I want especially to thank Mr. Takahashi Toshirō for his kindness and encouragement over many years, and John Pierson and Linda Meyer, who have been constantly supportive, yet consistently valuable critics.

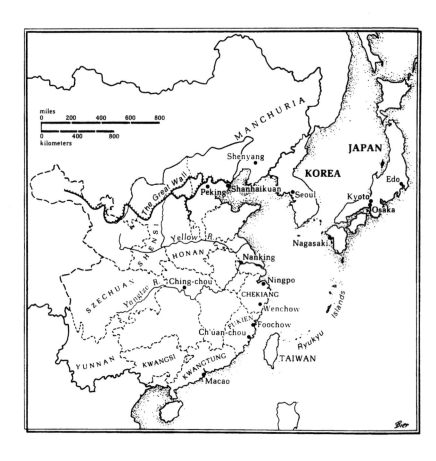

miles
0   200   400   600   800

0   400   800
kilometers

MANCHURIA

JAPAN

KOREA

Shenyang

The Great Wall

Peking Shanhaikuan

Seoul

Edo

Kyoto

Osaka

SHENSI

Yellow R.

HONAN

Nagasaki

Nanking

SZECHUAN

Yangtze R.

Ching-chou

Ningpo

CHEKIANG

Wenchow

FUKIEN

Ch'uan-chou

Foochow

Ryukyu Islands

YUNNAN

KWANGSI

KWANGTUNG

TAIWAN

Macao

Bier

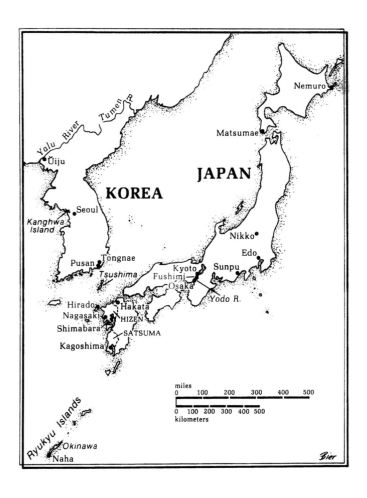

Yalu River

Tumen R.

Üiju

KOREA

JAPAN

Nemuro

Matsumae

Seoul

Kanghwa
Island

Nikko

Edo

Pusan Tongnae

Kyoto

Sunpu

Tsushima

Fushimi

Osaka

Yodo R.

Hirado

Hakata

Nagasaki

HIZEN

Shimabara

SATSUMA

Kagoshima

miles
0   100   200   300   400   500

0   100 200 300 400 500
kilometers

Ryukyu Islands

Okinawa

Naha

Bier

STATE AND DIPLOMACY IN
EARLY MODERN JAPAN:
Asia in the Development of the
Tokugawa Bakufu

CHAPTER ONE

Introduction

IN THE midsummer of 1639 a Portuguese ship left Nagasaki harbor for Macao, ordered out of the country by a government fearful of Christian subversion. With that voyage nearly a century of Japanese involvement with Iberian merchants and missionaries came to a close. After the English abandonment of trade to Japan in 1623, after the end of Spanish relations in 1624, the expulsion of the Portuguese left only the Dutch East India Company to link Japan to Europe. Chinese merchants remained, and an outbound trade with both Korea and the kingdom of Ryukyu was just beginning to blossom into economic significance, but, after a century of untrammeled international activity, order in Japanese international relations was restored only at the price of real restrictions on both the avenues and the agents of external contact.

If Japan's access to foreign trade, foreign ideas, and foreign contact in general had been totally, or even predominantly, dependent on European mediation theretofore, the Portuguese exodus would have left Japan severely isolated, not only from the blessings of early modern Western culture, but also from the benefits and the dangers of participation in the trade, diplomacy, and strategic affairs of the East Asian region and the world. This is all the more an issue of concern since the expulsion of the Portuguese was accompanied by the imposition of severe restrictions on the freedom of Japanese to voyage abroad. After 1635 Japanese voyages beyond Okinawa to the south and Korea to the west were prohibited by shogunal edict. But there were other avenues to trade, and other purposes to diplomacy.

Early Tokugawa period Japanese foreign relations have been

the object of much scholarly study. However, scholars have tended to treat almost exclusively Japanese relations with the approaching Western world, a relationship from which Japan retreated in the 1630s for reasons of state security. Indeed, this retreat has come to dominate popular Western impressions of Japan, to the point that it symbolizes for many the ultimate case of isolationism. In this atmosphere, Tokugawa Japan's relations with Asia, to the extent that they have received attention, have been treated as minor, exceptional, and generally irrelevant to the system as a whole. European relations, or the relative lack of them, have come to occupy a central role in the analysis of the entire Tokugawa period.

The development of Tokugawa foreign relations has almost uniformly been discussed in terms of developments in Japan's European policy, culminating in the expulsion of the Portuguese in 1639, the eradication of Christianity, and the establishment of the Dutch monopoly on European trade with Japan. After 1639, the traditional account tells us, " . . the Japanese Empire [was] shut up . . . and [did] not . . suffer its inhabitants to have any commerce with foreign nations, either at home or abroad."[1] Japan is said to have embarked on a policy of "seclusion" (*sakoku*), or what C. R. Boxer calls "the closed country."[2] This policy is taken to describe one of the defining characteristics of the Tokugawa polity and of Edo period culture as a whole.[3]

---

[1] The quotation is from Engelbert Kaempfer's *The History of Japan together with a Description of the Kingdom of Siam 1690-1692*, tr. J. G. Scheuchzer, 3 vols. (James MacLehose and Sons, 1906), 3:301. This line, the title of an essay in the appendix, is particularly relevant to the discussion of early Tokugawa foreign relations since it is the source of the historiographic perception of Tokugawa Japan as closed.

[2] C. R. Boxer, *The Christian Century in Japan, 1549-1650* (University of California Press, 1951), p. 362.

[3] E.g., Howard Hibbett, *The Floating World in Japanese Fiction* (Charles E. Tuttle Company, 1975), p. 8; Thomas C. Smith, "Pre-Modern Economic Growth: Japan and the West," in *Past and Present*, 60 (1973): 146–150. Cf. George Elison, *Deus Destroyed: The Image of Christianity in Early Modern Japan* (Harvard University Press, 1973), pp. 1-3.

Seclusion, taken as the totality of Tokugawa foreign relations, has been linked causally to the establishment of the Tokugawa state system in two different and complementary ways. Some have regarded it as a necessary precondition to the stability of the *bakuhan* state.[4] Others have taken the bakufu's ability to cut Japan off from the rest of the world as evidence that the Tokugawa system was already established in the 1630s.[5] Closure, that is, has been considered a definitive condition, described as either a necessary precondition to, or an inevitable outgrowth of, the whole polity which it supported.

There is merit in both of these views, but neither is sufficiently specific about the nature of the causality linking premise and result. More significantly, both are flawed by implicity viewing *sakoku* as the full range of Tokugawa foreign relations. The present study will take Tokugawa foreign relations in a broader sense. It emphasizes the examination of Asian relations in order to demonstrate that foreign relations were indeed significant in the early Tokugawa state.

Stated most broadly, it is the contention of this study that foreign relations, especially Asian relations, were intrinsically and organically significant to the nature of the Tokugawa bakufu, and to Tokugawa period history in general: Japan and Asia are inextricably intertwined. It is not possible to remove Asia from Japanese history after 1640 by the simple historiographic expedient of saying that Japan was "closed," for Japan was not closed to Asia, nor even entirely closed to Europe. Similarly, it is impossible to remove Japan from Asian history after 1640 simply because Japanese ceased to voyage to the south seas. Japan remained a significant economic and strategic fact in East Asia, as the petitions of Ming loyalists

---

[4] E.g., Iwao Seiichi, *Shuinsen bōeki shi no kenkyū* (Kōbundō, 1958), pp. 1, 369ff.

[5] E.g., Miki Seiichirō, "Chōsen eki ni okeru kokusai jōken ni tsuite," in *Nagoya Daigaku kenkyū kiyō*, 62 (1974): 15; John W. Hall, "Tokugawa Japan: 1800-1853," in James B. Crowley, ed., *Modern East Asia: Essays in Interpretation* (Harcourt, Brace & World, Inc., 1970), p. 64.

to Japan would show, while Japan remained attuned to developments in Asia.

A "seclusion" analysis ignores the fact that Japan is in Asia, and divorces European relations ("seclusion") from Asian relations and foreign policy in general. The "seclusion" approach sees a southward-expanding Japanese empire meeting the eastward- and westward-expanding European empires in the evening of the age of discovery in the mid–sixteenth century, and watches their intercourse grow until Japan is involved with four of Europe's imperial powers, and with the papacy. All this was aborted in the 1630s by Japan's abnormal rejection of foreign intercourse, with the initiation of policies designed to: (1) exterminate the subversive ideology of Roman Catholicism, (2) monopolize the profits of foreign trade in the hands of the bakufu, and (3) effect a total cessation of Japanese travel outside of Japan, a goal seen as essential to the achievement of goals 1 and 2. The policies of the 1630s, then, are seen as a great discontinuity in the natural course of Japanese history. This analysis has been achieved, however, by the expedient of ignoring Asian relations in order to examine European relations.

If, however, one takes a less parochial view and extends the analysis to include Japan's Asian environment, particularly Korea, Ryukyu, and China, there is less discontinuity in Japanese foreign relations in the 1630s. There is a greater disruption in the 1590s, when Japan invaded Korea, and found herself at war with all of East Asia. But war is at least a "normal" discontinuity, and examination of Japan's Asian relations prior to that war, and of postwar normalization efforts, shows no serious discontinuity. Even when relations are traced further, the same institutions can be seen functioning at least until the 1850s.

In fact, the bakufu did not attempt to monopolize foreign trade, but actually promoted the trading interests of certain daimyos. It was the bakufu that authorized Satsuma to trade with Ryukyu and China, and Tsushima to trade with Korea in the first decade of the seventeenth century, and every succeeding shogun reconfirmed those authorizations. These trading rights, moreover, were pointedly reconfirmed by the bakufu in conjunction with the more famous edicts of 1639 expelling the Portuguese.[6]

The bakufu, in fact, permitted Japanese to travel abroad, and allowed the repatriation of Japanese from abroad. The Tsushima daimyo maintained a permanent trading factory, "Japan House," and a ceramics manufactory in Pusan, Korea, continuously from 1611 into the Meiji period.[7] The population of Japan House at times reached one thousand, and there was constant traffic between Tsushima and Korea in pursuit of trade. Satsuma's political and commercial ties with Ryukyu required Satsuma to maintain a substantial overseas traffic as well.[8] There was constant traffic between Japan and the other countries of Northeast Asia to effect the repatriation of both Japanese and foreign distressed seamen.[9]

The expulsion of the Portuguese from Japan, and the re-

[6] Sō Yoshinari to Tongnae Magistrate, Kan'ei 16/9/X, in *Honpō Chōsen ōfukusho* (hereafter *HCO*), 120 vols., MS copy, coll. Historiographical Institute, Tokyo University, vol. 4. (Letters of this period often did not specify the day of the month. I have indicated this by "X.")

[7] Oda Seigo, *Chōsen tōjishi bunken kō (tsuketari) Fuzan Wakan kō* (Gakugei Shoin, 1936), pp. 117-163. For the apt phrase "Japan House," as a translation of the term *Waegwan* (Korean)/*Wakan* (Japanese), I follow Martina Deuchler, *Confucian Gentlemen and Barbarian Envoys: The Opening of Korea, 1875-1885* (University of Washington Press, 1977), p. 4, and Key-Hiuk Kim, *The Last Phase of the East Asian World Order: Korea, Japan, and the Chinese Empire, 1860-1882* (University of California Press, 1980), p. 19, *et passim.*

[8] See Mitsugu Matsuda, "The Government of the Kingdom of Ryukyu, 1609-1872" (unpublished Ph.D. dissertation, University of Hawaii, 1967), and Mitsugu Sakihara, "The Significance of Ryukyu in Satsuma Finances during the Tokugawa Period" (unpublished Ph.D. dissertation, University of Hawaii, 1971), contain extensive discussions; Robert Sakai, "The Satsuma-Ryukyu Trade and the Tokugawa Seclusion Policy," *Journal of Asian Studies*, 23.3 (May 1964): 391-403, gives a more focused discussion of the Satsuma-Ryukyu trade.

[9] Okada Nobuko, "Kinsei ikoku hyōchakusen ni tsuite—toku ni Tō Chōsen sen no shogū," in *Hōsei shigaku*, 26 (March 1973): 39-49. For a full discussion of Tokugawa practice in aiding distressed seamen, see Kanezashi Shōzō, *Kinsei kainankyūjo seido no kenkyū* (Yoshikawa Kōbunkan, 1968), especially Section 2, Chapter 1, Part 6, "Gaikokusen kyūjo gimu" (The Obligation To Aid Foreign Ships).

sulting limitations on Japanese external relations, especially with the West, were of course significant in the development of Tokugawa history. But if those relationships which Japan rejected were significant by their absence, then it is even more important to examine in some detail the relationships that the bakufu chose to maintain and to foster. Indeed, this study will show that the external relationships which survived 1639, and the form which they took, were important elements in creating and maintaining stability in the Tokugawa bakufu. Korean and Ryukyuan diplomatic missions to the shogun's court, which continued into the nineteenth century, were important to the structure of the bakufu's legitimacy, both in the bakufu's policy calculations and in the response of the political public. These same diplomatic exchanges also served to augment official and unofficial ideology in the creation of a new perception of the organization of international society, and of Japan's place in that society. Shogunal policy further mobilized institutions of diplomatic and strategic intelligence which, if they were not entirely successful in the maelstrom of the mid-nineteenth century, kept the bakufu abreast of strategic developments in the region in the seventeenth century, and were instrumental in shogunal policy responses to piracy on the high seas and to civil war in China through the end of the seventeenth century.

The Tokugawa bakufu pursued a reasoned, comprehensive set of goals in its foreign policy from the early years of the seventeenth century; these goals were applicable to relations with all countries, and were continuous through the 1630s and beyond. The goals, deduced from examination of Asian relations, are fully consistent with what is known of the history of Japan's European relations at the same time. The generalizations about Japan's foreign relations based on "the Christian century" are inadequate to explain Asian policy. In sum, the bakufu never intended entirely to isolate Japan from foreign intercourse.

Any doubt that the bakufu did not intend simply to close the country can be laid to rest by noting the careful investigation the senior council made prior to the 1639 order expelling the Portuguese, and the orders to the daimyos of Satsuma and Tsushima immediately after the expulsion. In the weeks before the order the roju were busy with discussions with the Dutch in order to be sure that expulsion of the Portuguese would not endanger the continuation of the Dutch trade.[10] Immediately after the Portuguese were ordered expelled, the shogun commanded that the Dutch in Hirado be given the best treatment possible,[11] and ordered the daimyo of Tsushima to tell the Korean government that, "because commerce with [the Portuguese] has . . . been banned from this year, we must seek more broadly trade with other foreign nations besides them, and [the shogun] has ordered us to trade with your country [for medicines and textiles] even more than in the past. . . ."[12] This is not a declaration of seclusion, but part of a careful effort to balance the political and security needs of the state against the bakufu's continuing interest in the maintenance and expansion of foreign trade.

The bakufu soon faced another crisis in which security interests and trade interests had to be balanced against each other, for the Ch'ing conquest of China in 1644 was attended by substantial civil war and by the disruption of maritime trade. In the midst of this chaotic situation, while the bakufu dealt with the security implications of the fall of Ming,[13] Edo still found that Japanese interests were best served by the maintenance of trade. On 23 July 1646 the roju ordered Shimazu Mitsuhisa of Satsuma to continue trading via Ryukyu for Chinese silks, despite the uncertanties of war.[14]

[10] Nagazumi Yōko, tr., *Hirado Oranda shōkan no nikki*, 4 vols. (Iwanami Shoten, 1969-1970), 4:208-218; cf. Nagazumi, "Orandajin no hogosha to shite no Inoue Chikugo no kami Masashige," in *Nihon rekishi*, 327 (August 1975): 2.

[11] *Tokugawa jikki*, 10 vols. (Yoshikawa Kōbunkan, 1964), 3:164.

[12] Sō Yoshinari to Tongnae Magistrate, Kan'ei 16/9/X (27 September to 26 October 1639). *HCO*, vol. 4.

[13] The bakufu's strategic response to the Chinese civil war is discussed in detail in Chapter IV.

[14] Abe Shigetsugu, Abe Tadaaki, and Matsudaira Nobutsuna to Shimazu

Nor was even the decision to terminate trade to Southeast Asia in Japanese ships beyond reconsideration. Documents found in a junk shop in 1980 show that sometime in the 1650s the merchant house of Suminokura proposed to Edo the reopening of the licensed trade, suspended in 1635, and, contrary to what one would expect, had the anti-trade attitudes of Edo been so unshakeable as *sakoku* conceptions suggest, the bakufu replied that there was indeed precedent for outgoing trade under the first three shoguns, but that, "Whereas [the trade] has been in suspension for some time, it would be difficult to give a quick response [to your suggestion]. But since [a shogunal official] will be returning to Kyoto shortly, discuss the matter with [him and another shogunal official]," and the bakufu would then reconsider the petition.[15] In any event there is no indication that Edo finally relented and permitted the reopening of the licensed trade, but what is at issue here is an *attitude*, a sense of what was possible, or conceivable in the Edo of the 1650s. As Hayashiya Tatsusaburō remarked in reacting to the discovery of these documents, "We had no idea." The accepted view that the " 'Seclusion Edicts' [of the 1630s] put a stop· to all outward movement has now collapsed. This even raises doubts about the absolute nature of the seclusion system."[16]

Mitsuhisa, Shōhō 3/6/11, in *Kagoshima ken shiryō, Kyūki zatsuroku tsuiroku*, 8 vols. (Kagoshima Ken, 1971-1978), 1:45.

[15] So[ne] Genzaemon Yoshitsugu (cipher), Mura[koshi] Jizaemon Yoshikatsu (cipher), and I[tami] Kurōdo [Katsunaga] (unable to sign due to absence from the Castle) to Hirano Tōjirō, Suminokura Yoichi, and Sueyoshi Hachirōemon, dated the third month, first day (signature MS letter, Suminokura Collection, Kyōto Shishi Hensansho). I am grateful to the Kyōto Shishi Hensansho, and to Professor Hayashiya Tatsusaburō and Mr. Kawashima Masao for supplying me with photographs of this letter and the five other letters found with it. Mr. Kawashima's introduction of the letters, "Sakokugo no shuinsen bōeki-ka," in *Kyōto Shishi Hensansho tsūshin*, 143 (April 1981), identifies the senders of the letter as shogunal Commissioners of Finance, and transcribes this letter and two others into modern print. On internal evidence Kawashima dates this letter between 1652 and 1659; more precise dating is impossible at this time.

[16] Hayashiya's remarks are quoted in *Asahi shinbun*, 23 November 1980.

The bakufu's careful preparation of alternate avenues of trade as part of the groundwork before terminating Portuguese trade with Japan, the promotion of trade in the face of war in East Asia, and the willingness to consider reopening Japanese outbound trade in the 1650s, all suggest that the *limits* of behavior, the *possibilities* of the system, were far more open-ended, more manifold, than what has been visible in the received vision of the Tokugawa past. It is therefore apposite to turn for a moment to the development of that vision before proceeding further.

THE IDEA OF THE TOKUGAWA SECLUSION AND THE TERM *Sakoku*

The idea of the Tokugawa seclusion was not born at the same time as the phenomena which that idea purports to describe. Although the "closing of the country" is usually depicted as a conscious policy upon which the bakufu embarked in the 1630s, it is doubtful whether the bakufu's councillors would have recognized at the time that they had set a course for the closing of the country. The measures, which are said to comprise the seclusion policy—prohibitions on Japanese overseas voyages, restrictions on the export of weapons, bans on Christianity and on Catholic travel to Japan, and the like—were indeed promulgated by the bakufu, but they did not conceive of their actions as shutting Japan off from the rest of the world, nor would they have recognized the term we most commonly see for their policy. That term *sakoku*, a term which has dominated the modern historiography of the Tokugawa period, was not a contemporary seventeenth-century term.[17] Furthermore, that term does not represent the perceptions of Japanese about their own policies and history, but rather the mistranslated perception of a European visitor of the 1690s. The concept was

---

[17] The contemporary terms were *kaikin* ("maritime prohibitions," a Ming term), and *go-kinsei, go-genkin,* or simply *go-kin,* all of which mean "prohibitions."

transported to Japan only much later, in the nineteenth century, and in a distorted form.

The familiar history of early-seventeenth-century European relations with Japan culminated in the issuance of a series of orders from the senior council to the magistrate of Nagasaki in the years 1633 to 1639.[18] These five sets of edicts are collectively referred to by Japanese historians as the "Seclusion Edicts," and one of the edicts is listed under the title *Sakoku rei* in the standard bibliography of Japanese writings of the pre-modern period.[19] While these edicts, did, in fact, expel the Portuguese from their long-standing trading relationship with Japan and effectively limit Japanese contact with Europe to the presence of a few Dutch traders in Nagasaki, there is nothing in them to indicate that they were intended to close Japan to the world, and much to indicate, as will be seen below, that the bakufu anticipated ongoing, if carefully controlled, foreign relations with compatible foreign peoples.[20]

The Term *Sakoku*

The earliest attested appearance of the term *sakoku*, "the closed country," is its use as the title of an essay, a privately circulated polemic, by the Nagasaki Dutch interpreter Shizuki Tadao, in 1801: "Ima no Nihonjin wa zenkoku o tozashite kokiimin o shite kokuchū kokugai ni kagirazu aete iiki no hito to tsūshō sezarashimuru jijitsu ni shoeki naru ni ataureri ya ina ya no ron" was too long for convenient use as a title, so Shizuki

---

[18] Ishii Ryōsuke, ed., *Tokugawa Kinrei kō zenshū*, 6 vols. (Sōbunsha, 1959), 6:375–379.

[19] *Kokusho sōmokuroku*, 8 vols. and index (Iwanami Shoten, 1964–1976), 3:692.

[20] The office logs for the summer of 1639 from the Hirado Dutch trading factory for the weeks just prior to the expulsion of the Portuguese show that before Edo expelled the Portuguese the bakufu carefully assured itself that it would have unhindered access to the Dutch trade. The original records are in Nagazumi Yōko, tr., *Hirado Oranda shōkan no nikki*, 3:331–333, 348; 4:208–218. Cf., Nagazumi, "Orandajin no hogosha," p. 10.

reversed the characters "kuni o tozasu" to form the neologism "sakoku," calling his work "Sakokuron."[21]

This work was not, however, original with Shizuki. He had merely translated into Japanese an appendix from the German physician Engelbert Kaempfer's *The History of Japan*, which he found useful to buttress his opposition to the argument, current in Japan around 1800, that Japan ought to permit trade with the Russians in the north, develop a colonial empire, and the like. Such policies had been advocated over the previous two or three decades by intellectuals like Honda Toshiaki, Hayashi Shihei, and others in a semi-public debate (for matters of state policy were not considered appropriate subjects for public discussion), precipitated by Russian approaches in the north and by the proposals of the late bakufu councillor, Tanuma Okitsugu.[22]

In his translation, Shizuki relied on the Dutch translation of Kaempfer's essay, entitled in English "An Enquiry, whether it be conducive to the good of the Japanese Empire to keep it shut up as it now is, and not to suffer its inhabitants to have any Commerce with foreign nations, either at home or abroad."[23] Shizuki's translation is an accurate rendition of the Dutch, as the Dutch is of the English on which it had been based, but the English version was not faithful to the original German text: "Beweiss, das im Japanischen Reiche aus sehr guten Gründen den Eingebornen der Ausgang, fremden Nationen der Eingang, und alle Gemeinschaft dieses Landes mit übrigen Welt untersagt sey."[24] The phrase "to keep it shut

---

[21] In *Shōnen hitsudoku Nihon bunko*, 12 vols. (Hakubunkan, 1891-1892), vol. 5. Itazawa Takeo was the first to credit Shizuki with the creation of the term *sakoku*, in his *Mukashi no nanyō to Nihon* (Nihon Hōsō Shuppan Kyōkai, 1940), p. 145.

[22] This point is discussed in Inobe Shigeo, *Ishin zenshi no kenkyū* (Chūbunkan Shoten, 1935), pp. 275-295.

[23] Engelbert Kaempfer, *The History of Japan*, 3:301.

[24] Engelbert Kaempfer, *Geschichte und Beschreibung von Japan*, 2 vols. (Stuttgart: F. A. Brockhaus Komm., 1964), 2:385. These errors in translation are discussed in Kobori Keiichi, *Sakoku no shisō* (Chūō Kōron Sha, 1974), pp. 58ff.

up," which is the basis for Shizuki's "kuni o tozasu" and "sakoku," is absent from the original German.

Yet as Shizuki read Kaempfer, and as he understood the history of Tokugawa foreign policy, he had found in Kaempfer a European who approved of the supposed closing of Japan. Kaempfer had served as the physician of the Dutch factory in Nagasaki in 1690-1691, and at that time it may well have appeared that Japanese foreign policy prohibited all European contacts except those with the Dutch, for by the 1690s the Dutch were the only Europeans allowed in Japan. Less than twenty years earlier an English ship, the *Return*, had appeared in Nagasaki harbor and applied for the reopening of the Anglo-Japanese trade, which the English had abandoned as unprofitable fifty years earlier.[25] The *Return*'s application was rejected, which may have seemed to Kaempfer merely a confirmation of the rejection of any non-Dutch European contacts with Japan. Kaempfer was perhaps unaware that the *Return* was sent away primarily because of the fact that the English King, Charles II, had married a Portuguese princess, so that Japan now regarded England as a Catholic collaborator and an enemy. While it is difficult to speculate what the bakufu's reaction would have been had Charles married, say, a Dutch woman, we know that in the 1670s Japan was still receptive to foreign proposals for relations. For, in 1674, the very year after the *Return*, the bakufu responded to the overtures of the King of Siam, and reopened relations that had been interrupted for over forty years.[26]

The seclusion of Japan of which historians write is often coupled with another element said to characterize the foreign policy of Japan laid down in the 1630s. That is, Japan is said to have established two categories of foreign relations in the 1630s, i.e., diplomatic relations (*tsūshin*) and trade relations

[25] The *Return* incident is described briefly in Iwao Seiichi, *Sakoku* (Chūō Kōron Sha, 1966), pp. 431-434. Documents in Hayashi Akira, comp., *Tsūkō ichiran*, 8 vols. (Kokusho Kankōkai, 1913), 6:352-398. (Cited below as *TKIR*.)

[26] Iwao Seiichi, "Reopening of the Diplomatic Relations between Japan and Siam during Tokugawa Days," in *Acta Asiatica*, 4 (1963): 1-31.

without diplomatic relations (*tsūshō*). The former category comprised relations with Korea and the Ryukyuan Kingdom, the latter, relations with Holland and China. The flaw in this attribution is that it, like the term *sakoku*, is a creation of the period following the downfall of Tanuma, which has since been read back and applied to the Tokugawa period as a whole.[27]

The earliest appearance of the classification of Tokugawa foreign relations into the two categories, *tsūshin* and *tsūshō*, was in 1793, when the bakufu rejected the petition of Adam Laxman for the opening of Russo-Japanese trade. In rejecting Laxman's request, Matsudaira Sadanobu ruled that Japan's foreign relations were limited to those countries with which Japan had traditionally maintained either diplomatic or trading relations.[28] Twelve years later, when the bakufu rejected the appeals of Count Rezanov for the opening of Russo-Japanese trade, the implicit information was made explicit: those countries with which Japan had diplomatic relations were limited to Korea and Ryukyu; trading relations were limited to Holland and China.[29] By 1853, when Hayashi Akira compiled the *Tsūkō ichiran*, this reading of history had become entrenched, and was represented as the norm of Tokugawa foreign relations.[30]

Thus by the early 1850s the political responses of the pe-

[27] These categories are still viewed by some Japanese historians as if they were part of the policies of the 1630s, and hence appropriate *a priori* for the analysis of seventeenth-century foreign relations, rather than terms of art derived in the 1790s and early 1800s. See, for example, Arano Yasunori, "Bakuhansei kokka to gaikō—Tsushima han o sozai to shite," in *1978-nendo Rekishigaku Kenkyūkai taikai hōkoku*, p. 95.

[28] *TKIR*, 7:94ff; Matsudaira Sadanobu, *Uge no hitokoko; Shugyōroku* (Iwanami Shoten, 1942), p. 164. See also Herman Ooms, *Charismatic Bureaucrat: A Political Biography of Matsudaira Sadanobu 1758-1829* (University of Chicago Press, 1975), pp. 119-121.

[29] *TKIR*, 7:192-193.

[30] *TKIR*, 1:1. Hayashi prepared this work on shogunal orders to serve as a handbook of the diplomatic precedents of the Tokugawa bakufu prior to 1825. A sequel, *Tsūkō ichiran zokushū*, 5 vols. (Osaka: Seibundō Shuppan, 1967-1973), covers the years from 1825 into the 1850s.

riod from 1790 to 1805, which had become part of the debate over foreign relations, began to enter the historiography of those relations, with the terms *tsūshin* and *tsūshō* entering the vocabulary first. When the term *sakoku* was first used historiography is not clear. Its earliest use in bakufu documents dates from the 1850s as well, but the term was still unusual at that time.

The inspectors for coastal defense use the term as a matter of historical fact in an 1857 memorial to the senior council on the forthcoming visit to Edo of the American consul, Townsend Harris: ". . . In 1636 the third shogun established the honorable prohibitions and thereafter . no barbarians but the Dutch could voyage [to Japan] . and after the Shimabara rebellion . . . he established the law of seclusion (*sakoku no go-hō*). . .".[31] This may be the first use of the term *sakoku* in an official document, and thus the start of a historiographic tradition. At least, four years earlier, during the debate over the response to be made to Perry, Ii Naosuke, the shogun's senior vassal, did not use the term, although the editors of the foreign relations papers of the years from Perry to the Meiji Restoration have labelled Ii's memorial, "We should not keep to the law of *sakoku*."[32]

By the 1850s, then, the idea of *sakoku* as a description of

[31] *Dai Nihon komonjo bakumatsu gaikoku kankei monjo*, 44 vols. (Shiryō Hensanjo, 1910-   ), 16:549-552, dated Ansei 4/6/X (July-August 1857). The Shimabara rebellion of 1637-1638 was a massive uprising of peasants in western Kyushu in which many of the rebels were Japanese Christians. Modern writers have debated the relative importance of Christian protest and excessive exploitation by an ambitious local daimyo in causing the revolt, but the bakufu seems to have regarded it as a Christian uprising, and dealt with it accordingly. On the rebellion in general, see Boxer, *The Christian Century in Japan*, pp. 375-383; Elison, *Deus Destroyed*, pp. 217-222; and Asao Naohiro, *Sakoku* (Shōgakkan, 1975), pp. 279-325, who gives careful consideration to the significance of both the daimyo's harsh governance and Christian fervor. For one view of the relationship between the rebellion and foreign policy, see Nakamura Tadashi, "Shimabara no ran to sakoku," in *Iwanami kōza Nihon rekishi*, 2 (1975): 227-262.

[32] *Dai Nihon Komonjo bakumatsu gaikoku kankei monjo*, 2:255, dated Ka'ei 6/8/2 (4 September 1853).

the foreign policy of the 1630s—as an historical fact—had made its way into the public consciousness of Japan. By 1890, when Shigeno Yasutsugu, Kume Kunitake, and Hoshino Hisashi introduced it in their *Kokushigan* (A *Look at National History*), the term had made its way into the professional historian's vocabulary. Yet Shigeno, Kume, and Hoshino were careful not to use the term to describe the policies and historical developments of the 1630s, where they speak rather of the selective closing of ports to foreign commerce.[33] They speak of *sakoku* only retrospectively; in their discussion of the Meiji Restoration, they speak of the "old law of *sakoku*,"[34] or of the "customs of seclusion (*sakoku*) being deeply ingrained in the hearts of the people,"[35] in contexts where they are clearly quoting or paraphrasing the political arguments of the last years of the Tokugawa bakufu. Shigeno and his co-authors thus introduced the idea of the Tokugawa seclusion in a context roughly appropriate to the era in which the modern term was coined, and although there is but passing reference to foreign affairs after the 1640s, neither is there any suggestion that foreign affairs had lapsed altogether with the expulsion of the Portuguese. Indeed, even their discussion of Engelbert Kaempfer is devoid of any reference to his "Sakoku ron."[36]

A quarter-century later, however, the idea of the "seclusion policy" was so firmly entrenched that Nakamura Kōya titled his study of Tokugawa period foreign relations *On the History of the Closing of the Country by the Tokugawa Bakufu* (*Edo bakufu sakoku shi ron*).[37] Nakamura carefully explains in his introduction that *sakoku* was a slogan of the late Tokugawa period that requires careful definition.[38] He goes on to qualify the concept of the national seclusion by noting that,

---

[33] *Kōhon kokushigan* (Shigakkai, rev. ed., 1908), pp. 436f.

[34] *Ibid.*, p. 451.

[35] *Ibid.*, p. 463.

[36] *Ibid.*, pp. 396f.

[37] Nakamura Kōya, *Edo bakufu sakoku shi ron* (Hōkōsha, 1914).

[38] *Ibid.*, p. 1.

"prior to the so-called seclusion, Japan's foreign relations were chiefly with Korea, Ming, Annam, Siam, and the South Sea Islands [Indonesia and the Philippines] amongst the Oriental [nations], and amongst the Occidentals, the Portuguese, Spanish, Dutch, and English. Even after the so-called seclusion we continued to have intercourse with Korea, China, and the Dutch. Material culture [continued to] arrive; spiritual culture [continued to] arrive; there were political relations and economic relations. The only total seclusion was against Christianity. It did not affect all foreign relations, but merely sealed [Japan] off against some of them. . . In fact, [Japan] certainly did not even come close to being isolated, and this was not the intent of bakufu policy. Therefore it is careless and lax to call five-sixths of the foreign relations of the Edo period the 'age of the closed country.' "[39]

Having thus asserted the thesis of the present study, however, Nakamura then argues that the seclusion policy was an essential precondition for the survival of the Tokugawa polity, and for the formation of Edo culture and society.[40] The remainder of Nakamura's work deals almost exclusively with relations with the European trading powers in the first four decades of the seventeenth century, culminating in the "final seclusion edict of 1639" and in the "policy of seclusion."[41]

In sum, then, students of Edo period foreign relations have taken the expulsion of the Portuguese, and the generally defensive external posture of the Tokugawa bakufu, as license virtually to ignore foreign relations after 1640, relegating them to the realm of the exceptional or the curious, with no sys-

[39] *Ibid.*, pp. 5f.
[40] *Ibid.*, pp. 6-14.
[41] *Ibid.*, pp. 290-310. The exception to Nakamura's concentration on European relations is a brief look at the request of Cheng Chih-lung for Japanese aid in the effort to restore the Ming dynasty, pp. 358-365. Nakamura argues that the bakufu's rejection of Cheng's request was due to the strength of *sakoku*. Not only does Nakamura thus undermine his own caveats about the limited intent of the restrictions on foreign relations. I believe he is also wrong about the subtance of the particular issue, and that other factors determined the decision. See below, Chapter IV.

temic significance for Edo period history as a whole. Even students of Japanese-Korean relations have fallen into this trap. Nakamura Hidetaka, the leading authority on pre-modern Japanese-Korean relations, to whom the present study owes a great debt, terminates his study of Edo period Japanese-Korean relations, "Edo jidai no Nissen kankei," in the 1630s, and his "Gaikōshi jō no Tokugawa seiken" (The Tokugawa Regime in Diplomatic History), lapses from the 1640s to the 1840s as if nothing occurred in the intervening two centuries.[42] Yet Nakamura well knows how much passed between, and nestled between those two studies in his collected works are monographic articles on several topics in Japanese-Korean relations from those years, which he does not integrate into the period as a whole.

The impact on Western accounts of Japanese history left by the expulsion of Christianity has been similar. James Murdoch's *A History of Japan During the Century of Foreign Relations, 1542-1651*[43] focusses its attention on foreign affairs almost exclusively on European relations, with scarcely a reference to Asia after the end of the Korean campaigns of the 1590s. Then, having pursued Japan's "foreign intercourse" to the expulsion of the Portuguese, Murdoch in his next volume, which brings Japan down to the end of the Tokugawa period, devotes his long chapter on "foreign relations" almost entirely to the situation of the Dutch trade in Nagasaki, with but passing reference to the Chinese, and that mostly for their impact on the Dutch.[44] He dismisses Korean relations, hidden in a chapter on the politics of the early eighteenth century, as a "tempest in a teacup."[45]

The use of the "Christian century" as a means to approach the foreign relations of early Tokugawa Japan found its best

---

[42] Nakamura Hidetaka, *Nissen kankei shi no kenkyū*, 3 vols. (Yoshikawa Kōbunkan, 1965-1969), 3:245-336, 465-563. (Cited below as *NKSK*.)

[43] James Murdoch, *A History of Japan*, 3 vols. (Kobe, 1903, 1910; London, 1926), vol. 2.

[44] *Ibid.*, 3:259-312.

[45] *Ibid.*, p. 252.

expositor in C. R. Boxer, who paints a vivid and exciting picture of Japan's relations with Europe in the period 1549-1650.[46] Boxer speaks of those relations coming to an end—save for the Dutch left in Nagasaki—in a chapter on "Sakoku, or the Closed Country,"[47] in which he examines the reasons why the bakufu adopted "the Sakoku, or closed country policy . . . in 1633-1640."[48] George Elison, Boxer's able successor in analyzing Japan's first hundred-year clash with Christianity, crystallizes the unfortunate effects of this concern with Japan's estrangement from an aggressive, threatening West: "The Tokugawa policymakers extended the principle of distrust to a sweeping generality. The causes of Sakoku were complex, but a nurtured stage of alarm at Christianity as the external threat was prime matter in the policy's justification. *And Sakoku became the sum total of the shogunates's approach to foreign affairs*"[49] (emphasis added). Since ". . . this measure could not be effective unless external Christian influences were denied entry. And contacts with the outside world were cut.   Tokugawa Japan is a culture under isolation."[50]

In writing more general treatments of Japanese history, writers have been led by summations such as Elison's, by a belief in the centrality of Western culture and ideas in modern development, and by rhetorical convenience, to dismiss Tokugawa period foreign affairs in a similar vein. Honjo Eijiro, writing of the "Facts and ideas of Japan's overseas development prior to the Meiji Restoration," said that, "Under [the seclusion] policy, the visit of foreigners to this country was prohibited, while Japanese nationals were strictly forbidden to go abroad. Thus, 'seclusion' characterized the country's foreign relationship in the Tokugawa period."[51] Wil-

[46] C. R. Boxer, *The Christian Century in Japan*.

[47] *Ibid.*, pp. 362-387.

[48] *Ibid.*, p. 362.

[49] George Elison, *Deus Destroyed*, p. 3.

[50] *Ibid.*, p. 2.

[51] Eijiro Honjo, *Economic Theory and History of Japan in the Tokugawa Period* (Russell & Russell, Inc., 1965), p. 215.

liam Beasley, summarizing the Tokugawa period, said that "For two hundred years this system of *sakoku*, 'the closed country,' was maintained."[52] Honjo's debt to Kaempfer and Beasley's to Boxer are apparent in their language.

For the concept of "seclusion" or "isolation" to have any utility as an analytical device, after all, it must be defined. We must know, that is, the *limits* of isolation, the *degree* of isolation, and the full range of possibilities it offered to contemporary Japan, and to the rest of the world, in its own time. And, in order to do that, we must, in effect, define also the extent of Japan's openness during the Tokugawa period. For if we are to contend that Tokugawa Japan was not nearly so isolated as it has hitherto been portrayed, we must also acknowledge that it was on the other hand not nearly so open as, for example, contemporary Elizabethan England. The analogy with England is perhaps useful for comparison, for England, too, was confronted by what she perceived as a Catholic menace, and yet dealt with it in a way quite different from the response of the Tokugawa bakufu.

In attempting to define the limits of Tokugawa foreign relations in the areas of politics, ideology, and security, we are in a fashion pursuing the path of several historians of American foreign policy since William Appleman Williams' "The Legend of Isolationism in the 1920s"[53] began to challenge the sufficiency and the utility of "isolationism" as an analytical category in the understanding of the American experience. For even in the United States, as Stephen Peter Rosen has observed, the conflict in American foreign policy has not been "a battle between isolationists and interventionists but a fight between two camps with opposing understandings of the proper relationship between the domestic

[52] W. G. Beasley, *The Modern History of Japan* (Frederick A. Praeger, Inc., Publishers, 1963), p. 2.

[53] William A. Williams, "The Legend of Isolationism in the 1920's," in *Science & Society*, 18 (Winter 1954): 1-20, reprinted in *Issues in American Diplomacy*, ed. Armin Rapoport (The Macmillan Company, 1967), pp. 215-228.

political system and foreign policy."[54] As was the case in the American experience in both the Federal period and the 1920s, so also in Tokugawa Japan before Perry, the issue at hand was not simply the choice between some sort of rampant interventionism, on the one hand, and a total, hermetically sealed isolation, on the other. Rather, both were trying, and succeeded in their ways, to resolve their ambivalence about external relations into workable policies that could be existentially acceptable to their peoples, preserve essential values, and serve the political, ideological, security, and economic needs of their countries, while preserving their domestic institutions and sense of national identity.

It is the contention of this book that Japan remained integrated into the East Asian region to a significant degree throughout the Tokugawa period, even after the "completion of Japan's isolation" in the 1630s. The modes of that integration extended from the political and diplomatic realms to the intellectual, cultural, and scholarly, into areas of national security, defense, and intelligence, and to trade and the economy in the largest sense. Furthermore, these areas of integration, of interconnectedness, were two-way streets: the mutual significance of Japan and Asia for each other is a continuous datum in the history of each; Japan cannot be removed from Asia, nor Asia from Japan, whether by shogunal edict or by historiography.

[54] Stephen Peter Rosen, "Alexander Hamilton and the Domestic Uses of International Law," in *Diplomatic History*, 5.3 (Summer 1981): 183-202.

CHAPTER TWO

Post-Hideyoshi Normalization

WHEN Toyotomi Hideyoshi died in late 1598 and the Five Elders (*go-tairō*) emerged as the caretaker government of Japan, Tokugawa Ieyasu was clearly the most powerful among them,[1] even willing to act alone in foreign affairs.[2] Hideyoshi's seven-year war with Korea and China had left Japan isolated from Asia, alienated from even her near neighbor, the Ruykyuan kingdom, and dependent upon freebooters, independent Japanese traders, and Europeans for the bulk of her external relations. Thus the most urgent diplomatic business at hand was what in modern terms would be called the normalization of relations with East Asia.

The situation called for a variety of approaches. Prewar relations with Korea had involved a long-standing exchange of embassies, trade, and cultural intercourse, occasionally interrupted by Japanese pirate raids in Korea. The embassies had been exchanged between the Ashikaga shoguns in Kyoto and the Yi kings in Seoul, treating each other as peers. Trade had been conducted primarily by daimyos in western Japan, and after 1551, when the Ōuchi clan of western Honshu was destroyed, the Sō family of Tsushima were left as the only Japanese permitted to trade in Korea. As a result there was a

---

[1] Ieyasu's status as *primus inter pares* is evident from Hideyoshi's testament, in *Dai Nihon komonjo iewake dai ni Asano ke monjo* (Tōkyō Teikoku Daigaku, 1906), pp. 135-138.

[2] An example of Ieyasu's acting alone in foreign affairs in 1598 is Tokugawa Ieyasu to Asano Nagamasa, Keichō 3/11/15, in *ibid.*, pp. 119f; cf. Nakamura Kōya, comp., *Tokugawa Ieyasu monjo no kenkyū* (4 vols., Nihon Gakujutsu Shinkōkai, 1958-1961), 2:357, and Tokugawa Ieyasu to Tōdō Takatora, Keichō 3/11/4, in *ibid.*, p. 356.

single, easily identifiable entity through whom negotiations could be conducted, if only Korea could be reconciled.[3]

Restoring relations with Ryukyu ought to have been less difficult, since Ryukyu had not suffered invasion at the hands of Japan, But Ryukyu had developed into a thriving commercial power in the previous centuries, jealously guarding her independence from Japan. Although Ryukyu had sent a congratulatory embassy to Hideyoshi in 1589, it had not submitted to Japan as it had to Ming, and King Shō Nei refused Japanese demands for cooperation in the invasion of Korea.[4] As in the case of Korea, there was an easily identifiable intermediary in Ryukyuan relations, the Shimazu lords of Satsuma, who would be called on again by Ieyasu.

Relations with China were a more complex problem, and were never really restored, as will be seen in Chapter III. Ashikaga Yoshimitsu had opened formal diplomatic relations with the Ming dynasty in 1401, by accepting subordinate status in the Chinese diplomatic order, and had thereby obtained control over the right of Japanese to trade in China. These rights had lapsed in 1547, however, and Japanese had been excluded from China, while Chinese were forbidden by Chinese law from going to Japan. Thus, the Sino-Japanese trade had been taken over by Europeans and Ryukyuans, and by Chinese and Japanese who met in non-Chinese ports. In large part because of the unacceptability of subordinate status in relations with China, the Tokugawa bakufu would never enter into formal relations with China, as it would with other states of East Asia, but would admit Chinese traders to Japan on terms similar to those China imposed on foreign traders coming to Chinese ports.

In the pages that follow, we shall examine briefly the proc-

[3] Nakamura, *NKSK*, 1:141-302, gives a comprehensive review of Japanese-Korean relations in the pre-Hideyoshi period. See also Tanaka Takeo, *Chūsei taigai kankei shi* (Tōkyō Daigaku Shuppankai, 1975), pp. 53-94.

[4] George H. Kerr, *Okinawa, The History of an Island People* (Charles E. Tuttle Company, 1958), pp. 151-156; Shin'yashiki Yukishige, *Shinkō Okinawa issennen shi*, 2 vols. (Yūzankaku, 1961), 2:420.

ess of reestablishing relations with Korea and Ryukyu. The diplomacy between Japan and China in the early years of the Tokugawa period will be treated separately in Chapter III, since the failure of diplomacy between these two is inseparable from the early Tokugawa bakufu's use of diplomacy as a legitimating device.

RESTORING RELATIONS WITH KOREA

Immediately following the death of Hideyoshi on 18 September 1598, Ieyasu and the other elders ordered the withdrawal of Japanese troops from Korea.[5] While the withdrawal was neither so easy nor so glorious as Japanese public-school history textbooks have made it seem, it was indeed effected in a short time, though not without heavy Japanese losses. The Japanese field generals, particularly Konishi Yukinaga, Katō Kiyomasa, and Shimazu Yoshihiro, immediately began to negotiate with their Chinese counterparts to arrange the exit of their troops. They arranged a series of hostage exchanges between Japanese and Ming forces that was intended to guarantee a quick end to the war, and safe exit for the Japanese.[6] The hostages were exchanged, but there was further fierce fighting along the southern coasts of Korea before the Japanese were able to make good their escape.[7]

By 1599, Tsushima records claim, Tokugawa Ieyasu had authorized the daimyo of Tsushima, Sō Yoshitoshi, to negotiate with Korea for the restoration of relations between the two countries, something which Yoshitoshi, Yukinaga, Kiyomasa et al., had thought to be included in their hostage-exchange agreements of the year before.[8] Even before

[5] *Dai Nihon komonjo iewake dai ni Asano ke monjo*, pp. 117-120; Nakamura, *NKSK*, 3:253.

[6] Nakamura, *NKSK*, 3:254.

[7] The final battles of the Japanese invasions of Korea are briefly described in Yi Pyŏngdo et al., *Han'guksa*, 7 vols. (Seoul: Ŭryu Munhwasa, 1959-1965), 3:657-669.

[8] *Chōsen tsūkō taiki*, MS, 10 vols. (Sō Collection, Banshōin, Tsushima), *kan* 4; cf. the recently published edition of *CTT*, edited by Tanaka Takeo

this Yoshitoshi had begun to attempt negotiations with Korea, sending an envoy to Pusan in the last month of 1598, but the envoy never returned to Japan, and the attempt came to naught. That Korea was not yet ready to negotiate with Japan should not be surprising. In fact, the court in Seoul was at that very time discussing reprisal raids against Tsushima.[9] Now authorized by Ieyasu, Yoshitoshi sent another envoy, who brought with him not only letters from Yoshitoshi's chief adviser, Yanagawa Shigenobu, but a number of Koreans who had been taken captive during the war.

Tsushima's interest in the restoration of relations between Japan and Korea was more than accidental. Located in the straits between Hakata and Pusan, and agriculturally poor, Tsushima had for centuries relied upon its position in the Japanese-Korean trade as the foundation of its economy.[10] If relations with Korea, and Tsushima's right to trade in Pusan, were not restored, Tsushima would be unable to survive economically. It was in recognition of this fact, we may suppose, that Ieyasu made grants of rice lands to Tsushima in the years prior to the restoration of trade.[11]

and Tashiro Kazui (Meicho Shuppan, 1978), p. 147. For the reader's convenience citations of the *CTT* MS are hereafter cross-referenced to this edition. This MS of this work, hereafter cited as *CTT*, has notations indicating portions of the work to be deleted from the copy to be presented to the bakufu. Since Tsushima had to keep track of what had actually happened, this version may be taken as a fairly reliable record of what Tsushima knew to have occurred, and of what Tsushima knew to be in bakufu records. Tanaka Takeo, *Chūsei taigai kankei shi*, pp. 249, 261, and Tashiro Kazui, *Kinsei Nitchō tsūkō bōeki shi no kenkyū* (Sōbunsha, 1981), p. 37, question the authenticity of Tsushima's claim here of authorization from Ieyasu.

[9] *Sŏnjong taewang sillok*, 107:20a-21b (hereafter cited as *STS*), in *Chosŏn wangjo sillok*, 48 vols. and index (Seoul: Kuksa P'yŏnch'an Wiwŏnhoe, 1955-1963), 23:547f (hereafter cited as *CWS*).

[10] *NKSK*, 1:311-338, "Tsushima no rekishi teki ichi," and for a vivid reminder of the historical agricultural poverty of Tsushima, see the third-century *Wei chih* account in *San-kuo-chih*, Ch'en Shou, ed., 5 vols. (Peking: Chung-hua Shu-chü, 1971), translated in L. Carrington Goodrich and Ryusaku Tsunoda, *Japan in the Chinese Chronicles* (Pasadena: Perkins Oriental Books, 1968), p. 9.

[11] Nakamura, *NKSK*, 3:257.

It was not until mid-1600, after several attempts by Tsu-shima, that Korea responded to these feelers, setting the re-patriation of Korean prisoners of war still in Japan as a con-dition for further negotiations.[12] Tsushima began repatriating Koreans the next year.[13] Korean reluctance was due not only to continuing resentment of the damage suffered at the hands of the Japanese during seven years of war and partial occu-pation, and the large numbers of Koreans still held in Japan, but also to the presence of Ming officers in Korea, who were directing parts of the Korean government and delaying ne-gotiations. Moreover, Tsushima had at times resorted to threats as a means of "encouraging" Korea to negotiate, a tactic which proved counterproductive. However, the Ko-rean reply arrived on the eve of the decisive battle of Seki-gahara, so that it brought no immediate result, Japanese pol-itics being focussed elsewhere for the moment.

The battle of Sekigahara gave evidence to Korea that Ja-pan's concerns for the near term would be domestic, hence not externally aggressive, and seems to have turned the Ko-rean court in a direction more favorable to negotiations. Ko-reans taken prisoner in the war who had been returned through the good offices of Tsushima, or who had managed to es-cape, provided Seoul with timely information on the domes-tic Japanese situation.[14]

Negotiations continued slowly over the next few years, with Tsushima sending repeated entreaties to Korea, always

[12] *TKIR*, 1:303, citing *CTT, kan* 4, pp. 148-150.

[13] *Ibid.*

[14] *Ibid.* For specifics, see Naitō Shunpo's massive study of war-prisoner repatriation, *Bunroku Keichō no eki ni okeru hiryonin no kenkyū* (Tōkyō Dai-gaku Shuppankai, 1976). See also, for example, *STS*, 136:2b, in *CWS*, 24:228, for the 1601 report of Kyŏngsang Left General Kim T'aehŏ that he had learned from a group of returnees of the death of Konishi Yukinaga "in battle" (he was actually executed). On 26 May 1601 one of these repatriates, a certain Kang Sajun, presented a memorial with a detailed review of polit-ical developments from the death of Hideyoshi through the Battle of Seki-gahara. "Now," he concluded, "all [the Japanese] want is peace." Kang also reported that Tsushima's peace feelers had the backing of Tokugawa Ieyasu. *STS*, 136:21b-23b, at *CWS*, 24:237f.

accompanied by repatriated prisoners. Korean reluctance stemmed from resentment, and from continued uncertainty as to Japanese intentions. But the departure of the Chinese resident general, Wan Shih-te, and his troops in late 1600, which removed direct Chinese interference in negotiations,[15] the increased flow of information from Japan through the repatriates, and the Korean desire to know the enemy—all prevailed to prompt the Korean government to send a reconnaissance mission to Tsushima in early 1602, after repeated urgings by Yi Tŏkhyŏng, who was soon to become Chief State Minister.[16] Later that year, therefore, Chŏn Kyesin and Son Munik went to Tsushima to talk with Sō Yoshitoshi, and attempt to estimate Japanese intentions.[17]

The following year Yoshitoshi located a Korean royal relative, one Kim Kwang, who had been taken captive by Shimazu Yoshihiro in 1597. Yoshitoshi brought Kim to Tsushima in 1603, and seems to have convinced him of the positive need for a restoration of full relations between Korea and Japan, for when Kim returned to Seoul he argued that position to the court.[18] At the same time, Seoul sent Son Munik back to Tsushima once more, and it is possible that it was Son who took Kim home to Korea.[19]

In 1604 Korea responded to further pressure from Tsushima, and to her own expectation of further prisoner repa-

[15] NKSK, 3:257.

[16] NKSK, 3:260. Yi Tŏkhyŏng's memorials are in STS, 144:19b-20a (CWS, 24:330); STS, 145:8a-9b (CWS, 24:335f); etc. Yi was promoted to Chief State Councillor on 26 March 1602 (Sŏnjo 24/12/3), STS, 147:3a, in CWS, 24:350.

[17] TKIR,1:308f.

[18] STS, 171:19b-20a, in CWS, 24:572f; STS, 171:22a-24a, in CWS, 24:575f. See Nakamura's study of Kim Kwang, "Chōsen eki no horyo Kin Kō no sōkan," in NKSK, 2:477-496. Kim's discussions with Keitetsu Genso, a Zen monk advising Sō Yoshitoshi on diplomacy, seem to have been decisive. The conversations are quoted in NKSK, 2:479ff. On Genso, and for a fuller understanding of the role of Zen monks in Japanese diplomacy, see Osa Masanori, "Keitetsu Genso ni tsuite—ichi gaikō sō no shutsuji to hōkei," in Chōsen gakuhō, 29 (1963): 135-147.

[19] TKIR, 1:308-313.

triation, by sending Son to Tsushima once more. This time, however, he went as an aide to the prominent monk-politician Song'un, who had been an active defender of the throne during the war, and who had experience negotiating with Japanese generals like Katō Kiyomasa.[20] The major impetus to the dispatch of so prominent a figure seems to have been that Ming had finally countenanced Korean reconciliation with Japan, after six years of opposition.[21]

Song'un and Son arrived in Tsushima in the late fall of 1604 to investigate conditions in Japan, as a preliminary to deciding what further steps toward peace would be warranted.[22] The envoys did not bring a letter of state from the Korean king, Sŏnjo, to Ieyasu, and thus may not be regarded as an embassy of normalization. In fact, it appears that Seoul did not expect them to go beyond Tsushima, for they carried only a letter from the Third Minister on Rites, Song Imun, to Yoshitoshi. The letter expressed Korean gratitude for the return of the prisoners, especially for the repatriation of Kim Kwang, who was mentioned by name. Song made clear that Korea was acting in consultation with Ming, and offered to reopen both diplomatic relations and trade, "if only Japan would demonstrate her good faith."[23] Thus it is clear that the goal of the mission of Song'un and Son was the normalization of relations between the two countries.

[20] *TKIR*, 1:314-327, has materials on Song'un's mission. On Song'un and Katō Kiyomasa, see Yi Wŏnsik, "Jinran sōshō Shōun Taishi bokuseki no hakken ni yosete—Katō Kiyomasa jin'ei e no ōhen o chūshin ni," in *Kan*, 5.5-6 (1976): 218-234.

[21] *STS*, 174:9b, in *CWS*, 24:611. Letter from the inspector of Liaotung.

[22] *STS*, 175:7b, in *CWS*, 24:617; *TKIR*, 1:314.

[23] *CTT*, *kan* 4. Song Imun to governor of Tsushima, dated fourth lunar month of Wan-li 32 (27 July to 24 August 1604), also reproduced in *TKIR*, 1:315. Tsuji Zennosuke, *Zōtei kaigai kōtsū shiwa* (Naigai Shoseki, 1930), pp. 466f., says that, "In 1604 Koreans accepted the request of the Sō clan of Tsushima and permitted people from Tsushima to go to Pusan to trade," and Song's letter indeed says, "We will temporarily allow [Japanese] to bring goods and trade," but I have seen no evidence of regular trade prior to 1611, other than as an ancillary activity of diplomatic missions. Perhaps the next clause, "if Japan will but demonstrate good faith," governs the offer.

Yoshitoshi immediately sent Yanagawa Shigenobu to Edo, where he arranged, through Ieyasu's foreign affairs advisers, Honda Masanobu and the Zen monk Saishō Shōtai, to have Yoshitoshi bring the Korean emissaries to Kyoto to meet Ieyasu.[24] Yoshitoshi and the Korean envoys arrived in Kyoto on 5 March 1605, and lodged in the Hōkōji temple to await Ieyasu's arrival.[25] They were received in audience with Ieyasu at Fushimi Castle on 22 April 1605, and then discussed Korean-Japanese reconciliation with Shōtai and Masanobu. The Japanese seem to have stressed the fact that Ieyasu took no part in the invasion of Korea, and was therefore not in any sense an enemy of Korea. They therefore asked that the two countries be reconciled.[26] Multiple references in the Japanese sources make it seem probable that Ieyasu was primarily interested in arranging for a Korean embassy to come to Edo in the near future, according to one source, to serve as a mission to congratulate Ieyasu's son Hidetada on his impending succession to the shogunal office.[27] As an incentive, and as the demonstration of good faith which Song Imun had sought, Ieyasu ordered that over 1,300 Koreans who had been captured during the war to be repatriated to Korea with Song'un.[28]

While there is no doubt that Song'un's mission and Ieyasu's response—especially the repatriation of so many prisoners—served to accelerate reconciliation, Seoul was still not satisfied with Japan's attitude. Thus, in 1606 the Korean court set two preconditions for the dispatch of a formal embassy:

[24] *CTT*, kan 4; *TKIR*, 1:317-322; "Hō Chōrō Chōsen monogatari tsuketari Yanagawa shimatsu," in *Shintei zōho shiseki shūran* (41 vols., Kyoto: Rinsen Shoten, 1967), 28:455; *Kansei chōshū shokafu*, 22 vols. plus 4 index vols. (Gunsho Ruijū Kanseikai, 1964-1968), 8:255; Tsuji, *Zōtei kaigai kōtsū shiwa*, pp. 466f.

[25] *Rokuon nichiroku* entry for Keichō 10/2/28 (16 April 1605) in *Dai Nihon Shiryō*, 293 vols. to date, in 12 series (Shiryō Hensanjo, 1901-   ), 12.2:989f.

[26] *Kosa ch'waryo* (Keijō: Keijō Teikoku Daigaku Hōbun Gakubu, 1941), p. 112.

[27] *TKIR*, 1:317-322.

[28] *CTT*, kan 4, pp. 173-174.

an official state letter from Ieyasu as "king of Japan" requesting an embassy, and the extradition of the Japanese soldiers
who had desecrated the tombs of some of the former monarchs of the Yi dynasty.[29] As Japanese scholars have been
quick to note,[30] such a letter would have indicated a Japanese
admission of defeat in the late war, and Ieyasu, as a non-
participant in the war, would of all Japanese be least likely
to write it.

Tsushima was in a most difficult position, for while it was
clearly unlikely that Ieyasu would send the letter that Seoul
was demanding, full resumption of the trade upon which
Tsushima's very survival depended would not come until
there was a reopening of state-to-state diplomatic relations,
which in turn would not come until the two conditions were
met. Thus, while a further Korean exploratory mission was
in Tsushima in late 1606, Yoshitoshi, Yanagawa Shigenobu's
heir Kagenao, and Yoshitoshi's diplomatic adviser Keitetsu
Genso, forged a letter from the "king of Japan" to the king
of Korea, which met the Korean conditions, and also sent to
Korea two young criminals, to be executed as the desecrators
of the royal tombs.[31] It was obvious to the Korean court that
the "criminals" were too young to have been soldiers in the
war, and, likewise, that the letter was a forgery, because it
was totally at variance with normal Japanese protocol, particularly in being signed and sealed as if it came from the
"king of Japan," and in using the Ming calendar. But they
nonetheless decided that the time was ripe for an embassy to
go to Edo and reopen relations with Japan.[32] Miyake Hide-

[29] The tombs were those of Chungjong (r. 1506-1544), and the consort of
King Sŏngjong (r. 1469-1494). NKSK, 3:265.

[30] Tsuji, Zōtei kaigai kōtsū shiwa, p. 467.

[31] NKSK, 3:264f. The forged letter from Ieyasu is recorded in STS, 205:10a
(CWS, 25:284, Sŏnjo 39/11/12). Korea reported the letter to the Ming court,
and it is recorded in the Huang-ming shih-lu, quoted in Kondō Morishige,
comp., Gaiban tsūsho (hereafter GBTS), in Kondō Seisai zenshū, 3 vols. (Kokusho Kankōkai, 1906), vol. 3. Each of Kondō's works in this collection is
separately paginated. GBTS, p. 15.

[32] NKSK, 3:264f; STS, 205:14a-14b (CWS, 25:286). Vice-Ambassador

toshi argues convincingly[33] that Seoul was interested in restoring relations with Japan at this moment because of the increasingly frequent Manchu attacks on her northern border,[34] which made a peaceful southern flank imperative.

Since the Korean embassy was purportedly being sent in response to an invitation from Ieyasu, it was designated a "Response Embassy" (haedapsa), with the additional title of "Repatriation Embassy" (soehwansa). Ambassador Yŏ Ugil and his retinue of five hundred left Seoul in the first lunar month of 1607, and arrived in Edo in the fifth lunar month.[35] It is important to note that the Japanese public, and even the bakufu, was unaware of the Korean court's purposes, or of the official title of the mission—to say nothing of the forged letters to which the embassy was responding. The Kyoto courtier Mibu Takasuke thought the embassy had come "to present greetings to the shogun, and to discuss peace,"[36] which was not entirely untrue, while the abbot of the memorial temple for Ashikaga Yoshimitsu, the Rokuon'in, recorded that the embassy was sent "because the two countries have been reconciled."[37] Others presented the embassy as a mission to congratulate Hidetada on his succession to the office of shogun,[38] which had occurred shortly after Song'un had

---

Kyŏng Sŏn was convinced that the 1606 letter was a forgery when he saw Hidetada's 1607 response to Sŏnjo's letter. Kyŏng Ch'ilsŏng haesarok, in Kaikō sōsai, 4 vols. (Keijo: Chōsen Kosho Kankōkai, 1914), 2:49. Kaikō Sōsai hereafter cited as KKS.

[33] Miyake Hidetoshi, "Tokugawa seiken shokai no Chōsen shinshi," in Chōsen gakuhō, 82 (January 1977): 109.

[34] STS, 185:10a, at CWS, 25:63; STS, 187:3a, at CWS, 25:63; etc.

[35] Kyŏng Sŏn, Kyŏng Ch'ilsŏng haesarok, in KKS, 2:1, 43. The fifth month in Korean reckoning corresponded to the intercalary fourth month of Keichō 12 in the Japanese calendar. Sources disagree on the exact number in the mission. See Miyake, "Tokugawa seiken shokai no Chōsen shinshi," pp. 119f; 130, ɴ. 85.

[36] Takasuke no sukune hinamiki, Keichō 12/4/8, quoted in Dai Nihon shiryō, 12.4:785.

[37] Rokuon nichiroku betsuroku, Keichō 12/4/8, quoted in Dai Nihon shiryō, 12.4:785.

[38] "Hō Chōrō Chōsen monogatari tsuketari Yanagawa shimatsu," in Shintei zōho shiseki shūran, vol. 28, p. 456.

left Kyoto in 1605, or even to pay tribute to Japan,[39] which is certainly not what Seoul had in mind. Ambassador Yŏ Ugil bore with him a letter from Sŏnjo which began: "The King of Korea, Yi Kong, offers a Response to His Majesty, the King of Japan."[40] This forced Tsushima to substitute a forgery which would not imply the existence of a prior letter from Ieyasu to Sŏnjo. Yoshitoshi's agents somehow accomplished this forgery, and thus the letter that Yŏ presented to the bakufu on 20 June 1607 was written as if it were a spontaneous greeting from Sŏnjo to Hidetada.[41] The embassy also delivered letters from Vice-Minister of Rites O Ŏngnyŏng to the bakufu's senior councillors, and letters from Song'un to Shōtai, Hayashi Razan, and senior officials of the bakufu. The embassy's chief interpreter, Pak Taegŭn, delivered these to Honda Masanobu the following day.[42]

There are but scanty records of the issues which Ambassador Yŏ and his party may have discussed with bakufu officials while they were in Edo. Clearly, however, questions of how firmly established the bakufu was, and how secure would be the peace between the two countries, were uppermost in the minds of the Koreans, while prisoner repatriation was another major issue, since this was a specific task assigned to the embassy. On 7 July 1607 the embassy discussed the repatriation issue with Honda Masanobu in Edo, and Honda reported about it to Ieyasu. Since some of the

[39] Keichō nikki, quoted in TKIR, 1:318. The divergent Korean and Japanese views on the nature of the 1607 Korean embassy are exhaustively examined by Miyake, "Tokugawa seiken shokai no Chōsen shinshi," pp. 110-113.

[40] GBTS, pp. 9-15. The compiler of GBTS, Kondō Morishige (1771-1829), who held several research and archival posts under Tokugawa Ienari, including Shogunal Librarian (Shomotsu bugyō), was the first in Japan to discover the forgeries of 1606-1607. The original of this letter is preserved in CTT, kan 5, pp. 173-174, with a note to indicate that it was not to be shown to the bakufu, and the comment, "Yanagawa Kagenao forged both state letters at this time."

[41] The reception at Edo Castle is detailed in Kyŏng Sŏn, Haesarok, in KKS, 2:48-50.

[42] CTT, kan 5, p. 176, and TKIR, 3:87, give the text of O's letter. Kyŏng Sŏn, Haesarok, in KKS, 2:48, reports its delivery.

Koreans taken prisoner during the war had by this time been resident in Japan for as long as fifteen years, it was quite likely that not all would wish to return home, and so Ieyasu ordered only that the daimyo should allow those who wished to return home with the embassy.[43] By the time the embassy left Tsushima it had gathered 1,418 repatriates from all over Japan.[44]

A further issue of importance to the Korean embassy was how Japan fitted into the Ming-centered East Asian diplomatic order. Although the forged letter that Tsushima had sent in 1606 had been dated in the Ming calendar, Hidetada's response to Sŏnjo was not, apparently signifying Japan's rejection of the centrality of China. The draft reply shown to the Koreans in Edo was apparently dated in the Japanese calendar,[45] but the letter which was finally sent used no calendar, simply avoiding the issue.[46] Hidetada's letter also failed to call the shogun "king," as the letter which Tsushima had fabricated had done. Had Hidetada signed himself "king" he would have placed himself, together with the king of Korea, as a subordinate of China.[47] Shōtai, in fact, reportedly urged Hidetada that the mere existence of the Japanese emperor ranked Japan on a par with China, whose status was based on the presence of the "son of heaven."[48] This question was left unsettled in 1607, but was obviously important to both Japan and Korea.

After the Korean embassy left Edo it stopped to pay a courtesy call on Ieyasu, in "retirement" in Sunpu (present-day Shizuoka).[49] By insisting that the embassy present its credentials to, and conduct its formal diplomatic business with,

[43] Miyake, "Tokugawa seiken shokai no Chōsen shinshi," p. 113.

[44] Kyŏng Sŏn, Haesarok, in KKS, 2:65.

[45] Ibid., p. 49.

[46] TKIR, 3:88f.

[47] See below, Chapter III, for a discussion of the significance of these two issues.

[48] Kyŏng Sŏn, Haesarok, in KKS, 2:55.

[49] Ibid., p. 54.

Hidetada in Edo, Ieyasu stressed the institutionalized nature of bakufu power and the hereditary nature of the shogunal office, both of which were of concern to the Korean government.[50]

The 1607 Korean embassy served to restore state-to-state relations between Japan and Korea. Although there was never any clear definition of the occasions on which such embassies would be sent in the future, there were in fact eleven more embassies during the Tokugawa period, the last of them in 1811, and further missions were discussed as late as the 1850s. Below is a tabulation of these embassies, their scale, and their stated purposes. It will be apparent that most of these embassies were sent to congratulate a newly enthroned shogun on his succession, but they served many other purposes as well, from Korea's point of view.[51] And the embassies functioned to Japanese advantage both as legitimating propaganda for the bakufu, and as a channel of political and strategic intelligence on continental affairs, as the political foundation for trade, and as one element in an emerging diplomatic manifestation of Japan's ideal vision of the structure of international order.

It is also important to note that no equivalent embassies were ever sent from Edo to Seoul during the Tokugawa period, except for an intelligence mission dispatched to investigate the first Manchu invasion of Korea, and to offer military assistance.[52] Korean writers argue that this is evidence of the superior status of Korea in the relationship, while Japanese often argue the reverse. It is true that Seoul rejected all Tsushima's requests, other than the mission of 1629, which was clearly on orders from Edo, for permission to send an envoy to Seoul. But it is also true that there was no party in

---

[50] *Ibid.*, p. 49, quotes the Tsushima adviser Kihaku Genpō as stressing this.

[51] Miyake Hidetoshi's works show this divergence clearly, e.g., "Genna Chōsen tsūshinshi raihei riyū e no gimon," in *Kyūshū shigaku*, 52 (1973): 31-42.

[52] This intelligence mission is discussed further in Chapter IV.

KOREAN EMBASSIES TO JAPAN DURING THE TOKUGAWA PERIOD*

Year	Shogun	Korean King	Ambassador	Purpose of Embassy**	Number in Retinue
1607	Hidetada	Sŏnjo	Yŏ Ugil	Reconciliation (J); Prisoner Repatriation and "response" (K)	467
1617	Hidetada	Kwanghaegun	O Yun'gyŏm	Prisoner repatriation (K); Congratulations on the victory at Osaka (J)	428
1624	Iemitsu	Injo	Chŏng Ip	Repatriation (K); Congratulations on succession to office (J)	300
1636	Iemitsu	Injo	Im Kwang	Congratulations on the peace (J)	475
1643	Iemitsu	Injo	Yun Sunji	Congratulations on the birth of a shogunal heir	462
1655	Ietsuna	Hyojong	Cho Hyŏng	Congratulations on succession	488

1682	Tsunayoshi	Sukchong	Yun Chiwan	Congratulations on succession	475
1711	Ienobu	Sukchong	Cho T'aeŏk	Congratulations on succession	500
1719	Yoshimune	Sukchong	Hong Ch'ijung	Congratulations on succession	479
1748	Ieshige	Yŏngjo	Hong Kyehŭi	Congratulations on succession	475
1764	Ieharu	Yŏngjo	Cho Ŏm	Congratulations on succession	472
1811***	Ienari	Sunjo	Kim Igyo	Congratulations on succession	336

* Compiled from NKSK, 3:302f; KKS; TKJR; and Yi Wŏnsik, "Chōsen Shunso shinmi Tsushima no hōnichi ni tsuite—Tsushima ni okeru Nikkan bunka kōryū o chūshin ni," in Chōsen gakuhō, 72 (1974): 4.

** (J) indicates Japanese views; (K), Korean views. See the works of Miyake Hidetoshi listed in infra, n. 75, for exhaustive analyses of the divergent Korean and Japanese purposes in these embassies.

*** The 1811 embassy was delayed for 27 years after the succession of Ienari because the bakufu was unwilling to bear the expense it would require, and because of doubts, first raised by Arai Hakuseki in 1710 (Arai Hakuseki zenshū [6 vols., Kokusho Kankōkai, 1905-1907], 4:628f) about the propriety of receiving Korean embassies in Edo when Japanese who went to Korea did not go beyond Pusan. See Tabohashi Kiyoshi, Kindai Nissen kankei no kenkyū (2 vols., Keijo: Chōsen Sōtokufu, 1940), 2:639-894, for a thorough treatment of this embassy.

Korea analogous to Tsushima to whom diplomatic relations were so crucial. Furthermore, every Korean embassy to Japan in this period was sent in response to a specific Japanese request, rather than on the initiative of Seoul.

By contrast, the Korean government never requested an embassy from the shogun, and the bakufu never sought to send one. Tsushima did send congratulatory missions to Pusan on the occasion of royal births and successions, and condolence missions on the occasion of royal deaths.[53] The Korean government responded with similar expressions of felicity and regret on the passing, birth, or succession of a new daimyo in Tsushima, and Korean envoys who came to or passed through Tsushima in later years are said to have paid their respects before the memorial tablets of the shoguns in the Sō family temple. All of this must simply be regarded as a lower order of diplomatic contact than that between the rulers of the two countries in their respective capitals. If any assessment of the relative status of Japan and Korea is to be drawn from their diplomatic relationship, this must be based upon an analysis of the protocol used in the relationship. Both the format of diplomatic correspondence, and the nature of the protocol employed in diplomatic receptions, reflect an essential parity between Japan and Korea.[54]

The 1607 Korean embassy, by reestablishing state-to-state relations, also provided a framework of authority for Tsushima to negotiate the reopening of officially sanctioned trade between herself and Korea. Korea had permitted petty trading by Tsushima's envoys during the negotiation period preceding 1607, but this had been a courtesy, and had not been on a scale that was economically significant to the hard-pressed island fief.

The following year, 1608, Yanagawa Kagenao claimed to have received authority to send an answering embassy to

---

[53] *HCO, passim, CTT, passim.*
[54] See below, Chapter V, for further discussion.

Seoul,[55] but the sudden death of Sŏnjo on 8 March[56] gave the Korean court an excuse to refuse the envoys permission to leave Pusan and to pay a call in Seoul, even if only for the purpose of offering incense at the late monarch's tomb.[57] Kagenao and his party were restricted to Pusan, where they presented a letter from Ieyasu—not extant, but certainly a forgery. The following year Kagenao returned with another letter, which requested access to Ming so that Japan could pay tribute,[58] in an unfortunate choice of phrase echoing Hideyoshi's request that Korea "lend him a road" so that he could attack Ming.[59]

However, while these envoys were in Pusan, they negotiated the reopening of Tsushima's trade with Korea. These negotiations resulted in the conclusion of a set of articles, the Articles of 1609 (k. *Kiyu yakcho*; j. *Kiyū yakujō*), which set forth the terms under which Tsushima's trade at Pusan would thenceforth be conducted, These articles were clearly regarded as successors to a series of earlier sets of articles established in 1443, 1512, and 1547, which had governed the conduct of the sanctioned Japanese-Korean trade for nearly two centuries.[60] The articles permitted Tsushima to trade at

[55] *TKIR*, 3:403.

[56] *STS*, 221:4a (*CWS*, 25:395; Sŏnjo 41/2/1).

[57] *T'ongmun'gwanji* (Keijo: Chōsen Sōtokufu, 1944; repr. Seoul: Kyŏng'in Munhwasa, 1973), p. 81; *Chŭngjŏng Kyorinji* (Seoul: Tongmunsa, 1974), p. 158.

[58] *Kosa ch'waryo*, p. 120.

[59] *CTT, kan.* 3, p. 127.

[60] The texts of the articles of 1443, 1512, and 1609 are in *T'ongmun'gwanji* pp. 81f, and *Chŭngjŏng Kyorinji*, pp. 171ff. On the 1443 articles, see Seno Bayū, "Seitō kigai jōyaku ni tsuite," in *Shigaku zasshi*, 26.9 (1926): 103-123; *CTT, kan* 1; *Sejong taewang sillok, kwŏn* 100-104, *passim*. On the 1512 articles, *NKSK*, 3:9-12, and Yi Hyŏnjong, *Chosŏn chŏn'gi tae-Il kyosŏp-sa yŏn'gu* (Seoul: Han'guk Yŏn'guwŏn, 1964), pp. 278-293; and on the 1547 articles, *NKSK*, 3:170-183, and Yi Hyŏnjong, *Chosŏn chŏn'gi*, pp. 294-299. On the 1609 articles, *NKSK*, 3:282-300, and Yi Hyŏnjong, "Kiyu choyak sŏngnip simal kwa segyŏn sŏnsu," in *Hangdo Pusan*, 4 (1964): 229-312. Yi Hyŏnjong, "Kiyu choyak naeyong ŭi sasŏ-byŏl ch'ongnam kŏmt'o," in *Taegu sahak*, 7-8 (1973): 281-300, collates all the extant texts of the Articles of 1609,

an outpost to be established in Pusan, Japan House (j. *Wakan*; k. *Waegwan*), analogous to the Dutch trading factory that would later be established in Nagasaki.

The Articles of 1609 established the number of official ships which Tsushima might send each year to engage in the "official trade"(k. *kong muyŏk*; j. *kō bōeki*), representing the "king" of Japan—the shogun, who in fact never sent a trading ship—the daimyo of Tsushima, and various residents of Tsushima who were authorized by Korea (and Tsushima) to engage in trade. Also specified were the sizes of the various types of ships and of their crews, the length of time that they were permitted to remain in Pusan, what provisions they were to receive,[61] and the credentials that they were to carry.

This official trade was in the form of tribute trade between the daimyo of Tsushima and the Korean government, and served to legitimate broader-ranging trade between them. Tsushima also engaged in private or non-official trade, not anticipated in the articles, and exerted every effort to expand that trade. In the late seventeenth century, the profit from the private trade between Tsushima and Pusan produced profits for Tsushima occasionally exceeding 10,000 *kan* of silver, worth as much as the rice-tax revenues of all but the very largest daimyo.[62]

The Articles of 1609 have been frequently misconstrued, as to both their content and their function. George McCune regards them as a "treaty" between two sovereign states, which established "treaty relations," suggesting that the articles involved the bakufu, which they did not, and argues that although "[d]irect relations were also conducted with

---

from *T'ongmun'gwanji*, *kwŏn* 5; *Chŭngjŏng kyorinji*, *kwŏn* 4; *Pyŏllye chibyo*, 2 vols. (Seoul: Tamgudang, 1973), *kwŏn* 5; *Kosa ch'waryo*, *kwŏn* 2; *Chŏptae waein sarye*, *kwŏn* 1, and the documents in the Sō Collection, National History Compilation Committee, Seoul. Yi proposes a variorum text, "Kiyu choyak naeyong," pp. 279ff.

[61] Protocol dictated that Korea feed Japanese in Korea on diplomatic missions, and that Japan provide for Korean diplomats in Japan.

[62] Tashiro Kazui, "Kinsei Tsushima ni okeru Nissen bōeki no ichi kōsatsu," in *Nihon rekishi*, 268 (1970): 88-114.

the Tokugawa government during the seventeenth and eighteenth centuries, these were relatively unimportant."[63] But direct relations between Seoul and Edo were the foundation of the entire Japanese-Korean relationship, and it was only *after* these relations were reestablished in 1607 that there could even be negotiations for the Articles of 1609. Likewise, McCune among others, argues that Korean-Japanese relations were in a tributary pattern, with Korea in a superior position.[64] However, one must distinguish between the relationship of the Korean central government and Tsushima—merely a local baron in Japan, and one whom Korea regarded as vassal[65]—and relations between Seoul and Edo. That Korea was superior to Tsushima in status is beyond dispute. But the relative status of Japan and Korea is very much in dispute, and not at all clear. Many Japanese writers of the Edo period called the Korean embassies "tribute missions" (*raikō; raichō*), or saw Korea as "submitting" to Edo,[66] while

[63] McCune, "Korean Relations with China and Japan, 1800-1864" (unpublished Ph.D. dissertation, University of California, Berkeley, 1941), p. 12. James B. Palais, "Korea on the Eve of the Kanghwa Treaty, 1873-1876" (unpublished Ph.D. dissertation, Harvard University, 1967), p. 537, also argues that the "treaty" set the pattern of Korean-Japanese relations until 1876. Key-Hiuk Kim, *The Last Phase of the East Asian World Order*, pp. 15-16, takes the same position. While exchanges between Seoul and Edo were irregular, they constituted the foundation of the relationship between the two countries.

[64] McCune, "Korean Relations," p.12. Cf. Key-Hiuk Kim, *The Last Phase of the East Asian World Order*, p.23.

[65] *Sŭngjŏngwŏn ilgi*, 115 vols. (Seoul: Kuksa P'yŏnch'an Wiwŏnhoe, 1961-), 25:10ba, and my "Korean-Japanese Diplomacy in 1711: Sukchong's Court and the Shogun's Title," in *Chōsen gakuhō*, 74 (January 1975), pp. 10, 23, n. 40.

[66] *Kokusho sōmokuroku*, 5:694-698, lists over fifty contemporary items relating to Korean embassies in the Edo period which call the embassies either *raichō* or *raikō*, both of which suggest submission or tribute. Two of these, "Chōsen raikō ki," describing the embassy of 1617, and "Chosen shinshi raikō ki," about the 1624 embassy, are by Hayashi Razan, and therefore semi-official in character. In a letter he drafted for Honda Masazumi to send to China in 1611, Razan described Korea as paying tribute to Japan. Honda Masazumi to governor of Fukien, in *Hayashi Razan bunshū* (Osaka: Kōbun-

others clearly saw the loss of Japan's right to visit Seoul as a diminution of Japanese status.[67] While it is more difficult to find Koreans who admired Japan than Japanese who admired Korea, or specific Korean cultural achievements,[68] it is no problem whatsoever to find disparaging remarks by each about the other, and each continually tried to assert superior status vis-à-vis the other in their relations throughout the Edo period. However, the protocol of the relationship between the two capitals was essentially that of a peer relationship.

Some scholars have also asserted that the Articles of 1609 signify the reestablishment of "national intercourse" (*kokkō*),

sha, 1930), p. 130. Local authorities also were under the impression that Korea came to pay court, e.g., *Chōsenjin raichō ni tsuki muraura atemono kakiage chō* (MS, 1710, collection of the author), a register of assessments for support of the 1711 embassy levied on villages along the Tokaido road in the vicinity of Hamamatsu. Cf. Nakai Chikuzan's *Sōbō kigen*, in *Nakai Chikuzan to sōbō kigen* (Taishō Yōkō, 1943), p. 165.

[67] Arai Hakuseki proposed remedying this situation by receiving Korean embassies in Tsushima. *Arai Hakuseki zenshū*, 6 vols. (Kokusho Kankōkai, 1905-1907), 4:682. This proposal was enthusiastically taken up seventy-five years later by Matsudaira Sadanobu, on the advice of Nakai Chikuzan, when Ienari succeeded as shogun in 1787, and actually implemented in 1811. See Tabohashi Kiyoshi, *Kindai Nissen kankei no kenkyū*, 2:639-894.

[68] Yi Ik (1682-1763) was impressed with Japanese attainments in the virtues of loyalty and duty. See his "Ilbon chung'üi" in *Sŏngho saesŏl*, 2 vols. (Seoul: Kyŏng'in Sŏrim, 1967), 1:602, also quoted in Japanese in *NKSK*, 3:314-315. Yi Ik had predicted a revolt of loyal men to overthrow the shogun and to restore the emperor to his rightful place of power, proposing a scenario remarkably like the actual downfall of the bakufu over one hundred years later. His scenario is based on a reading of the Kimongaku scholars Yamazaki Ansai (1618-1682), his disciple Asami Keisai (1652-1711), and Keisai's disciple Wakabayashi Kyōsai (1676-1732), coincidentally demonstrating the availability of Japanese works of scholarship in early-eighteenth-century Korea. Conversely, Yamazaki Ansai was an admirer of the Korean Confucian scholar Yi Hwang (T'oegye, 1501-1570), which he acknowledges in his "Principles of Education," in Ryusaku Tsunoda et al., comp., *Sources of Japanese Tradition* (Columbia University Press, 1958), p. 356. More open admiration is evident in the eagerness with which Hayashi Razan sought the advice of members of the Korean embassy on matters of Neoconfucianism, *ibid.*, pp.350f.

that is, of full diplomatic relations,[69] but since Edo was not a party to the articles, this seems to overstate their significance. Relations were restored between the two states by the embassy of 1607, and the exchange of letters between the king and the shogun. Only predicated on this were the trade articles concluded.

McCune also argues that it was "one of the most important features of the 1609 treaty that it recognized the discontinuance of the reception in Korea of envoys from the Shogun," while "[a]nother feature . . was that no Japanese envoys could travel to the Korean capital but were entertained by [Korea] in [P]usan. Japanese could not pass beyond the confines of the trading post provided for them."[70] McCune has here confused the text of the articles with the commentary on the accumulated precedents and protocol as recorded in the Korean diplomatic and bureaucratic handbooks, T'ongmun'gwanji and Kyorinji. The Articles themselves contain no such provisions.[71] Seoul did in fact refuse Genso and Kagenao permission to go to Seoul in 1609 to offer incense at Sŏnjo's tomb,[72] and this refusal came to have the force of precedent in later years, hence its inclusion under precedents, not as part of the articles.

[69] Tashiro Kazui, "Jūshichi jūhachi seiki Nissen bōeki no suii to Chōsen tokō sen," in Chōsen gakuhō, 79 (April 1976): 14, for example.

[70] McCune, "Korean Relations," pp. 156f.

[71] Compare the texts in Yi Hyŏnjong, "Kiyu choyak ŭi sasŏ-byŏl ch'ongnam kŏmt'o," pp. 291-295, and his variorum text, pp. 297ff, with the texts in T'ongmun'gwanji, pp. 82f and Chŭngjŏng kyorinji, pp. 12-17. In particular, McCune has construed part of the commentary in the latter source, p. 14, "Each [of the above types of Japanese official trade ships] shall constitute a category. They are not permitted to proceed to Seoul, and shall be received in the Pusan factory," to be an integral part of the articles (which he regards as a treaty). My understanding of this passage as part of the commentary and accumulated protocol is consistent with Yi Hyŏnjong's analysis, and with Nakamura Hidetaka, "Kiyū yakujō saikō," in Chōsen gakuhō, 101 (October 1981): 49-50.

[72] Board of Rites notice, dated Wan-li 8/3/1 (25 March 1610), in CTT, kan 5, pp. 180-183.

By 1614 Tokugawa Ieyasu was again seeking an embassy from Korea,[73] but the embassy did not actually appear until 1617, after the fall of Osaka and Ieyasu's death.[74] A further embassy came to Japan in 1624, and embassies continued at irregular intervals into the early nineteenth century. The bakufu labelled most of these missions "congratulatory missions" of one sort or another, usually to congratulate a new shogun on succession to office. As will be shown in detail in Chapter III, these embassies also served an important legitimating function for the bakufu, and, by extension, for each new monarch, while we shall see in Chapter IV that continued relations with Korea provided an important channel of intelligence on contemporary developments in continental Asian politics.

However, Korean purposes in these embassies frequently differed from Japanese goals in the seventeenth century, with greater emphasis on Korean security, prisoner repatriation, and intelligence about the political situation in Japan.[75] But, in another sense, perhaps what is most significant about these embassies is that they provided a context of state-to-state relations that legitimated the conduct of more mundane matters, such as trade, aid to distressed seamen and fishermen, and the like, while further constituting a major element in the set of diplomatic structures which would provide Japan with a world order of her own in which to function and locate herself.

---

[73] *CTT, kan* 5, pp. 199-200.

[74] See below, Chapter III.

[75] Miyake has examined the differing goals of the shogunate and the Korean government in these embassies in a series of articles: "Tokugawa seiken shokai no Chōsen shinshi," "Genna Chōsen shinshi raihei riyū e no gimon," "Kan'ei shokai no Chōsen shinshi," in *Kyūshū shigaku*, 53-54 (1974): 63-78; "Kan'ei jūsannen Chōsen shinshi kō," in *Kitakyūshū Daigaku Bungakubu kiyō*, 6 (1970): 1-20; "Sakoku chokugo no Chōsen tsūshinshi," in *Kitakyūshū Daigaku Bungakubu kiyō*, 51-52 (1971): 23-52; "Rishi Kyōso-chō Nihon tsūshinshi kō," in *Kitakyūshū Daigaku Bungakubu kiyō (B keiretsu)*, 3.1 (1969): 1-32; and "Tenna Chōsen shinshi kō," in *Shigaku ronshū—taigai kankei to seiji bunka*, 2 vols. (Yoshikawa Kōbunkan, 1974), 1:163-192.

RELATIONS WITH THE RYUKYUAN KINGDOM

The post-Hideyoshi "normalization" of relations with the Chūzan kingdom of Ryuku was achieved by means even less subtle than the forgeries that Tsushima had perpetrated in Ieyasu's name in order to reopen relations with Korea. Repeated—if historically unfounded—requests, threats, and commands were made to Naha by the Shimazu family, lords of Satsuma in southwestern Kyushu, who had a tradition of commerce with Ryukyu, in an attempt to obtain from King Shō Nei an embassy of tribute and an expression of submission to Ieyasu. Shō Nei, however, merely ignored these overtures, as he had earlier ignored Hideyoshi's command that Naha aid the Japanese invasions of Korea.[76]

Matters were finally resolved when, in 1609, Shimazu Iehisa received authorization from Ieyasu to force the submission of Ryukyu, even by sending an expeditionary force to the island kingdom. In the early summer of that year a force of about 3,000 troops left Satsuma and invaded Okinawa, quickly bringing the tiny country to its knees. A small occupation force was left in the capital city of Naha, while Shō Nei and his principal councillors were taken as prisoners to Kagoshima, the Shimazus' seat of power. The following year Shimazu was able to fulfill the commands of the bakufu, bringing Shō Nei before Ieyasu and Hidetada in submission.[77]

Shortly after the conquest Ieyasu granted the Shimazu clan the right to "rule" over Ryukyu,[78] and soon thereafter the Shimazus received the right to incorporate the *kokudaka* (pro-

[76] George H. Kerr, *Okinawa*, p. 155; Shin'yashiki Yukishige, *Shinkō Okinawa issennen shi*, 1:420.

[77] Sources on the Satsuma conquest of Ryukyu and the mission of King Shō Nei to Edo are collected in *TKIR*, 1:5-291. Brief accounts in English may be found in Kerr, *Okinawa*, pp. 151-166, and Robert K. Sakai, "The Ryukyu (Liu-ch'iu) Islands as a Fief of Satsuma," in John K. Fairbank, ed., *The Chinese World Order* (Harvard University Press, 1968), pp. 115-118.

[78] Honda Masazumi to Shimazu Iehisa, Keichō 14/7/13, and Honda Masazumi to Shimazu Yoshihisa, same date, in *Dai Nihon komonjo iewake dai jūroku Shimazu ke monjo*, 2 vols. (Tōkyō Teikoku Daigaku, 1942-1966), 2:336f.

ductivity as calculated in terms of rice) of Ryukyu into their own holdings, thus giving the Shimazu clan a higher status among the daimyos of Japan.[79] Some contemporary Japanese even referred to the Shimazu clan as "lords of four provinces," which could only mean that they were including the Ryukyuan kingdom in their calculations.[80]

However, this does not mean that Ryukyu ceased to be a foreign country, or that relations between Naha and Edo ceased thereby to be foreign relations. While the material on the mission of 1610, when Shō Nei was brought before the shogun, is scanty, there is ample material on the later missions of royal Ryukyuan envoys to the bakufu, starting in 1634 and continuing into the *bakumatsu* period. From these documents it is clear that in terms of institutional arrangements and protocol the missions from Naha were consistently treated as diplomatic missions. Both institutionally and in terms of protocol, the situation was analogous to the arrangements made for embassies from Korea, except that Ryukyu was accorded distinctly lower status than was Korea.[81]

A significant criterion for the assertion that Ryukyu was a foreign country for diplomatic purposes is the way in which the Hayashi family, from Hayashi Razan to Hayashi Fukusai, dealt with that country, for the Hayashis were the chief diplomatic protocol officers for the bakufu from the 1630s until the 1850s (with a brief exception in the early eighteenth century). When Hayashi Gahō, Razan's son, edited his father's papers, he established a category for "Letters to Foreign

[79] Discussed in Sakai, "The Ryukyu Islands," pp. 118f.

[80] *Hitomi Chikudō zenshū* (abridged MS copy, 3 vols., collection Historiographical Institute, Tokyo University), v. 3. This tension is well illustrated by Ogyū Sorai's treatment of the Ryukyuan embassy of 1711 in his *Ryūkyū heishi ki* (MS copy, Nanki Bunko, Tokyo University Library), in which he clearly deals with Ryukyu as a foreign country, yet feels constrained to note that, "[Ryukyu] is in fact a vassal-state of Satsuma, and her ambassadors are of the same rank as the house elders [of Satsuma]."

[81] My conclusions about the relative diplomatic status of Korea and Ryukyu in Japanese perception are explained in detail below, Chapter V.

Countries," in which he included Ryukyuan correspondence along with diplomatic correspondence that Razan had drafted to China, Macao, Siam, Korea, and other countries whose status as foreign lands cannot be in doubt.[82] In 1674, when Gahō began to compile the intelligence reports that Edo was receiving from foreign sources, Ryukyu again appears alongside China, Korea, and other foreign countries.[83] In 1670, when the Taiwan-based pirate and Ming loyalist Cheng Ch'eng-kung (Coxinga) attacked Ryukyuan tribute ships voyaging to and from China, the Nagasaki magistrate negotiated with Coxinga for reparations, and when, a few years later, the bakufu cautioned the Dutch against interfering with Ryukyuan shipping, the reason was not that Ryukyu was a part of Japan, but that "Ryukyu is a vassal state of [Japan]."[84] Korea occasionally referred to Tsushima in the same terms,[85] without implying that Tsushima was Korean territory.

That the bakufu regarded Ryukyu as a foreign country is vividly illustrated by Oliver Statler's anecdote that in October 1857, when the bakufu was discussing the proper protocol for the reception of Townsend Harris before the shogun, the two models of diplomatic protocol offered were those of the Korean and Ryukyuan embassies![86] Even in the Tokugawa law codes, the reception of Koreans and the re-

[82] *Hayashi Razan bunshū*, pp. 130-163.

[83] Hayashi Gahō, comp., *Ka'i hentai*, 3 vols. plus suppl. (Tōyō Bunko, 1958-1960), 1:79-91 *et passim*. Hereafter cited as *KH*.

[84] Mitsugu Sakihara, "The Significance of Ryukyu in Satsuma Finances during the Tokugawa Period" (unpublished Ph.D. dissertation, University of Hawaii, 1971), p. 11, and *Tokugawa jikki*, 5:403.

[85] *Sŭngjŏngwŏn ilgi*, 25:10ba, and Ronald P. Toby, "Korean-Japanese Relations in 1711: Sukchong's Court and the Shogun's Title," in *Chōsen gakuhō*, 74 (1975): 10; 23, n. 40.

[86] Oliver Statler, *Shimoda Story* (Random House, 1969), p. 491. Statler's citations for this passage are in error, but the documents in *Dai Nihon komonjo bakumatsu gaikoku kankei monjo*, 16:42 (Shimoda Magistrate to Senior Council, Ansei 4/7/21, and *ibid*., 16:158 (Kaibō gakari, Ōmetsuke, and Ometsuke to Senior Council, Ansei 4/7/16), demonstrate that senior bakufu officials involved in a serious diplomatic crisis were referring to Ryukyuan relations as well as Korean relations for precedents.

Year	Shogun	Ryukyuan King	Ambassador	Purpose of Embassy
1610	Hidetada	Shō Nei	Shō Nei	Submission to Japan (Shō Nei brought as captive)
1634	Iemitsu	Shō Hō	Princes Sashiki, Tamagusuku, Kin	Congratulations on Iemitsu's succession Gratitude for investiture of Shō Hō
1644**	Iemitsu	Shō Ken	Prince Kin	Congratulations on birth of shogunal heir
1644**	Iemitsu	Shō Ken	Prince Kunigami	Gratitude for investiture of Shō Ken
1649	Iemitsu	Shō Shitsu	Prince Gushikawa	Gratitude for investiture of Shō Shitsu
1653	Ietsuna	Shō Shitsu	Prince Kunigami	Congratulations on Ietsuna's succession
1671	Ietsuna	Shō Tei	Prince Kin	Gratitude for investiture of Shō Tei
1682	Tsunayoshi	Shō Tei	Prince Nago	Congratulations on Tsunayoshi's succession
1711**	Ienobu	Shō Eki	Princes Miri, Tomigusuku	Congratulations on Ienobu's succession Gratitude for investiture of Shō Eki
1714	Ietsugu	Shō Kei	Prince Kin	Gratitude for investiture of Shō Kei
1714	Ietsugu	Shō Kei	Prince Yonagusuku	Congratulations on Ietsugu's succession
1718	Yoshimune	Shō Kei	Prince Goeku	Congratulations on Yoshimune's succession
1748	Ieshige	Shō Kei	Prince Gushikawa	Congratulations on Ieshige's succession

Year	Shogun	Ryukyuan King	Ambassador	Purpose of Embassy
1753**	Ieshige	Shō Boku	Prince Nakijin	Gratitude for investiture of Shō Boku
1764	Ieharu	Shō Boku	Prince Yomitanzan	Congratulations on Ieharu's succession
1791**	Ienari	Shō Boku	Prince Ginowan	Congratulations on Ienari's succession***
1797**	Ienari	Shō On	Prince Ōgimi	Gratitude for investiture of Shō On
1806	Ienari	Shō Kō	Prince Yomitanzan	Gratitude for investiture of Shō Kō
1832	Ienari	Shō Iku	Prince Tomigusuku	Gratitude for investiture of Shō Iku
1842	Ieyoshi	Shō Iku	Prince Urasoe	Congratulations on Ieyoshi's succession
1850	Ieyoshi	Shō Tai	Prince Tamakawa	Gratitude for investiture of Shō Tai

* Compiled on basis of *TKIR*, 1:1–250, *passim*; *TKIR zokushū* (5 vols., Osaka: Seibundō Shuppan, 1968–1973), vol. 1, *passim*; Ōshima Nobujirō, "Ryūkyū shisetsu no Edo sanrei," in *Rekishi chiri*, 61.3(1933): 50; Shunzo Sakamaki, *Ryukyu: A Bibliographic Guide to Okinawan Studies* (Honolulu: University of Hawaii Press, 1963), p. 90; *Jinmei Daijiten* (10 vols., Heibonsha, 1953–1955). Ryukyuan name readings follow Sakamaki, ed., *Ryukyuan Names: Monographs on and Lists of Personal and Place Names in the Ryukyus* (Honolulu: East-West Center Press, 1964).

** Diplomatic Reception occurred in the last month of lunar year corresponding to prior Gregorian year.

*** Ōshima mislabels this a gratitude embassy. Cf. *TKIR*, 1:198.

ception of Ryukyuans were treated under the same general
heading as other foreign relations.[87]

Modern scholarship is divided on the question of the status
of Ryukyu. "The status of the Ryukyu kingdom in early
modern times was puzzling not only to Western observers,"
writes Robert Sakai, "but also to Japanese."[88] For even while
the Ryukyuan king paid tribute to Satsuma and to Edo, he
also continued to pay tribute to the Ming and Ch'ing thrones.
He might then be considered as a subvassal in the Tokugawa
polity, or as a foreign prince in dual vassalage. Takeno Yōko
deals with Satsuma's Ryukyu trade as a form of foreign
country.[89] Toguchi Masakiyo, on the other hand, argues that
the inclusion of Ryukyu in the Satsuma *kokudaka* and the
application of that system of land assessment to Ryukyu, the
application of certain aspects of bakufu law to Ryukyu, and
the inclusion of Ryukyu within the supposed "closing of Japan," all require that Ryukyu be included in Japan from the
date of the Satsuma expedition of 1609.[90] Both these positions have become identified also with positions regarding
the proper status of Ryukyu in modern times, so that modern politics have come to complicate the issue.

A more subtle position was offered some fifty years ago
by the Japanese colonial theorist Yamamoto Mieno, who argued that Sastuma had subjected Ryukyu to what he called
a "mistaken colonial policy."[91] Yamamoto thus recognized

---

[87] *Tokugawa kinrei kō zenshū*, 6 vols. (Sōbunsha, 1959), 6:375–439; *Ofure-gaki kanpō shūsei* (Iwanami Shoten, 1934), pp. 1336–1356, etc., regularly make
this grouping.

[88] Robert K. Sakai, "The Ryukyu Islands," pp. 112–115.

[89] Takeno Yōko, "Satsuma han no Ryūkyū bōeki to bōeki shōnin Ishi-moto ke no kankei," in Hidemura Senzō, ed., *Satsuma han no kiso kōzō*
(Ochanomizu Shobō, 1970); and her *Han bōeki shi no kenkyū* (Mineruva Shobō,
1979), chs. 5, 9.

[90] Toguchi Masakiyo, *Kinsei no Ryūkyū* (Hōsei Daigaku Shuppankyoku,
1975), pp. 359–373.

[91] Yamamoto Mieno, "Ayamareru shokumin seisaku no kikeiji—Ryū-kyū," in *Keizaigaku ronsō*, vols. 23 (1926), 24 (1927), 25 (1927), 28 (1928).

the temporal sway of Satsuma while affirming the de jure foreign status of the islands.

If one decides, with Toguchi and his partisans, that Ryukyu has been a part of Japan proper since 1609, then, while eliminating the problem of Japanese-Ryukyuan relations as an issue in Tokugawa diplomatic history, one is suddenly faced with an entirely new set of problems. For then one must analyze Ryukyuan-Chinese relations, and the issue of Ryukyuan submission to China with knowledge and consent of Edo, as aspects of Japanese foreign relations. Instead of the question of Ryukyuan missions to Edo, and their significance as part of Tokugawa foreign policy, one would have to deal with Ryukyuan missions to Peking and royal investiture by the Chinese emperor,[92] the presence in China of Ryukyuan exchange students, and the possession by Ryukyu of ocean-going vessels, in apparent violation of bakufu law. This is not to suggest that by dealing with Ryukyuan missions in Edo as diplomatic missions one has resolved the dilemma, but one of these issues must be faced.

Ryukyu, like Korea, was an intentional, not an accidental, element in the system of Tokugawa foreign relations. Satsuma's colonial exploitation of Ryukyu was, to be sure, different from Tsushima's role in Korea, but in trading privileges granted by the bakufu, and in protocol and intelligence functions in diplomacy, Satsuma's role was analogous to that of Tsushima in Korea, and the authority granted Satsuma by the bakufu was similar. "Through the Ryukyu islanders," as Robert Sakai writes, "the Shimazu daimyo obtained valuable Chinese commodities which were then sold for a profit to other parts of Japan,"[93] exactly as the daimyo of Tsushima did. But it is difficult to agree that "This commercial activity was a breach in the shogun's monopoly of foreign trade,

[92] These missions and Ryukyuan investiture by China are treated in detail in Ch'en Ta-tuan, "Investiture of Liu-Ch'iu Kings in the Ch'ing Period," in Fairbank, *The Chinese World Order*, pp. 135-164.

[93] Robert K. Sakai, "The Satsuma-Ryukyu Trade and the Tokugawa Seclusion Policy," in *Journal of Asian Studies*, 23.3 (1964): 391.

which was supposed to be confined to the single port of Nagasaki."[94] For, as we have seen, the bakufu had clearly authorized foreign trade elsewhere than in Nagasaki, and by agents not under its direct control, when it authorized, later confirmed, and ultimately underwrote with especially minted silver[95] Tsushima's Korean trade. The shogun did not maintain a monopoly on foreign trade, and the Satsuma-Ryukyu trade was not a breach in a seclusion policy, but a *part* of foreign policy.

[94] *Ibid.*

[95] Tashiro Kazui, "Tsushima han's Korean Trade, 1684-1710," in *Acta Asiatica*, 30 (1976): 97.

CHAPTER THREE

The Lens of Recognition: Diplomacy in the Legitimation of the Bakufu

UNDERSTANDING and analysis of the mechanisms and processes of legitimation of the Tokugawa bakufu have been complicated by the ideological and historiographical conceit that political legitimacy resided in the imperial office, and that all other legitimate secular authority derived therefrom. If this conceit has occasionally misled modern scholars in their pursuit of a fully satisfying picture of the development of shogunal legitimacy, it also created sometimes awkward theoretical problems for Tokugawa period scholars trying to fit contemporary Japanese institutions and practices to normative Confucian models of legitimacy imported from China, problems which became critical political issues in the waning years of Tokugawa rule. For the most part, however, they found evidence of the bakufu's legitimacy in its mastery of the traditional indices of temporal power derived from imperial patents to the shogunal office, properly transmitted in the Tokugawa line. They usually buttressed these indices with arguments grounded in Confucian ethical and political theory, applying the moral tests of a recipient of the Mandate of Heaven to the shogun while attempting to keep the ideal position of the imperial office intact.[1] How the Tokugawa bakufu legitimated itself, that is, how it established that it possessed legitimacy, which is " . the foundation of such

[1] Itō Tasaburō, "Edo bakufu no seiritsu to buke seijikan," in *Rekishigaku kenkyū*, 131 (January 1948): 1-11; 132 (February 1948): 29-47, gives a concise discussion.

governmental power as is exercised both with a consciousness on the government's part that it has a right to govern
and with some recognition by the governed of that right,"[2]
is one of the important questions facing modern historians
of the Tokugawa period. Until recently this inquiry was
largely confined to the questions referred to above: how the
bakufu gathered to itself the imperial patents of temporal authority, and how possession of these patents and their attendant powers were attractively clothed in the trappings of
Confucian ideology.[3] Less attention has been accorded the
political actions, both domestic and international, undertaken
by the bakufu in the first decades of its existence to give
more concrete expression to the sense of legitimacy that it
was trying to foster. This is despite the fact that self-legiti-
mation is one of the most important tasks facing a new government, the more so when that government is attempting
to build a new type of political order. In this task new governments may turn to devices of foreign diplomacy as a form
of propaganda for domestic legitimation. Charles P. Korr
has shown how considerations of legitimacy operated to help
to shape the foreign policy of Oliver Cromwell as he attempted to establish an ongoing government in mid-seven-

[2] Dolf Sternberger, "Legitimacy," in *International Encyclopedia of the Social
Sciences* (1968), 9:244.

[3] David Margarey Earl, *Emperor and Nation in Japan, Political Thinkers of
the Tokugawa Period* (University of Washington Press, 1964), pp. 15ff; John
Whitney Hall, *Government and Local Power in Japan, 500-1700, A Study Based
on Bizen Province* (Princeton University Press, 1966), pp. 345-353; Conrad
Totman, *Politics in the Tokugawa Bakufu, 1600-1843* (Harvard University
Press, 1967), pp. 39f; Herschel Webb, *The Japanese Imperial Institution in the
Tokugawa Period* (Columbia University Press, 1968), pp. 168-174. The examination of shogunal legitimation has developed rapidly over the last decade. See especially the essays in *Japan before Tokugawa: Political Consolidation
and Economic Growth, 1500-1650*, ed. John W. Hall et al. (Princeton University Press, 1981), by Asao Naohiro, "Shogun and Tennō," Fujiki Hisashi, "The Political Posture of Oda Nobunaga," John Hall, "Hideyoshi's
Domestic Policies," Katsumata Shizuo, "The Development of Sengoku Law,"
and Sasaki Junnosuke, "The Changing Rationale of Daimyo Control in the
Emergence of the Bakuhan State."

teenth-century England.[4] It is the concern of this chapter to show how the interplay of foreign policy and legitimation of a new regime functioned in Japan in the first half of the seventeenth century.

Political legitimacy rests on a complex foundation consisting of the possession of power, the appearance of orthodoxy in obtaining that power, and the recognition of these two factors by significant elements of political society. Political society consists of both the domestic political constituency—in early-seventeenth-century Japan comprising the imperial court, the upper reaches of *bushi* society, and a very few Buddhist monks, scholars, and merchants—and international society, which had in this case been traditionally centered on the Ming tribute system.

In 1600 Tokugawa Ieyasu found himself without recognized legitimacy in either domestic Japanese political society, where such temporal legitimacy as existed on the national level was entrusted to Toyotomi Hideyoshi's seven-year-old son Hideyori, even after Sekigahara, or in international society, where Hideyoshi's seven-year war in Korea had left Japan the outlaw of Northeast Asia, unwelcome anywhere closer than Annam. Yet, by the time of the death of Ieyasu's grandson Iemitsu in 1651, the bakufu had gained control over foreign relations, both domestic and international legitimacy had been established beyond serious question, and Japan was again accepted in East Asia.

NORMALIZATION EFFORTS IN NORTHEAST ASIA

The narrative details of the restoration of diplomatic and economic relations with the kingdom of Korea, from the earliest negotiations in the 1590s through the missions of 1604–1605 and 1607, the Trade Articles of 1609, and the reopening of

[4] Charles P. Korr, *Cromwell and the New Model Foreign Policy* (University of California Press, 1975), pp. 5, 7.

trade in 1611, have been discussed in Chapter II.[5] There is evidence that one of Ieyasu's motives in restoring relations with Korea was his hope of gaining admission to the Chinese world order, from which Japan had been excluded for over half a century, through Korean mediation.[6]

Through the combined efforts of Ieyasu and his advisers, on the one hand, and of Sō Yoshitoshi (1567-1615), as daimyo of Tsushima, the traditional mediator between Japan and Korea, and his advisers, on the other, the new bakufu was successful in bringing to Edo and Sunpu an extravagant embassy of some 467 persons, bearing letters and presents from Korea's King Sŏnjo (r. 1567-1608) to the shogun. This act was to be interpreted by some Japanese as recognition of Ieyasu's unification of Japan;[7] unification was one of the classical criteria of governmental legitimacy in the region which based its ideology on the Chinese classics.[8] Indeed, Hayashi Razan, the bakufu's chief ideologue, used this embassy as evidence of Tokugawa legitimacy when trying to win direct recognition from Ming three years later.[9] The bakufu regarded the restoration of Korean relations as a major victory.

[5] Original sources for the normalization process, and the standard accounts of it are in Tsuji, *Zōtei kaigai kōtsū shiwa*, pp. 465–480; *GBTS*, pp. 9-21; *TKIR*, 1:241-328; Nakamura, *NKSK* 3:234-336.

[6] Requests had been made on Ieyasu's orders that Korea "lend Japan a tribute route to Ming" as early as 1609. Ŏ Sukkwŏn, comp., *Kosa Ch'waryo* (Keijo: Keijō Teikoku Daigaku Hōbungakubu, 1941), pp. 120f. A letter repeating the request is included in *CTT*, *kan* 5. Tsuji, *Zōtei kaigai kōtsū shiwa*, p. 473, and Tanaka, *Chūsei taigai kankei shi*, p. 54, also present evidence to this effect, but Tsuji avoids the implications of the term "tribute."

[7] See Hayashi Gahō, "Chōsen raiō gaishū jo," in *Gahō Sensei Hayashi Gakushi bunshū* (contents, prefaces 1 and 2, and 120 *kan*, in 51 fascicles, 1689), 90:3b.

[8] Ou-yang Hsiu, "Cheng-t'ung lun," in *Ou-yang Wen-chung-kung-chi, Ssu-pu ts'ung-k'an (SPTK)* edition, 59:5a-18a; Su Shih (Su Tung-p'o), "Cheng-t'ung lun," in *Ching-chin Tung-p'o wen-chi shih-lüeh, SPTK* ed., 11:5b-11a; Ssu-ma Kuang, *Tzu-chih t'ung-chien*, 11 vols. (Peking: Hsin-hua Shu-tien, 1956), 3:2185-2188. For convenience the reader may wish to consult the punctuated texts in Morohashi Tetsuji, comp., *Daikanwa jiten*, 13 vols. (Taishūkan Shoten, 1955-1956), 6:673ff.

[9] Honda Masazumi to governor of Fukien, in *Hayashi Razan bunshū*, p. 130.

The conquest of Ryukyu in 1609 and the embassy of King Shō Nei (r. 1589-1612) to Edo in 1610 may be analyzed in a similar manner. After Ieyasu's appointment as shogun in 1603, the daimyo of Satsuma began urging Shō Nei to send an embassy of congratulation. When these exhortations bore no fruit, Shimazu Iehisa sought and received Ieyasu's order to chastise Ryukyu and force submission and an embassy. The ostensible reason for attacking the Ryukyu was that the country had failed to pay tribute, i.e., to submit as a vassal of Japan. Once the conquest had been accomplished, and Shō Nei had visited Edo, this "submission" to "vassal-state" status was used as further evidence of the legitimacy of the ba-kufu in correspondence with Ming,[10] although Ming was fully informed of the true state of affairs vis-à-vis Ryukyu,[11] and could hardly be expected to regard the invasion of one of her own vassal states as an indicator of legitimacy.

We will return to Korean and Ryukyuan relations below, but first we must examine post-Hideyoshi approaches to Ming, especially since it was the "Chinese world order" which had been the principal determinant of Japanese foreign relations prior to 1600. Although there are few direct documentary sources on this question prior to Honda Masazumi's letter to the governor of Fukien Province in Keichō 15 (1610), there is little doubt that Ieyasu was intent upon obtaining the right to trade directly with China, a right which had been suspended since 1547.

Since Ieyasu was interested in direct trade with Ming, we should recall the format of the trade traditionally practiced

[10] *TKIR*, 1:9-39; *Kagoshima kenshi*, 5 vols. (Kagoshima Ken, 1940-1943), 4:660-679. For Ieyasu's attempts to contact Ming through Ryukyu, see Kimiya Yasushiko, *Nisshi Kōtsūshi*, 2 vols. (Kinshi Hōryūdō. 1926-1928), 1:459f. Brief English language accounts of the Satsuma conquest of Ryukyu are in George H. Kerr, *Okinawa*, pp. 156-166; Robert K. Sakai, "The Ryukyu (Liu-ch'iu) Islands as a Fief of Satsuma," in John King Fairbank, ed., *The Chinese World Order* (Harvard University Press, 1968), pp. 115-118.

[11] *Ming-shih*, 6 vols. (Kuo-fang Yen-chiu Yuan, 1962), 1:145f; 6:3700. The Ryukyu-Ming correspondence is in *Rekidai hōan*, quoted in Miyata Toshihiko, "Kinsei shoki no Ryūmin bōeki," in *Nihon rekishi*, 340 (September 1976): 2-6.

between Japan and Ming and consider the implications for Tokugawa legitimacy. Japanese ships had been allowed to trade in China in the fifteenth and sixteenth centuries only if they carried a license, a *kangō* (ch. *k'an-ho*), originally issued by the Ming government to the "king of Japan"—the shogun—who in turn distributed them to Japanese who wished to trade. Ashikaga Yoshimitsu had accepted "vassal-state" status in the Ming tribute system in order to obtain investiture as king of Japan, and thereby control the *kangō*, the *sine qua non* of direct access to China.[12] Yoshimitsu's control of the distribution of *kangō* thus gave him a powerful tool with which to control recalcitrant *shugo* and religious institutions.[13] At a time when he had overcome but not necessarily reconciled his opposition, Yoshimitsu sought to promote his constituents' interests as a means of convincing them of the legitimacy of his position. By entering the Ming tribute system Yoshimitsu had sought to enhance his prestige, but acceptance of the title "king" from Ming was a two-edged sword: critics accused him of compromising Japanese sovereignty, and this criticism has followed him down through history.[14]

In the seventeenth century, there were two major difficulties in obtaining admittance to the Chinese tribute system. First, it required that Ieyasu, as the representative of Japan, compromise the very independent legitimacy and sovereignty that he was seeking to establish, by petitioning the Ming emperor in a formal document, a *piao*, in which he called himself a "subject" of Ming, dated in the Ming calendar.[15] To do so would subject him to the same type of

[12] The relationship also involved irregular embassies from Japan to Peking. For a full discussion see Wang Yi-t'ung, *Official Relations between China and Japan, 1368-1549* (Harvard University Press, 1953), and Tanaka Takeo, *Wakō to kangō bōeki* (Shibundō, 1961).

[13] Zuikei Shūhō, *Zenrin kokuhō ki*, in *Kaitei shiseki shūran*, 33 vols. (Kondō Shuppanbu, 1900-1902), 21:37f.

[14] Satō Shin'ichi, "Muromachi bakufu ron," in *Iwanami kōza Nihon rekishi*, 23 vols. (Iwanami Shoten, 1962-1964), 7:48.

[15] Tanaka, *Chūsei taigai kankei shi*, pp. 23f, 55f explains the *piao*.

criticism that Yoshimitsu had received. Second, not only were the Korean invasions still fresh in China's memory, but *wakō* (Japanese pirate) activity, noted frequently in the *Ming shih*, continued into the 1610s.

Thus Ieyasu would have a difficult time establishing his legitimacy in Ming eyes, and could do so only at the price of injuring that legitimacy in the eyes of Japanese political society. The early correspondence with Ming substantiates this conflict and helps to establish the overt relationship between Asian diplomacy and bakufu legitimacy.

In late 1610 Hayashi Razan, on orders from Ieyasu, consulted with Ieyasu's main foreign-policy advisers, Honda Masazumi and Ishin Sūden, and then drafted a letter for Masazumi's signature and Ieyasu's seal, addressed to the governor of Fukien Province. This letter, dated 29 January 1611,[16] is the first in a series of letters from 1611 to 1625 bearing on the reopening of direct trade and relations with Ming.

In order to demonstrate Ieyasu's sincerity and legitimacy to Ming, the letter would have had to meet certain Chinese standards unacceptable to him. First, and most important, the letter is not a *piao*; it is not signed by the ruler, but by his subordinate, and is thus in unacceptable form. The letter also fails to use the Chinese calendar, which Razan knew was an obligatory sign of acceptance of Chinese suzerainty. Razan does use the properly reverential terms for China, but by calling the Chinese emperor the "Son of Heaven of Great Ming," he was reserving Japan's own "Son of Heaven in Kyoto," and denying the universality of the Chinese monarchy. Razan makes but a qualified apology for the invasion of Korea, and no mention of more recent transgressions like the 1609 *wakō* raid on Wen-chou.[17] Rather than apologize for the invasion of China's vassal state, Ryukyu, he tries to make it a virtue, proclaiming that "Ryukyu calls herself Japan's vassal." By asserting, in an attempt to establish Tokugawa

[16] *Hayashi Razan bunshū*, p. 130.
[17] *Ming-shih*, 1:145.

claims of legitimacy, that a whole list of Chinese vassal states, from Korea to Siam, has begun to pay tribute to Japan, Razan does no less than declare that Japan is trying to usurp China's place in the world order.

Razan, Ieyasu, and Masazumi asked that Ming issue them *kangō*, something which they knew required less equivocal earnests of Japanese desire for admittance to the Chinese order through investiture. But since one of the requirements for investiture was to demonstrate that Ieyasu was the legitimate ruler of Japan, Razan tried to establish such a claim. Yet Ieyasu's most potent symbol of domestic legitimacy was his Japanese imperial appointment as shogun, and this not only would carry no weight with Ming, but would harm the Japanese case. Razan therefore did not mention it. Instead, he offered three classical criteria for the identification of legitimacy: Ieyasu had unified the country; he had rectified administration and brought prosperity to the people; and his dynasty had already attained its third generation (*sic*). This last is clearly making more of the seven-year-old Iemitsu than is warranted, but each of these is an index of legitimacy with roots deep in the classical tradition. Ou-yang Hsiu's treatise on legitimacy, cited above, is divided into two sections, one on the unification criterion, and one on the three-generation standard.[18] It will be seen below that these indicators are critical functional criteria for the determination of political legitimacy, and appear for the purpose frequently in early Edo period diplomatic correspondence.

There is no need to examine every letter to China; it is more important to analyze the response of the bakufu to the first response received from China.[19] As the bakufu's do-

---

[18] *Supra*, n. 8. For an excellent discussion of the three-generation criterion, see Ojima Sukema, *Chūgoku no kakumei shisō* (Chikuma Shobō, 1967), pp. 25-28.

[19] Most of this correspondence is in *GBTS*, *kan* 8-9, pp. 52-62. All approaches to China prior to 1620 sought entry, in one form or another, to the Ming investiture system and direct access to trade with China; all of it reflected the Japanese ambivalence toward recognition of China's ecumenical

mestic resistance melted away, and as the *shuin* license system,[20] the bakufu's own system for licensing trade and guaranteeing security to international maritime commerce, proved itself a viable substitute which did not require compromising Japanese legitimacy or sovereignty, the bakufu's interest in entering the Chinese world order waned. This is clear from the following events of 1619-1621.

In the third month of Genna 7 (1621) Sūden records that a Chinese merchant named Tan Feng-hsiang[21] brought to Nagasaki a letter from the military governor of Chekiang Province addressed to the shogun, and another letter addressed to the magistrate of Nagasaki, dated in 1619. These letters, particularly the one to the shogun, Tokugawa Hide-

---

legitimacy, an ambivalence visible in Honda Masazumi's letter to the governor of Fukien, in *Hayashi Razan bunshū*, p. 130. After the events of 1619-1621 described below, however, Japan no longer sought access to direct trade with Ming, and Japanese correspondence with it thereafter focussed on the issue of Christianity, as typified by Suetsugu Heizō to the governor of Fukien, dated eighth month of 1625, at *Hayashi Razan bunshū*, pp. 136f. *GBTS*, pp. 58f. Hayashi Razan drafted both these letters, so they may be presumed to reflect shogunal policy.

[20] The *shuin* licenses were patents issued by authority of the shogun, and bearing his red seal, authorizing a particular bearer to undertake a specific overseas voyage. Prior to the issuance of such patents, which Ieyasu had issued from at least 1604, the shogun had been in communication with the rulers of many of the states of East Asia, as far away as Luzon and Siam, urging that these letters patent be accepted as evidence of the bearers' bona fides, and that the bearers be permitted to trade freely at their licensed destinations; any Japanese ships lacking such patents, Ieyasu urged, should be treated as pirates. See, e.g., Ieyasu to Lord of Annam, spring 1601, in *GBTS*, p. 73. This system, which continued in force, with modifications, until 1635, was at its height capable of guaranteeing safe passage on the high seas, even in war zones. See the brief discussion in Boxer, *The Christian Century in Japan*, pp. 261-267, and the authoritative study by Iwao Seiichi, *Shuinsen bōeki shi no kenkyū*.

[21] The entire affair is recorded by Ishin Sūden in *Ikoku nikki*, 4 vols., MS copy, collection Historiographical Institute, vol. 2, and reprinted in *TKIR*, 5:555-561, which also gives the text of the Chinese letter. Other relevant information is in Sūden's diary, *Honkō kokushi nikki*, 7 vols. (Zoku Gunsho Ruijū Kanseikai, 1970), 5:103-117. The following discussion is based on these sources.

tada, precipitated a three-month debate among the bakufu's elders and its chief foreign policy advisers, Ishin Sūden, Hayashi Razan's younger brother Eiki (Razan was in Kyoto at the time), and the Nagasaki Deputy (*daikan*) Hasegawa Fujihiro over whether to accept the letter, and how to deal with it. This letter appears to be the first Ming response to the long series of Japanese feelers dating back at least to 1605-1606, and probably back before the battle of Sekigahara; as such one would have expected that, despite the strong wording of the letter, the bakufu would be pleased at this opening to China. The principal actors, save Hidetada himself, were all men from Ieyasu's cabinet, most of them involved in his approaches to China, and it was these men, not the shogun, who set the terms of the decision. The Chinese letter is not entirely clear, but it seems to offer direct trade with China, seeking in exchange suppression of Japanese piracy, a diplomatic exchange which had been offered to Japan often in the past.[22]

Sūden and others debated the disposition of this letter for three weeks, and frequently discussed it with the *rōjū*. The bakufu found the letter unacceptable for two principal reasons. The letter to Hidetada was identical with that to Hasegawa as Nagasaki Deputy; thus it violated the distinction between superior and inferior. It also addressed Hidetada as "Nihon shōgun sama," which they deemed disrespectful in a diplomatic context. Former Nagasaki Deputy Terasawa Hirotaka even argued that any direct negotiations with Ming on the question of peace would violate the Japanese constitution (*Nihon no gohatto*), and that China should be commanded to make its approach through Korea. On 26 June 1621 Hidetada approved the issuance of this humiliating demand, which was incorporated into his rejection of the Ming approach. The response was passed unofficially to the Chinese envoys in Kyoto: "Correspondence between Great Ming and Japan has in recent years been reported via Korea and Tsu-

[22] *NKSK*, 1:141-202.

shima; Tsushima then memorializes [Edo] about it. Now you have impertinently and unreasonably appealed directly. Return to your land and communicate what you wish through the Korean interpreters."[23]

After all the energy expended on attempts to open direct relations with China, and gain access to the China trade during Ieyasu's lifetime, why did Hidetada now reject this opportunity? All the principals in this case, except Hidetada, who appears merely to have ratified the decision of his councillors, had been advisers to Ieyasu in his campaign for admission to the Chinese order until a few years before. Was it simply that Hidetada was less interested in trade and foreign relations than his father, as is often supposed?

The involvement of so many experienced advisers, with demonstrable interest in foreign relations and cognizance of the potential benefits of trade for the bakufu, argues against such reasoning and demands some more substantive change in the situation to explain it. In the wake of the settlement of Osaka, the death of Ieyasu and the consequent elimination of the strains inherent in the so-called "bifurcated bakufu"; the death of Goyōzei-in, which had lessened the potential for domestic challenges to shogunal legitimacy; the stunning diplomatic success of the reception of the 1617 Korean embassy at Kyoto; with the success of the *shuin* license system in protecting Japanese traders abroad and bringing troublesome Europeans to heel; with the vigorous competition between the Dutch and the Portuguese reducing the commercial and strategic pressures on the bakufu abroad, the bakufu no longer felt the need to compromise a burgeoning autonomous structure of legitimacy for the marginal advantage of direct dealings with Ming. Indeed, it is precisely direct dealings with Ming that the bakufu rejected in its 1621 decision.

Four years later, when Razan drafted a reply for Nagasaki Deputy Suetsugu Heizō to a 1624 letter from the Fukien inspector, he made no mention either of tallies or of Japanese

<hr>

[23] *Ikoku nikki*, vol. 2; *GBTS*, p. 58; *TKIR*, 5:558.

participation in the Chinese trade or tribute system. He concentrated instead on another critical issue for Japan in East Asia, the control of Christianity, which was to be a frequent subject of diplomatic correspondence over the next six decades.[24] "Normalization" with Ming had been abandoned in the interests of bakufu legitimacy.

FOREIGN EMBASSIES AND BAKUFU LEGITIMACY

The relationship between the diplomatic developments discussed above and the creation of a structure of bakufu legitimacy is clear. But even though much of the most important correspondence would later be made public in such forms as Razan's collected works, the bulk of it was screened from public view. In the last analysis the most important public use of diplomacy as propaganda was in the reception of foreign embassies at the shogunal court, starting with Ieyasu's negotiations with the Korean monk-politician Song'un in Kyoto in 1605.

Among the clearest cases of this propaganda-oriented diplomacy were Hidetada's 1617 reception of a Korean embassy at Fushimi Castle in Kyoto, and Iemitsu's reception of a Ryukyuan embassy at the newly completed Nijō Castle in Kyoto in 1634. Asao Naohiro has suggested that a relationship exists between these two embassies and the enhancement of shogunal legitimacy, but nearly all the evidence that he adduces, as well as the bulk of his analysis and discussion, are devoted to the domestic political acts of Hidetada and Iemitsu coinciding with these embassies. He has not in fact demonstrated that the bakufu used these embassies to this purpose, nor that they had the desired effect.[25] Discussion here must, therefore, focus on evidence for the specific manipulation of foreign embassies as propaganda for the enhancement of shogunal prestige and legitimacy.

[24] *Hayashi razan bunshū*, pp. 136f; *GBTS*, pp. 58f, etc.
[25] Asao Naohiro, *Sakoku*, pp. 359f; Asao, "Shōgun seiji no kenryoku kōzō," in *Iwanami kōza Nihon rekishi*, 10 (1975): 5, etc.

Tokugawa Ieyasu, having eliminated the greatest remaining threat to the Tokugawa dynasty with the conquest of Osaka in early 1615, died less than a year later, leaving his son Hidetada as shogun in his own right, without his father pulling the strings from Sunpu. Hidetada was left with an effectively "unified feudal state," his father's advisers (many of whom he proceeded to eliminate), and a few potentially serious contenders as alternative centers of power: the imperial court and certain western daimyos. There were serious questions as to whether Hidetada, who had been such an embarrassment at Sekigahara in 1600, could hold the coalition together.

As Asao has pointed out, Hidetada's trip to Kyoto the following summer, his first such trip as sole secular ruler of Japan, was a crucial act in his creation of a structure of legitimacy and authority for his own rule. His journey to Kyoto was one of ten shogunal visits in the first thirty years of the Edo period. Besides serving the ancient *kunimi* (country-viewing, i.e., laying claim to the land) function incumbent on a sovereign, and giving Hidetada a chance to visit his father's shrine at Kunōzan, modern Shizuoka, it gave him an opportunity to impress the court and daimyos with his majesty and power, to work on his structure of legitimacy. That Hidetada chose to journey to Kyoto at this time, and to remain there for nearly three months, underscores Tsuji Tatsuya's point that the relationship between emperor and shogun was the most pressing issue on Hidetada's political agenda.[26]

It was a combination of good luck and hard work that enabled Hidetada at the same time to parade before the country, and particularly the capital, an embassy of some 428 persons from the king of Korea.[27] Ieyasu had been trying since

[26] Tsuji Tatsuya, "Kan'ei-ki no bakufu seiji ni kan suru jakkan no kō-satsu," in *Yokohama Shiritsu Daigaku ronsō*, 24.2/3 (1973): 31-35. Compare Totman, *Politics in the Tokugawa Bakufu*, pp. 38f.

[27] On the background of this embassy, see Miyake Hidetoshi, "Genna Chōsen shinshi raihei riyū e no gimon." On the embassy itself, *TKIR*,

1614 through the daimyo of Tsushima to get Korea to send an embassy. Tsushima's representations had become more and more urgent, even suggesting that Tsushima's position would be endangered by failure to produce a Korean embassy for the shogun. The Koreans in fact sent their embassy in response to a forged "royal letter" purportedly from the shogun, sent by Tsushima in Genna 2/11 (9 December 1616 to 8 January 1617), which Korea thought was a suit for peace.[28] The official Japanese view was that the embassy had been sent to congratulate Hidetada on the conquest of Osaka and the unification of Japan; the Korean government thought it was responding to a letter from Hidetada suing for peace, and so commissioned this a "response embassy," with the additional mission of repatriating Korean prisoners from the Hideyoshi invasions.

Although the Korean embassy had been long delayed, it is probable that Sūden knew that Hidetada's departure for Kyoto in the middle of the sixth month would bring about the reception of the anticipated embassy in the midst of the shogun's sojourn in the imperial capital. Hidetada arrived in the capital in the sixth month and at once began attending to the business of impressing the court and the daimyos,[29] tasks which kept him occupied until the arrival of the Korean embassy late in the eighth month. The daimyos had been ordered by the bakufu to participate;[30] the daimyos of the major *tozama* houses and lords of the collateral houses of the Tokugawa clan were all in attendance. They gathered in Kyoto to give witness to the grandeur of Hidetada's rule.

Because the arrival of the Korean embassy had been so

1:381-384; 2:303f; 3:90ff, 209-213. Diaries of Korean Ambassador O Yun'gyŏm, *Tongasang illok*, in *KKS*, 2:78-110, and Vice Ambassador Yi Kyŏngjik, *Pusangnok*, in *KKS*, 2:111-205.

[28] *Kwanghaegun ilgi*, 112:9b, at *CWS*, 32:565; *TKIR*, 1:381-384.

[29] *Honkō kokushi nikki*, 4:143; *Dai Nihon shiryō*, 12.27:417-656. For Hidetada's red-seal license to the Dutch, p. 606; his reception of the Portuguese, pp. 581-588.

[30] *Dai Nihon shiryō*, 12.27:308-360. *Honkō kokushi nikki*, 4:135, for the orders to the daimyo.

long delayed, rumors were rife about the precise significance of the embassy. Richard Cocks, director of the English trading factory at Hirado until its demise in 1623 and an indefatigable observer of the contemporary Japanese scene, noted in his diary for 31 August 1617 (O.S.) that "the Emperour" (the shogun) had given orders throughout the land that the Koreans were to be accorded properly respectful treatment. He continued: "Some report (& are the c'mons) that they are com to render obaysance & pay tribute, otherwaies themperour would haue made wars against them againe."[31] Cocks was in Kyoto himself at the same time as the Korean embassy, seeking Korean permission to open English trade with that country.[32] On 20 September (O.S.) he reported,

Yt is said the Coreans sent a pr'sent to themperour (Hidetada) . ., and made their case knowne wherefore they were sent from the King of Corea to hym; w'ch was, first to vizet the sepulcre, or doe funerall rights to the deceased Emperour Ogosho Samma (Tokugawa Ieyasu), and next to reioyce w' his Ma[tie] that now is in that he had soe quietly succeaded his father w'thout wars or bloudshed, and lastly to desire his Ma[tie] to haue the Coreans vnder his protection as his father had before hym, & to defend them against forraine envations, yf any other nation did seeke to disturbe their quiet, &c.[33]

These rumors do not represent Korean thinking on such questions, but they are an index of the value that such embassies had in enhancing the bakufu's prestige, and thus bolstering shogunal legitimacy. Later, in 1643, one Kyoto cour-

---

[31] Richard Cocks, *Diary Kept by the Head of the English Factory in Japan: Diary of Richard Cocks, 1615-1622*, 3 vols., ed., Historiographical Institute (Tōkyō Daigaku Shuppankai, 1978-1980), 2:156-157 (31 August 1617 [O.S.]). This edition supersedes the Murakami edition, *Diary of Richard Cocks*, 2 vols. (Sankosha, 1899), but readers may locate passages in that edition by reference to entry dates.

[32] Cocks, *Diary*, 2:171 (21,22 September 1617 [O.S.]).

[33] *Diary*, 2:170 (20 September 1617 [O.S.]).

tier (*kuge*) similarly interpreted the arrival of a Korean embassy as evidence of the long reach of shogunal power. Two days later the rumors had escalated to the point that the shogun was supposed to be trying to lure Korea out of the orbit of the Ming tribute system, as Cocks reported that "all the Japon lordes . . . be set on p'r the Emperour to w'thdraw [Korea] from favouring the King of China."[34]

Richard Cocks was not, however, the only person to be impressed by the Korean embassy's appearance before the shogun. When over 400 Koreans had an audience with Hidetada at Fushimi Castle on 25 September 1617, the prominent Buddhist priest Gien noted the occasion in his diary,[35] and the compilers of the genealogies and records of many *tozama* and other daimyos considered the event of such significance that they recorded at length their lords' participation. The courtier Mibu Takasuke recorded in his diary the presents showered on the ambassadors by the shogun, for ranking members of the court had been summoned to Fushimi for the ceremonial presentation of Korean King Kwanghae's state letter to the shogun,[36] and on 17 October the Kyoto *shoshidai*, Itakura Katsushige, was dispatched to

[34] *Diary*, 2:171 (22 September 1617 [O.S.]). Although such rumors were of course not in accord with Korean thinking, still, they were common. Eighteen years later they were reiterated by Senior Councillor Sakai Tadakatsu, who notes reports of similar rumors in Seoul in 1629. Sakai Tadakatsu to Sō Yoshinari, MS signature letter dated (Kan'ei 12)/8/29, (10 October 1635), in Sō Collection, Historiographical Institute, Tokyo University. According to Sakai, the rumor had been that Korea would "attach itself to Japan."

[35] *Gien Jugō nikki*, 12, Genna 3/8/26 (25 September 1617), and Genna 3/9/18 (17 October 1617), quoted in *Dai Nihon shiryō*, 12.27:884; 12.28:12. Gien was born into a very high-ranking *kuge* family, and later was adopted as the son of the last Ashikaga shogun. He had strong ties to the Toyotomi family and their cause, and the family had reciprocated with financial support for Gien's temple, the Sanbōin. Abbots of the Sanbōin had served in a ceremonial legitimating capacity in the Muromachi period in the transmission of the imperial patent to the shogun, and Ieyasu had used Gien in this way in 1603. Itō Tasaburō, "Edo bakufu no seiritsu," p. 31.

[36] *Hayashi Razan bunshū*, p. 248.

the court to underscore the importance of the embassy and to make sure that the *kuge* were properly impressed.[37] In addition, the daimyos of western Japan, mostly *tozama* lords, had been ordered by the bakufu to serve as hosts for the embassy en route to Kyoto and back, thus involving more elements of the nation in this event.[38] It is dangerous to overinterpret the fact that all the daimyos in Kyoto had been ordered to participate in the audience of the Korean embassy, since a ruler could not very well appear in audience without his court. Still, it seems clear that the shogun, newly liberated from his father, was trying to impress them with his majesty and to enhance his legitimacy in their eyes.

Surely when Hayashi Razan called the mission "tribute,"[39] he showed that he was concerned about the need to enhance the legitimacy of this particular shogun and of the bakufu as an institution. Two years earlier Sō Yoshinari of Tsushima, intermediary in negotiations with Korea, had given as one of Ieyasu's reasons for requesting the embassy the fact that "even now His Majesty has not forgotten the splendid brilliance of the embassy of a few years ago (1607)."[40] Moreover, the official reason for the embassy, calculated from the Japanese point of view, was to congratulate Hidetada on the pacification of Osaka and the unification of all of Japan, a reason calculated to enhance shogunal prestige, even though negotiations for this embassy antedate the fall of Osaka by at least half a year.[41] Furthermore, unification of the country was

[37] Otsuki (Mibu) Takasuke, *Takasuke no Sukune hinamiki*, 5, Genna 3/9/18 (17 October 1617), quoted in *Dai Nihon shiryō*, also records the embassy. Even when Korean embassies did not stop in Kyoto, they must have impressed the court, as they "dressed in official uniform and passed through the center of the city." *T'ongmun'gwanji*, p. 91.

[38] E.g., *Hosokawa kaki*, 21 ("Tadotashi fu," 1), and *Takayama-kō Tōdō Takatora jitsuroku*, 42, in *Dai Nihon shiryō*, 12.27:885. The best account of the audience is in Yi Kyŏngjik, *Pusangnok*, in *KKS*, 2:149-153.

[39] *Hayashi Razan bunshū*, p. 248.

[40] Sō Yoshinari to Board of Rites, Genna 1/11/X (21 December 1615-18 January 1616), in *GBTS*, p. 19.

[41] Miyake Hidetoshi, "Genna Chōsen shinshi," explores this point fully.

one of the classical indicators of legitimacy stressed by Ou-yang Hsiu, Ssu-ma Kuang, and the other theorists cited above in the discussion on legitimacy theory.

Indeed, the self-legitimating motivations inherent in the invitation of Korean embassies to Japan became explicit in 1624, when Tsushima's protocol envoy to Korea, Taira To-shimasa, called the request for an embassy from Korea "a plan to pacify the hearts of the people."[42] This phrase would be repeated some months later on the embassy's return to Seoul, when Korean Ambassador Chŏng Ip reported to the throne the reason why Hidetada had chosen to abdicate in favor of his son Iemitsu,[43] so clearly the concept of winning popular favor in political society was of concern to the ba-kufu at that time.

While the 1624 embassy was in Edo, Andō Shigenaga, who was in charge of lodging the embassy, explicitly linked the legitimation of the shogunate to the arrival of the Korean embassy, and, incidentally, to the three-generation criterion Razan had raised in 1611:

Although Ieyasu thoroughly annihilated [Toyotomi] Hi-deyori, there were still many factions. Then he transmitted [his office] to his son, and transmitted it to his grandson, thus reaching the third generation, so that he established [the hereditary nature of his office]. But the shogun is even now not yet supreme, and so the hearts of the people are even today not yet submissive. Therefore we awaited the arrival of your embassy most eagerly. We thought we would subjugate the land by a boastful display, conducting an embassy well suited to the situation. The shogun is deeply pleased. Had the embassy failed to arrive, the Japanese people might have doubted that we were totally at peace. The generals of all the provinces [the daimyos] were all gathered in the nation's capital, and there were some who were of a mind to raise troops and attack to the west. Thus

---

[42] *Injo cho sillok*, 5:19a, at *CWS*, 33:598.

[43] *Injo cho sillok*, 8:51a, at *CWS*, 33:692.

Hidetada feared that they might take advantage of a momentary situation to foment strife. The shogun does not want war.[44]

A high-ranking *fudai* daimyo with close ties to the policy councils of the bakufu has here proclaimed the high degree of importance that the bakufu placed on Korean embassies, and has laid out in unambiguous form the relationship in bakufu thinking between Asian diplomacy and legitimation of the bakufu.

Ten years later, in 1634, Hidetada's son and successor Iemitsu made a progress to Kyoto, the last shogunal visit to the imperial city until the *bakumatsu* period. In many ways Iemitsu's trip was analogous to his father's visit in 1617. Hidetada had just died, terminating the second period of "dual monarchy" in the bakufu, and leaving Iemitsu to demonstrate that he could control the government. To be sure, time and institutional development made Iemitsu far more secure than his father had been, but it remained for him to demonstrate that he could seize the opportunity. The death of the bakufu's senior foreign policy adviser, Sūden, in early 1633 had made demonstrations of control in the diplomatic arena a particularly pressing matter. Iemitsu responded to the challenge by placing his own men in key foreign policy posts, particularly "wise Izu" Matsudaira Nobutsuna at the roju level, and Sakakibara Tsunenao and Kamio Motokatsu as the new Nagasaki magistrates. It was this team that began to deal positively with the subversive threat of Catholicism, issuing the second of the five sets of edicts noted above immediately after their appointment.[45]

---

[44] Kang Hongjung, *Tongsarok*, in *KKS*, 2:256. Andō was the son of the late bakufu councillor Andō Shigenobu. He later became the first Commissioner of Shrines and Temples (*jisha bugyō*), and frequently held protocol posts when the shogun received foreign diplomats.

[45] The five "Sakokurei," more properly a series of memoranda and orders to the Nagasaki *bugyō* issued in 1633, 1634, 1635, 1636 and 1639, appear in *Tokugawa kinrei kō zenshū*, 6:375-379. Even so responsible and widely used

Iemitsu's demonstration of supreme control over foreign relations, however, followed closely on the pattern established by his father. He took the opportunity of his trip to Kyoto to summon an embassy from the Ryukyuan kingdom, which he could parade before the court and the daimyos just as Hidetada had done with a Korean mission, thus producing "the illusion that the shogun's grace extended beyond the seas."[46] This Ryukyuan embassy served much the same function for Iemitsu as the 1617 Korean mission had for Hidetada, helping to confirm the legitimacy of his sole possession of the shogunal office following the death of his father.

Indeed, just as the first three Tokugawa shoguns used the devices of pre-mortem succession, and dual monarchy or associative monarchy to help to guarantee the establishment of Tokugawa claims to dynastic legitimacy through the establishment of a chosen, competent heir, and hence also to establish the legitimacy of the hereditary transmission of the shogunal office within the Tokugawa line,[47] they regularly employed the pomp and ceremony of foreign embassies to mark critical transitions in the dual monarchy of the first few decades of the dynasty. The first steps in establishing Hidetada as a viable successor to Ieyasu were, of course, Ieyasu's retirement and Hidetada's formal elevation to the office of shogun. But to mark this transition, to declare to both Japan

---

a text as Ōkubo Toshikane et al., eds. *Shiryō ni yoru Nihon no ayumi, kinsei hen* (Yoshikawa Kōbunkan, 1955), identifies these collectively as "sakokurei," without further explanation, pp. 127-131. For a recent analysis of Iemitsu's reorganization of the bakufu councils see Tsuji Tatsuya, "Kan'ei ki." The best chronology of the Nagasaki magistrates is Shimizu Hirokazu, "Nagasaki bugyō ichiranhyō no saikentō," in *Kyōto Gaikokugo Daigoku kenkyū ronsō*, 40 (1974): 14-22.

[46] Asao, *Sakoku*, p. 259.

[47] On pre-mortem succession see Jack Goody, "Introduction," in Goody, ed., *Succession to High Office* (Cambridge University Press, 1966), esp. pp. 9-11. For another case of pre-mortem succession by association of the chosen heir, see Andrew W. Lewis, "Anticipatory Association of the Heir in Early Capetian France," in *American Historical Review*, 83.4 (October 1978): 906-927. The Capetian case forms a close parallel to the Tokugawa case in both timing and purpose.

and to the rest of East Asia that Hidetada was now, at least formally, shogun, ruler of Japan, Ieyasu made his successor the focus of foreign diplomatic recognition. When the Korean embassy of 1607 came to Japan, they expected to perform their formal ceremonial duties before Ieyasu. Ieyasu, however, insisted that since Hidetada was now shogun it was to him that they should make formal obeisance, and to him that they should present King Sŏnjo's letter of state. It was Hidetada who should represent the country of Japan internationally. As if to underscore the transition, the Korean embassy merely made an informal courtesy call on Ieyasu in Sunpu, on their way home from Edo. By pointing to Hidetada in this way as the technical locus of authority, even though it was clear to all politically aware persons in Japan at the time that Ieyasu remained in fact supreme, the elder, the "senior monarch," could expedite the transfer of charisma and power from himself to his chosen successor while he was still alive to reenforce the transfer by less metaphysical means if need should arise. Similarly, Hidetada displayed the panoply of his powers, his full possession of his late father's charisma, immediately after Ieyasu's death by displaying his reception of the Korean embassy of 1617 before court and camp together in Kyoto. As the following chart shows, Hidetada and Iemitsu continued this practice, mobilizing diplomatic display to the beginning of the fourth generation of Tokugawa shoguns. In fact Iemitsu's deployment of both Korean and Ryukyuan embassies to mark the birth of his first son and heir, Ietsuna, suggests that Iemitsu intended also to retire when Ietsuna was of an age to succeed, and replicate the pattern of dual or associative monarchy in the shogunal office, and that only his early death in 1651 prevented him from doing so.

The bakufu could get along without direct relations with China, since it had developed substitute trading patterns, but it could not tolerate complete isolation in Northeast Asia. Relations with Korea and Ryukyu were an essential part of the growing Tokugawa world order. One of the purposes of that order was the enhancement of the bakufu's legitimacy.

Year	Sole Monarch/ Senior Monarch	Junior Monarch
1600	Ieyasu's victory at Sekigahara	
1601		
1602		
1603	Ieyasu takes title Sei'i taishōgun	
1604	Ieyasu receives Korean embassy, Kyoto	
1605	Ieyasu retires to Sunpu as Ōgosho (senior monarch)	Hidetada becomes shogun at Edo
1606		
1607		Hidetada receives Korean embassy at Edo
1608		
1609		
1610		
1611		
1612		
1613		
1614	Battles of Osaka; destruction of	
1615	Toyotomi/anti-Tokugawa coalition	
1616	Ieyasu dies/Hidetada as sole monarch	
1617	Hidetada receives Korean embassy in Kyoto	
1618		
1619		
1620		
1621		
1622		
1623	Hidetada retires as Ōgosho	Iemitsu succeeds as shogun
1624		Iemitsu receives Korean embassy at Edo

Year	Sole Monarch/ Senior Monarch	Junior Monarch
1625		
1626		
1627		
1628		
1629		
1630		
1631		
1632	Hidetada dies/ Iemitsu as sole monarch	
1633		
1634	Iemitsu receives Ryukyuan embassy in Kyoto	
1635		
1636	Iemitsu receives Korean embassy in Edo	
1637	First Korean pilgrimage to Nikko	
1638		
1639		
1640		
1641		Birth of shogunal heir, Ietsuna
1642		
1643	Korean pilgrimage to Nikko; presentation of bell for Yōmeimon	Korean embassy of congratulations on birth of Ietsuna
1644	Ryukyuan embassy makes pilgrimage to Nikko; presents offertories for Ieyasu's tomb	Ryukyuan embassy of congratulations on birth of Ietsuna

The ability of the early shoguns to produce ostentatious foreign embassies on Japanese soil, thereby demonstrating international legitimacy, was a powerful propaganda tool in the building of domestic legitimacy.

PLACING BAKUFU CONTROLS ON THE DAY-TO-DAY CONDUCT OF KOREAN RELATIONS

We must now return to institutional considerations to examine the extension of direct bakufu control over the conduct of the day-to-day affairs of Korean relations through the establishment of a system of rotating-duty monks from the chief Rinzai Zen temples of Kyoto. These monks, stationed in the Iteian hermitage in Tsushima's castle town, came to be entrusted by the bakufu with the management of all correspondence with Korea, as a result of a suit and counter-suit between the daimyo, Sō Yoshinari, and his chief retainer, Yanagawa Shigeoki, argued before the bakufu in 1634-1635. This lawsuit, known as the "Yanagawa Affair," deserves detailed treatment as a well-documented case in the adjudication before the shogun of disputes between daimyos and their retainers, but discussion will be limited here to an essential outline.[48]

The seeds of the Yanagawa Affair lie in the tumultuous period between the withdrawal of Japanese troops from Korea in 1598 and the arrival of the first full Korean royal embassy in 1607. Tsushima's economy was almost entirely dependent on the entrepôt trade between Japan and Korea for survival, and after the war Tsushima was without adequate revenue. Following the departure of King Sŏnjo's special envoys, the monk Song'un, and Son Munik, from Japan in 1605, Korea presented Tsushima with the demand that Ieyasu submit a letter to the Korean king requesting an embassy—tantamount to an admission of defeat—prior to the reestablishment of formal relations. Tsushima found itself faced

[48] The following discussion is based on Nakamura, *NKSK*, 3:267-269.

with a dilemma: it could not survive without the full restoration of Korean trade, which must be predicated on the normalization of relations at the national level, but this was now in turn predicated on a letter from Ieyasu which Tsushima knew he would not write.

Tsushima solved the problem by forging a letter addressed to the Korean king, signed "Tokugawa Ieyasu, King of Japan," and dated in the Ming calendar, in the thirty-fourth year of the Wan-li era (1606). The forgery was masterminded by Yanagawa Kagenao, Sō Yoshitoshi, and the monk Keitetsu Genso, probably with the connivance of a Korean emissary to Tsushima, Chŏn Kyesin. The letter did not deceive King Sŏnjo, who was aware of the Japanese aversion to the title "king," since his embassy had been at Hideyoshi's court in 1596 when Hideyoshi angrily rejected a Ming offer of investiture as "king of Japan" in the Chinese tribute system.[49] Sŏnjo also knew that Japan had its own calendar and did not recognize the Ming calendar. Yet he chose to accept the letter and to respond with a "response embassy," which left Seoul in the first lunar month of 1607 and arrived in Edo in the fifth month (intercalary fourth in the Japanese calendar).[50]

Since Sŏnjo was pretending to respond to a letter from Ieyasu, he opened his letter, "The King of Korea, Yi Kong,[51] respectfully *replies* to His Majesty, the King of Japan" (emphasis added), clearly implying the existence of a letter that

[49] Diary of Korean Ambassador Hwang Ch'up'o, *Tongsarok: Mallyŏk pyŏngsin ch'utong t'ongsinsa ilhaeng Ilbon wanghwan illok* (MS, 1596, in Kawai Bunko, Kyoto University Library), entries for ninth month, and *NKSK*, 3:266f.

[50] Diary of Korean Vice-Ambassador Kyŏng Sŏn, *Kyŏng Ch'ilsŏng haesarok*, in *KKS*, 2:1, 2:43.

[51] The given names of kings in Korea were taboo, and not intended to be pronounced. Sŏnjo's true name is a rare character, of uncertain reading. Contemporary Japanese sources would suggest reading it "Yŏn," but I follow modern Korean usage here. The implications of using the royal name in letters to the shogun are quite important, for the only other instance in which a reigning Korean king's true given name was used was in his correspondence with the Chinese emperor.

the bakufu would not recognize, thus threatening the exposure of Tsushima's deception. Thus the 1606 forgery engendered a long series of further prevarications, forgeries, and schemes by Tsushima in its intermediation between Edo and Seoul in order to hide the first falsehood. Having established the precedent of "shogun-as-king," Tsushima then had to maintain that deception, repeatedly forging the character "king" in shogunal letters. Shogunal titles were destined to remain a major issue in relations with Korea, reappearing in 1617, 1624, 1636, 1711, and 1719.[52]

Use of the title "king" might be interpreted as Japanese acceptance of the concept of universal Chinese sovereignty in the Confucian world order. We have already seen that it was the unwillingness to compromise autonomous Japanese sovereignty and Tokugawa legitimacy in this manner that ultimately prevented Japan from gaining direct access to China.

However, in 1631 a rift developed between Sō Yoshinari (r. 1615-1658) and his chief retainer, Yanagawa Shigeoki, apparently over the latter's growing power and his desire to abandon his ties to Tsushima and to become a *hatamoto*.[53] In the course of the investigation and adjudication of this dispute over the next four years the forgeries of 1617 came to light, and the original issues were superceded by the question

[52] On this question in 1617 see the diary of Yi Kyŏngjik, *Pusangnok*, in *KKS*, 1:156; *Ikoku nikki*, vol. 2; *HKN*, 4:163; and "Hō Chōrō Chōsen monogatari," in *Kaitei shiseki shūran*, 28:455-470. I have examined the significance of shogunal titles in diplomacy in the brief diplomatic reform of 1711 in my "Korean-Japanese Diplomacy in 1711: Sukchong's Court and the Shogun's Title."

[53] There is no satisfactory published account of this affair, but it is treated briefly in *NKSK*, 3:483-486, and *Nagasaki kenshi hansei hen* (Yoshikawa Kōbunkan, 1973), pp. 845-851. The Sō Collection at the Historiographical Institute, Tokyo University, has a number of primary MSS, including *Yanagawa Shigeoki kuji no toki Hō Chōrō narabini Matsuo Shichiemon e otazune nararu seitō no chō*, 1 vol., *Yanagawa kuji kiroku*, 3 vols., and a packet of letters also titled *Yanagawa kuji kiroku*. Other sources are in the same institute's MSS for unpublished portions of *Dai Nihon shiryō*, the *Shiryō kōhon*, vols. 169-171, *passim*. and *TKIR*, 1:328ff. For the information transmitted to Korea see *Sŭngjŏngwŏn ilgi*, 50:273-278.

of responsibility for this act of *lèse majesté*. Even though the earlier forgeries of 1606-1607 were not revealed in the trial, the forgeries in 1617 and 1624, alleged misconduct by the Tsushima monk-official Kihaku Genpō in Seoul in 1629, while on a mission for the bakufu, and the very fact that conflict between Yoshinari and one of his retainers had become so severe as to require shogunal attention, gave Edo sufficient reason to have confiscated the Tsushima fief and extirpate the Sō and Yanagawa houses.[54] Daimyos were at this very time being extirpated, confiscated, and transferred for far lesser offenses, such as incompetence demonstrated by inability to maintain harmony in the *kashindan* (corps of retainers), of which the very suit under consideration should have been prima facie evidence.[55] Yet, despite the overwhelming evidence against all parties concerned, it was only the Yanagawa faction that was punished. Yoshinari was given a stern reprimand, but was reconfirmed in his special rights to trade with Korea and to mediate between Seoul and Edo.[56]

Lest the message of the case be lost on the daimyos, all those in Edo at the time were ordered to witness the sentencing,[57] and many leading daimyos had the trial and decision recorded in their family chronicles and genealogies, so that their descendants would not forget the lesson.[58] It should be noted that this case occurred at the peak of confiscations

[54] Genpō went to Seoul in 1629 on Iemitsu's orders to investigate the 1627 Manchu invasion of Korea. See below, Chapter IV, for a fuller discussion of Genpō's mission to Seoul, and Tashiro Kazui, "Kan'ei 6 nen (Jinso 7; 1629) Tsushima shisetsu no Chōsen-koku 'Go-jōkyō no toki mainikki' to sono haikei," in *Chōsen gakuhō*, nos. 96, 98, 101 (1980-1981).

[55] Kurita Motoji, *Edo jidaishi jō* (Naigai Shoseki, 1928), pp. 279-302; Fujino Tamotsu, *Shintei bakuhan taiseishi no kenkyū* (Yoshikawa Kōbunkan, 1961), pp. 251-264. The years following Hidetada's death in 1632 were the peak years of daimyo confiscations.

[56] For this decision see *Tokugawa jikki*, 2:674f.

[57] There is a seating diagram of the trial, "Kuji taiketsu goza-kubari ezu" (MS, Sō Collection, Historiographical Institute).

[58] *Hosokawa kaki*, "Tadatoshi-fu" (Kan'ei 12/3/12; 16); *Date (Jōzan) chika kiroku* (Kan'ei 12/3/12); *Maeda (Kanazawa) kafu*; *Ogasawara Tadazane ichidai oboegaki (ken)*, etc. in *Shiryō kōhon*, 170.3.

of daimyo domains, and that in the eight months since the departure of the Ryukyuan embassies Iemitsu had for the first time made the *sankin kōtai* system of alternate attendance and hostagery obligatory for all the daimyos. The news quickly spread, and on 30 March 1635 François Caron reported from Hamamatsu to Nicholaes Couckebacker, the head of the Dutch factory in Hirado, on the progress of the case. On 25 April Couckebacker recorded the final decision.[59] Nothing was left to chance; every detail of the Yanagawa decision must be seen as deliberate and calculated.[60]

The revelation of malfeasance in a matter which so intimately affected shogunal legitimacy in the international and domestic spheres showed that certain aspects of foreign relations had escaped shogunal control. It required quick and clear action on the part of the bakufu. First, it demanded that the bakufu establish institutional controls over Korean relations in a way that would make less likely such violations of shogunal authority in the future. Second, the revelation that the shogun had been identified with an unacceptable title demanded that the bakufu decide officially the title to be used by the shogun in foreign relations, and formalize the complete protocol of diplomatic correspondence with Korea.

Before we proceed to these two questions it would be well to note the significance of the general nature of the bakufu's solution to the Yanagawa case: extension of appropriate supervision over Korean affairs, and maintenance of the Sō monopoly on trade and mediation with Korea.

The main thrust of studies of the diplomatic history of the early Tokugawa period has been in the area of European re-

[59] Nagazumi Yōko, tr., *Hirado Oranda shōkan no nikki*, 3:205, 232.

[60] Sō Yoshinari was very well connected for a daimyo of a small fief. His father-in-law was Hino Sukekatsu, the bakufu's man in the imperial court (*buke densō*), while his eldest daughter was the wife of another *kuge*, Minister of the Left Denbōin Kintomi, *Kansei chōshū shokafu*, 8:262. Kim Seryŏn, Korean vice-ambassador in the next year's embassy, reported that the great daimyo Date Masamune and the Tokugawa cadet daimyo Tokugawa Yoshinao worked to save Yoshinari because they saw Shigeoki as a threat to all the daimyos' positions. Kim, *Sasangnok*, in *KKS*, 2:471.

lations; hence it has been most common to view the 1630s as the bakufu's last big push toward isolation. Indeed, we have noted that the orders given to the two new magistrates of Nagasaki in mid-1634 were the second set of so-called "seclusion edicts." If the isolation of Japan had been the bakufu's true overriding goal, then the logical solution to the Yanagawa affair would have been the extirpation of the Sō clan, confiscation of its fief by the bakufu, and the garrisoning of Tsushima, as the western marchland of Japan. The bakufu instead went out of its way to continue relations with Korea—the Sō clan was the only intermediary recognized by Korea—and we have seen that the bakufu reconfirmed Tsushima's rights in conjunction with the promulgation of the 1639 policy on Catholicism and on Portuguese trade.[61] These facts should serve to lay to rest some of the misconceptions that exist about the direction of early Tokugawa foreign policy: the bakufu actively sought contact with Korea and the rest of Japan's international environment, pulling back only when it perceived real danger.

To return to the question of institutional controls over Korean affairs: Iemitsu, ostensibly in response to a request of Sō Yoshinari,[62] appointed a Gozan monk to oversee Korean diplomatic correspondence, and decreed that this system should involve the rotating appointment of Gozan Zen monks, who would be responsible to the bakufu, and who would reside in Genpō's now empty hermitage in Tsushima, Iteian.[63] The first appointee was the monk Gyokuhō Kōrin of the Hōshōin in Tōfukuji, who arrived in Tsushima in the tenth month of 1635.[64] At the same time, on 16 September

[61] Sō Yoshinari to Magistrate of Tongnae, Kan'ei 16/9/X (September-October 1639), in HCO, vol. 4.

[62] TKIR, 1:328, 365; Taishū hennen ryaku (Tōkyōdō Shuppan, 1974), p. 256.

[63] Kansei chōshū shokafu, 8:260.

[64] Ibid.; TKIR, 1:367ff, has a list of the first 63 appointees. Nikkan shokei (MS copy, 8 vols., Historiographical Institute) gives more detailed information. The diplomatic correspondence under the Iteian system, 1635-1871, was compiled as HCO.

1635 (Kan'ei 12/8/5), Yoshinari was required to present to Iemitsu a seventeen-article oath, promising that he would honestly carry out his duties in Korean relations and acknowledging that any further malfeasance would lead to extirpation.[65]

On 6 January 1635 the bakufu had ordered the suspension of all contact between Tsushima and Korea pending the outcome of the trial.[66] Now it was necessary to reopen communications with Pusan. Permission to do so was granted, and at the same time Yoshinari was ordered to inform the Korean government of the conviction of the Yanagawa faction.[67] An envoy from Tsushima arrived in Korea in the sixth month with preliminary notification,[68] but detailed reports awaited the establishment of the Iteian rotation system, and the return to Korea of a troupe of equestrians who had performed before Iemitsu in Edo on 21 May 1635, just three weeks after the settlement of the lawsuit.[69]

In the tenth month of 1635 Yoshinari returned to Tsushima and sent official notification of the lawsuit to the Korean Board of Rites.[70] The letter is of signal importance in Tokugawa diplomatic history for several reasons. First, it was written and countersigned by the newly appointed bakufu overseer, Gyokuhō Kōrin, and thus represents the first extension of direct bakufu control over day-to-day correspondence with Korea. Just as the institution of the Nagasaki magistrate had marked the bakufu's invasion of an area of developing independent rights, so now it was taking authority over rights in which Tsushima had heretofore enjoyed unfettered freedom for centuries. Second, the letter disclaims

[65] *Kan'ei jūsan heishinen Chōsen shinshi kiroku* (3 vols., MS, collection Historiographical Institute), vol. 1 for text of the oath.

[66] *Ibid.*, Kan'ei 11/10/19, 29; 11/11/8, 10, 30; 11/12/1.

[67] *Kansei chōshū shokafu*, 8:260; *NKSK*, 3:484.

[68] *NKSK*, 3:485, citing *Tongnaebu chōbwae samok ch'o.*

[69] *TKIR*, 3:51-54. The Korean discussions of the Yanagawa case are in *Sŭngjŏngwŏn ilgi*, 50:271-278.

[70] *HCO*, vol. 1. Sō Yoshinari to Board of Rites, 1635, fifth lunar month.

all previous correspondence with Korea as forgeries perpetrated by Yanagawa and his party. The disclaimer gave the bakufu the opening to do what it had not done before: to set about a detailed and deliberate reordering of its identity in international affairs. And, third, as one step in that direction, this letter marks the first use in diplomatic correspondence of the title "great prince" (taikun), by which the shogun was to be known in foreign relations. Assumption of this title, as Nakamura Hidetaka has argued, is one of the most significant developments in Tokugawa diplomatic history, as the following discussion should make clear.[71]

KING OR GREAT PRINCE: WHAT'S IN A NAME?

As noted often above, diplomatic titles for the shogun had been disputed frequently—at least as early as 1401—in the course of Japanese history, and had been a specific issue of debate on the occasion of the 1617 Korean embassy in Kyoto. Ieyasu and Hidetada had in the past been willing to be addressed as "king" by Korean, Annamese, and other foreign rulers.[72] And in certain instances their own Japanese subor-

[71] NKSK, 3:482, suggests that the first use of the term "great prince" in Japanese diplomatic letters is in late 1636, but there are at least three earlier occurrences. The title had been applied to Tokugawa shoguns in informal domestic parlance at least as early as 1610; e.g., Honda Tadakatsu testament, "Honda Heihachirō kikigaki," in Naramoto Tatsuya, ed., Kinsei seidō ron (Iwanami Shoten, 1976), p. 22.

[72] E.g., King of Annam to King of Japan (1605), fifth month, sixth day, in GBTS, p. 76; King of Annam to King of Japan, (1610), second month, twentieth day, in ibid., p. 81. The title "king" (j.ō; k; ch. wang) had developed complex and far-reaching significance in East Asia. Diplomatically, when viewed from the Chinese standpoint, proper use of the title "king" by a foreign ruler, or between foreign rulers, implied a linkage of those rulers to the Chinese emperor and, through the Son of Heaven, a relationship to heaven and to the cosmic order itself. "Kings" were subordinate to the Son of Heaven, and derived their legitimacy from him, just as the Son of Heaven derived his from the mandate of heaven. For the shogun to sign a letter as "King of Japan" would thus declare to the East Asian world order Japan's subordination to China, and the shogun's acknowledgment of ex-

dinates had referred to them as "king" in their diplomatic correspondence as representatives of the bakufu.[73] These Tokugawa shoguns, however, had never signed any letters referring to themselves as "king." In both 1617 and 1624, in fact, Ishin Sūden had specifically rejected that title even in the face of strong pressure from Korean embassies.[74] It is clear from Sūden's private office log for that date that he had referred to the *Zenrin kokuhō ki* in the matter, the fifteenth-century compendium of diplomatic documents noted above, which severely criticized Ashikaga Yoshimitsu for accepting and using the title when granted by Ming. A key point in this criticism had been that it was improper to imply that Japan was subordinate to China, which the use of "king" did, and that both that act and the use of the Ming era name denied the Japanese emperor.[75] For similar reasons Doi Toshikatsu, senior member of the roju, speaking for the bakufu in 1636, specifically rejected use of Chinese era names in Japanese diplomatic correspondence.[76]

Having rejected the title "king," and in 1621 the title "shogun," as diplomatic appellations, the bakufu was forced to

ternal sources of legitimacy. Conversely, King Sǒnjo's insistence on such an act could be interpreted as seeking to repay Ming for military aid against Japan in the 1590s, on the one hand, while trying to locate Japan conveniently in the China-centered hierarchy on the same diplomatic level as Korea. If one removed China from consideration, and relied on Mencius' arguments of ethical kingship, it was possible to argue that the title "king" was indeed appropriate for the shogun, and Arai Hakuseki was to attempt to use the title that way in 1711. See John K. Fairbank, "A Preliminary Framework," in Fairbank, *The Chinese World Order*, pp. 1-14, and Benjamin I. Schwartz, "The Chinese Perception of World Order, Past and Present," in *ibid.*, pp. 276ff.

[73] *TKIR*, 3:207, Honda Masazumi to Korean Vice-Minister of Rites O Ǒngnyǒng (1607), fifth month, says, "I have received the august order of our king," etc.

[74] Yi Kyǒngjik, *Pusangnok*, in *KKS*, 2:156; *HKN*, 4:163. etc.

[75] *Zenrin kokuhō ki*, pp. 36–38.

[76] *Injo cho sillok*, 31:72b, at *CWS*, 34:618, reporting the first letters under the Iteian rotation, observes that Japan "will not use Ming era names since, they say, Japan is not subject to Ming."

come up with its own choice. The result of this identity crisis was the title *Nihon-koku Taikun* (Great Prince of Japan), which became the standard diplomatic title for the shogun in Korean relations until the nineteenth century, with one exception; the title was used less consistently in Ryukyuan relations.[77]

Nakamura Hidetaka has argued, on the basis of Razan's wide learning and scholarship, that Hayashi Razan was the originator of the title "great prince" in diplomatic usage. He suggests that the first use of this title in a Japanese diplomatic document was in the letters of Kan'ei 13/12/27 (23 January 1637) which Razan had drafted for Ii Naotaka and Matsudaira Nobutsuna, in reply to Vice-Minister of the Board of Rites Pak Myŏngbu.[78]

Naotaka's and Nobutsuna's letters were written in response to letters from Pak delivered at the time of the visit of the 1636 Korean embassy to Edo, at the same time that the envoys presented the state letter from King Injo (r. 1623-1649) to Iemitsu. Injo's letter was addressed to "His Majesty, the Great Prince of Japan," and the letters from Pak to the senior councillors spoke of "your esteemed Great Prince."[79] The Korean court was not clairvoyant: if the title "great prince" was in fact a Japanese decision, then Japan must have notified the Korean court at some time prior to the departure of this embassy from Seoul if Injo and Pak were to write it in their letters. Failing that, it would be equally reasonable that the title was a Korean selection. But, if such notification did occur, then that and not Naotaka's and Nobutsuna's letters should constitute the first appearance of the title "great prince" in Japanese diplomatic correspondence.

Such notification of course did occur, and is recorded in Korean sources for the last lunar month of 1635, a full year

[77] The exception was in 1711. See my "Korean-Japanese Diplomacy in 1711." On Ryukyuan usage, Mitsugu Matsuda, "The Government of the Kingdom of Ryukyu, 1609-1872," p. 36.

[78] *NKSK*, 3:482. The letters are in *Hayashi Razan bunshū*, pp. 140f.

[79] *TKIR*, 3:102, 219f.

earlier than the letters that Nakamura proposes as the first appearance of the term in Japanese diplomatic documents.[80] Moreover, there are at least three appearances of the title "great prince" applied to the shogun in extant Japanese letters to Korea that antedate the letters cited by Nakamura. The first of these, Sō Yoshinari to the Board of Rites, dated in the tenth lunar month of 1635, is the official announcement to Korea of the outcome of the Yanagawa trial. As the first letter bearing the countersignature of the first Iteian abbot, Kōrin, we may assume a high degree of fidelity to Edo's wishes, and the letter itself cites as its authority "our Great Prince." The second letter, dated in the second lunar month of 1636, is the bakufu's request for the Korean embassy which would arrive in Edo at the end of 1636 bearing Injo's and Pak's letters. It called Iemitsu "our Great Prince," and Hidetada "our late Great Prince." The third letter, dated five months later, reports Yoshinari's audience of 20 July 1636 with Iemitsu, citing specific authority from the "Great Prince" for the invitation to the embassy, and confirming the expected date of the embassy's departure from Korea.[81] It is noteworthy that none of these letters bears the Japanese era name, Kan'ei, although Iemitsu's state letter to Injo of 23 January 1637 would do so.[82] This is a significant point, which will be discussed in some detail below.

The decision to identify the shogun as "great prince" must have been made no later than the tenth month of 1635, and probably before that, since the decision was certainly made in Edo. As to the identity of the person who selected the title, I can find no direct evidence to confirm Professor Nakamura's inference that it was Hayashi Razan. There is, however, indirect evidence giving reason to doubt the attribution. When the time came for the bakufu to compose a reply to Injo's 1636 letter to Iemitsu, it was reported to the Korean embassy that Razan was incapable of understanding

[80] *T'ongmun'gwanji*, p. 87; *Pyŏllye chibyo*, 1:301; 2:512f.
[81] These letters are in *HCO*, vol. 1, and *Nikkan shokei*, vol. 1.
[82] *Hayashi Razan bunshū*, pp. 140f.

the text of Injo's letter, and had written a reply so unsatis-
factory that Iemitsu had rejected it, and reassigned the com-
position of a reply to Sūden's successor as abbot of Konchiin,
Saikaku Genryō.[83] This casts some doubt on Razan's attribution of the reply to his own brush, and renders at least
problematical Nakamura's inference that it was Razan who
selected the title "great prince."

This newly adopted title has no diplomatic precedents in
the East Asian culture sphere,[84] and therefore does not denote any predetermined relationship to China or to the Chinese
world order. It seems to be for precisely these reasons that
the title was chosen. The Tokugawa bakufu had had ambiv-
alent feelings about participation in the Ming world order
from the very beginning of the century. It desired to partake
of the fruits of membership, both in the form of trade and,
perhaps, in its earlier, insecure years, in the form of the derivative legitimacy available through diplomatic recognition
and investiture as "king of Japan." But, conversely, it had
been increasingly unwilling to compromise its growing autonomous structure of legitimacy. Professor Nakamura has
argued convincingly that the establishment of "Great Prince
Diplomacy" in the 1630s represented a declaration of independence from the sinocentric world order dominating East
Asia, and suggests that this fact was a critical determinant of
the ability of Japan alone of the nations of East Asia to escape
colonization or parcelling among the powers in the wake of
the collapse of the Ch'ing world order in the nineteenth century.[85] I would be more specific and link the very structure
of mature Tokugawa foreign relations to the maturation of
the idea of "Japan-as-central-kingdom," which grew from
native and Confucian roots in the seventeenth century, nurtured by the diplomatic system: Japan dealt only with ritual

[83] Im Kwang, *Pyŏngja Ilbon ilgi*, in *KKS*, 2:352.

[84] However, we have seen that it had been used domestically in Japan,
and it was used in Korea to denote royal princes. *Kyŏngguk taejŏn* (Gakushūin Tōyō Bunka Kenkyūsho, 1971), p. 36.

[85] *NKSK*, 3:464ff.

peers and inferiors, and was not subordinate to any other power, so that there was no empirical barrier to the equation noted here. Maruyama Masao and Uete Michiari have linked this equation directly to both nineteenth-century anti-foreign sentiment and to the ability of this xenophobia to metamorphose into the movement to join the community of nations in the nineteenth century,[86] thus avoiding colonization or dismemberment.

Both the Nakamura and the Maruyama/Uete positions are convincing, but one might go a bit further in an attempt to link the two. The choice of "great prince of Japan" was indeed a declaration of independence from the sinocentric order which had dominated East Asia for centuries, and in which Japan had participated, but it was still more. It represented the declaration of a new, self-sufficient domestic legitimacy structure willing to meet with others autonomously in the diplomatic arena. When followed a year later, in Iemetsu's letter to Injo noted above, by the use of the Japanese era name, "Kan'ei," the declaration of independence was complete. Doi Toshikatsu had made this explicit in 1636 in his debate with Korean ambassador Im Kwang,[87] and a year earlier Kōrin had asked that Korea also refrain from using Chinese era names because "Japan was not a vassal of Ming."[88]

The legitimating thrust of the diplomacy of the first thirty years of Tokugawa rule, then, was crystallized in these acts of 1635-1636. Both the inferential evidence and the explicit statements of the most senior bakufu officers directly involved in Korean affairs argue not only for the removal of Japan from the Chinese world order, as urged by Nakamura, but for the establishment of an alternative order, a "great

---

[86] Maruyama Masao, "Kindai Nihon shisōshi ni okeru kokka risei no mondai (1)," in *Tenbō* (January, 1949), pp. 4-15; and Uete Michiari, "Taigai kan no tenkai," in Hashikawa Bunsō and Matsumoto Sannosuke, eds., *Kindai Nihon Seiji shisō shi*, 2 vols. (Yūhikaku, 1971), 1:33-74. This point will be examined at length below, in Chapter V.

[87] Im, *Pyŏngja Ilbon ilgi*, in *KKS*, 2:351f.

[88] *Injo cho sillok*, 31:72b, at *CWS*, 34:618.

prince" order, a Japan-centered order of international relations. In this order, however reliant it was on Chinese traditions in the establishment of its norms and terms, Japan relied on no external agency, such as China, for its definition of itself or for its location of itself in the cosmos, except insofar as these agencies either recognized the bakufu as a peer, as Korea seemed to do, or as a suzerain, as Ryukyu did.

The bakufu was weaving a world order out of those diplomatic partnerships which served to enhance its own aura of authority and legitimacy under mutually acceptable norms of diplomatic behavior. Korea, under attack from the rising Manchu forces on her northern border, was—as the bakufu knew—[89] in no position to risk diplomatic disputes with Japan in the 1630s and 1640s.[90] Ryukyu had been bludgeoned and colonized into cooperation as a vassal. Holland, after a period of exclusion from 1628 to 1633 for what was perceived as a threat to Japanese sovereignty,[91] was woven into the fabric at the very time that the Catholic countries were being excluded, although there was a moment of danger in 1640 due to a violation of the Japanese era name.[92] Similarly, acts of violence against the Japanese community in Siam in 1630 led to a forty-year rupture in relations between these countries, repaired only after a long series of earnest representations of sincerity by several Siamese kings to the bakufu.[93] Government level relations with Ming had been rejected as compromising legitimacy, but trade with Chinese ships coming to Nagasaki was encouraged; it required no compromise of sovereignty, and later proved both a useful

[89] *TKIR*, 3:576-591.

[90] *Pyŏllye chibyo*, 2:512. For a discussion of the Manchu pressures on Korea, *NKSK*, 3:500-536, and Miyake, "Kan'ei jūsannen," pp. 1-8.

[91] On the Hamada Yahei affair, see Iwao, *Sakoku*, pp. 262-268; and Tsuji Zennosuke, *Zōtei kaigai kōtsū shiwa*, pp. 552-572.

[92] *Hirado Oranda shōkan no nikki*, 4:428ff (1640/11/9).

[93] See Iwao, "Reopening of the Diplomatic and Commercial Relations," p. 31.

channel for intelligence and a potential means to assert sovereignty.

WHAT'S IN AN ERA NAME?[94]

There have been frequent references to era names—Japanese, Chinese, and others—in the analysis so far. Let us now make a frontal attack on the problem, commencing with a brief discussion of the significance of these seemingly exotic devices.

From Han times the Chinese have calculated periods of time longer than the month or single year in relatively short, discontinuous sequences of years labelled by *nien-hao* (j. *nengō*, "era names") of felicitous import. The first use of an era name, as distinct from the name of the emperor, appears to have been the Hou-yüan era, proclaimed by the Han emperor Wen-ti in 163 B.C. After a brief hiatus under Wen-ti's successor, the era Chung-yüan was proclaimed in 149 B.C., and era names appear to be continous thereafter, down to the present day.

Since one of the principal functions of the Son of Heaven was to intermediate between Heaven and Man, and since the performance of rituals at the proper times was deemed essential to proper ordering of the universe, proclamation of the calendar had early become one of the prerogatives of the Son of Heaven, the emperor of China. Thus the right to proclaim the calendar and the era name was an index of the locus of legitimacy. Acceptance of the Chinese calendar was one of the prerequisites of admission into diplomatic relations with China at most times in her history for just this reason; it provided Chinese sovereigns with external confirmation of the legitimacy of their tenure in the office of cosmic mediator.[95] As noted in the discussion above, Hayashi Razan's fail-

---

[94] See Mary C. Wright, "What's in a Reign Name: The Uses of History and Philology," in *Journal of Asian Studies*, 18.1 (November 1958): 103-106.

[95] See Tanaka's discussion on this point, *Chūsei taigai kankei shi*, pp. 11, 20.

ure to write the Ming era name was one of the factors that made his letter unacceptable to China.

Japan began to use era names of her own in the great wave of sinification in the seventh and eighth centuries, and from 701 to 1868 used over 200 era names, ranging from less than three months (Ryakunin, 1238-1239) to thirty-five years (Ōei, 1394-1428), all proclaimed under the prerogatives of the imperial court.[96] The imperial court may have used Chinese era names in its dealings with the T'ang court, but the records are not extant,[97] and thereafter Japan, separated by a hazardous ocean voyage from China, seems, with the exception of the early-fifteenth-century Ashikaga shoguns, to have relied exclusively on her own era names, or to have finessed the problem by avoiding the use of any era name. Zuikei Shūhō's analysis in *Zenrin kokuhō ki* shows that Japanese political society was aware of the implications of these facts for Japanese sovereignty and legitimacy.[98]

If we apply this discussion to the immediate problem of the relationship between diplomacy and the legitimation of the early Tokugawa bakufu, it will be recalled that in 1606

[96] On Japanese era names see Herschel Webb and Marleigh G. Ryan, *Research in Japanese Sources: A Guide* (Columbia University Press, 1965), pp. 20-23.

[97] *Koji ruien*, 56 vols. (Yoshikawa Kōbunkan, 1969), 26:840-886. The only letters included are from T'ang, dated Yuan-ho 1/1/28 (806 A.D.).

[98] *Zenrin kokuhō ki*, pp. 36ff. This "era names" custom is not uniquely East Asian; it also exists in the West. It was much more common to specify the era name, *Anno Domini*, in past ages, but it remains implicit in any document we write. The "Christian" world did not universally accept the change from the Julian to the more accurate Gregorian calendar, proclaimed in 1582, until after the Russian Revolution of 1917. The Russian and Greek churches still reject it for ecclesiastical purposes. Jews in the Diaspora had little choice but to follow Christian practice, but at least in the 20th century many reject the "A.D." and "B.C." labels, replacing them with "C.E." (Common Era) and B.C.E. (before C.E.), rather than appear to admit the validity of Jesus' birth as a starting point. And the Hebrew ecclesiastical calendar, in which 1980 = 5740, is still in use, while Islam has an independent calendar dating from the Hegira. Era names are very much with us.

Sō Yoshitoshi and Yanagawa Kagenao had conspired to forge a letter from Ieyasu to Sŏnjo, king of Korea, and that Sŏnjo had recognized it as a forgery, in part because he knew that Japan did not recognize the Ming calendar. Korea, then, was aware of Japan's possession of an independent calendar, and explicitly linked it to Japanese autonomy. Still, Korea tried at various points, as in the discussions between Doi Toshikatsu and Im Kwang in 1636, to get Japan to use the Ming era name.

Even later, however, the bakufu seems to have been inconsistent in its use of era names. There is no record of an authentic bakufu-acknowledged document dated in a foreign calendar, but there are many which do not specify the era name, relying on the Chinese locution *lung-chi* (in the year), and the symbols of the sexagenary cycle; such letters are extant addressed to China, Korea, and Siam.[99] Even after the establishment of the Iteian rotation system in late 1635, the first few letters written by Kōrin did not use the Japanese era name until *after* the journey of the Korean embassy to Edo. That is to say, the decision to use the Japanese era name in all diplomatic correspondence was a separate, and later, policy decision from the establishment of the title "great prince," and of equal importance as a declaration of independence from the Chinese world order. That Korea was surprised, not to say angered, by this is evident from Im Kwang's argument with Doi Toshikatsu.

Letters both to and from Ryukyu, on the other hand, were always dated in the Japanese calendar, clearly indicating Ryukyu's "acceptance" of Japanese suzerainty.[100]

It is not clear what the bakufu intended by its failure to use Japanese era names in its letters to Korea in 1607, 1617, and 1624. But, taken in conjunction with similar behavior in

---

[99] E.g. *Hayashi Razan bunshū*, pp. 130, 134f; *TKIR*, 3:89, 92, 98; *GBTS*, pp. 113-122, *passim.*

[100] *TKIR*, 1:12-77, *passim.*

correspondence with Siam and Ming, they represent the ambivalence of the bakufu over how best to build legitimacy, whether through endogenous or exogenous means of support. Placing Japan too hastily under the Ming umbrella could have led to the type of problems faced by Ashikaga Yoshimitsu, i.e., creating the appearance of a compromise of Japanese sovereignty, without concomitant benefits. Japan therefore refrained from the use of Ming era names. Yet too hastily and unequivocally asserting independence from the Ming order might have cut off Japan, and in particular the bakufu, from the potentially valuable perquisites of membership: the right to trade directly on the China coast, and the attendant power to purchase domestic recognition of authority by distributing trading tallies to appropriately placed Japanese.[101]

As was the case with the question of the shogunal title, so with the era name problem. The Yanagawa Affair and its aftermath forced the issue for the bakufu. Moreover, in 1636 the rising power of the Manchus was apparent even in Japan, and may have been a factor in the decision, as it demonstrated a weakening of Ming power. The bakufu had learned of the first Manchu invasion of Korea in 1627, rather quickly after the event, and had even discussed the possibility of sending aid to Korea.[102] The second, decisive Manchu invasion occurred at the very time that the 1636-1637 Korean embassy was in Japan.

[101] I have omitted any detailed discussion here of the "red seal" ship system (shuinsen), through which the bakufu by the 1620s was providing Japanese and foreign merchants with substantial security on the high seas and the right to trade at specified ports from Hirado to Ayuthia (Siam). The implications for Tokugawa legitimacy of the ability to make these guarantees and to have them recognized by merchants and princes 4,000 miles from Japan should be apparent. The standard treatment is Iwao Seiichi, Shuinsen bōeki shi no kenkyū, by now a classic. See also Robert Innes, "The Door Ajar: Japan's Foreign Trade in the Seventeenth Century" (unpublished Ph.D. dissertation, University of Michigan, 1980), pp. 105-156, and Boxer, The Christian Century, pp. 261-267.

[102] TKIR, 3:576ff.

The question of era names was not settled without debate. After arguing the question with Korean Ambassador Im at the embassy's lodgings on 23 January 1637, Doi Toshikatsu had discussed the matter with the shogun. He returned to the ambassador's lodge at the Honseiji temple in Bakurōchō, Edo, the next day to tell Im that the shogun felt that omission of the Japanese emperor's era name would be insincere. He insisted that Japan would not use the Ming era name, as Im was demanding, because Japan was not a vassal of Ming. Japan could only agree to the omission of the Japanese era name if, as a quid pro quo, Korea would enter into a written agreement to cease using Ming era names.[103]

Here is a clear statement of the bakufu's purpose. It is identical to that which motivated the choice of the title "great prince" the previous year. Japan was demanding that Korea agree to the removal of China as a referent in Japanese-Korean relations, and the bakufu seems even to substantiate the rumors that Richard Cocks had reported in 1617 that the shogunal purpose was to cause Korea "to w'thdraw from favoring the King of China."[104] When Im refused, Iemitsu insisted on asserting Japan's sovereignty on the same level as China's. Im Kwang had to accept Iemitsu's letter and those of the senior councillors or return to Korea empty-handed. It was a Hobson's choice. When Im took the former option, the bakufu had succeeded in putting Japanese era names on the same plane as those of China. The ability so successfully to assert Japanese sovereignty in the international community inevitably redounded to the benefit of the bakufu's legitimacy. Hayashi Gahō, by including these letters in Razan's collected works, made the success public knowledge.[105]

In an ironic turn of history, the Manchus cut off Korea

---

[103] Im, *Pyŏngja ilbon ilgi*, in *KKS*, 2:350-353. Vice-Ambassador Kim Seryŏn, *Sasarignok*, in *KKS*, 2:447-450; and Third Ambassador Hwang Ho, *Tongsarok*, in *KKS*, 3:89f.

[104] Cocks, *Diary*, 22 September 1617 (O.S.), 2:171.

[105] *Hayashi Razan bunshū*, pp. 140f.

from Ming at the very time that her ambassadors were earnestly trying to get Japan to recognize Ming era names, and eight years later they marched into Peking to succeed the Ming dynasty as the Ch'ing dynasty. Korea, which had been proud to be associated in the Ming world order, and which had been saved from the Japanese invasions of the 1590s with Ming assistance, was not quickly reconciled to the fall of Ming. Although Seoul had no alternative but to accept the Ch'ing calendar in her dealings with Peking—the Manchu invasions were even fresher in Korean memory than the Japanese invasions; the Ch'ing now had legitimacy-building problems at least as great as had been those of the Tokugawa bakufu—Korea proceeded to omit the Chinese era name whenever possible, and one of the first places was in correspondence with Japan. Korea dropped Chinese era names from letters to Japan in early 1645, within months of the fall of Peking, and never restored them. In their stead Korea used only the cyclical signs for the years, month specified, day left blank.[106]

Thus, with the establishment of "great prince" diplomacy in 1635-1636, and the disappearance of China as an implicit diplomatic reference point in 1645, the bakufu had succeeded in creating an autonomous system of diplomacy, independent of China, and consonant with the demands of Japanese sovereignty and of bakufu legitimacy. Even prior to this, in 1639, the bakufu had expelled the Portuguese, and in 1640-1641 had removed the Dutch from their relative freedom in

---

[106] HCO, vols. 9, 10. The day was left blank lest it violate any taboo days of the recipient. Some letters were actually dated "Year. Month. Lucky Day," and the recipient could pick his own. The first extant letter without an era name is Third Minister, Board of Rites, Yu Sŏngjŭng to Sō Yoshinari (1645), third month, HCO, vol. 10. The decision to omit Chinese era names from letters to Japan was taken on Injo 23/3/11 (7 April 1645). Pibyŏnsa tŭngnok (28 vols., National History Compilation Committee, 1959-1960), 1:794f. Nakamura Tadashi is wrong to state, "Korea used Ming (later Ch'ing) era names in correspondence with Japan." "Shimabara no ran to sakoku," p. 240. This is an error beclouding the very nature of the "Kan'ei diplomacy" Nakamura seeks to explain.

Hirado to their long imprisonment on the man-made island of Deshima, in Nagasaki harbor. It is not the purpose here to trace European policy in detail, but it is germane to note that the proximate cause of the destruction of the Hirado Dutch factory and the move to Nagasaki was the discovery under the gable of a newly built warehouse of the alien—nay, Christian!—era name, "A.D. 1640."[107] It was not just with Korea that the bakufu would dispute era names to protect its legitimacy.

One might argue that the expulsion of the Catholics from Japan in 1639 should be regarded in a different light than it has to date. It constituted not the *sui generis* "isolation" policy of a xenophobic Japan, toward which all Japanese foreign policy had been moving ineluctably for the full twenty-seven years since Ieyasu's first anti-Christianity edict, divorced from all other foreign policy, and at the sacrifice of a promising foreign trade. Neither was it unprecedented; it was nearly identical in many ways to the policy that Ming had carried out against Japan at several points in the past. Rather, the so-called "isolation" policy should be seen as part of a much larger foreign policy embracing all of Japan's world. That foreign policy made tradeoffs; all rational foreign policies do. The Tokugawa tradeoff was between unrestricted foreign commerce, on the one hand, and the demands of sovereignty, security, and legitimacy, on the other.

Trade has been shown to have increased after "isolation," and the bakufu ordered the daimyos of Tsushima and Satsuma to ensure that there be no decrease in total silk imports as a result of the expulsion of the Catholics. What was gained in the expulsion of the Catholics was a sense of bakufu legitimacy enhanced by the removal of those elements that seemed to challenge it. One might even argue that the abandonment of the *shuin* trading license system was also in the interest of bakufu legitimacy. By the mid-1630s, with the English and the Spanish gone, and with relations with Siam

[107] *Hirado Oranda shōkan no nikki*, 4:428ff.

ruptured, the bakufu was no longer in a position to issue guarantees of passage and trade with any expectation that they would be respected or could be enforced. With no further expectation of the rewards of trade with Japan, these foreigners had no further reason to refrain from preying on Japanese ships, and the bakufu was unwilling to test its ability to enforce them by arms two or three thousand miles from home. The payoff was not sufficient to risk the integrity of so carefully nurtured a system of legitimacy.

RING IN THE NEW: A BELL FOR IEMITSU

The bakufu's efforts to assert legitimacy through diplomacy did not stop with the establishment of "great prince" diplomacy and the expulsion of Catholicism. Rather, they continued for many years thereafter, with energy decreasing as the perception of need declined.

The Korean embassy of 1636-1637 was bullied into a pilgrimage to Ieyasu's tomb at Nikko, much as Cocks had suggested might happen nineteen years earlier, making the trek in the midst of a heavy blizzard.[108] Sō Yoshinari first broached the subject, at the request of Iemitsu, on the day after the embassy arrived in Edo, 3 January 1637. Iemitsu wanted the embassy to make a sightseeing trip to Nikko "as an act of splendor for the whole country,"[109] that is, as a demonstration of the power and majesty of the bakufu. Im Kwang

---

[108] TKIR, 3:23-28; Shiryō kōhon, vol. 171, part 15. The bakufu did not plan the blizzard, but it did mobilize a small army of corvee labor to shovel the snow. Kurokawa Dōyū, Enpekiken zuihitsu (Kan'ei 13/12/17), in the Shiryō Kōhon, vol. 171, part 15. Some Japanese records pretend that the Korean pilgrimage was at the earnest request of the Korean embassy. See "Chōsen ōrai" in TKIR, 3:26; or Hayashi Razan bunshū, in ibid., p. 28. Some daimyos believed this as well, a fact which could not fail to enhance shogunal prestige. Hosokawa Tadatoshi to Soga Matazaemon (Nagasaki magistrate), Kan'ei 14/1/26 (20 February 1637), in Hosokawa kaki, "Tadatoshi-fu," quoted in Shiryō kōhon, vol. 170, part 15. But other records show this was not so. TKIR, 3:23.

[109] Im, Pyŏngja Ilbon ilgi, in KKS, 2:338f.

1. Im Kwang's arrival at the entrance to Tōshōgū, the first of three visits by Korean ambassadors, as depicted by Kanō Tan'yu in the shrine's history

objected, but ultimately, on 13 January, a 214-man contingent of the Korean embassy, including the three principal envoys, departed for Nikko. They presented incense at Ieyasu's shrine at Nikko on the 17th, and were back in Edo on the 20th.[110]

How did Tokugawa political society respond? Hosokawa Tadatoshi, who had reason to be grateful to the bakufu, having received the 540,000 koku Kumamoto fief only four years earlier, described the event in a letter to the Nagasaki magistrate Soga Matazaemon a month later, calling Iemitsu's success "laudable," and the event was recorded in Tadatoshi's genealogy.[111] Niwa Nagashige, receiving the senior council's order to supply horses for the procession to Nikko, thought the event was evidence of the excellence of Iemitsu's

[110] *TKIR*, 3:23-28; Im, *Pyŏngja Ilbon ilgi*, pp. 345-348; Kim Seryŏn, *Sasangnok*, pp. 441-444; Hwang Ho, *Tongsarok*, pp. 84-87. One hundred sixty-nine Koreans stayed behind in Edo. *TKIR*, 3:28.

[111] In *Shiryō kōhon*, vol. 171, part 15.

1. *continued*

rule.[112] The day after the embassy returned to Edo, Iemitsu personally thanked Yoshinari,[113] who gave this reason for the pilgrimage in his official biography: "The Three Ambassadors paid their respects at [Ieyasu's] shrine solely because the three generations of peace [which have prevailed between our two countries] and the peace of Korea are due entirely to the high grace of Tōshōgū [Ieyasu]."[114] Clearly political society had been impressed. [115]

Seven years later the bakufu was able to take advantage of Korea's weakened position under Manchu pressure to get Korea to agree to an unprecedented mission to congratulate Iemitsu on the birth of his son and heir, the future shogun

[112] *Niwa monjo*, quoted in *Shiryō Kōhon*, vol. 171, part 15 (Kan'ei 13/12/17).

[113] *TKIR*, 3:28 (*Chōsen ōrai*).

[114] *Kansei chōshū shokafu*, 8:260.

[115] Nakamura has noted the value of these Nikko pilgrimages—there were three by Korean embassies, in 1637, 1643, and 1655, and one by a Ryukyuan mission, in 1644—for Iemitsu's authority as a ruler. *NKSK*, 3:305.

Ietsuna.[116] The previous year, 1642, the bakufu had arranged to cap the newly completed Nikko complex with a congratulatory inscription written by the Korean king himself. The inscription, "The Hall of Religious Practices in Nikko Calms the World and Illumines Filial Piety," was hung over the Yōmei Gate, main entrance to the shrine, where for many years it impressed daimyos on their pilgrimages there, with this high praise from a foreign king.[117] "Nikko" in this inscription of course also represents Ieyasu himself. An anonymous Korean diarist with the 1643 embassy asserts that the bakufu's request for this plaque had orginated with the superannuated Tendai monk Tenkai (1536–1643), who had been a zealous guardian of Ieyasu's memory and of Tokugawa legitimacy for two generations.[118] One even wonders whether the splendors of foreign recognition showered on Tōshōgū may have helped to encourage the imperial court to grant the shrine the coveted *miya* status, highest for a shrine, in 1645.

In early 1642 the bakufu, through Tsushima, arranged for the casting in Korea of a bronze bell, which would be sent with the 1643 embassy to Nikko. Japan even supplied the

---

[116] On the differing Korean and Japanese reasons for the embassy, see Miyake, "Sakoku chokugo no Chōsen tsūshinshi," especially pp. 32–37. Korea was under heavy Manchu pressure to mediate the opening of diplomatic relations with Japan, but Korea had no desire to see these two barbarian nations communicate with each other. *NKSK*, 3:500–524.

[117] See Matsuda Kinoe, "Richō Jinso yori kizō seru Nikkō Tōshōgū no hengaku to kane, tsuketari, Daiyūbyō no Chōsen tōrō," in *Nissen shiwa*, 2 (1926): 48–77, and Nakamura Hidetaka, "Nikkōzan Tokugawa Ieyasu byōshadō hengaku no mohon ni tsuite," in *Chōsen gakuhō*, 49 (1968): 241–257. Nakamura shows that the calligraphy on the plaque was not in fact Injo's, but since Japanese thought for 320 years that it was Injo's royal hand (a Nikko catalogue of 1694 lists it as a "plaque written in eight characters by the king of Korea;" *Odōguchō*, quoted by Matsuda, p. 59), the effect is undiminished. *TKIR*, 3:30.

[118] *Kyemi tongsa ilgi*, in *KKS*, 3:227f. Tenkai, who had served the Tokugawa family since 1589, was instrumental in the establishment of the Nikko shrines. In 1636, then a spry centenarian, he was at Nikko for the first Korean pilgrimage there.

bronze. We shall here pass over the negotiating process which enabled Japan to persuade Injo's court to accede to this latest Japanese request; let us merely repeat that Korea was under severe pressure from the Manchu emperor Abahai (Ch'ing T'ai-tsung) to help him to open relations with Japan. Abahai had taken two Korean princes hostage, so Injo could ill afford a rupture with Japan over any issue, and certainly not over a bell.

The Korean bell bore an inscription of nearly 150 characters, composed by the second minister of the Board of Rites; the calligraphy was by a prominent Korean calligrapher. The inscription celebrates Ieyasu's splendor in terms so effusive that even Iemitsu would have been hard put to outdo it. An extract:

> The hall of religious practice at Nikko was constructed for the Great Avatar Tōshō [Ieyasu]. The Great Avatar was possessed of infinite merit and virtue; he receives infinite reverence. . . . The filial piety inherent in succeeding to his work and expanding thereupon increasingly glorifies the illustrious deeds of this ancestor. Our King has heard of this and, overjoyed, has caused this Dharma Bell to be cast in order to offer it as a supplement to the Three Treasures at his sepulchre. . . .[119]

It is worth noting that the inscription makes no mention of the request for the bell, making it appear that the virtue of the Tokugawa house simply overflows the shores of Japan and is evident even as far away as Korea. This accords quite literally with one of the claims made by Hayashi Razan in the letter to China that he drafted for Honda Masazumi in 1611.[120]

[119] Inscription, Korean bell, Tōshōgū, Nikko, Tochigi Prefecture. In order to indicate respect for the denotee of a particular character, the writer changed lines, so that no other character appeared above, e.g., the character for king. The humility of the character for subject was indicated by writing that character in a smaller size. *TKIR*, 3:29f, gives the full text but omits these significant details.

[120] *Hayashi Razan bunshū*, p. 130.

2. Bronze bell presented by King Injo for the shrine to Tokugawa Ieyasu, hung before the Yōmei Gate, Tōshōgū, Nikko

On the day that the Korean embassy of 1643 passed through Kyoto, 462 strong, the bell was apparently the talk of the town. Kujō Michifusa, then the Naidaijin and later imperial regent, recorded the entire scene in his diary. He also recorded the complete inscription on the bell, including the untranslatable calligraphic honorifics, and a catalog of the offertory objects being brought by the embassy. Michifusa was nearly overwhelmed, exclaiming, "Has this shogun's military might already reached to foreign countries! Recently they have been sending embassies on every felicitous occasion."[121]

The bell and offertory objects were sent to Edo by sea and, when they arrived there, on 1 August 1643, they put Iemitsu

[121] *Michifusa kō ki*, 10 vols. (MS copy, Historiographical Institute, Tokyo University), vol. 5 (Kan'ei 20/6/14). It is only fair to mention that Michifusa set a record for the briefest tenure as *sesshō* in Japan's history, only five days, in 1647.

"in superb humor."[122] The following month an anonymous Korean diarist attached to the embassy recorded the reason for Iemitsu's elation: the bell had arrived on the memorial day of Ieyasu's death. Exclaiming that it was "surely a Heaven-sent blessing that this bell and the offertories had arrived on that day," Iemitsu had marked the felicity of the event by pardoning six criminals who had been scheduled for execution that day.[123]

Iemitsu had good reason to be pleased. He may never have learned of Michifusa's effusive reaction, though it would have gratified him. Hereafter every daimyo, every imperial envoy making the pilgrimage to Nikko, as they were not infrequently required to do, would be greeted upon his approach to the shrines with tangible, graphic evidence of the far-reaching power and majesty of the bakufu. Just as its institutional base was being put in order, so its legitimacy was being made manifest. The bell stands even today, to the right of the Yōmei Gate, opposite an ornate bronze chandelier presented by the Dutch, a durable symbol of the successful manipulation of diplomacy by the first three Tokugawa shoguns in the building of their foundations of legitimacy. Twelve years later Ietsuna would likewise obtain from Korea matched bronze lanterns, inscribed with suitably laudatory prose, which stand before Iemitsu's memorial shrine at Nikko, Daiyūin.[124] But this was merely gilding the lily, for the bakufu no longer felt insecure in its legitimacy. Never again was the bakufu to demand this type of symbol from Korea.

CHRISTIANITY AND LEGITIMACY-ORIENTED DIPLOMACY

The development of Japan's anti-Catholic policies from 1587 to 1639 and beyond is too well known to bear repeating

---

[122] *Yūbyō nikki*, quoted in *TKIR*, 3:31.

[123] *Kyemi tongsa ilgi*, in *KKS*, 3:229. I have not yet found confirmation of this amnesty in Japanese records. *Tokugawa jikki*, 3:317, merely notes that the bell was sent on to Nikko on the nineteenth.

[124] The text is reproduced in *TKIR*, 3:47.

here.[125] That policy sought the preservation of three interdependent desiderata: Japanese security, Japanese sovereignty, and Tokugawa legitimacy. To the extent that Christianity might make the bakufu appear unable to guarantee either of the first two, the third was undermined. We have made the same sort of observation as a tentative explanation of the abandonment of the *shuin* trading license system. In order to assure the success of this policy the bakufu sought the cooperation of neighboring governments. Hayashi Razan's letter for Suetsugu Heizō to the governor of Fukien, 1625, is one of the best known of these efforts,[126] but this letter antedates the all-out attack on Christianity by several years, and is the last such letter to Ming. Again, Chinese merchants coming to Nagasaki were thoroughly warned about both the evils of Christianity itself and the dangers that the bearer of this "disease" would have to risk should he dare come to Japan.[127]

In regard to Korea, however, Japan carried out a thoroughgoing campaign for support of the anti-Christian policy, starting as early as 1639 and continuing, with diminishing intensity, at least into the 1680s. The earliest extant letter, dated in the ninth lunar month of 1639, addressed to the magistrate of Tongnae (now part of Pusan), gets right to the point: "The southern barbarians are trying to seduce the people with their base doctrine [Christianity], and so the Great Prince has from this year prohibited the Southern Barbarians from coming to Japan." A scant two months later Tongnae Magistrate Kang Taesu replied that, "To suppress the vile and foster the right is the great essential in governing the

[125] C. R. Boxer, *The Christian Century in Japan*, is a classic treatment of early Japanese reactions to the west, as is G. B. Sansom, *The Western World and Japan* (Alfred A. Knopf, 1950), especially pp. 115-131 and 167-196; George Elison, *Deus Destroyed*, is a challenging examination of the impact of Christianity on Japanese ideology in the early Tokugawa period.

[126] *Hayashi Razan bunshū*, pp. 136f.

[127] Yano Jin'ichi, *Nagasaki shishi Tsūkō bōeki hen Tōyō shokoku* (Nagasaki Shiyakusho, 1938), pp. 50-64; Yamawaki Teijirō, *Nagasaki no Tōjin bōeki* (Yoshikawa Kōbunkan, 1964), pp. 297f.

land. Were it not for the sternness of your Great Prince's Government, what then might things come to?"[128]

When the Korean embassy of 1643 was in Edo, Hayashi Razan and Andō Shigenaga, now Commissioner of Shrines and Temples, called on Ambassador Yun Sunji at his lodgings in the Honseiji temple. Razan raised the question of Christianity, explained the prohibition in force in Japan, and asked whether Korea also had such a policy. The embassy replied through Chief Interpreter Hong Hŭinam, somewhat disingeniously, that Korea had never even heard of Christianity until Tsushima had broached the issue.[129] This is a very rare instance in the history of Korean embassies to Japan, for discussions of substantive issues were seldom recorded, except those issues relating to postwar normalization. It is an index of the importance that both sides placed on this problem.

Like the United States seeking support for the war in Vietnam, or mobilizing the Organization of American States behind its embargo on Cuba, the bakufu continued, through Tsushima, to bombard Korea with letters on the evils of Christianity. The bakufu was seeking support and cooperation in keeping the menace under control.

In 1644 those efforts bore fruit. The magistrate of Pusan turned over to the chief of the Japanese factory there a Ming merchant ship and its crew of fifty-two, although it is not clear why Korea should turn Chinese seamen over to Japan. Upon examination by the Nagasaki magistrate, five of the fifty-two were found to be Christians. This affair was reported to Iemitsu himself, who was described as "greatly pleased and deeply obliged" by Korea's sincere cooperation in this Christian problem. These statements are contained in a letter from Sō Yoshinari to the Board of Rites. That they

---

[128] These letters are found in *HCO*, and were collected by Tsushima's Edo officials as *Kan'ei Shōhō no tabi Yaso shūmon go-genkin ni tsuki Chōsen koku go-ōfuku shokan utsushi* (MS, Sō Collection, Historiographical Institute), which contains twelve letters, sent 1639-1645, and Korean replies. Most of these letters were sent on bakufu orders.

[129] *Kyemi tongsa illok*, in *KKS*, 3:225f.

reflect bakufu policy is clear from the fact that the letter was written, not by the Iteian resident, as one would expect, but by Hayashi Razan.[130] Third Minister of the Board of Rites Yu Sŏngjŭng replied a month later that such cooperation was only natural in the pursuit of friendly relations.[131] There were at least two further occasions when Tsushima communicated with Korea on the Christianity question on the order of the bakufu.[132]

The bakufu was of course trying to build international legitimacy for its foreign policy. There was the added prestige value of the appearance that Korea had been bent to the will of Japan. With Korea turning Chinese over to Japan it might even be made to seem that Richard Cocks's rumors of 1617 had come true, and that the shogun had succeeded in getting Korea "to withdraw from favoring the king of China." But in the long run the blatant failure of a policy could do even more to harm the aura of legitimacy than the failure to act in the first place, as the failure to "repel the barbarians" would in the nineteenth century. It was against this prospect that the bakufu sought to guard. I suggest that similar considerations operated in the abandonment of the *shuin* license system for trade, the ban on foreign travel except that by Tsushima and Satsuma, and the embargo on travel to Japan from the Catholic countries.

The Tokugawa bakufu in its first half century of existence had a consistent, developing interest in using its foreign relations powers as a tool of legitimation. In the early stages serious consideration was given to entering the Chinese world order for the purpose of clothing the bakufu in the type of derivative legitimacy that system could provide; had the ba-

---

[130] Sō Yoshinari to Board of Rites, *HCO*, vol. 10; *Hayashi Razan bunshū*, p. 148; *Ikoku nikki*, vol. 4.

[131] Yu Sŏngjŭng to Sō Yoshinari, *ŭryu*, 3rd month, *HCO*, vol. 10; *Kan'ei Shōhō no tabi Yaso shūmon*.

[132] *Yoshizane kō go-kafu*, MS, n.d., Sō Collection, Banshōin, Tsushima.

kufu in fact done so it would have been in the interesting position of using two external legitimators, its Japanese imperial mandate and Chinese investiture.

But with the growing success of the bakufu in other areas of domestic and foreign policy the need to borrow legitimation was diminished. Conversely, the need to protect the nascent autonomous/endogenous legitimacy of the bakufu grew to take precedence. In 1621 the bakufu rejected an opportunity for relations with China for just these reasons. By centralizing the source of authority in foreign affairs in the hands of the bakufu even as it delegated certain segments of that authority to subordinate entities, the Tokugawa bakufu was at once expanding and strengthening the authority of shogunal government in foreign affairs which had been initiated by the Kamakura bakufu nearly four centuries earlier. But where the earlier bakufus, as well as Nobunaga and Hideyoshi, had failed to bring all competing centers of competence in foreign affairs under their control, by the time of Iemitsu the Tokugawas had made all rights to external contact dependent on written authority from them, and had incorporated that authority into the general structure of authority of the Tokugawa state system.[133]

One might say that the early Tokugawa shoguns had suc-

---

[133] Tsushima's, Satsuma's, and Matsumae's special rights in foreign relations, whether for trade, voyages, or foreign residence, or to act as overseas representatives of the bakufu, were uniformly dependent upon inclusion in written instruments of enfeoffment (*andojō*) issued at the start of each shogunal or daimyo reign, and the articles of each daimyo's blood oath to the shogun. This arrangement was regularized in the period 1634-1636, shortly after the death of Hidetada, when so many critical institutional and policy changes were being made in foreign affairs. Satsuma's rights in Ryukyuan relations were so ordered during Iemitsu's Kyoto progress, immediately after the reception of the 1634 embassy. Matsumae's rights were made dependent on such documents in late 1634 after Iemitsu's return to Edo. *Shiryō kōhon*, vol. 169, part 10; Asao, *Sakoku*, 257-264. The authorization of Tsushima's rights and obligations was part of the settlement of the Yanagawa affair. *Yanagawa Shigeoki kuji kiroku*, vol. 2.

ceeded at what Oliver Cromwell attempted a few years later in England:

> Cromwell recognized that the Stuart monarchs had weakened their position in England by not understanding that foreign affairs played a role in domestic politics and could be used to bolster the government. Cromwell did not make the same mistake . . [in the] priorities that [he] established for his government. Once he realized that foreign policy gave him a means by which he could assert aggressive leadership . he devoted much of his energy toward a diplomatic structure whose overriding purpose was to insure his position as the political leader of England.[134]

By 1650 the bakufu had succeeded in generating a portfolio of legitimating assets which were new in Japanese history. When Edo Castle was rebuilt in the 1650s the donjon was not replaced. This act of military confidence symbolized the bakufu's success in establishing principles of legitimacy independent of and supplemental to the imperial mandate. That it had done this in the domestic arena both ideologically and politically is widely recognized.[135] By the astute use of power and manipulation of classical indices of legitimacy in diplomacy as well, and by the artful use of diplomacy for propaganda at home, the bakufu had further assured its independent bases of legitimacy. Kujō Michifusa's reaction to the inscription on the Korean bell and the spectacle of the 1643 Korean embassy's passage through Kyoto merely echoed the rumors reported years earlier by Richard Cocks and Sakai Tadakatsu. Through diplomacy the bakufu was generating recognition of its independent rights to power in the very core of the classical center of legitimation.

The establishment of a bakufu monopoly of authority in the realm of foreign relations was a major building block in

[134] Charles P. Korr, *Cromwell and the New Model Foreign Policy*, p. 5.
[135] Kitajima Masamoto, *Edo bakufu no kenryoku kōzō* (Iwanami Shoten, 1964), pp. i–ii; and Abe Yoshio, *Nihon shushigaku to Chōsen* (Tōkyō Daigaku Shuppankai, 1965), pp. 24–32.

the foundations of the early bakufu's authority, and the ability to manipulate those foreign relations served the early shoguns as a significant device of legitimating propaganda. The importance of this linkage between the early bakufu's monopolization of authority in foreign relations and the establishment of bakufu legitimacy is perhaps best seen in relief against precisely the converse relationship at the end of the Tokugawa period. By polling the daimyos in 1853 for advice in the disposition of the American letters and demands communicated by Commodore Matthew C. Perry, Abe Masahiro surrendered the bakufu's putative monopoly over the determination of foreign policy.[136] When Hotta Masayoshi went even further, in 1858, referring the draft of the Harris Treaty to the imperial court for approval, he was not only admitting impotence within the confines of samurai society, which had monopolized the right of action in political affairs since the start of the Tokugawa dynasty, he was inviting the imperial institution to reenter the political arena once more as an active principal.[137] Moreover, he had thereby substantially, and ultimately, perhaps, mortally undercut the shogunal claims of exclusive competence in foreign relations which helped to undergird the bakufu's legitimacy.[138]

[136] W. G. Beasley, *Select Documents on Japanese Foreign Policy, 1853-1868* (Oxford University Press, 1955), pp. 23, 102-107; also Harold Bolitho, *Treasures among Men: The Fudai Daimyo in Tokugawa Japan* (Yale University Press, 1974), p. 221.

[137] Herschel Webb discusses the significance of foreign developments in the repoliticization of the imperial institution in the 1850s, *The Japanese Imperial Institution in the Tokugawa Period*, pp. 223-259.

[138] Beasley, *Select Documents*, p. 36. See pp. 183-189 for the treaty text; pp. 180f for the court's response.

CHAPTER FOUR

The World Through Binoculars: Bakufu Intelligence and Japanese Security in an Unstable East Asia

REBUILDING Edo Castle in 1657 without the great tower of its central keep stood as fitting symbol of the bakufu's success in the domestic arena, and of its concomitant sense of security from any credible internal threat. Domestic affairs were, after all, reasonably within the sphere of shogunal competence, and they caused little concern to Edo for the next century and a half or more. Yet there remained beyond Japan's shores potential sources of danger that the bakufu could not keep directly under control, but only under careful scrutiny.

The threat from Europe was effectively contained after the 1630s by the expulsion of the Iberians from the Japan trade, by the limitations placed on Japanese overseas travel, and by the restriction of Dutch access to Japan to the single port of Nagasaki. Danger from Japan's maritime and continental neighbors in East Asia, however, could not be so readily contained, nor could it be lightly dismissed.

The massive physical size of China, and the geographic proximity of Japan to the entire East Asian region, were simple facts of the Japanese environment, but in the seventeenth century the region was particularly volatile. This volatility was not only a result of the presence of the Europeans; massive civil wars in Japan, in the late sixteenth century, had spilled over into Asia, while international and civil wars in and around China were a virtual constant from the mid 1610s to the mid 1680s. These wars the bakufu could not ignore, for they might at any time overflow the continent and wash upon the shores of Japan. They imposed upon the bakufu a continuously threatening international environment, which made Asian affairs, especially continental affairs, a source of constant security concern to the Edo authorities, for Japan inevitably became peripherally involved in these contests, either as a haven for refugees, or as a potential source of military assistance to one belligerent or another. Several times, indeed, the bakufu was forced to debate the question of whether to involve Japan directly in the conflict, either as a combatant, or as a supplier of arms and materiel. The answer to those questions was not consistently negative.

For even though Japan has never been successfully invaded, in fully historical times, from the Asian mainland, nor subject to a dynasty of foreign conquest, at least after the sixth century,[1] still, despite this high degree of apparent security, changes in the strategic balance in continental East Asia have often affected Japan in significant ways. Some modern scholars, for example, credit a perceived threat from the unifying Sui and T'ang dynasties in China, and the Silla unification of Korea, in the sixth and seventh centuries, with catalyzing the emergence of the first unified Japanese state.[2] But more recent, and of much greater significance in the consciousness of the Japanese of Tokugawa times, were the thirteenth-century Mongol invasions of Japan, the only fully historic, and therefore clearly remembered, attempt by a foreign power to conquer Japan.[3]

[1] See Gari K. Ledyard, "Galloping Along with the Horseriders, Looking for the Founders of Japan," in *Journal of Japanese Studies*, 1.2 (Spring 1975): 217-254, for an illuminating discussion of the thesis that Japan was under a conquest dynasty in the fourth and fifth centuries.

[2] It is the position of Inoue Mitsusada, for example, that, "Japan's direct motive in adopting the *ritsuryō* system [of Chinese-style centralized bureaucratic state] was the foreign rather than the domestic situation." See his "The *Ritsuryō* System in Japan," in *Acta Asiatica*, 31 (1977): 93.

[3] For an introduction to the impact of the Mongol invasions of 1274 and 1281, see Kyotsu Hori, "The Economic and Political Effects of the Mongol

The rise of the Manchus to form a unified state, their struggle for control of China proper, and the final total victory of the Ch'ing dynasty (1644-1911) in the 1680s forcefully recalled for contemporary Japanese the Mongol invasions of four centuries earlier. The Manchu conquest of China forced Tokugawa Japan to remain sensitive to the shifting strategic balance in the region, to remain vigilant, and to be constantly aware of the fact that she could not avoid a strategic relationship to her environment. While perceived threats to the security of the Tokugawa state had led to increasingly stringent restrictions on European relations, and on European and Chinese access to Japan, no amount of passive isolationism could deny the fact that Japan remained dangerously close to China. As the strategic events in the East Asian region unfolded, therefore, the bakufu responded with intelligence and security policies that were designed to defend Japan. That response was at the same time a tacit, and sometimes an explicit, acknowledgment of the manifest truth: Japan is in Asia, and cannot isolate herself from it.

The consolidation of the Manchu tribes into a state had begun in the late sixteenth century, and the great state-builder Nurhaci (1559-1626) had even offered in the early 1590s to help Ming fight off the invading Japanese in Korea.[4] Japan appears to have taken little notice of the rising power in the steppes until early 1627, however, when Nurhaci's son Abahai invaded Korea.[5] In that year, Manchu forces drove quickly south from the Yalu to Seoul, forcing King Injo to flee to Kanghwa Island, off the coast west of the capital, traditionally a refuge of Korean royalty in times of crisis. On 18 April

Wars,'' in John W. Hall and Jeffrey P. Mass, eds., *Medieval Japan: Essays in Interpretation* (Yale University Press, 1974), pp. 184-198.

[4] Immanuel C. Y. Hsü, *The Rise of Modern China* (Oxford University Press, 1970), p. 21.

[5] There is a brief account of the 1627 Manchu invasion of Korea in William E. Henthorn, *A History of Korea* (The Free Press, 1971), pp. 186ff. For a more detailed account see *Han'guksa*, vol. 4, *Kŭnse hugi pyŏn*, pp. 87-94. The Manchu armies entered Korea at Ŭiju, on the Yalu River, on 4 March 1627.

1627 Injo took an oath of fealty to the Manchu ruler and capitulated to the invaders.[6]

The Korean government quickly informed the director of Tsushima's trading outpost in Pusan of the invasion, in part because the Japanese would soon find out in any case, but also because the Korean government thought it might use the invasion as an excuse to terminate, or at least to suspend, the Pusan trade.[7] This Tsushima was not willing to do, nor could Korea, an enemy at her back, effectively resist. But while Tsushima was attempting to exploit Korea's weakness to expand her trading privileges, it was also incumbent upon Sō Yoshinari as a diplomatic agent of the bakufu to inform the shogunate of the Manchu invasion of Korea. Exactly when Yoshinari reported the invasion to Edo is not clear from the extant records, but the following year, just before Yoshinari left Edo to return to his domain, Iemitsu summoned the Tsushima lord to Edo Castle. Through Tōdō Takatora he ordered the daimyo to send a reconnaissance mission to Seoul, and apparently told Yoshinari that if Seoul was still in military danger he would send troops to Korea to help to resist the Manchus:[8]

---

[6] *Injo cho sillok*, 15:50a-51a, at *CWS*, 34:181.

[7] *Injo cho sillok*, 13:31a, at CWS, 34:119, reports that on 25 March 1627 the Pibyŏnsa (Border Defense Agency) suggested, and the king agreed, that the invasion be reported to the Japanese at Pusan. Tongnae Magistrate Yu T'aehwa then wrote to Yoshinari asking him to suspend trading activities until the emergency had ended, *CTT, kan* 6; p. 222; *TKIR*, 3:577, but, as Yu noted in his report to Seoul in mid-April, the Japanese refused to suspend the trade, but showed their sympathy with the Korean cause by presenting some weapons to Korea. *Chŏptaesa mongnok ch'o*, quoted in *Chōsenshi* (36 vols. and index, Keijo: Chōsen Sōtokufu, 1933, repr., Tōkyō Daigaku Shuppankai, 1976), vol. 5, pt. 2, p. 102.

[8] *Tokugawa jikki*, 2:451. This notice is based on the Sō family genealogy, in *Kansei chōshū shokafu*, and should be treated with caution, but the compilers of both the *Tokugawa jikki* and *TKIR* (3:577) accept it as genuine. Compare *CTT, kan* 6, p. 222, which says that Iemitsu sent Tōdō Takatora, long a patron of Yoshinari's interests, to convey his orders to Yoshinari, *Taishū hennen ryaku*, pp. 249-250, and *Kōrin kōryaku*, quoted in Ura Yasukazu, "Minmatsu Shinsho no Senman kankei shijō ni okeru Nihon no chii

Since the Shogun has heard that the Tatars recently invaded the western frontier of Korea, he personally ordered Sō Yoshinari, the Governor of Tsushima, to send an envoy to the Korean royal capital immediately upon his return [to Tsushima] to reconnoiter the situation there in detail. [He said that] if the Korean royal capital was in danger [Japan] would send an expeditionary force.

Tsushima had frequently presented arms and ammunition to Korea as tribute articles over the previous decade, or offered them for sale at the trading post in Pusan, so it is not surprising that she should do so once more in this time of crisis. In the fourth lunar month of 1627, for example, before Iemitsu's orders, or even before Iemitsu could have known of the Manchu invasion of Korea, Tsushima presented two hundred catties of gunpowder, and five hundred long swords, to Korea. What total volume of arms was sent to Korea at this time is difficult to reconstruct from the fragmentary records, but the true figure is certainly still higher.[9]

Tsushima's actions had anticipated in part Iemitsu's reaction to the news of the Manchu invasion, but by the time Edo responded to the crisis, hostilities in Korea had long since ceased. Now, sending arms and materiel to a hard-pressed Korea was a relatively easy task, but sending an embassy to Seoul would not be so simple. The Ashikaga shoguns had sent several ambassadors to Seoul in the fifteenth and sixteenth centuries, as had several of the daimyos engaged in the Korea trade prior to 1550. But since the reso-

(1)" in *Shirin*, 19.2 (April 1934): 47. "Hō Chōrō Chōsen monogatari," p. 458, gives Genpō's version of these events as recalled some thirty years later.

[9] The shipment of the lunar fourth month is recorded in *Chŏptaesa mongnok ch'o*, quoted in *Chōsenshi*, vol. 5, pt. 2, p. 69; Henthorn gives the figures 300 muskets, 500 long swords, and 300 catties of gunpowder, in *A History of Korea*, p. 188; cf. *Injo cho sillok*, 15:60b, at *CWS*, 34:186, 16:39a, at *CWS* 34:208, and 17:32, at *CWS*, 34:234, for shipments in the fifth, seventh, and twelfth months of 1627. Earlier, in 1619, a Ming envoy to Seoul had noted that Korea was supplied with firearms from Japan, *Kwanghaegun ilgi* (T'aebaeksan copy), *kwŏn* 143, at *CWS*, 30:186. For some reason, the other surviving copy of the *Kwanghaegun ilgi*, the Chŏngjoksan copy, 143:9a, at *CWS*, 33:253, has excised the relevant sentence.

lution of the wars of the 1590s and the normalization of relations, no Tokugawa shogun had sought to send an embassy
to Seoul. The only shogunal responses to Korean embassies
to date had been in the form of letters to the Korean kings,
gifts, and the repatriation of Korean war prisoners. Envoys
from Tsushima, on the other hand, had frequently sought to
go to Seoul, but had always been denied permission to do
so. Even in 1608-1609, when Yanagawa Kagenao and Kihaku Genpō had gone to Pusan to negotiate the trade articles,
and had sought to go to Seoul to pay respects to the recently
deseased King Sŏnjo, they had been refused.

Edo's response to the crisis may have come after the end
of hostilities in Korea. Still, Yoshinari had received his orders, and he was not reluctant to use the opportunity to expand his own trading interests in Korea, and so, on his return to Tsushima in the winter of 1628-1629, following
Iemitsu's order, he began to assemble an embassy. After extended discussions in Tsushima, Yoshinari named as ambassador Kihaku Genpō, who had been an adviser on diplomatic
matters since the time of Yoshinari's father, and Sugimura
Uneme Toshihiro, an elder of the Tsushima domain, as vice-
ambassador. Their retinue of nineteen comprised two more
Zen clerics, and fifteen other Tsushima samurai experienced
in Korean affairs. They crossed to Pusan on 4 April 1629,
representing themselves quite properly as a shogunal embassy, seeking to become the first Japanese diplomats to go
to Seoul since the end of the invasions of the 1590s.[10] Earlier
envoys from Tsushima had also sought to go to Seoul to

[10] "Hō Chōrō Chōsen monogatari," p. 459; *Sŭngjŏngwŏn ilgi*, 2:146 (Injo
7/3/24), records the report of Tongnae Magistrate Yu Yŏgak; *Injo cho sillok*,
20:18a, at *CWS*, 34:322. Genpō's embassy is treated in some detail in Tashiro Kazui, "Kan'ei 6 nen (Injo 7; 1629) Tsushima shisetsu no Chōsen-
koku 'Gojōkyō no toki mainikki' to sono haikei." The diary kept by one of
Sugimura Uneme's retainers, who accompanied him to Seoul, "Kan'ei rokunen gojōkyō no toki mainikki," edited by Tashiro, appears in *Chōsen gakuhō*, no. 95 (April 1980), pp. 73-116. Genpō's recollections of the mission
are in "Hō Chōrō Chōsen monogatari." Ishihara Michihiro, "Chōsen gawa
yori mita Minmatsu no Nihon kisshi ni tsuite," in *Chōsen gakuhō*, 4 (March
1953): 122-125, quotes extensively from Korean sources on this mission.

negotiate, but they had all been refused, and required to remain in Pusan, kept at arm's length by the Korean government.[11]

Moreover, as Yoshinari well knew, the Manchu invaders had long since withdrawn, in the summer of 1627, and Yoshinari had even written to congratulate Injo on the "pacification of the barbarian invasion," and had sent along a gift of swords and siege cannon.[12] The problems raised by Genpō's mission to Seoul were, from the Korean government's viewpoint, all the more delicate for the fact that King Injo had himself come to the throne in a coup focussed on the issue of relations with the rising Manchu state, and his accession had been followed almost immediately by a brief internal rebellion.[13]

Genpō and Sugimura Uneme were therefore greeted with considerable suspicion when they arrived in Pusan claiming to have shogunal orders to go to Seoul, for they brought no letter from Iemitsu to King Injo, only one from Sō Yoshinari to lesser Korean authorities. Yet, after lengthy pleading and persuasion by the Japanese, and substantial debate by their Korean hosts in both Pusan and the capital, the pair seem to have convinced the Korean officials that they were indeed a bona fide mission authorized by Edo, and for that reason they were permitted to proceed to Seoul—the only Japanese mission to the Korean capital in the Tokugawa period.

In Seoul for a month, from mid-May to mid-June 1629,

[11] *Kwanghaegun ilgi* (T'aebaeksan MS), *kwŏn* 14, at *CWS*, 26:301-302, dated *kiyu/3/kiyu* (30 April 1609), for example, or *ibid.*, *kwŏn* 15, at *CWS*, 26:304, dated *kiyu/4/kyech'uk* (4 May 1609).

[12] *Injo cho sillok*, 16:46b, at *CWS*, 34:211, dated Injo 5/6/*imsul* (20 July 1627); *Chŏptaesa mongnok ch'o* entry of the same date, quoted in Ura Yasukazu, "Minmatsu Shinsho no Senman kankei shijō okeru Nihon no chii (1)," p. 45, or *Chōsenshi*, vol. 5, pt. 2, p. 135.

[13] On the importance of Manchu relations in the domestic politics of Korea in the decade prior to the first Manchu invasion, see especially Inaba Iwakichi, *Kōkaikun jidai no Mansen kankei* (Keijo: Ōsakayagō Shoten, 1933); on the revolt of Yi Kwal, which sought to overthrow Injo and restore Kwanghaegun, see Yi Sangbaek, *Han'guksa, Kŭnse hugi pyŏn*, pp. 12-15.

Genpō and Sugimura separately paid their respects to King Injo at the Royal Audience Hall (Sŭngjŏngjŏn), but the bulk of their business was conducted through the Board of Rites. When they returned to Tsushima they brought Injo's reply: although the Japanese offer of assistance was most generous, the Manchu threat had been turned back (this was a bit disingenuous) and the danger had passed. Besides, there was no precedent for accepting the assistance of a Japanese expeditionary force, so no matter how strong the Manchus might be, Korea would decline the offer.[14]

Barely thirty years after the end of the Japanese invasions of Korea, such Korean reluctance is hardly surprising. When Genpō returned to Tsushima on 6 August, he reported the Korean refusal to Yoshinari.[15] The daimyo and the monk wrote to Ishin Sūden in Edo, who received their letters on 14 September, while Yoshinari wrote separately to Sakai Tadakatsu, a member of the rōju.[16] Sūden later noted that Iemitsu was pleased with the results of Genpō's mission.[17]

Iemitsu may have been pleased with Genpō's diplomatic performance, but he ought not to have mistaken a temporary Korean reprieve from Manchu pressure for the disappearance of the Manchus as a threat to Korea or as a security concern of Japan. The Manchu armies had withdrawn from Korea, it is true, but they had not ceased to be a force in the region. Rather, they would continue as a factor in East Asian affairs for several centuries, and they remained an active, ongoing security interest of the shogunate for most of the remainder of the seventeenth century. The strategic turmoil in East Asia that attended the rise of Manchu power would occupy Jap-

[14] TKIR, 3:576; "Hō Chōrō Chōsen monogatari," pp. 460–461; "Kan'ei rokunen gojōkyō no toki mainikki," p. 115.

[15] "Hō Chōrō Chōsen monogatari," p. 462; CTT, kan 6, p. 223.

[16] Honkō kokushi nikki, 6:229. Sūden received both reports on 25 September. Notice of Yoshinari's report to Sakai Tadakatsu is in Kansei chōshū shokafu, 8:257, where it is recorded that Yoshinari sent a retainer to report "orally in detail" to Tadakatsu.

[17] Honkō kokushi nikki, 6:253, entry of 11 November 1629.

anese attention for many decades, stimulate the development of systems of strategic intelligence-gathering and analysis that became the bakufu's strategic sensory system in East Asia until the fall of the shogunate in the nineteenth century, and at times again bid fair to involve Japan in continental warfare.

The Ch'ing Conquest of China

At the same time that the Manchus were consolidating their position in Northeast Asia, Ming China was being rent by a succession of internal rebellions. When one rebel leader, Li Tzu-ch'eng, took Peking in April 1644, Wu San-kuei, the Ming general in charge of the eastern terminus of the Great Wall, Shanhaikuan, turned to the Manchus to help combat the rebels. Manchu armies flooded into north China, and took Peking on 6 June.[18] The Manchu emperor's entry into the palace marked the beginning of the Ch'ing dynasty in China.

No sooner did the Manchus take China than pretenders to the Ming throne began to appear, for the last emperor had died by his own hand during Li Tzu-ch'eng's siege. Meanwhile, Ming loyalist movements sprang up to resist the alien conquerors and to fight for a restoration of the old dynasty.[19]

News of the fighting reached Japan fairly rapidly. By 4 September 1644. before the Ch'ing court had been formally moved from Shenyang (Mukden) to Peking, Chinese merchants arriving at Nagasaki were reporting the warfare.[20] The vividness, detail, and accuracy of the first reports are noteworthy. They included the background of Li Tzu-ch'eng's revolt and the late emperor's suicide, Wu San-kuei's opening of the gates at Shanhaikuan and the Manchu capture of Peking, the southward progress of the Manchu armies, and the emergence of the first pretender to the Ming throne, the Prince

[18] Hsü, *The Rise of Modern China*, p. 27.
[19] *Ibid.*, pp. 28f.
[20] *KH*, 1:3-8.

of Fu. A much briefer report came from Tsushima, containing information picked up in Pusan.[21] All these reports were sent to Edo and processed within the bakufu, in a manner to be described below, which was eventually to become standard bakufu procedure for handling foreign intelligence reports.

More significant for the bakufu, however, was the arrival of a Chinese trader named Lin Kao in Nagasaki, in the last lunar month of 1645. Lin presented the Nagasaki magistrate with letters from the Ming loyalist admiral Ts'ui Chih, requesting Japanese military assistance in the restoration of the fallen Ming dynasty.[22] Lin's mission was but the first of more than a dozen embassies from Ming pretenders and loyalist forces that would come seeking Japanese military aid, in the form of either expeditionary forces or materiel, over the next forty years.[23] As a result, strategic and political developments in China and on the China Sea were kept before the bakufu as active issues for many years after the "closing of the country" in 1639.

Lin and Ts'ui were both subordinates of Cheng Chih-lung (1604-1661), who was now the principal supporter of the Ming pretender in Foochow, the Prince of T'ang. But he was already well known to the bakufu, for he had had a colorful career in the 1620s and 1630s, first as an aide to the chief of the Chinese residents in Hirado, Li Tan, then as an interpreter for the Dutch, as a pirate, and as an officer in the

---

[21] *KH*, 1:10f; *Tōheiran fūsetsu kōgi e ōseagerare sōrō hikae narabini Chōsenkoku sanzoku totō goannai ōseagerare sōrō hikae* (MS, ca. 1734, Sō Collection, Keio University), cited below as *Tōheiran fūsetsu*, gives a nearly identical text under date of fourth month, 1647, but a letter from Third Minister of the Board of Rites, Yu Sŏngjŭng, to Sō Yoshinari, dated in the first month of 1646, makes it clear that Korea had notified Tsushima of the Ch'ing advance prior to this date. See *HCO*, vol. 9.

[22] *KH*, 1:11-14. Ts'ui Chih was an alias of Chou Ho-chih. See Ishihara Michihiro, *Minmatsu Shinsho Nihon kisshi no kenkyū* (Fuzanbō, 1945), pp. 13f.

[23] Nakamura (Nakayama) Kyūshirō has tabulated these embassies to Nagasaki in his "Minmatsu no Nihon kisshi oyobi kisshi," in *Shigaku zasshi*, 26.5 (May 1925): 3f.

defense of the China coast against piracy. If his experience as a mediator among the principals active in the maritime trade in East Asia suggested to him the idea of dispatching Lin to Nagasaki in the first place, his notorious past as a veritable Vicar of Bray would make him suspect in the eyes of the bakufu, and ultimately undermine the purpose of his mission, as will be apparent below.[24]

Lin Kao presented to the Nagasaki magistrate two long letters from Ts'ui requesting Japanese aid in restoring the Ming dynasty. "I humbly observe that the people of the great country of Japan are all brave, are all well versed in bow and blade, and are all practiced in [the arts of] ships and rudders. . . We beg to borrow a force of three thousand . . ." which would form an eternal alliance between China and Japan.[25]

Nagasaki Magistrate Yamazaki Gonpachirō forwarded these letters directly to Edo, where Hayashi Razan translated them into Japanese for presentation to the rōju and the shogun. After Razan read the letters to Iemitsu, the shogun ordered

[24] On Cheng Chih-lung see C. R. Boxer, "The Rise and Fall of Nicholas Iquan," in *T'ien Hsia Monthly*, 11.5 (April-May 1941): 401-439 (Nicholas Iquan was one of Cheng's aliases, his Christian persona); Donald Keene, *The Battles of Coxinga* (London: Taylor's Foreign Press, 1951), pp. 45-49, and the brief biography in Arthur Hummel, comp., *Eminent Chinese of the Ch'ing Period* (United States Government Printing Office, 1943; repr. Taipei: Ch'eng Wen Publishing Company, 1975), pp. 110-112, and ibid., pp. 196-198, for a sketch of the Prince of T'ang. See also John E. Wills, Jr., "Maritime China from Wang Chih to Shih Lang—Themes in Peripheral History," in Jonathan D. Spence and John E. Wills, Jr., eds., *From Ming to Ch'ing: Conquest, Region, and Continuity in Seventeenth-Century China* (Yale University Press, 1979), especially pp. 216-228, for an enlightening analysis of Cheng Chih-lung and his role in East Asian affairs. In his final vicar-like turnabout, Cheng abandoned the Ming cause and surrendered to the Ch'ing forces on 21 September 1646, but his son Ch'eng-kung, famous in Europe (and Japan) as Coxinga, and his grandson Ching held out on Taiwan until 1683. See Hummel, *Eminent Chinese*, pp. 108-112. Keene has translated the popular mid-Tokugawa puppet drama based on the life of Ch'eng-kung, *Kokusenya kassen*, in his *Battles of Coxinga*, pp. 100-160. On Li Tan, see Iwao Seiichi, "Li Tan, Chief of the Chinese Residents in Hirado," in *Memoirs of the Research Department of the Toyo Bunko*, 17 (1958): 27-83.

[25] *KH*, 1:11-12.

senior councillor Matsudaira Nobutsuna to seek the opinion of Ii Naotaka, lord of the senior *fudai* domain of Hikone, and a close adviser to the shogunate since the time of Hidetada.[26] After what was apparently a long and heated debate, the shogun and his advisers decided to reject the request for the moment, awaiting further developments. The *ōmetsuke* (Inspector General), Inoue Chikugo no kami Masashige, and the second Nagasaki magistrate, Baba Saburōzaemon, who was in Edo at the time,[27] were directed to instruct Yamazaki how to reply to Lin:

> Your letter of the 26th of last month (14 January 1646) has arrived. We see that it contains the letter which Lin Kao brought with him, and [your transcript of] Lin Kao's verbal communication. When we reported to the roju that this was a request for a [Japanese] expeditionary force and arms [to put down] the rebellion in China [the roju replied that] Japan and China have not had formal relations (lit. "there has been no tally trade") for one hundred years, and Japanese no longer voyage in and out of China; and even when Chinese ships have come to Nagasaki to trade, as they have for some years now, they have done so in a private capacity (or, "in secret"). Therefore [you are to reply that] even though Lin Kao has come this time with his petition, the matter is not worth presenting suddenly to the shogun. Tell Lin Kao the above, and order him to return to his country forthwith.[28]

Actually, Matsudaira Nobutsuna had dictated this letter embodying the shogunal will to Hayashi Razan, and it was signed by Inoue and Baba, in order to make it appear that the request was handled at a lower level of government than was in fact the case, and to make it seem that the request was unacceptable on its face. In any event, the bakufu had clearly rejected the request for the time being.

[26] *KH*, 1:13.
[27] *Tokugawa jikki*, 3:429, 430.
[28] *KH*, 1:13–14.

With these instructions Yamazaki also received from Edo a "restatement in Chinese of the purport of Inoue's and Baba's letter to Yamazaki,"[29] which was to be given to Lin over Yamazaki's signature, again to make it appear that the matter had been deemed worthy of only the lowest level of attention.

Defeated, Lin left for home, but not without leaving behind a "Reply to the King of Nagasaki" (the Nagasaki magistrate), acknowledging the contents of Yamazaki's letter, as well as what appear to have been Yamazaki's verbal comments that, "the council of elders [the roju] found it difficult to present [Lin's request] to His Majesty," and that "in the matter of military weapons, although in the current instance we wish we could permit you to take some back with you, Japanese law strictly forbids any such thing, not merely with regard to China, but indeed to any country."[30]

In adding this reference to Japanese legal proscriptions of the export of armaments, Yamazaki was apparently exceeding his instructions, but he was certainly on firm ground. As early as 1621 Edo had begun to restrict the export of Japanese arms, which had been a staple of Japan's foreign trade in the fifteenth and sixteenth centuries.[31] In that year the bakufu

[29] *KH*, 1:14. The editors of *KH* regard these reasons as designed for public consumption, implicitly supporting the explanation given in *Nanryūkun iji*. *Ibid.*, p. 13n; *infra*, n. 35.

[30] *KH*, 1:14. Between 1633 and the 1680s there were usually two Nagasaki magistrates at any one time, one on duty in Nagasaki, the other resident in Edo, where he could be called on for advice on foreign affairs questions. See Sasama Yoshihiko, *Edo bakufu yakushoku shūsei (zōhoban)* (Yūzankaku, 1974), p. 272, for a brief review of the changes in the staffing of the Nagasaki magistracy. On Inoue as inquisitor in the persecution of Christians, see Elison, *Deus Destroyed*, pp. 191-209, *passim*, but for a picture of him as protector of the Dutch in Japan, see Nagazumi Yōko, "Orandajin no hogosha."

[31] See, for example, Tanaka Takeo and Robert Sakai, "Relations with Foreign Countries," in *Japan in the Muromachi Age*, ed. John W. Hall and Toyoda Takeshi (University of California Press, 1977), pp. 170-171, noting that as many as 364,000 catties of sulfur, as many as 30,000 swords, might be taken to China in a single expedition.

had issued orders to the great daimyos of northern Kyushu, Hosokawa Tadatoshi and Ōmura Suminobu, to the Nagasaki magistrate Hasegawa Fujihiro, and, it can be inferred from the dairy of Richard Cocks, to the daimyo of Hirado, Matsuura Takanobu.[32] While these acts seem to have been limited in scope, intended to prevent weapons exports by European traders in Japan at that time, in 1634 the bakufu broadened the prohibition to include any "transportation of Japanese weapons to foreign countries (ikoku)."[33]

But Iemitsu had suggested sending arms, and even an expeditionary force, to aid Korea against the Manchus, in 1628, after the earlier proscriptions on weapons exports. Moreover, some thirty years hence the bakufu would approve the export of war materiel through Okinawa to anti-Ch'ing forces on the China coast, again despite the proscriptions on the books.[34] There is strong reason to believe that Iemitsu had the same thing in mind now, too, despite both the somewhat disingenuous reply to Lin Kao, and the weapons-export proscription of 1634, as will be apparent below.

Rather, Iemitsu's refusal was a ruse to test the bona fides of Lin's request, for he doubted that Lin was in fact an ambassador from the Ming government,[35] largely because of the involvement of Cheng Chih-lung. Since there was no clearly constituted Ming government at this time, and since there were several pretenders competing for the throne, even had Cheng not been involved, such circumspection would be easy

[32] Dai Nihon shiryō, 12.38:1-24; 138-139.

[33] Tokugawa kinreikō zenshū, 6:377.

[34] Kagoshima ken shiryō Kyūki zatsuroku tsuiroku, 8 vols. (Kagoshima, 1971-1978), 1:673, 675, 684; KH, 1:159-162. In this instance, in 1676, the request from pro-"Ming" forces in Fukien was explicitly for "sulfur for military purposes." Perhaps Edo only permitted the exportation of sulfur this time because the shipment would be through Okinawa, and would thus allow Japan a margin of what, in the Nixon White House, was known as "deniability."

[35] Nanryūkun iji, the biography of Iemitsu's uncle Tokugawa Yorinobu, lord of Wakayama, quoted in TKIR, 5:390.

to understand.[36] The lack of any recognized Ming government, the dubious prospects of any of the pretenders for success at retaking China, and the involvement of Cheng in this
particular request—all were clearly factors inducing caution
on the part of the shogunate, and yet, as will be seen, there
was still substantial enthusiasm for sending an expeditionary
force to China.

Shortly after the bakufu had made its decision, however,
on 27 February 1646, the day that Baba and Inoue had written telling Yamazaki to order Lin Kao back to Foochow,
Itakura Shigemune, the shogun's deputy for Kyoto (shoshidai), who often participated in shogunal policy discussions
when he was in Edo, wrote to his nephew Shigenori, out-
lining a rather different understanding of the shogun's position. Rather than being disinterested in responding to the
Chinese request, according to Itakura, the shogun was not
only interested, but there was even a plan of battle for an
anticipated Japanese expeditionary force to China! The plan
outlined in Itakura's letter called for a total force of 20,000
Japanese soldiers to land on the Chinese coast, to establish
fortified positions there, and to continue to establish fortifi-
cations as they moved inland.[37]

Other participants in the discussions at the castle appear to
have shared Itakura's view of Iemitsu's intentions, for nine
days later one of these, Tachibana Tadashige, the daimyo of

[36] Some of these pretender courts have recently been studied by Jerry
Dennerline, "Hsü Tu and the Lesson of Nanking: Political Integration and
Local Defense in Chiang-nan, 1634-1645," in Spence and Wills, ed., *From
Ming to Ch'ing*, pp. 89-132, and Ian McMorran, "The Patriot and the Par-
tisans: Wang Fu-chih's Involvement in the Politics of the Yung-li Court,"
in *ibid.*, pp. 133-166.

[37] Itakura Shigemune to Itakura Shigenori, Shōhō 3/1/12, quoted in Tsuji
Zennosuke, *Zōtei kaigai kōtsū shiwa*, pp. 640-641; also cited in Iwao Seiichi,
Sakoku, p. 405, Asao Naohiro, *Sakoku*, pp. 378-379. Shigenori himself later
served on the roju, 1665-1668 and 1670-1673, and as shogunal deputy in
Kyoto, 1668-1670. See his biography in *Kansei chōshū shokafu*, 2:140-141;
150, 151.

Yanagawa, in northwestern Kyushu, wrote from Edo to one of his retainers:[38]

According to what I have heard about [this] from the roju, the matter has been reported to the Castle. But relations with China lapsed more than a hundred years ago

[38] Quoted in Tsuji, *Zōtei kaigai kōtsū shiwa*, pp. 644-646. This letter is also discussed in Iwao, *Sakoku*, pp. 404-405. Tsuji, who found the original letter in the otherwise unpublished "Soga Collection," attributes this letter to Tadashige's father, Tachibana Muneshige, and Iwao accepts this attribution as well. There are, however, a few problems with this letter which are overlooked by Tsuji and Iwao, but which may help to explain why Asao has not cited it. I have chosen to reject this ascription, and attribute the letter to Tadashige (1612-1676). Attribution to Muneshige is clearly in error, since he had died on 15 January 1643 (Kan'ei 19/11/25 [See the notice in *Tokugawa jikki*, 3:133, under date of Kan'ei 16/4/3, when Muneshige retired, or the biography in *Kansei chōshū shokafu*, 2:372]). While Muneshige was dead, and so could not have written the letter, his son Tadashige was not only alive and well at the time, but was involved in the bakufu's deliberations on the appropriate response to the requests of the Ming resistance for military aid from Japan. By December 1646 (Shōhō 3/10/24) he was one of over a dozen daimyos placed on alert for the possible approach of Chinese refugee ships, after the fall of Foochow: "In the latest report from Nagasaki, it was learned that the Ming armies were defeated at Foochow, and the Ming ruler killed, and therefore [the following list of daimyos] were ordered on alert for the approach of foreign ships." (*Tokugawa jikki*, 3:460-461.) Tsuji's misattribution is probably due to a combination of good-faith error, and wishful thinking. At his coming-of-age ceremony in 1624, Tadashige had received the courtesy title *Sakon-no-shōgen* (Captain of the Left Guards) from Hidetada, and so shared use of that title with Muneshige, who had held it since 1587. Tsuji does not reproduce the signature on the letter in question, but in a letter to a retainer a quickly dashed-off "Sakon" would be an entirely appropriate signature. In ascribing the letter to Muneshige, "the hero of the Battle of Pyŏkchegwan" (Tsuji, p. 646; for details of the battle, near Seoul on 28 February 1593, see *Chōsenshi*, vol. 4, pt. 10, pp. 32-33), Tsuji makes the writer's resolve to go to China and die a glorious death seem all the more heroic: had he been alive, Muneshige would have been seventy-nine years old, by Japanese count, and already a war hero. There is an extensive biography of Muneshige in Fujino Tamotsu, *Bakusei to hansei* (Yoshikawa Kōbunkan, 1979), pp. 215-237, which does not, however, allude to this letter. Tadashige's official biography is in *Kansei chōshū shokafu*, 2:372.

and even more to the point [China] won't allow Japanese ships to approach [their shores]; they even post picket ships [to prevent that]. Therefore, it is hardly proper for them to come, now that their country has fallen into civil war, and say, "We are having some trouble, so could you please send some troops." Furthermore, while it might be proper to respond to them if the request came from the [Chinese] emperor or his general, we don't really know who this messenger is. [The shogun] also has some reservations about sending Japanese weapons overseas, so he has [instructed] the two Nagasaki magistrates to respond that the request was not even reported to the shogun, nor even fit to be reported to the roju.

Therefore, I think it unlikely that an expeditionary force will be sent. Still, we cannot tell whether there might be a further request, although that is how things stand now.   But, even though an expeditionary force seems unlikely, still Peking has already fallen, and we have even heard that Nanking may also have been taken, so it is impossible to tell whether there might not suddenly be another request from the Chinese emperor or his general for an expeditionary force, so we cannot afford to be caught napping (*yudan arumajiku sōrō*). And if we do send forces, I am of a mind to go with them, even if I have to make up an excuse to go. . . . I told them that [when the order comes to] ship arms to Nagasaki, I want to buy some arms [for the assault] myself. I have also heard that if there is an attack on Korea from China, [Korea also] will request an expeditionary force. . . .

If it was Iemitsu's intention to test the *bona fides* of this Ming request for Japanese aid by waiting to see if further requests were forthcoming, he was not to be disappointed, nor would he have long to wait. In the autumn of 1646 a second emissary from Cheng Chih-lung, Huang Cheng-ming, arrived in Nagasaki once more to seek Japanese aid.[39] Through Huang, Cheng and the Lung-wu pretender sent letters to the shogun and to the Nagasaki magistrate, along with gifts of Chinese silks and brocades. The letters asked once more for military aid against the Manchus in the fight to restore the Ming dynasty, but, they said, "although we formerly asked for five thousand troops, it would be difficult to defeat the enemy with just that number, so please send more."[40]

The Lung-wu pretender's letters recalled the fact that the Tatars had been enemies of Japan from ancient times, having attacked Japan "four or five times,"[41] and reminded the shogun that it was the Ming dynasty which had ousted the Mongols from China. Implying that there was a debt therefore to be paid, the pretender argued that in light of the historic friendship between Japan and Ming it was only proper that Japan should accede to this request and send troops.[42]

The Nagasaki magistrate forwarded these letters to Edo, where Iemitsu ordered Hayashi Razan to prepare a memorandum on all previous official communications received from China. Razan presented his list to the shogun on 23 November 1646,[43] a list which began with the rescript from the Emperor Ming of the state of Wei to the "Empress Jingū" in

[39] *KH*, 1:15-25.

[40] *KH*, 1:17.

[41] In fact, there were only two attempted Mongol invasions of Japan, in 1274 and 1281, both of which failed. See Kyotsu Hori, "The Mongol Invasions and the Kamakura Bakufu" (unpublished Ph.D. dissertation, Columbia University, 1967).

[42] *KH*, 1:19, summarizes the Lung-wu letters. It is ironic that Ming should invoke the friendship of Japan and China as a reason for the call, when Ming law had discriminated against Japan in foreign affairs for a century, and "Japanese pirates" (*wakō*, not all of whom were Japanese) had plagued the Chinese coast for even longer. The bakufu had cited this hiatus in relations with Ming as one reason for rejecting the previous year's request for troops. On the *wakō* see Tanaka Takeo, *Wakō to kangō bōeki* (Shibundō, 1961), and Kwan-wai So, *Japanese Piracy in Ming China During the Sixteenth Century* (Michigan State University Press, 1975).

[43] *KH*, 1:22.

A.D. 238,[44] and ended with the letter from Tan Feng-hsiang of 1619.[45]

When Razan's memorandum was presented to the shogun, the roju, the collateral Tokugawa lords of Wakayama, Owari and Mito, and Ii Naotaka, there was support among the three collateral houses for the dispatch of an expeditionary force,[46] support which was even reported to Korea before the year was out.[47] However, opponents of the expeditionary force argued that there was nothing to be gained by such an expedition, and that it was only likely to create more enemies for Japan.[48] This was the position of Iemitsu's great-uncle Yorinobu of Wakayama, and of Ii Naotaka, the senior retainer of the shogunal house.

The reactions of Itakura Shigemune and Tachibana Tadashige the previous spring also suggest the existence of substantial interest in sending an expeditionary force to China. But any inclination that Iemitsu may have had to send troops was dampened considerably by a report from the Nagasaki

[44] This is the rescript to "Pimiko, Queen of Wa," given to Pimiko's ambassador to the Chinese state of Wei in the last lunar month of 238, recorded in the *Wei-chih*, in *San-kuo-chih*, 3:857. See the translation in Ryusaku Tsunoda and L. Carrington Goodrich, comp., *Japan in the Chinese Dynastic Histories*, pp. 220-221. The legendary "Empress Jingū" was probably modelled on the Pimiko of the *Wei-chih*. See Gari K. Ledyard, "Galloping Along with the Horseriders," esp. pp. 235-242.

[45] See above, Chapter III.

[46] *Tokugawa jikki*, 3:460; Hayashi Nobuatsu, *Kan'ei shōsetsu*, in *Zoku shiseki shūran*, 10 vols. (Kondō Shuppanbu, 1930), 6:274-275.

[47] *Injo cho sillok*, 47:70a, at *CWS*, 35:289; 47:75a, at *CWS*, 35:292. Tsushima's envoy to Pusan, "Fujiwara" Toshitsuna (Arita Mokubei), told Korean officials that "two of the Great Prince's uncles" (the heads of the three Tokugawa collateral houses were all Iemitsu's uncles) had urged the shogun to "borrow a road from Korea to send troops" to the aid of the Ming pretender's cause, but that Sō Yoshinari had argued against that, reminding Iemitsu that Korea was still economically exhausted from the Manchu invasion of 1636, and would not be able to provision the Japanese army as it passed through.

[48] *Tokugawa jikki*, 3:459-460; Hayashi Nobuatsu, *Kan'ei shōsetsu*, pp. 274-275; Shionoya Tōin, "Shōdaiki," quoted in Ishihara Michihiro, *Minmatsu Shinsho Nihon kisshi no kenkyū* (Fuzanbō, 1945), p. 40.

magistrate that arrived in Edo as the debate was in progress. The magistrate had news from the most recent Chinese junk to arrive from the coast that Cheng Chih-lung had been defeated at Foochow, and was negotiating acceptable terms for his submission to Ch'ing.[49]

The fall of Foochow and the surrender of Cheng Chih-lung helped Iemitsu to choose between the conflicting advice of his councillors. He had recently sent Sō Yoshinari home to Tsushima with instructions to seek further intelligence on the Chinese civil war from Korean sources, and it can be inferred that the other daimyos of western Japan were also placed on alert. But on 27 and 28 November the roju wrote to Nabeshima Katsushige, daimyo of Hizen, the province where Nagasaki was located, to Hosokawa Mitsunao of Kumamoto, just south of Nagasaki, to Sō Yoshinari, and probably to all other western daimyos not in Edo at the time, advising them of the change in shogunal intentions:

As China is in the midst of a civil war, a letter arrived from Hirado Ikkan [Cheng Chih-lung requesting] that we send troops. However, it was not formally addressed, and there were some parts that seemed suspicious, so His Majesty intended to send a shogunal envoy to Nagasaki to investigate matters with Ikkan's envoy. But just then a letter dated the 4th [11 November] arrived from the Nagasaki [magistrate], reporting that Foochow has fallen, and that the Prince of T'ang [the Lung-wu pretender] and Ikkan are surrendering the city. Therefore there is no purpose to further investigation [of the request for aid.] All [the daimyos] now in Edo will also be so commanded. This that

[49] *KH*, 1:24–25. The news travelled fast, for the defeat was on 6 October (Hummel, *Eminent Chinese*, p. 110), and the news reached Nagasaki on 11 November, where it was duly recorded by the director of the Dutch factory (*Nagasaki Oranda Shōkan no nikki*, tr. Murakami Naojirō, 3 vols. [Iwanami Shoten, 1956-1958], 2:115), and immediately reported by the magistrate to Edo, where the message arrived on the 24th. *Tokugawa jikki*, 3:460; *TKIR*, 5:399-400.

we have commanded you is in accordance with the sho-gunal will.[50]

Once they had decided to reject the appeals for aid, the bakufu composed a list of twenty-one "reasons" why the requests were unacceptable. These reasons, reminiscent of those given in the rejection of the Tan Feng-hsiang letter in 1621, concentrate on protocol issues which affected the status of Japan and the locus of the shogun in the Japanese polity.[51] These, however, were merely the reasons for refusing to is-sue a formal reply to the appeals, not the reasons for reject-ing them, as the tantalizing extant fragments of the debate make clear.

Indeed, discussion of the proposal for an expeditionary force had gone so far as Iemitsu's consulting with Sō Yoshinari as to whether Korea would allow Japanese troops to pass through Korea on the way to aid the Ming cause. But Yoshitoshi had discouraged the idea since, he said, Korea was too exhausted from the recent Manchu invasions to feed a Japanese army on its way to China.[52] Needless to say, Korea would have

---

[50] The text translated here is A[be] Tsushima no kami [Shigetsugu], A[be] Bungo no kami [Tadaaki], and Matsu[daira] Izu no kami [Nobutsuna] to Nabeshima Shinano no kami [Katsushige], Shōhō 3/10/20 (27 November 1646), in *Go-tōke reijō; Ritsuryō yōryaku*, vol. 2 of *Kinsei hōsei shiryō sōsho*, ed., Ishii Ryōsuke (Sōbunsha, 1959), p. 102; cf. the same letter in *TKIR*, 5:400–401, which also contains Abe Tsushima no kami, Abe Bungo no kami, Matsudaira Izu no kami to Hosokawa Higo no kami [Mitsunao], dated Shōhō 3/10/21 and the letter of Matsudaira Hizen no kami to Matsudaira Izu no kami and Abe Bungo no kami (n.d.) acknowledging receipt of, and quoting verbatim, the letter of 10/21 received by Matsudaira Hizen no kami. Simi-larly, although the letter of the rōjū to Sō Yoshinari seems to be lost, Yoshi-nari's acknowledgment of receipt quotes the order in full: Sō Yoshinari to Matsudaira Izu no kami, Abe Bungo no kami and Abe Tsushima no kami, dated Shōhō 3/12/19 (21 January 1647) is preserved in the Tsushima office log, *Mainikki issatsu Edo go-rōjū narabini katagata e tsukawasu gojō hikae issatsu nisatsu gatchō* (MS, dated Shōhō 3 [16 Feb. 1646 to 4 Feb. 1647], collection Sō Archives, Kenritsu Tsushima Rekishi Minzoku Shiryōkan, Izuhara, Tsushima). Boxer, "The Rise and Fall of Nicholas Iquan," p. 436, discusses Cheng's surrender at Foochow.

[51] *KH*, 1:22-24.

[52] *Injo cho sillok*, 47:70a, in *CWS*, 35:289.

been unwilling to welcome Japanese troops on her soil in any case.

After this meeting with Iemitsu, discussions continued in Edo to resolve the bakufu's response to this second round of appeals from Cheng. Yoshinari meanwhile returned to Tsushima with orders from Edo to seek further intelligence from Korea on the progress of the Chinese civil war. He arrived home on 3 December, less than a week after the roju had written to say that the news of the fall of Foochow had rendered moot for the time being the question of Japanese military involvement. Yet, contrary to what the group of letters would lead one to expect, Yoshinari soon received a flurry of orders from Edo to continue and even to intensify his intelligence-gathering efforts.

Immediately upon his return home, Yoshinari wrote back to Edo to inform the roju of his safe return,[53] and at once wrote also to the Korean Board of Rites, the prefect of Tongnae, and the magistrate of Pusan to inform them that he had been granted leave from the shogun's court and had arrived home on the third of December. But, more importantly, he said that he had "learned that officials of the Interpreters' Office will soon come as an embassy to my province. I have made all preparations, and look forward to receiving them."[54] The interpreters arrived in Tsushima on 21 January, the same day that Yoshinari received the roju's letter of two months earlier,[55] and on the twenty-second Yoshinari wrote Edo that he expected to interview the inter-

[53] Sō Yoshinari to Matsudaira Izu no kami, Abe Tsushima no kami and Abe Bungo no kami, Shōhō 3/10/27, with copy to Makino no kami and Matsudaira Izumi no kami; Yoshinari to Ii Kamon no kami (Naotaka), Sakai Sanuki no kami (Tadakatsu) and Hotta Kaga no kami (Masamori), Shōhō 3/10/27, in *Mainikki issatsu* (1646). Yoshinari wrote to over 130 other daimyos at this time to inform them of his safe return home.

[54] Sō Yoshinari to the Two Governors of Tongnae and Pusan, Shōhō 3/11/X, in *HCO*, vol. 11. The text of the letter to Board of Rites, at *ibid.*, differs slightly, but only in style, not in substance.

[55] *Mainikki issatsu* (1646), entry for Shōhō 3/12/16, in separate entries for the same day, records the arrival of the Korean mission and the roju letter.

preters momentarily and then report fully.[56] On the twenty-eighth Yoshinari received interpreters Yi Hyŏngnam and Han, and six of their retinue, at his castle,[57] but, as Yoshinari reported two days later to Matsudaira Nobutsuna and to the tairo Sakai Tadakatsu, "In former years Korea fought a war with the Tatars, but then made peace, and . . . the [two] interpreters would not speak freely about Korean relations with the Tatars since [they made peace], even when I inquired about it." The interpreters protested that they were not authorized to discuss such matters, and needed evidence that Yoshinari was himself acting with proper authority from Edo. Yoshinari told them he would get written authorization from Edo, by the beginning of the second month, he hoped, but that he was scheduled to return to Edo in the middle of the third month. Therefore, Yoshinari sought written evidence that he could send to Korea, of the instructions he had received before leaving Edo.[58]

While Yoshinari waited for a reply from Edo, in the early spring of 1647, he began to increase pressure on Korea for some useful information on the Chinese civil war. If he could not serve Edo's intelligence needs, after all, his future tenure in Tsushima might be threatened. He therefore wrote to the magistrates of Tongnae and Pusan to warn them that he needed information quickly: "I am about to leave Tsushima for [Edo]. Even though we have repeatedly asked you about the situation in China recently, you have reported nothing whatsoever to us. . . The Overseer of Japan House will explain the details to you orally."[59] Yoshinari hoped that the dead-

[56] Sō Yoshinari to Matsudaira Izu no kami, Abe Tsushima no kami and Abe Bungo no kami, Shōhō 3/12/17, in *Mainikki issatsu* (1646).

[57] *Mainikki issatsu* (1646), entry for Shōhō 3/12/23. "Interpreter Han" is listed without his given name.

[58] Sō Yoshinari to Sakai Sanshū [Tadakatsu, the tairo], and Matsudaira Zushū [Nobutsuna], Shōhō 3/12/25, in *Mainikki issatsu* (1646).

[59] Sō Yoshinari to the Magistrates of Tongnae and Pusan, dated Shōhō 4/2/X, in *HCO*, vol. 11.

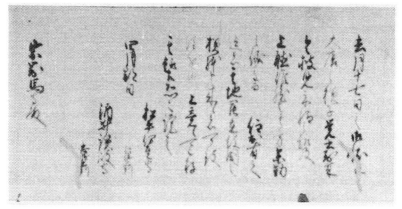

3. Matsudaira Nobutsuna and Sakai Tadakatsu's letter relays Iemitsu's order to Sō Yoshinari to remain in Tsushima to gather Korean intelligence on the progress of the Ch'ing conquest of China, and to "report whatever you hear about that country"

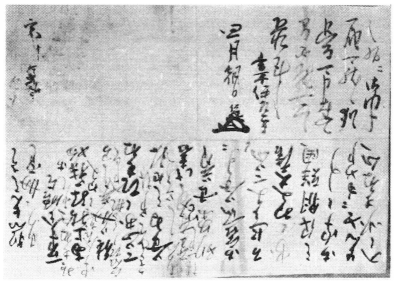

4. Matsudaira Nobutsuna orders Sō Yoshinari "to enquire to Korea about the situation in China and report" back to Edo on the Ch'ing conquest

line imposed by his impending departure for Edo would accelerate Korean cooperation.

Matsudaira and Sakai replied to Yoshinari's 30 January report promptly on 12 March 1647 (Shōhō 4/2/6). After recapitulating the information that they had already received, they told Yoshinari: "We have presented our correspondence with you for the Royal Viewing. Thereupon [it was decided that] since Korea should have knowledge of the situation in China, you are hereupon to send [an envoy] to Pusan in order to learn about the situation. You are to report when you have learned something."[60] With this authorization Yoshinari immediately sent an envoy to Pusan to request information on the Chinese civil war, writing to both Tongnae and Pusan: "The other year we had reports that the Tatars had taken China. What is the state of civil administration in that country now?" He added, tantalizingly, "I have entrusted the details orally to my envoy."[61]

The envoy, Arita Mokubei, told Tongnae Magistrate Min Yŏnghyŏp that the shogun had sent a letter to Yoshinari saying that he had repeatedly sought news of the situation in Nanking and Peking. If Tsushima was on such good terms with Korea, then why, Iemitsu wondered, had not Yoshinari reported? Iemitsu wondered whether Korea was not now a vassal state of Ch'ing, just as she had been Ming's vassal.[62] Arita was suggesting that Korea's continuing failure to cooperate was calling into question Yoshinari's competence to mediate between Edo and Seoul. In tandem with Yoshinari's suggestion to the interpreters that the roju were so irritated at the apparent Korea cooperation with the Manchus that

[60] Matsudaira Izu no kami Nobutsuna (cipher) and Sakai Sanuki no kami Tadakatsu (cipher) to Sō Tsushima no kami, [Shōhō 4]/2/6 (signature MS letter, Sō Archives, Banshōin, Tsushima).

[61] Sō Yoshinari to the Two Governors of Tongnae and Pusan, Shōhō 4/2/X, in *HCO*, vol. 11. This letter is remarkable for its total lack of the usual polite greetings, and its impatient tone. This, as will momentarily be clear, reflected Yoshinari's concern that failure to come up with some useful intelligence would negate his value to Edo as a mediator with Seoul.

[62] *Injo cho sillok*, 48:9a, at *CWS*, 35:297.

they were considering sending an army,[63] this presented Korea with the unlikely, but thoroughly unpalatable, Scylla and Charybdis of either a renewed Japanese invasion, or the loss of Tsushima as mediator. Never had Yoshinari pressed so hard.

Indeed, while Yoshinari was waiting for a response from Seoul, he appears to have sent an interim report to Edo, for on 5 May 1647 the two senior men, Sakai and Matsudaira, wrote Yoshinari acknowledging that "Your letter of the [21st] last, and the accompanying memorandum on the situation in China, have arrived. Upon reading and discussing them, we presented their contents to the Royal Hearing, whereupon it was commanded that despite your [impending obligation] to come to Court, you are to remain in that locale until further orders. It is the Royal Will that you are to report whatever you hear about that country."[64] At the same time Matsudaira wrote separately: "As we ordered you in our previous letter, you are to enquire to Korea about the situation in China, and then report as ordered."[65]

[63] *Injo cho sillok*, 48:2b, at *CWS*, 35:293, has Interpreter Yi Hyŏngnam's report to the Korean court.

[64] Matsudaira Izu no kami Nobutsuna (cipher) and Sakai Sanuki no kami Tadakatsu (cipher) to Sō Tsushima no kami [Shōhō 4]/4/1 (copy MS letter, Sō archives, Banshōin, Tsushima). It is possible that even before this Yoshinari made a report to Edo on the China situation, for on Shōhō 4/3/24 (28 April 1647) Arita Mokubei returned from Korea with information that prompted Yoshinari to send an express report to Edo; since the content of Arita's report to Yoshinari, and Yoshinari's to Edo, is not recorded, it is impossible to know whether the information related to the Chinese civil war. *Mainikki issatsu* (1647) (MS, Sō Archives, Kenritsu Tsushima Rekishi Minzoku Shiryōkan). An express messenger arrived from Edo on 22 May, probably delivering the letters from Sakai and Matsudaira. *Ibid.*, entry of [Shōhō 4]/4/18. See Plate 3.

[65] Matsudaira Izu no kami Nobutsuna (cipher) to Sō Tsushima no kami, [Shōhō 4]/4/1 (signature MS letter, Sō Collection, National History Compilation Committee, Seoul). It is unclear why Nobutsuna wrote separately to Yoshinari on the same day that he wrote jointly with Tadakatsu. Perhaps the efforts of Yoshinari's friends Matsudaira Uemon and, Matsudaira Shuzen, relatives of Nobutsuna's to whom Yoshinari sent copies of the correspondence, had made Nobutsuna solicitous of Yoshinari's welfare. See Pl. 4.

Yoshinari certainly realized the delicacy of his position, afraid that too extreme pressure on Korea could cost him future rights to trade, while failure to produce results might win him the fate that he had so narrowly escaped over a decade earlier in his dispute with Yanagawa. The cancellation of his journey to the shogunal court, and the repetition of shogunal orders so frequently and so forcefully, however, underscored the seriousness of Edo's interest in following the situation in China, and ensured that Yoshinari would press the matter with renewed vigor. Finally, toward the end of May, Yoshinari's efforts were rewarded. He received a letter from Min Yŏnghyŏp, the prefect of Tongnae, which outlined the development of the Ch'ing takeover of China, and a memorandom from an Interpreter Kim, giving a bit more information on civil affairs in China after the Ch'ing takeover.[66] Yoshinari, undoubtedly greatly relieved to have something substantial to report, sent a long report to Matsudaira and Sakai on 1 June 1647, along with Min's letter of a few days earlier.[67] Neither the report nor Min's letter contained much that was new to the bakufu, but it at least accomplished two other important objectives: it opened Korea as an avenue of strategic intelligence for the bakufu, and it demonstrated that Yoshinari was able to perform. That may have saved him his position.

[66] Tongnae Magistrate [Min Yŏnghyŏp to Sō Yoshinari], *chŏnghae*/4, and Hundo Kim Ch'ŏmji memorandum, both contained in *Tōheiran fūsetsu*. Neither memorandum is recorded in *HCO*. Comparison with *Ka'i hentai*, 1:10, report of Yoshinari based on messages from Tongnae in 1645, shows how little new information Korea was willing to add even two years later. Korea was caught in the middle here, and was simultaneously sending reports to Ch'ing on Japanese conditions and intentions. *Injo cho sillok*, 47:73a, at *CWS*, 35:291, records Injo ordering a report to Peking on the "Japanese situation."

[67] Sō Tsushima no kami to Sakai Sanuki no kami and Matsudaira Izu no kami, [Shōhō 4]/4/28, in *Tōheiran fūsetsu*. Yoshinari's report is missing from *Ka'i hentai*. Yoshinari sent another "secret report" to Edo on 4 September, the contents of which are not recorded, but which probably gave further intelligence on the Chinese situation. *Mainikki issatsu* (1647), entry of Shōhō 4/8/6.

Historians attempting to account for the bakufu's repeated refusals directly to aid the Ming loyalist cause have suggested that the response had been in some sense predetermined by a policy of isolation formulated in the 1630s and finalized in 1639, which would not change until the 1850s. Tsuda Hideo, for example, argues that the rejection of involvement was "common sense: Japan did not aid [the Ming loyalists] because the *sakoku* policy had just been initiated."[68] Inobe Shigeo likewise argues: "When Cheng Chih-lung requested troops in 1645, and again when [his son] Cheng Ch'eng-kung repeated the same request in Keian [1648] and in Manji [1658]," the bakufu's rejection of involvement was a foregone conclusion because of its desire "to support its policy of *sakoku*," which he summarizes as directed at the goal of internal peace, in support of which the bakufu would shun involvement abroad.[69]

These explanations, however, are unconvincing, at least as regards the bakufu's behavior in 1646-1647, when it rejected the appeals of Cheng Chih-lung. The bakufu may have rejected these appeals, but its first rejection was clearly designed to buy time to allow the situation to develop further, and to gather sufficient information on which to base a decision—information both about the strategic situation in China and about the legitimacy of the request for aid. As Ura Yasukazu notes,[70] there was "considerable sentiment within (the bakufu) for the dispatch of an expeditionary force to the continent, and it was hotly debated by the shogun and his principal advisers." And Tsuji Zennosuke argues, with considerable evidence, as has been seen, that Iemitsu, urged on by the Tokugawa collaterals and by Itakura Shigemune, the Kyoto deputy, had even formulated a "plan for the invasion of China," a scheme aborted only by the inability of the Ming loyalist forces to gain a victory that would keep them a "vi-

[68] In *shinpojiumu Nihon rekishi 11 bakuhan taisei ron* (Gakuseisha, 1974), p. 139.

[69] Inobe Shigeo, *Ishin zenshi no kenkyū*, p. 24.

[70] *KH*, 1:23-24n.

able alternative" long enough to benefit from Japanese assistance, and by the vigorous opposition of his senior *fudai* retainer, Ii Naotaka.[71] As the roju wrote to several daimyos on 27 November 1646: "According to the report of the [eleventh] from Nagasaki, Foochow has fallen, and the Prince of T'ang [the Lung-wu pretender] and [Cheng Chih-lung] Ikkan have surrendered, so there is no point to further study" of the matter.[72]

At the least, therefore, it is difficult to accept the "closing of the country" as the reason for the bakufu's decision to reject the petitions of self-styled Ming loyalists for Japanese military aid in the restoration of the dynasty. Nor can the decision be written off as a foregone conclusion that Japan's desire for peace forbade Japan from fighting for the restoration of the Ming dynasty. For the bakufu seems to have tottered on the brink of this decision, with some people close to the policy councils believing that military movement was imminent. Others were strongly disposed toward non-involvement, and when the Ming resistance suffered its great defeat at Foochow, any thought of sending a force became suddenly moot. However interested Itakura, Tachibana—and who knows how many others—were in sending forces, there was little point in sending them off to certain failure.

But, indeed, the bakufu and most Japanese were hostile to the Manchus, and favored the Ming loyalists in any way that they could. The shogunate, for example, allowed Ming loyalists to trade in Nagasaki, while for a time discriminating against Chinese merchants under the Ch'ing government. Shortly before Cheng Chih-lung's embassy arrived, two Chinese junks had arrived from Nanking to trade.[73] The crew had pigtails, and because this seemed strange the matter was referred to Edo. On 10 September 1646 the Dutch opperhoofd recorded that ships from Nanking had been barred

[71] *Zōtei kaigai kōtsū shiwa*, pp. 646-654.

[72] See above, note 50.

[73] Murakami Naojirō, tr., *Dejima Rankan nisshi*, 3 vols. (Bunmei Kyōkai, 1938-1939), 3:34 (27 July 1646).

from trading because their crews wore their hair in Manchu-decreed pigtails, but would be pardoned this once. In the future, however, they would be permitted to trade only "if they come in Chinese style."[74] Since it was known that no Chinese operating from an area under Manchu control could do this, the clear intention of this decision was to favor traders not under Manchu control, that is, either overseas Chinese or those operating from Ming loyalist strongholds.

As Ishihara Michihiro has shown,[75] it seems to have remained possible for Cheng Chih-lung's son Coxinga (Cheng Ch'eng-kung), the most famous loyalist leader, to have continued access to Japanese weapons well into the 1650s. While this may reflect the anti-Ch'ing sympathy evident in the above decision, it could represent the fruits of smuggling as well as legal trade. For although Coxinga sent at least four requests to Japan for aid from 1647 to 1660, the bakufu never responded to these, although the roju debated at least the first and the third.[76]

The bakufu had chosen to avoid direct involvement in the Ming-Ch'ing conflict, and continued to turn away Ming loyalists, real or pretended, who sought Japanese aid. Ideologically, however, the bakufu was strongly predisposed to the Ming loyalists,[77] and gave practical expression to this support, not only by favoring only those Chinese merchants under anti-Ch'ing auspices, but also by serving as a haven for loyalist refugees who preferred to settle in Japan rather to remain in a China controlled by barbarians.[78]

Yet the level of fighting after the 1640s was essentially limited, and rarely sufficient to encourage any serious hope

[74] *Dejima Rankan nisshi*, 3:50.
[75] Ishihara Michihiro, *Minmatsu Shinsho Nihon kisshi no kenkyū*, pp. 55-67.
[76] *KH*, 1:28, 45; Nakamura Kyūshirō, "Minmatsu no Nihon kisshi oyobi kisshi," pp. 3-5.
[77] Hayashi Gahō, "Go Tei ron," in *Gahō Sensei Hayashi Gakushi bunshū*, kan 48.
[78] Probably the best known of these was the Confucian scholar Chu Shunshui, who became an adviser to the lord of Mito, Tokugawa Mitsukuni.

of a Ming revival. Japanese eyes continued to focus on the situation because it could have endangered Japan's foreign trade, and might explode into a more serious war at any time. The bakufu continued to permit Coxinga's ships access to Nagasaki, and to the profits of trade with Japan, but refused all petitions for more direct assistance. However, in the waning days of 1673 there began in China an open rebellion of major proportions, this time no longer confined to coastal areas, which refocussed Japanese attention on the strategic relationship to mainland Asia, and rekindled hopes in both Japan and Korea of a Ming restoration.

THE REVOLT OF THE THREE FEUDATORIES AND THE TOKUGAWA INTELLIGENCE APPARATUS

The Revolt of the Three Feudatories erupted when the K'ang-hsi Emperor accepted petitions from Wu San-kuei and other Chinese generals, who had been enfeoffed in reward for their service in the founding of the dynasty, that their fiefs be abolished.[79] Wu, enfeoffed in Yunnan, had not expected that this petition would be accepted. Therefore, from his fief in Yunnan, he immediately communicated with Coxinga's son and heir, Cheng Ching. Cheng controlled Taiwan, from which he made pirate raids on the China coast, and on Dutch and Chinese shipping. Wu raised the standard of revolt, claiming to seek restoration of the empire to the Ming imperial house of Chu, in the person of a pretender in the custody of Wu.

By the fourth month of 1674 Cheng Ching and the enfeoffed prince of Fukien, Keng Ching-chung, threw in their lot with Wu, and the war was on in earnest. The Ch'ing dynasty and its young K'ang-hsi emperor faced the most serious threat to dynastic survival that it was to meet until the onslaught of the West nearly two centuries later. To many

---

[79] The following two paragraphs are based on Tsao Kai-fu, "The Rebellion of the Three Feudatories against the Manchu Throne in China, 1673-1681: Its Setting and Significance" (unpublished Ph.D. thesis, Columbia University, 1965), pp. 70-112.

observers in Japan and Korea who longed for a Ming restoration, it seemed that the Ch'ing dynasty might fall in the
third generation, thus rendering its historical claim to legitimacy doubtful.[80] Later historians have borne out this judgment of the seriousness of the threat to the Ch'ing dynasty's
survival posed by Wu's revolt. [81]

News of the revolt travelled rapidly. First notice reached
the Korean court in the third month of 1674 in the form of
advance dispatches from an embassy returning from Peking.[82] Later the same year, on 8 July 1674, copies of Wu's
and Cheng's manifestoes of revolt, the latter dated but two
months earlier, as well as a report from the Nagasaki interpreters' office based on their interrogation of Chinese merchants, arrived in Edo via express messenger from Nagasaki.
The roju on duty, Kuze Hiroyuki, passed these manifestoes
to Hayashi Gahō, the chief scholar and archivist, with orders
to bring them to the castle on the ninth. When Gahō arrived,
the roju were assembled, and they considered the implications of the rebellion for Japan.[83] Unfortunately, the contents
of these discussions, like most bakufu policy deliberations,
have not been recorded.

Thereafter reports began to flow regularly from Nagasaki
to Edo on the progress of the revolt, as every Chinese ship
that called at Nagasaki was interrogated (we would say de-
briefed) by the interpreter's office upon arrival. All reports
were sent to Edo, there to be processed by Gahō and examined by the roju.

On 9 September roju Inaba Masanori forwarded to Gahō
two more Chinese intelligence reports and a map of the military situation in China, showing Yunnan, Szechuan, Shensi,

[80] Hayashi Gahō, "Go Tei ron," in Gahō Sensei Hayashi Gakushi bunshū,
kan 48.

[81] E.g., Lawrence D. Kessler, K'ang-hsi and the Consolidation of Ch'ing Rule,
1661-1684 (University of Chicago Press, 1976), p. 83; Kanda Nobuo, "Sanpan
no ran to Chōsen," in Shundai shigaku, 1 (March 1951): 60-75.

[82] Hyŏnjong taewang kaesu sillok, 28:1a, at CWS, 38:176.

[83] KH, 1:68; TKIR, 5:424.

Kwanghsi, Taiwan, and most of Kwangtung, Honan, and Fukien in anti-Ch'ing hands.[84] Comparison of other maps of the military situation prepared by modern scholars, and with narratives, shows this map to be fairly accurate. Perhaps the Korean government was not unjustified in expecting the early demise of the Ch'ing government.[85]

The following month Inaba sent Gahō the first extant reports to arrive through the Ryukyu-Satsuma route, which Gahō proceeded to translate into Japanese and to return to Inaba for rōju action.[86] On 15 and 23 November Sō Yoshizane, daimyo of Tsushima, submitted to the bakufu the first intelligence reports on the war gleaned from Korean sources. These reports had been drawn up in Tsushima four months earlier, reflecting the information that the Korean government had gotten from its Peking embassy.[87] It is unclear why it took four months for these reports to reach Edo when others reports normally arrived in two months, and since the daily logs of the Tsushima Edo residence for the last nine months of 1674 are not extant, there is little information to follow up with.[88]

Before we examine the substance of these reports and the mechanics of their handling in Edo, it is important to outline briefly the main routes of foreign intelligence gathering available to the bakufu, some of their characteristics and some of their problems.

Route 1: "Chinese" merchants arriving in Nagasaki → Nagasaki Tō tsūji (Chinese interpreter's office) → Nagasaki bugyō → Edo (rōju/Hayashi). This route provided the greatest volume of data throughout the period covered by the Ka'i

---

[84] KH, 1:78.

[85] See Kanda Nobuo, "Sanpan no ran to Chōsen."

[86] KH, 1:79-91

[87] Tōheiran fūsetsu; KH, 1:93-96.

[88] The Sō Collection at the Historiographical Institute contains the 1,077 extant volumes of the fair copy of the daily logbooks of the Tsushima Edo residence, cited below as Edo Mainikki. Those for the first half of Enpō 2 are missing.

hentai (1644–1724), due simply to the fact that Chinese ships constituted the largest number of foreign entries into Nagasaki. For several reasons these reports seem generally to have been the most accurate: they were not controlled by any articulated intervening interest, such as a foreign government or corporation, and each ship's captain knew that his reports could be checked for accuracy against the reports of other captains, with possible punishment for false information. Moreover, the interpreters were dealing with a language they knew well, Chinese, which was not the case with the reports of the Dutch. On the other hand, most of the ship captains never themselves visited the Chinese interior any farther inland than Nanking, so that much of their information may have been little more than harbor gossip or information planted by harbor officials, unless the captains had their own intelligence networks in China. For themselves, the captains were more worried about Cheng Ching, who controlled the sea lanes and threatened them directly, than they were about Wu San-kuei, who was several hundred miles inland. The fact that Chinese merchants were interrogated in Nagasaki was sufficiently widely known in China that European Jesuits wrote of it in their reports to their superiors.[89] The Jesuit reports naturally emphasized Japanese interest in discovering Christians trying to smuggle themselves into Japan.

Route II: Peking → Fukien → Ryukyu → Satsuma → Edo. Since the Ryukyuan kingdom was subject to Satsuma control in most matters, and at the same time had regular access to Peking through tribute missions, as well as having Ryukyuan students studying in China,[90] one would have hoped for a secure, relatively accurate, essentially direct route of intelligence via Ryukyu. The earliest reports received on this route are dated in August 1674 and arrived in Edo in Octo-

[89] Père Fontaney to Père P. C., London, 15 Janvier 1704, in *Lettres édifiantes et curieuses*, 8 vols. (Paris: Société du Panthéon Littéraire, 1843), 3:124ff.

[90] Mitsugu Matsuda, "The Ryukyuan Government Scholarship Students to China," in *Monumenta Nipponica*, 23.3-4 (1966): 271-304.

ber,[91] with both original Chinese documents and highly accurate reports, but no other information was received from this source until two years later. Most of the information duplicates the manifestoes received via Nagasaki earlier in the year, but the two reports of the tribute ship returning from Fukien in 1674 contain sugnificant and accurate information on the building of the alliance between Wu and Keng Ching-chung, and a detailed, accurate narration of Keng's capture of Fan Ch'eng-mo, governor of Foochow.[92] Ryukyuan intelligence gathering was hampered by the interruption of access to China due to the activities of Cheng Ching and to the war itself.

Route III: Dutch merchants (*Oranda kapitan*) → Nagasaki *Oranda tsūji* (Dutch interpreter's office) → Nagasaki *bugyō* → Edo. These reports were least important in the collection of intelligence on mainland Chinese affairs, since Dutch interests were primarily maritime. The Dutch did provide substantial information from time to time on the activities of the Chengs on Taiwan, but far less on mainland China. Just as both sides in the rebellion sought Ryukyuan involvement, the "viceroy" of Fukien, probably Keng, sought Dutch trade in 1675, a fact which the Dutch duly reported to Nagasaki.[93] After the traders returned to Batavia, the opperhoofden reported their dealings to the bakufu in 1677,[94] while reporting that some Hollanders had remained in Foochow at the request of Cheng Ching and Keng Ching-chung, where a nominal Dutch naval showing would be made. The Dutch

---

[91] *KH*, 1:79-91.

[92] *KH*, 1:87; Tsao, "The Rebellion of the Three Feudatories," p. 104; Hummel, *Eminent Chinese*, pp. 228-229.

[93] Itazawa, *Oranda fūsetsugaki no kenkyū* (Yoshikawa Kōbunkan, 1974; repr. of Nihon Kobunka Kenkyūsho, ed., 1937), pp. 73-74, gives a report from the Opperhoofd Martinus Caezar, dated 20 August 1675. The Dutch were not entirely frank about the extent of their involvement in the civil war in China. For a fuller discussion of Dutch-Chinese relations during the revolt, see John E. Wills, Jr., *Pepper, Guns and Parleys: The Dutch East India Company and China, 1622-1681* (Harvard University Press, 1974), pp. 154-193.

[94] *Oranda fūsetsugaki*, p. 85.

reports are very thin on details of the overall situation in China, but by restricting themselves to matters in which the Dutch were directly involved, they managed to retain a high degree of accuracy. Unfortunately, that accuracy was regularly dimished by the intervention of the Nagasaki *Oranda tsūji* (Dutch interpreter's office), whose ineptitude in the Dutch language at this time was justly famous.[95] Even in the 1670s and 1680s, the Nagasaki interpreters had first to request the Dutch to translate their reports into Portuguese, in which the Japanese were more proficient. Thus it is not surprising that a Dutch reference to the K'ang-hsi emperor, referred to in the Dutch text as the "Kayser," should appear in the interpreters' report as "The General of Peking" (*Pekin no taishō*).[96] Besides, Dutch intelligence was never entirely reliable, for they had a habit of distorting their reports for their own political ends.[97]

Route IV: Peking → Seoul → Pusan → Tsushima → Edo. One of the uses to which the bakufu put its relationship with Korea was the gathering of intelligence on continental developments. Korea sent regular embassies to Peking each year to congratulate the emperor on the turn of the New Year and to receive the Ch'ing calendar, the ultimate symbolic act of vassalage in the Chinese world order. These embassies regularly returned to Seoul with reports of the latest developments in China. Korea also maintained a border trade with China at Ŭiju on the Yalu River, and this market area served

[95] C. R. Boxer, *Jan Compagnie in Japan* (The Hague: Martinus Nijhoff, 1950), p. 59. Kaempfer observed that, "there is scarce one in ten, that understands a Dutch word, excepting some few, who had been servants to the Dutch formerly." *The History of Japan*, 2:204. Kaempfer discusses the Dutch-language interpreters at length, pp. 198-204. Donald Keene, *The Japanese Discovery of Europe*, rev. ed., (Stanford University Press, 1969), p. 11, quotes "report cards for the 1693 interpreters: 'Barely knows any Dutch at all'; 'Because he is either stupid or lazy, he knows only the slighest amount of Dutch . . . ,'" etc.

[96] *Oranda fūsetsugaki*, pp. 104, 106.

[97] See Iwao Seiichi, "Reopening of the Diplomatic Relations."

as a second source of intelligence.[98] We have seen that Seoul's first notices of Wu San-kuei's revolt came from one of these embassies in the spring of 1674. Information deemed appropriate for the Japanese to know was passed down to the magistrate of Tongnae, where Japan House was located, and the information was then transmitted to the overseer of Japan House, who transmitted it to Tsushima. In certain instances, as in 1646 and late 1675,[99] Korean interpreters were sent to Tsushima to make reports on intelligence matters. In the 1675 instance, the report was entirely concerned with the Revolt of the Three Feudatories. These reports were then either sent by runner to the daimyo in Edo, who passed them to the roju as his own reports (after appropriate rewriting), or, when the daimyo was in Tsushima, sent to the *rusuigarō* (the elder in charge of the fief's Edo residence during the daimyo's absence) in the Edo residence, who then passed them to the secretary of the roju on duty. The earliest reports were actually made in person by Sō Yoshizane in conversation with the roju, while written reports were regularized after he returned to Tsushima in early 1675.[100]

As had happened thirty years earlier, at the time of the Ch'ing conquest of China, these incoming reports on the developing Revolt of the Three Feudatories also occupied the attention of the policy councils of Edo for nearly a decade. As Allen Dulles has observed, foreign intelligence information "is of little use unless it is got into the hands of the 'consumers,' the policymakers."[101] In this seventeenth-century context too, therefore, it is necessary to trace the handling of these reports, and to assess their contents, in order fully to understand the bakufu's intelligence apparatus. As seen above, the first notices of the revolt reached Edo on 8

[98] On the Sino-Korean trade see Chang Ts'un-wu, *Ch'ing-Han tsung-fan mao-i, 1637-1894* (Taipei: Chung-yang Yen-chiu-yuan Chin-tai-shih Yen-chiu-so, 1978).

[99] *KH*, 1:173-174.

[100] *Tōheiran fūsetsu.*

[101] Allen Dulles, *The Craft of Intelligence* (Harper & Row, 1963), p. 154.

July 1674 from Nagasaki. The Nagasaki magistrate sent them to the roju, who turned them over to Hayashi Gahō for translation into Japanese, so that the entire roju could consider them in council at the castle the next day. Included were the manifestoes of Wu San-kuei and Cheng Ching, and a debriefing report from the Nagasaki interpreters on the crew of the Number 2 Foochow junk.[102] This was followed three weeks later by interpreters' reports based on interrogation of the Number 6 Jakarta ship and the Number 8 and Number 9 Tung-ning ships, which followed the same route,[103] a route which subsequently proved to be regular.

On 9 September roju Inaba Masanori passed to Gahō a map of the strategic situation in China.[104] Unfortunately, there is neither any indication as to the source of this map, nor a precise date, although its placement indicates that it came from Chinese sources. However, comparison with maps in other works, and with narratives of the war, indicates that is a fairly accurate indication of the distribution of forces in South China in mid-1674.[105]

One month later, on 17 October, information began to flow to Edo from the Ryukyu route. Ryukyu was particularly sensitive to the situation, since its shipping to the China coast had been frequently victimized by the naval forces of the Cheng family on Taiwan. The most recent such incident had been resolved but a few months earlier by negotiations through Okano Magokurō, the Nagasaki *bugyō*.[106] Some of the information contained in these reports, originating as it did with Ryukyuans who had actually been in Foochow, was quite accurate. There is, for example, a detailed account of the events in the spring of 1674, when Keng Ching-chung finally joined Wu San-kuei in revolt, capturing Foochow and

---

[102] *KH*, 1:52-68.

[103] *KH*, 1:68-73.

[104] Inserted in *KH*, v. 1, between pp. 78 and 79. See Plate 5.

[105] Kessler, *K'ang-hsi*; Tsao, "The Rebellion of the Three Feudatories"; Masui Tsuneo, *Shin teikoku* (Kodansha, 1974), pp. 76-85, map, p. 82.

[106] *KH*, 1:72-75.

taking the governor, Fan Ch'eng-mo, captive.[107] The Ryu-kyuans even reported to the bakufu on Keng's secret attempt to suborn Fan.[108] Thus, so long as Ryukyuan ships were not barred from access to the China coast, they had the means, and the powers of observation, to provide high-quality intelligence to Edo.

The Ryukyuan route was of limited utility as an intelligence source, however, because Ryukyuan missions went to Foochow only in alternate years. But Ryukyu was useful in other ways. Because Ryukyu was a "foreign country," Edo could permit the shipment of war materiel to the rebel forces with whom the bakufu sympathized with the insulation of an "arm's length" transaction. Thus, in 1676 the reports from Ryukyu detailed the attempts by Keng to obtain supplies of sulfur from Ryukyu.[109] These were certainly intended for the manufacture of gunpowder, for that same year Keng purchased large quantities of sulfur, saltpeter, and lead from the Dutch East India Company.[110] The bakufu might readily have shrunk from shipping war materiel to Keng directly from Nagasaki, and might have cited Japanese statutory prohibitions on arms exports as justification if it had chosen to do so, as the Nagasaki magistrate had done in 1646. Although Keng's request was explicitly "for military use," the bakufu authorized Satsuma to ship sulfur to him through Ryukyu,[111]

---

[107] Hummel, *Eminent Chinese*, pp. 228-229; Tsao, "The Rebellion of the Three Feudatories," pp. 101-103.

[108] *KH*, 1:87-89.

[109] *KH*, 1:59-64.

[110] Wills, *Pepper, Guns and Parleys*, p. 160, puts the total value of Keng's arms purchases from the Dutch in 1676 at f256,937.

[111] [Roju] Tsuchiya Kazunao, Kuze Hiroyuki, Inaba Masanori to Matsudaira Ōsumi no kami (Shimazu Mitsuhisa), Enpō 4/9/3, in *Kagoshima ken shiryō*, 1:673; [Nagasaki Magistrate] Ushigome Chūzaemon to Matsudaira Ōsumi no kami, Enpō 9/4/17, in *ibid.*, 1:675; Shimazu Mitsuhisa to Ryūkyū Kokushi [Shō Tei], Enpō 5/6/22, at *ibid.*, 1:684, suggests that Keng's envoy returned to Foochow with the sulfur on Enpō 4/11/24. According to Ushigome, the authorization was from the shogun himself.

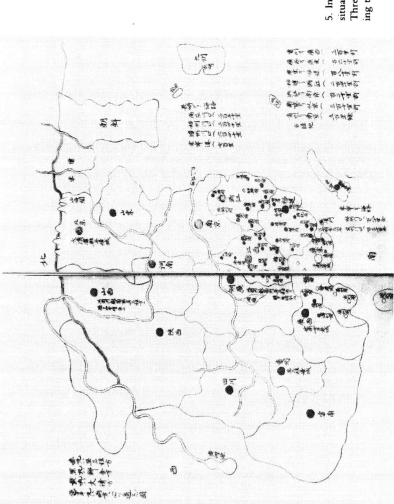

5. Intelligence map showing the strategic situation in China during the Revolt of the Three Feudatories, received in the Edo during the summer of 1674

perhaps the clearest strategic response that Edo would make to its intelligence estimates of the Chinese civil war.

By 1678, when the tide of battle had turned in favor of the Ch'ing forces, the only communications that Ryukyu had from China were from the emperor himself, while some of the K'ang-hsi's deputies were in correspondence with the Nagasaki *bugyō*.[112] While some of these exchanges were debated by the full membership of the roju,[113] the handling of other items, including an imperial rescript from K'ang-hsi to the Ryukyuan crown prince, is not even specified, and still other reports from Ryukyu and Satsuma were kept out of normal channels, being sent to Kira Yoshinaka, of *Chūshingura* fame, and never actually presented to the bakufu.[114] On the basis of content there seems to be no reason why these distinctions of handling should exist. For some reason, no further reports from Ryukyuan sources were recorded for later years.

The first suggestion from the Dutch that anything was amiss came in August 1675, in the report of Opperhoofd Martinus Caezar,[115] informing Edo that the "viceroy" of Foochow had sent emissaries to Batavia in an attempt to open trade with the Dutch. Since Keng Ching-chung at this time controlled the person of Fan Ch'eng-mo, governor of Foochow,[116] it is probable that this report indicates that Keng, at this time in a state of rebellion and in league with Wu, was the origin of this feeler. The version of this report reaching Edo[117] has slightly garbled the information. This was either because the interpreters did not know Dutch well enough, depreciating the value of the early Dutch *fūsetsugaki*, or because, although he recorded the truth in the *Daghregis-*

[112] *KH*, 1:260-274.

[113] Tairō Sakai Tadakiyo, with Inaba Masanori, Tsuchiya Kazunao, and Okubo Tadatomo, in consultation with Hayashi Gahō. *KH*, 1:260, 273f.

[114] *KH*, 1:264-270.

[115] *Oranda fūsetsugaki*, pp. 73f, 76.

[116] Hummel, *Eminent Chinese*, pp. 229, 416.

[117] *KH*, 1:122-126; *Oranda fūsetsugaki*, pp. 77-80.

ter, Caezar chose to keep from the Japanese the fact that the Dutch were in contact with the Chinese rebels. This sort of flaw was of course endemic to all the bakufu's sources of information.

Succeeding Dutch reports continued to give some attention to Chinese affairs, naturally emphasizing Taiwanese affairs where possible,[118] but also reporting dealings with Keng Ching-chung in Foochow, now "loyal" to the government. The skill with which the Nagasaki interpreters interpolated this report, identifying Keng from vague references in the Dutch, contrasts sharply with their earlier inept translations, and may indicate the increased amount of information that they now had about the progress of the revolt.

The movement of intelligence along Route IV, the Peking → Seoul → Tsushima → Edo route, is by far the best documented. The Tsushima versions of the reports are still extant in Tsushima archives, in addition to the bakufu's records included in the *Ka'i hentai.* Some of the information can be traced back to Seoul, in reports of the Korean embassies to Peking on their return to court. And the daily log of Tsushima's Edo residence makes it possible to trace some of the mechanics and politics of the presentation of these reports to the bakufu. Moreover, the existence of essentially the same report in both the Korean and the Tsushima versions enables us to locate with some precision the source of inaccuracies in this route of intelligence.

To turn first to the institutions involved in the Tsushima route, information was first picked up by the twice-yearly Korean embassies to Peking or, on occasion, by Korean officers along the Korean-Manchurian border. The ambassadors could send advance reports to Seoul in emergencies, as was done in 1674, but they always made a direct report to the throne on their return to Seoul. The first reports of Wu's revolt arrived in this manner. The information thus received was of course processed for use by the Korean government,

[118] *KH,* 1:154f; *Oranda fūsetsugaki,* pp. 82-83.

ever hopeful of a restoration of Ming, but selected information was also passed down to the magistrate of Tongnae, the administrative unit which included Pusan, and which was responsible for day-to-day Japanese relations. The magistrate then transmitted the information to the Tsushima trading factory. It was at this point, or rather between Seoul and Pusan, that the Korean government could edit or distort reports, for Korea preferred that Japan did not receive information which might sway her in favor of the Manchus. And, in fact, the volume of information reaching Edo along this route was substantially less than that reaching Seoul, indicating just such a culling process. An alternative procedure, used at various times throughout the Edo period, and employed in late 1675 in response to a Japanese request, was the dispatch of Korean interpreters to Tsushima, where they presented information orally.

Once information was in Tsushima hands it remained there until it reached Edo. Tsushima did not deal with or communicate with the bakufu through the Nagasaki *bugyō* on matters of security or intelligence. If the daimyo was in Tsushima, the report he issued was delivered by messenger to the Edo *rusuigarō*. The elder prepared multiple copies for delivery to the member of the roju on duty that month and to Hayashi Gahō. These are the versions that appear in bakufu records, and are analogous to those we have seen the roju discussing above. However, the fief elder also sent one copy of every report to Ōkōchi (Matsudaira) Masanobu. Masanobu's role seems to have been as Tsushima's expediter in Edo, for he was a brother-in-law of the daimyo of Tsushima, younger brother of the late roju Matsudaira Nobutsuna, and himself a master of shogunal ceremonies (*sōshaban*) since 1659, with extensive connections in Edo Castle.

If the daimyo was in residence in Edo, then he received the information from his fief elder in Tsushima, redrafted it as his own report to the bakufu, and presented it through the channels just noted. Exceptionally, in the early months of 1675, Sō Yoshizane reported directly, orally, to the tairo

Sakai Tadakiyo, and senior roju, and apparently understood it to be off the record, but bakufu records do not indicate such an understanding.[119]

The date of Yoshizane's meeting with Sakai and Inaba, and his return to Tsushima shortly thereafter, coupled with notations of handling of intelligence reports thereafter in the fief residence log, explain the importance of Ōkōchi Masanobu, for he appears in the records in relation to intelligence reports only from 16 March 1675, as Yoshizane was leaving for home. The daimyo could appear at the castle, or meet with the roju, on his own account, and could thus represent himself and get credit for his actions. But, with Yoshinari gone, his elders could not do more than pass materials to similar underlings at the councillors' residences; they could not come and go in the castle. It was part of every daimyo's job to be as well-connected as possible, and Yoshizane was successful at this.[120] Now he was using his connections to expedite his reports through the bakufu bureaucracy in his absence, and to see that he got credit.

Each time Tsushima sent an intelligence report to the roju, the roju responded with an official letter, a *hōsho*. Unfortunately, the texts of these letters are not extant, so no more can be stated with certainty than that the roju at least considered the reports and gave official acknowledgment. This reconfirms the fact that the roju believed these reports, and that the civil war in China was of sufficiently great concern to the Tokugawa state to merit consideration in the highest policy council of that state. Changes in the strategic situation in East Asia, even thousands of kilometers from Japan, were of concern to the bakufu at least as late as the 1670s.

In content, much of the information in the first Tsushima report is identical to the report that the Korean embassy in Peking had made to the Korean king three months earlier, but it includes substantive information of slightly later vin-

---

[119] *Tōheiran fūsetsu*, Enpō 3/1/6 (31 January 1675); cf. *KH*, 1:101-105.

[120] *Kansei chōshū shokafu*, 8:262-264. All Yoshizane's sisters had married into courtier or daimyo houses, as had his daughters.

tage as well. Yoshizane's report of July 1674 contains information received in Seoul as late as the end of the previous month, detailing Wu San-kuei's attack on Ching-chou, and includes other intelligence data not found in other reports to Edo.[121] It also contains some errors. Yoshizane's report says, "In order to capture Wu San-kuei, Peking has sent 100,000 Tatar troops to Yunnan." After an initial Manchu victory, Wu called up reinforcements and won a draw. Fang Chao-ying has calculated the force sent down at this time as comprising 10,551 men, Manchu, Mongolian, and Chinese, excluding officers,[122] so that the Tsushima report is exaggerated by a factor of ten. Moreover, Dr. Fang's calculation show that the total Ch'ing mobilization in the eight years of this war probably did not exceed 400,000, most of it after the initial stages of the war, making the figures in the Tsushima report all the more suspect. This kind of upward bias in the troop strength estimates in Tsushima's intelligence reports was not rare. On 2 February 1675 Sō Yoshizane reported that a force of 100,000 Mongols, joined by a large Manchu contingent, had lost over half their men in a defeat at the hands of Wu San-kuei.[123] Such figures are surprising. Fang's estimated total Mongol mobilization for the duration of the war is but 26,000,[124] and it is even unlikely that there were ever 100,000 Mongol troops at any one time. And, indeed, tracing this report back one stage to Seoul, where it originated, one finds that King Sukchong had received a report from Ambassador Prince Yŏngsin at Shanhaikuan, on his way home from Peking, on 4 December. Prince Yŏngsin reported that the K'ang-hsi emperor had sent down a force of 14,000 Mongol troops, over half of whom had died in battle

---

[121] *Tōheiran fūsetsu*; *KH*, 1:92-95.

[122] Fang Chao-ying, "A Technique for Estimating the Numerical Strength of the Early Manchu Forces," in *Harvard Journal of Asiatic Studies*, 13 (June 1950): 198f.

[123] *Tōheiran fūsetsu*; *KH*, 1:102.

[124] Fang, "A Technique," p. 202.

because they were unused to the subtropical climate of south China.[125]

If Yoshizane's report of 100,000 Mongol troops moving to the front under the Ch'ing flag suggests the degree of inaccuracy that could infect Tsushima's intelligence reports, his report of the previous week shows that at its best Tsushima could pass on to Edo information that was very accurate indeed. On 25 January, in a brief report, Yoshizane informed Edo that the K'ang-hsi emperor had requested the dispatch of Korean troops to help in the war effort.[126] The Korean ambassador to Peking, Yoshinari reported, had received a secret request from the "Tatar king" for Korean troops to aid in the fighting. The Korean court had received the report from the ambassador and debated it even before the ambassador himself had arrived back at Seoul. Sukchong's court thought that the "Tatar king [the K'ang-hsi emperor] looked like a loser" (makeiro ni aimie), and they worried about the effects of siding with the Tatars. They discussed the prospects for delaying tactics, making a show of preparing to send troops while in fact procrastinating in order to make an alliance with Wu San-kuei. For the moment, Yoshizane concluded, it seemed unlikely that Korea would enter the war.

This report of Yoshizane's is a remarkably accurate summary of the debate at the court in Seoul on 3 December 1674, when the chief ministers of state and officials of the Border Defense Agency discussed the Ch'ing request for Korean troops.[127] The court was in a difficult position: whatever the prospects for the Ming restoration they hoped for, at the moment they were separated from Wu San-kuei's troops by the full force of the Ch'ing army and the breadth of Ch'ing territory. Yet they feared that if they complied with the K'ang-hsi emperor's request, they would be hard put to refute charges of disloyalty after a Ming restoration. Chief State Councillor

---

[125] Sukchong taewang sillok, 1:25a, at CWS, 38:219.
[126] Sō Tsushima no kami [to the roju], Enpō 3/1/8, in Tōheiran fūsetsu; KH, 1:101.
[127] Sukchong taewang sillok, 1:26b-27a, at CWS, 38:219-220.

Hŏ Ch'ŏk even suggested that if the emperor continued to insist, Korea should reply that ever since the time of the first Manchu invasion of Korea in 1627, Korea had ceased to maintain an army.

These reports from Tsushima, their accuracy, and their relationship to the information available to Seoul, give a fairly clear picture of the advantages and the drawbacks of intelligence about the Chinese civil war that could be obtained from Korea. Since Korea shared a border with China, sent regular embassies to Peking, and traded regularly with China,[128] Korean observers had fairly regular access to whatever information was current in Peking, both in official circles and on the streets of the city. They also had an ample supply of border gossip, exchanged like any other commodity of value at the market at Ŭiju, on the Yalu River. Korea could choose either to pass all the information it received on to Tsushima, withhold information, or even distort information and add deliberate misinformation, as suited Korean purposes.[129] We know, for example, that in 1627, on the occasion of the first great Manchu invasion of Korea, the court considered withholding news of the invasion from Japan, and decided to inform Tsushima only because they would find out anyway, and in hopes of getting Tsushima to accept an interruption of trade.[130] On the other hand, Korea might intentionally supply inaccurate information to Japan, and it may well be that the inflation of the Mongol troop detachment from 14,000 to 100,000 between Seoul and Edo was the result of a deliberate Korean choice to misinform Japan.

It is at this point that the first evidence of overt bakufu

[128] See Chang Ts'un-wu's study of the trade, *Ch'ing-han tsung-fan mao-i, 1637-1894*.

[129] Allen Dulles, *The Craft of Intelligence*, Chapter 11, "Confusing the Adversary," discusses the value of disseminating misinformation. It is difficult to know in this instance what purpose Korea served by overstating Ch'ing troop strength. Perhaps the court hoped to dissuade Japan from sending troops via Korea.

[130] See *supra*, n. 7.

action appears in the records. (This is partially due to the lack of accessible records for any but the Tsushima route.) Why the bakufu waited so long is a matter for conjecture. In the late spring of 1675 the bakufu ordered Sō Yoshizane to gather more information on the progress of the civil war in China. This prompted Yoshizane to send an unusually long letter to the Korean Board of Rites, captioned "An Enquiry on the War in China."[131] Yoshizane, citing shogunal authority for his letter, asked Korea to take advantage of its proximity to China to gather information on the progress of the civil war and to pass the information on to Japan. He was particularly interested in the battles for the southern and northern capitals. He suggested that it was incumbent upon Korea as a good neighbor to provide Japan with intelligence. Since Korea had already supplied Japan with extensive, if faulty, information, the form of this letter, and the fact that it speaks only of the information received from Chinese merchants in Nagasaki, without acknowledging Korea's role, are puzzling.

Nam Ch'ŏnhan, Third Minister of Rites, responded the next month by letter[132] and two months later dispatched two interpreters to Tsushima. These men gave Yoshizane further information which he passed to the bakufu on 24 December.[133] Included was information regarding relations between Wu San-kuei and Cheng Ching, indicating pressure from Cheng to get Korea to spy on Japan, and from Wu for Korean support for his cause.

After Yoshizane's letter and the visit of the interpreters, information flowed from Korea to Edo with some regularity for about a year and a half. Then, as the war settled into a stalemate, Korean information lapsed for some time, while other more reliable sources took up the slack. When Tsu-

---

[131] [Sō] Taira Yoshizane to Third Minister Board of Rites, Enpō 3/5/X, in *HCO*, vol. 28.

[132] Nam Ch'ŏnhan to Governor Taira of Tsushima, *ŭlmo*/6/X, in *HCO*, vol. 28.

[133] *KH*, 1:135-138.

shima began again to submit reports toward the end of 1678, they were still incomplete and inaccurate. They omitted altogether, for example, the signal fact that Wu had proclaimed himself emperor of Chou, a blatant abandonment of the Ming cause which cost him heavily in moral support in Japan and Korea.[134] It may well be that it was this defective nature of the Korean intelligence route that made it increasingly difficult after 1678 for Tsushima even to get its reports accepted in Edo.[135] If this inference is valid, then there is some indication of the bakufu's ability to distinguish good information from bad, and to attempt to weed out the latter.

Only a small number of Japanese scholars have analyzed the bakufu's intelligence-gathering in the two centuries from the expulsion of the Portuguese to the arrival of Commodore Perry. But these writers have concentrated on Japan's interest in Europe, born of fear of Christianity, matters of which the bakufu was kept regularly informed by the Dutch. Katagiri Kazuo in his study of Tokugawa foreign intelligence attributes the bakufu's felt need to know about the outside world mainly to the presence of Europeans in East Asia, and their aggressive designs.[136] Itazawa Takeo also argues that the bakufu's interest derived from its fear of Christianity, and concentrates almost exclusively on Edo's interest in European affairs.[137] These scholars have understated the importance of Asian affairs in Tokugawa foreign relations in general, and of Asian intelligence in the overall intelligence picture and in Tokugawa security. Even Ura Yasukazu's study on the intelligence reports in the published edition of Ka'i hentai, the largest compendium of such materials, stresses the anti-Christian purposes of the bakufu's intelligence-gathering.[138]

However, at least through the end of the seventeenth cen-

[134] Hayashi Gahō, "Go Tei ron;" Kanda Nabuo, "Sanpan ran to Chōsen."
[135] Tōheiran fūsetsu; Edo Mainikki for Enpō 6-8 (1678-80).
[136] Katagiri Kazuo, "Sakoku jidai ni motarasareta kaigai jōhō," in Nihon rekishi, 249 (February 1969): 83-98.
[137] Itazawa, Oranda fūsetsugaki, "Introduction," pp. 5, 9.
[138] Ura Yasukazu, "Tōsen fūsetsugaki no kenkyū," in KH, 1:24-27.

tury, the bakufu maintained a continuing interest in the shifting power balance and strategic situation in East Asia. Even after the establishment of the so-called seclusion policy, the bakufu continued its close watch on the Chinese military situation. It could do no less, for China was not unified until 1683, and remained volatile until that time. And so long as the Chinese land mass and maritime China were in flux, Japan might somehow be drawn into the fray, while the unification of China by "barbarians" might mean a reenactment of the Mongol invasions. Self-proclaimed Ming loyalist forces repeatedly requested Japanese military aid between 1646 and the late 1650s. And in 1646, at least, powerful voices within the bakufu argued for the dispatch of a Japanese expeditionary force to China to aid in the restoration of the Ming dynasty. However, these requests for assistance, and the war in China itself, prompted the bakufu to initiate intelligence-gathering operations. With repeated applications for aid by Ming loyalists and with continued trade and piracy by the forces of Coxinga, especially after he wrested control of all of Taiwan from the Dutch in 1663, the international situation demanded that the bakufu arm itself with information.

The bakufu did gradually develop institutions to monitor foreign intelligence in general, and the China conflict in particular. Although these institutions existed in rudimentary form prior to the Revolt of the Three Feudatories, it was the outbreak of that revolt that spurred the bakufu's intelligence operations to their highest level of activity. This rebellion kept maritime and continental East Asia in turmoil for nearly a decade, and prompted some in both Japan and Korea to hope for a restoration of the Ming dynasty.[139] Despite the stipulations in the so-called "seclusion edicts" of the 1630s and earlier prohibitions against the export of Japanese arms, the rebellion prompted speculation in Peking that Japanese

[139] Hayashi Gahō, "Go Tei ron"; *Hyŏnjong taewang kaesu sillok*, 28:12b, at *CWS*, 38:181.

military aid might be introduced into the war zone.[140] Edo declined to send troops in response to the calls of Cheng Chih-lung and other Ming loyalist generals in the 1640s and 1650s, but when a request came for sulfur for "military use" in 1676, the bakufu approved the sale to Keng Ching-chung, and the sulfur was in fact shipped to Keng from Naha.[141]

In Japanese eyes, there was little to distinguish the Manchus from the Mongols; both were subsumed under the rubric of "Tatars." And for that reason if for no other, the prospect of a Manchu victory uniting China under Ch'ing rule raised the specter of a new round of Mongol invasions, a repetition of the experience of the thirteenth century. The Lung-wu pretender had explicitly recalled for the bakufu the connection between the Tatar invaders of the thirteenth century and the Tatars overrunning China in the seventeenth, both to suggest to Edo the renewed threat, and to remind Japan that it was his own Ming dynasty that had driven the Tatars out of China, exacting vengeance for Japan as well.[142] In the 1670s, the Revolt of the Three Feudatories stimulated Kumazawa Banzan to memorialize Edo for strengthened national defense, which would be necessary to stave off the Tatar invasion that he foresaw.[143] In so threatening an envi-

---

[140] "Oboe," Enpō 3/1/10, in *Tōheiran fūsetsu*. If these rumors of Japanese weapons shipments to Chinese rebels seem hard to credit three hundred years after the fact, they were clearly less incredible in their own time. Only the following year, as has been seen above, the bakufu allowed export of sulfur to Chinese rebels through Ryukyu. And in 1701, when the K'ang-hsi emperor heard rumors of Japanese military preparations for an invasion of China, he sent spies to Nagasaki to investigate the threat. Their reports are in *Wen-hsien t'sung-pien* (2 vols., Kuo-feng Ch'u-pan-she, 1964), pp. 856-857, and are noted briefly in Silas Wu, *Passage to Power* (Harvard University Press, 1979), p. 84, and discussed at length by Matsuura Akira, "Kōshū shikizō U-rin-tatsu Bo-ji-shin no Nagasaki raikō ni tsuite," in *Tōhōgaku*, 55 (January 1978): 62-75.

[141] *Supra*, n. 111.

[142] *Supra*, n. 42.

[143] Kumazawa Banzan, "Daigaku wakumon," in *Kumazawa Banzan*, ed., Gotō Yōichi and Tomoeda Ryūtarō, *Nihon Shisō Taikei*, vol. 30 (Iwanami Shoten, 1971), pp. 425-427.

ronment it was imperative that the bakufu be prepared to act and, as a first measure, to mobilize an intelligence network that would arm Edo with information that would keep the bakufu ready for any eventuality.

The bakufu's contemplation of active military involvement in support of the Ming resistance movement in China in the 1640s, and the construction and mobilization of a wide-ranging system of foreign intelligence in response to the Revolt of the Three Feudatories, alter the image of Japan's foreign policy in the period after the expulsion of the Portuguese, and demand some new readings of Japan's relationship to its Asian environment in the age of the mature Tokugawa bakufu.

The intelligence system devised by the bakufu is remarkably similar in both its methods and its organization and behavior to modern consular and military intelligence systems. If allowance is made for the inevitable difference in technology and communications, the intelligence network discussed here would be equally readily familiar to Sun Tzu, the progenitor of Chinese military theory in the Chou dynasty, or to Allen Dulles, a leading apostle of "the craft of intelligence" in mid-twentieth-century America, and certainly to anyone who has worked in a consulate or an intelligence agency.[144]

As befitted the principles of Tokugawa institutions, some of the organs in the bakufu's intelligence network—the domains of Tsushima and Satsuma, for example—were not entirely within the direct control of Edo, but they were generally sensitive to bakufu wishes and policy, at least in the gathering of intelligence. Others of them, particularly the

---

[144] See Dulles, *The Craft of Intelligence*, especially Chapter 2, "The Historical Setting," and Chapter 12, "How Intelligence Is Put to Use." Colleagues who have had experience in either the consular service or U.S. military intelligence have commented upon reading earlier drafts of this chapter that the Tokugawa intelligence system was essentially the same as the sorts of systems within which they had worked.

apparatus in Nagasaki, were more closely controlled by Edo, and staffed directly by shogunal personnel.

The way in which Edo deployed its intelligence-gathering apparatus, the way that information flowed to the periphery of Japan from abroad, and from the periphery to Edo, and the handling of intelligence information in Edo, suggest the outlines of the bakufu's nervous system. The roju did in fact perform the role of foreign-policy control center prescribed for it by Iemitsu in 1634 in his reorganization of administrative functions, a role reconfirmed by Ietsuna in 1662.[145] Operational directives for the gathering of intelligence flowed from Edo to Nagasaki, Tsushima, and Satsuma along regularized channels of communication. It was the duty of the Nagasaki magistrate and the daimyos of Tsushima and Satsuma then to activate their networks, either by interrogating new arrivals from overseas, as at Nagasaki, or by further directives to operatives overseas, in Naha and Pusan. These pathways for intelligence were essentially congruent to the major patterns of outgoing and incoming Japanese foreign trade.[146]

---

[145] *Tokugawa kinrei kō*, 2:142; *Tokugawa jikki*, 4:412; Kitajima Masamoto, *Edo bakufu no kenryoku kōzō*, pp. 462, 470, offers a brief discussion.

[146] See Tashiro Kazui, *Kinsei Nitchō tsūkō bōeki shi no kenkyū*, pp. 331-341, for a discussion of the structure of what she has termed the "East Asian trading sphere." Although Satsuma and Tsushima each traded directly only with Ryukyu and Korea, respectively, in each case China was the ultimate destination of much of the Japanese export payment, and the source of much of what was imported. Similarly, the most important object of ultimate interest to intelligence analysts was China, even if the immediate reporting agencies were Satsuma and Tsushima. Likewise, the Dutch, as the only Europeans trading in Japan, were expected to report on the affairs of all of Europe. See, for example, *Tokugawa jikki*, 5:439, where the Dutch are ordered to supply information on the doings of the Portuguese worldwide. For a fuller discussion of the intelligence duties of the Dutch, see Katagiri Kazuo, "Sakoku jidai ni motarasareta kaigai jōhō," which, despite the global implications of its title, deals only with European intelligence supplied by the Dutch; *Oranda fūsetsugaki shūsei*, ed., Iwao Seiichi, 2 vols. (Yoshikawa Kōbunkan, 1977-1979), 1:1-76, or Itazawa Takeo, *Oranda fūsetsugaki no kenkyū*, pp. 1-20.

The information that returned to Edo in response to these directives, or spontaneously, all flowed to the roju, either directly or through the incumbent head of the Hayashi family. The Hayashi role was essentially that of technical expert, translating Chinese-language documents into Japanese, doing research, and preparing reports for the roju. The deliberation on the intelligence received, however, and the authority to determine the appropriate policy response, rested with the roju, as specified in the 1634 reorganization, and as carried out in practice. The roju from time to time consulted also with the three main Tokugawa collateral lords, or with the daimyo of Hikone, the highest-ranking hereditary retainer of the shogunal house, and frequently also consulted with the shogun himself.

The roju responded to information with policy and action. When aid to the Ming restoration movement was an issue in 1646-1647, and some of the people privy to the roju's policy deliberations seemed to expect Edo to be sending troops to China in the near future, new reports from the war zone showed Edo that Cheng Chih-lung's cause had collapsed, and the roju scrapped further consideration of the mission. This course was surely preferable to that of prefiguring the Bay of Pigs by three centuries. To say that there was a strong predisposition among some shogunal policymakers not to intervene in any case does not negate the fact that intervention was clearly under consideration, and that the proponents of intervention in China had made substantial headway toward having their way. Perhaps the advocates of the more cautious policy were merely strengthened in their position by the new intelligence from Foochow, but the advocates of war found that these reports devastated their position.

Aborting what would have been a disastrous military adventure was one bakufu policy response to the flow of incoming intelligence information; orders to the Nagasaki magistrate and the daimyos of Kyushu and western Honshu to be on guard for Ming refugee ships and to heighten their military preparedness in the 1640s was another.[147] But as in the 1640s intelligence aborted one mission, in the 1670s the bakufu decided to accept a limited, arm's-length involvement in the Revolt of the Three Feudatories, authorizing the sale of sulfur to Keng Ching-chung. Mostly, however, the bakufu's response was to order its agents on the periphery to gather still more intelligence, and to direct further diplomatic action.[148]

Moreover, it is clear that these institutional arrangements remained vital and functional throughout the Tokugawa period, even if the policy responses were not as effective in the 1840s and early 1850s as they had been in the 1640s and 1670s. In the 1840s, for example, the roju Abe Masahiro engaged in long and intense correspondence with Tokugawa Nariaki, daimyo of Mito, a Tokugawa collateral, on the future course of foreign policy.[149] The issues were different from what they had been in the seventeenth century, but the actors—until the arrival of Perry, at least—were institutionally the same. Even the technical role of the Hayashi family did not erode, as the shogun ordered Hayashi Akira to prepare a compendium of the dynasty's diplomatic precedents, completed in the spring of 1853, just a few months before the arrival of Commodore Perry's fleet.[150] Even at that late date, the traditional intelligence network continued to supply Edo with information on developments abroad. Sō Yoshikazu, for example, forwarded reports to the roju on the progress of the Taiping rebellion in China.[151]

The quantity of intelligence information available to policy

---

[147] *Tokugawa jikki*, 4:460–461.

[148] For example, notations in the Tsushima office logs for Edo during the Revolt of the Three Feudatories, Edo *Mainikki* (1679) (MS, Sō Collection, Historiographical Institute), notice for Enpō 7/4/4 (1680/5/06) and *passim*.

[149] This correspondence is collected as "Shin Ise monogatari," and published in *Kyū bakufu*, vol. 4, nos. 6, 7 (June, July 1900).

[150] The result of this order was *Tsūkō ichiran*, which served as a diplomatic handbook for the bakufu in the 1850s and 1860s.

[151] *Dai Nihon komonjo bakumatsu gaikoku kankei monjo*, 1:433–434; 3:279–281.

planners, ancient or modern, may be massive, but it is of little use unless some judgments of quality are made to distinguish the good information from the bad.[152] The quality of information that the roju received was clearly mixed. Much of the information was quite timely and accurate.[153] Some of it contained original documents from China, particularly manifestoes from the rebels, rescripts from K'ang-hsi, and the like. But there was also a significant amount of erroneous information. Since the roju did not keep records of its deliberations, and very few of the directives that it issued in this regard survive, there is little information on the ability of the bakufu to distinguish good information from bad. The only evidence we have is inferential. Spot-checks show that information coming along the Tsushima route was biased upward, overstating troop levels and Chinese demands on Korea. In the later years of the war Tsushima found difficulty in getting its reports accepted by the bakufu; this may reflect the roju's recognition of the low quality of information on this route. Ryukyuan information, by contrast, was of very high quality when it was available, being based on the experience of Ryukyuans in China. Chinese information was of vast quantity and mixed quality. Dutch information was of small volume, mixed quality, and hampered by inept translation.

The Tokugawa foreign intelligence system, as seen in the years of the Revolt of the Three Feudatories, was essentially passive. So far as we can tell at this stage, the bakufu did not attempt to reach outside Japan in an active manner, except by exploiting the presence of Tsushima's agents in Pusan,

[152] Dulles comments on this difficulty frequently in *The Craft of Intelligence*, for example, p. 57.

[153] Masui Tsuneo says of *KH*, which contains most of the foreign intelligence available to the bakufu at the time of the Revolt of the Three Feudatories, that it "contains information, such as Wu San-kuei's manifestoes, and traces of the wavering of the Chinese masses between Ming and Ch'ing, which are unavailable in Chinese sources." He laments that historians of China have virtually neglected the *KH* and other Japanese intelligence reports for their value as sources. Masui, *Shin teikoku* (Kōdansha, 1974), pp. 34-35.

inviting Korean interpreters to Tsushima, and the like. No spies were sent to China. None of the coastal defense measures implemented at that time can be clearly demonstrated to be precautions lest the Revolt affect the Japanese home islands. But there clearly were negotiations between the Nagasaki *bugyō* and agents of Cheng Ching to protect Ryukyuan shipping against Cheng's raiding.

This passive posture is not entirely inconsistent with the traditional historiography of Tokugawa foreign relations. But the existence and vital operation of a foreign intelligence apparatus, and their degree of concern for strategic developments in East Asia, require modification of that view. It is difficult to say what level of threat the roju perceived at this time, even given knowledge of the Dutch contacts with both sides in the conflict. One can surmise, however, that they would have been much more alarmed had they been informed of the fact that the K'ang-hsi emperor was employing the German Jesuit Joseph Verbiest to cast cannon for his armies.[154] After the Ch'ing victory and final unification of China, the prospect of a monolithic, united China in "barbarian" hands was of great concern to many Japanese, who feared a repetition of the Mongol invasions of Japan. Kumazawa Banzan, a prominent Neoconfucian philosopher of the day, wrote to his son-in-law Inaba Hikobei to argue that this new situation demanded Japanese preparation for defense against just such an attack within the next year or two.[155] Banzan had hoped that he could discuss this crisis in national defense with the roju; the next year he elaborated his reasons

[154] Kessler, *K'ang-hsi*, p. 147.

[155] In *Banzan zenshū*, 6 vols. (Banzan Zenshū Kankōkai, 1940-1943), 6:197. For a discussion of this letter, its relationship to Banzan's *Daigaku wakumon*, and the relationship of Banzan's concerns over national defense to the larger scope of Banzan's thought, see Ian James McMullen's stimulating essay, "Kumazawa Banzan and 'Jitsugaku': Toward Pragmatic Action," in Wm. Theodore de Bary and Irene Bloom, eds., *Principal and Practicality: Essays in Neo-Confucianism and Practical Learning* (Columbia University Press, 1979), pp. 337-374, especially pp. 337-342.

in *Daigaku wakumon*, which he had intended as a memorial on strategy and national defense: "There have been numerous examples of the Northern Barbarians attacking Japan after they have taken China. Now they have already taken China."[156]

[156] "Daigaku wakumon," in *Kumazawa Banzan*, pp. 425-427.

CHAPTER FIVE

Through the Looking-Glass of Protocol: Mirror to an Ideal World

"Man tries to make for himself in the fashion that suits him best a simplified and intelligible picture of the world. He then tries to some extent to substitute this cosmos of his for the world of experience, and thus to overcome it. He makes this cosmos and its construction the center of his emotional life in order to find in this way the peace and serenity which he cannot find in the narrow whirlpool of personal experience. The supreme task of [the investigator] is to arrive at those universal elementary laws from which the cosmos can be built up by pure deduction. [O]nly intuition, resting on the sympathetic understanding of experience, can reach them."
—Albert Einstein, 1918

DIPLOMATIC protocol and diplomatic language are nothing if they are not a highly formalized, stylized set of symbols by which states attempt to represent the "order" between and among themselves. In a multi-state system such as that which existed in early modern Europe, that symbol system may evolve through a multilateral tug-of-war among the principal states involved, or it may be hammered out in a more explicit and willful process, such as the Congress of Vienna or the Versailles Conference.[1] The combination of protocol

---

[1] On the evolution of European multi-state diplomacy see Garrett Mattingly, *Renaissance Diplomacy* (Houghton Mifflin Company, 1971). On the Congress of Vienna see C. K. Webster, *The Congress of Vienna, 1814-1815* (Oxford University Press, n.d.), which was written as a guide for the use of British diplomats at the Paris Peace Conference. Section 15, pp. 60 and 68, deals with the issues of precedence and protocol in the organization of the Congress. See also Sir Ernest Satow, *A Guide to Diplomatic Practice*, 2 vols. (Longmans, Green and Co., 1917), at 2:75-79; also see Chapters 4 and 5, 1:13-51, on issues of precedence among states and among sovereigns.

and language employed in a particular diplomatic culture may be consciously reorganized, as at Vienna and Versailles, or evolve "naturally" through the accretion of practice over decades and centuries. In either case, they have in common that they constitute a formal system of behavior and language, which is perceived by some of its participants and observers to represent a realistic mirror of the moral, political, or military relationships of the several states involved. Diplomatic practice, that is to say, may be conceived of as being in some way isomorphic to the reality that it seeks to order, so that, "there may be a *patterned structure* binding . . . together"[2] the symbolic statements of a system of ritual. Indeed, because the meaning of symbolic statements is tied to their isomorphic relationship to some other reality, and because the degree of dispute and negotiation which attended the development of Tokugawa Japan's diplomatic symbology suggest that "the choice of symbols is a highly motivated one,"[3] we are not only entitled, but compelled, to "try to understand the relationship between what we call 'truth' . . ."[4] and symbol, for if there is any perceived isomorphism between the symbols—the behavior and the language—of the system and its structure, then the "[s]ymbols of [the] system, [even] though initially devoid of meaning, cannot avoid taking on a 'meaning' of sorts. . . ."[5]

The early Tokugawa bakufu was engaged in the develop-

---

[2] Douglas R. Hofstadter, *Gödel, Escher, Bach: An Eternal Golden Braid* (Basic Books, 1979), p. 59. Hofstadter is speaking of mathematics, not of diplomacy or protocol. However, he efficiently echoes the charge of the noted anthropologist Edmund Leach that, "In seeking to understand ritual we are, in effect, trying to discover the rules of grammar and syntax of an unknown language . ." (Leach, "Ritual," in *International Encyclopedia of the Social Sciences* [1968], 13:524), and that since, "Human actions can seem to *do* things, that is, they can alter the physical state of the world , or they can seem to *say* things . . ." it is therefore incumbent upon the observer to interpret ritual to discover its meaning. (*Ibid.*, p. 523.)

[3] Hofstadter, *Gödel, Escher, Bach*, p. 51.

[4] *Ibid.*, p. 54.

[5] *Ibid.*, p. 51.

ment of a system of behavior and language for the governing of Japan's relations with foreign countries in the seventeenth century, not only with the European intruders, but with Korea, the Ryukyuan kingdom, China, and the countries of Southeast Asia as well. This search for a set of norms and behaviors for the conduct of foreign relations proceeded in tandem with the development and establishment of the Tokugawa state. These canons of protocol would have to be acceptable both to Japan and to those countries which would maintain relations with Japan. During the early Tokugawa period Japan sought relations with all foreign countries active in East Asia. But in the end it was only with those countries which were willing to abide by a set of norms and protocol of Japan's own choosing that it was possible to establish relations which might survive beyond the 1630s.

The vocabulary and forms of international behavior on which Japan drew were those which constituted the experience of a Sinocentric international order dominant in East Asia during the Ming dynasty. This system has been termed "the Chinese world order,"[6] a term of convenience less cumbersome than the more literal "order based on the dichotomy between the civilized (i.e., Chinese) and the barbarian," and less judgmental than the "Chinese tribute system," or the "investiture system."[7] In the Chinese case, this system was founded on the assumption that the ethical norms of Confucianism constituted "civilization," and that these were embodied in the Chinese state, and personified by the Chinese

[6] Most significantly by John K. Fairbank, ed., *The Chinese World Order* (Harvard University Press, 1968).

[7] These are, respectively, renditions of the Chinese terms *hua-i*, "the civilized (*hua*) and the barbarian (*i*)," *ka'i* in Japanese; *ch'ao-kung* (j. *chōkō*), "paying tribute at court"; and *ts'e-feng* (j. *sakuhō*), "investiture." *Ka'i* is a term of great significance in the discourse of Tokugawa Japan; in order to avoid the cumbersome translation, this term will be preserved in the discussion that follows. There are several terms besides *chōkō*, e.g., *raikō*, "to come to pay tribute," which are largely interchangeable, and all will be rendered "tribute." *Ka'i*, *chōkō*, and *sakuhō* all have obvious normative and hierarchical implications which will be pursued in some detail below.

emperor, the Son of Heaven. It was his responsibility as possessor of the Mandate of Heaven to maintain order in the world by proper performance of ritual in his role as mediator between Heaven and Man. Non-Chinese monarchs were welcome to bring their states into participation in this "world order" by proclaiming themselves "subjects" of the Chinese emperor, in a document known as *piao*, by accepting the Chinese calendar, symbolic of acceptance of the emperor's mediation in the cosmos, and by receiving in return "investiture" or confirmation as monarchs of their countries.

For some of the monarchs of East Asia, participation in this exchange of symbols was an important element in the legitimation of dynasties and of monarchs. For Korea in the early Yi dynasty, for example, which accepted the ideology of Confucianism, "In the Chinese world order, only the Son of Heaven received the Mandate directly from Heaven. . . . The Yi throne [was] . . . [u]nable to receive its Mandate directly from Heaven, [and so] it turned to the Son of Heaven as a mediator. . . . Thus, the role of Ming investiture in the functional structure of the Yi state was to definitively affirm the legitimacy of the occupant of the throne."[8]

Other states on the periphery of China varied in their response to China's conceit of centrality in the cosmos for the emperor and centrality for China in the ordering of states.

---

[8] JaHyun Kim Haboush, "A Heritage of Kings: One Man's Monarchy in the Confucian World" (unpublished Ph.D. dissertation, Columbia University, 1978), p. 1. M. Frederick Nelson, *Korea and the Old Orders in East Asia* (Louisiana State University Press, 1945), especially pp. 11-20, is still a useful summary of the theory behind this. For a more thorough discussion, see Hugh Dyson Walker, "The Yi-Ming *Rapprochement*," especially Part I, "Traditional Sino-Korean Theories of Foreign Relations, 1392-1592" (unpublished Ph.D. dissertation, University of California, Los Angeles, 1971), pp. 6-86. Hae-jong Chun's "Sino-Korean Tributary Relations in the Ch'ing Period," in Fairbank, ed., *The Chinese World Order*, pp. 90-111, does not deal with the connection between Sino-Korean diplomacy and the legitimacy of the Yi kings, but Ta-tuan Chen, "Investiture of Liu-ch'iu Kings in the Ch'ing Period," in Fairbank, pp. 135-164, esp. pp. 135-149, deals with the actual mechanics and protocols of royal investiture.

Korea was perhaps the most enthusiastic participant in this "Chinese world order," while Japan was certainly among the most reluctant. Some states were able, like Siam, cynically to participate in the forms of submission to a Sinocentric conception of the world merely to partake of the benefits of trade and cultural relations.[9] Japan, on the other hand, had been historically reluctant to enter into such relations with China, for her own self-perception, in large measure bound up with the mythology of imperial divinity, made the acknowledgment of any supervening authority extremely difficult. Indeed, one of the earliest documents of Sino-Japanese diplomacy asserts the parity of the Japanese throne with the Chinese, and is addressed "from the Son of Heaven in the Land where the sun rises to the Son of Heaven in the land where the sun sets. The [Chinese] Emperor, it is recorded, looked at this, and was not pleased."[10] Only briefly, in the Muromachi period, did Japanese rulers acknowledge Chinese suzerainty in order to grasp the benefits of trade, and this initially by a shogun seeking to liberate himself from the need for Japanese imperial sanction.

Japan's participation in the "Chinese world order" of Ming came to an end in the mid-sixteenth century, when the last embassy went to Peking, and shortly thereafter the last trading tallies were lost in a fire. In any case, a relationship to China was a source of controversy, in both its own and in later ages. While Tokugawa Ieyasu contemplated, even sought, the reestablishment of such a relationship in the early seventeenth century, the benefits of autonomous modes of legitimation and alternative avenues of trade were rapidly becoming apparent. Hayashi Razan, for example, in his earliest letters to China for the bakufu, persisted in proposing that, "to restore the old relations between the two countries will surely bind together the joyous hearts of the two Heavens."[11] Razan was proposing a cosmos with two foci, one

[9] Mark Mancall, "The Ch'ing Tribute System: An Interpretive Essay," in Fairbank, pp. 68-70.

[10] *Sui-shu, chuan* 81, "Wo-kuo lieh-chuan," quoted in *Koji ruien*, 26:835.

[11] *Hayashi Razan bunshū*, p. 132; *TKIR*, 5:343; *GBTS*, p. 55.

Chinese and one Japanese, a conception unlikely to win Ming acquiescence. And, in the event, Japan did not join the "Chinese world order," but indeed withdrew from it instead. In its place Japan attempted to establish an alternative order of Japanese fantasy, a looking glass which might reflect the reemergent centrality of a newly reunified Japan.

Thus the bakufu sought a set of protocols and norms for the conduct of foreign relations which would be acceptable to a sufficient number of foreign states to sustain the levels of trade and cultural contact deemed essential, and which might constitute a symbolic mirror of the structure of an ideal "world order" of Japanese fantasy. In this manner Japan in the early Tokugawa period was able to reassert the conceit of Japanese centrality, clothed in the rhetoric of a "naturalized" Neo-Confucian ideology[12] and visibly represented by the protocol of the bakufu's external relations. In order to suggest the outlines of the structure of this "Japanese world order," it will be helpful, therefore, to examine certain aspects of the positive diplomacy conducted by the Tokugawa bakufu in its relations with Korea and the kingdom of Ryukyu, with Holland and China, while making reference to developments in the realm of Tokugawa thought. This will be done principally through an examination of the diplomatic documents exchanged by Japan with the monarchs and governments of Korea and Okinawa during the reign of the fifth Tokugawa shogun, Tsunayoshi (r. 1680-1709), by which time the forms to be observed had been largely settled,[13] and of the protocol developed for the reception of foreign embassies at the shogunal court.

[12] For the idea of Neoconfucianism as a naturalized ideology, see Kate Wildman Nakai's stimulating article, "The Naturalization of Confucianism in Tokugawa Japan: The Problem of Sinocentrism," in *Harvard Journal of Asiatic Studies*, 40:1 (June 1980): 157-199.

[13] Although Arai Hakuseki attempted a complete restructuring of protocol in the 1710s, his reforms were almost completely overturned in Yoshimune's restoration of tradition norms. On Hakuseki's reforms and the Korean response see my "Korean-Japanese Diplomacy in 1711," and Kate Wildman Nakai's forthcoming *Arai Hakuseki and Confucian Governance in Tokugawa Japan*, ch. 5, "Arai Hakuseki and the Meaning of Ritual."

By the time of Tsunayoshi, congratulatory embassies from Korea and Ryukyu had become integral elements in the succession rituals for new shoguns. In 1682 Tsunayoshi received both a Korean and a Ryukyuan congratulatory embassy (*gakei shisetsu*). Study of the protocol governing the reception of these two embassies at Edo, and of the language of the diplomatic documents exchanged on each occasion, illuminates the outlines of Japanese perception of the situation. It will also be useful in this regard to refer to the detailed account of the reception of the Dutch commercial agent in Nagasaki by Engelbert Kaempfer for the years 1691 and 1692, and to compare the relationship to the Chinese community of Nagasaki. The choice of years is governed in part by the fact that these embassies coincided with the final Ch'ing conquest of all of China (1683), but primarily by the fact that they are well-documented examples of the mature diplomacy and protocol of the Tokugawa period, representative of the bakufu's *preferred* forms and ceremonies from the reign of Iemitsu through the eighteenth century.[14] The diplomatic receptions of Tsunayoshi's reign, that is, represent the ideal protocol of most of the Tokugawa period, and as such constitute a good "text" for these purposes.

The congratulatory embassies of 1682 sent to compliment Tsunayoshi on his succession as the fifth Tokugawa shogun are typical examples of this phenomenon. In that year Tsunayoshi received two congratulatory missions: Yun Chiwan led an embassy of over 400 members from King Sukchong of Korea (r. 1674-1720), the first of three embassies that that king would send to Edo; King Shō Tei (r. 1669-1709) sent Ambassador Prince Nago from Okinawa with an entourage of nearly 100. Eleven years earlier he had sent an embassy to thank Ietsuna for investing him as King of Ryukyu.[15] The two embassies arrived in Edo, and were received by Tsunayoshi in succession.

[14] See *supra*, n. 13.
[15] See *TKIR*, vol. 1, pp. 59-68, for documentation on the 1671 embassy from Shō Tei to Ietsuna.

For its part, the bakufu, which was to receive these embassies as part of the ceremonial marking the transition of authority from the late Ietsuna to Tsunayoshi, did not wait idly by. The bakufu and its functionaries maintained the pretense that, as Hayashi Gahō put the case in regard to Korean embassies, they "spontaneously" sent embassies and tribute offerings,[16] but in fact preparations for the embassies from Ryukyu and Korea began in Edo long before their anticipated arrivals. Before the kings of Ryukyu, Korea, or any other neighboring state could "spontaneously" decide to send an embassy to congratulate the new shogun, they would have to be informed of the death of Ietsuna, which came on 4 June 1680, and the succession of his brother Tsunayoshi. Thus, shortly thereafter the bakufu had Sō Yoshizane set in motion the chain of events which would bring the Korean embassy to fruition, by writing to the Third Minister of the Board of Rites in Seoul:

> Our country is saddened, for our revered Great Prince has suddenly passed away, and the ministers and common people cannot contain their grief. Yet it was the August Command [of his late Majesty] first to establish his beloved younger brother, the Prince of Tatebayashi, to be the Heir, and therefore the State is at peace and undisturbed. But thinking of You from afar, we have dispatched [two envoys] to bring you the news.[17]

[16] *Gahō sensei Hayashi gakushi bunshū*, 90:3b. "Chōsen raiō gaishū jo." Similarly, the Confucian adviser to the daimyo of Tsushima, Amenomori Hōshū (1668-1755), noted that in 1663 the Korean government sent a mission to Tsushima, which "stated orally that two years later they wished to send an embassy to offer incense in commemoration of the fiftieth anniversary of the death of Tokugawa Ieyasu." Amenomori Hōshū, *Tenryūin-kō jitsuroku* (MS, Sō Archives, Banshōin, Tsushima).

[17] *HCO*, vol. 30, Sō Yoshizane to Third Minister of the Board of Rites, Enpō 8/7/x. Sō Yoshizane to Second Minister of the Board of Rites, Enpō 8/7/x, in *ibid.*, has substantially the same text. It is worth noting that both letters speak of Ietsuna in terms connoting the implicit assertion that he was the Son of Heaven. One letter says that he died, *anka* (Morohashi, no. 13914.13) the other, *shōka* (Morohashi, no. 2702.12[2]), both terms defined

Two months later Chŏng Yun, Second Minister of the Board of Rites, responded with expressions of condolence, while Yoshizane sent Chŏng notification of Tsunayoshi's "enthronement," which had taken place on 15 September.[18] The following year, after acknowledging Korea's condolences in the second month, in late summer Yoshizane wrote to the Board of Rites to begin the negotiations leading up to the actual embassy. First, on behalf of the bakufu, he summoned the embassy, as "precedent" dictated:

> Our revered Great Prince has succeeded to the State, reflecting the glorious deeds of the Ancestors. In accordance with precedent, send a full embassy to congratulate him and to renew amicable relations. Arrival in [Edo] should be at the juncture of the seventh and eight months of next year. The voyage is long, but let there be no error about the date. The current Great Prince already has a Royal Heir, so you should perform ceremonies to congratulate him as well.[19]

The next month Yoshizane wrote to ask Korea to send a mission to Tsushima to discuss the protocol for the forthcoming embassy.[20] By midwinter the protocol mission was able to return to Korea with a letter from Yoshizane confirming that the forthcoming embassy would be governed

---

as "referring to the death of the Son of Heaven" (*Daikanwa jiten*, 5:868; 2:533).

[18] Chŏng Yun to Sō Yoshizane, *kŏngsin*/9/x, and Sō Yoshizane to Second Minister of the Board of Rites, Enpō 8/9/x, in *HCO*, vol. 30. In this second notice, too, Yoshizane continued the conceit that the Shogun was the Son of Heaven: "Our esteemed new Great Prince has succeeded to the Treasured Position" (*hō'i*, Morohashi, 3:1114, no. 7376.6: "The position of the Son of Heaven") and conducted the ceremonies of succession to the office of the Son of Heaven" (*roku o tori*, Morohashi, 8:874, no. 26736.2: "to assume the post of the Son of Heaven").

[19] Sō Yoshizane to Second Minister, Board of Rites, Enpō 9/6/x, in *HCO*, vol. 31. Similar texts to Third Minister, to governor of Pusan, and to magistrate of Tongnae.

[20] Sō Yoshizane to Third Minister, Board of Rites, Enpō 9/7/x; to governor of Pusan and magistrate of Tongnae, Enpō 9/7/x, in *HCO*, vol. 31.

essentially by the protocols of the most recent embassy, that of 1655.[21]

The bakufu similarly communicated the salient information to the king of Ryukyu through the mediation of the daimyo of Satsuma, Shimazu Tsunataka, although the language of Tsunataka's communications to Shō Tei was of course less florid and less respectful of Ryukyu. Given the degree of administrative control that Satsuma exercised over Ryukyuan affairs, this is not surprising. By mid-November 1681, Shō Tei had sent a condolence mission to Kagoshima which, Shimazu Mitsuhisa reported to the roju, was conducted according to the precedents of the Shō'o period (1652), on the death of Iemitsu.[22] Two weeks earlier, Mitsuhisa's grandson and heir had acknowledged the king's intention of sending Prince Nago to congratulate the shogun on his succession.[23]

Meanwhile, just as Sō Yoshizane and the Korean Board of Rites were settling the protocol for the Korean mission, in mid-November 1681, ten months prior to the embassy's scheduled arrival in Edo, the roju appointed three of the most important shogunal officials to temporary superintendency of preparations for the embassy's reception: Mizuno Tadaharu, Commissioner of Shrines and Temples; Hikozaka Shigetsugu, the Chief Censor; and Ōoka Kiyoshige, the Commissioner of Accounts.[24] The following spring, Ōkubo Tadatomo, the senior member of the roju, was named Special Commissioner for Korean Affairs (*Chōsen goyō gakari*).[25]

Before we examine in detail the protocol for these two

[21] Sō Yoshizane to Third Minister, Board of Rites, Tenna 1/11/x, in *HCO*, vol. 31.

[22] *Shimazu kokushi* (MS copy, preface and 25 *satsu*, 1800, collection Historiographical Institute), 27:49b, entry for Tenna 1/10/18.

[23] [Shimazu] Tsunataka to Shō Tei, Tenna 1/10/4, in *Kagoshima ken shiryō Kyūki zatsuroku tsuiki*, 1:707, doc. 1816.

[24] *TKIR*, 2:417; *Tokugawa jikki*, 5:427; *Hiyōruku*, Tenna 1/9/28, in *Hiyōroku, Kōtoku ben, Han hiroku*, ed. Kitajima Masamoto et al. (Kondō Shuppan, 1971), p. 77.

[25] *Tokugawa jikki*, 5:437.

ambassadorial receptions before the shogun in Chiyoda Castle, it will be useful to compare the state letters that the bakufu exchanged with Korea, and those exchanged with Ryukyu. These letters, as Arai Hakuseki later noted,[26] were the most important standard of diplomatic relations between the states involved. Therefore, the examination of these documents exchanged between Japan and Korea, Japan and Ryukyu is critical to an evaluation of Japan's conception of the relations among these states.

Perhaps most significant in the letters exchanged between Tsunayoshi and King Sukchong[27]—and this was true of all exchanges between Seoul and Edo—is the fact that the two monarchs treat each other as peers, as is evident from their choice of language.

Whereas it was common for the true given names of East Asian monarchs to be surrounded with an aura of taboo—this was particularly true of China and Korea, more than of Japan—both monarchs open and sign their letters with their true given names. While the shogun's given name was relatively commonly used, for the Korean king, the only other time that he used his true given name—as opposed to a circumlocution—was in correspondence with the Chinese emperor.

Each addresses the other as "Your Highness" (j. *denka*, k. *chŏnha*), thus placing each other on exactly the same hierarchical plane, and expressing equal status and mutual respect. This title is immediately below that of "Your Majesty," which was used by Korea only to refer to the Chinese emperor, and by Japan only to refer to the Japanese emperor.

Sukchong's letter opens, "Yi Sun, King of Korea, *offers up a letter* (*pongsŏ*) to His Highness, the Great Prince of Japan," while in response, "Minamoto Tsunayoshi, Great Prince of Japan, *respectfully replies* (*keifuku*) to His Highness the King

[26] Arai Hakuseki, "Chōsen shinshi o gi su," in *Arai Hakuseki zenshū*, 4:675.
[27] Yi Sun, King of Korea, to His Highness, the Great Prince of Japan, *imsul*/5/X, in *TKIR*, 3:112; Minamoto Tsunayoshi of Japan to His Highness, the King of Korea, Tenna 2/9/x, in *ibid.*, 3:115.

of Korea." While the characters "pong" and "kei" are different, and therefore difficult to place on the same hierarchical continuum, nine shogunal responses both before and after this one employed the same character as the one chosen by Sukchong, "pong" (j. "hō"). The *Daikanwa jiten* also suggests that it is appropriate to consider these as peer terms.

The text of Sukchong's letter itself is an exceedingly ornate piece of Chinese, brocaded with complimentary phrases intended to express respect for the Japanese shogun, but it does not follow that it is in the least bit self-deprecating. In fact, the body of the text is essentially a boiler-plate of stock phrases, differing but little from the six royal letters of state which had preceded it, or from the five that would follow.[28] In this regard, the situation reflects the precedents and closely parallels the correspondence between the early Yi dynasty kings and the Ashikaga shoguns. At every level, correspondence between Japan and Korea was at a peer-to-peer level, so that shogun and king, roju and ministers of state, daimyo of Tsushima and third minister of the Board of Rites, etc., corresponded with each other, each with a putative peer.[29] It is also important to recall that after 1644—that is, after the fall of the Ming dynasty—Korean kings and ministers no longer used the Chinese calendar in their correspondence with Japan. This signified the removal of China's presence from any function of public significance in the Japanese-Korean relationship and, indeed, from Japanese foreign relations entirely.[30]

[28] The state letters are contained in *TKIR*, vol. 3, *passim*. The earliest letters, however, of 1607, 1617, and 1624, in particular, since they dealt also with the problems of normalization and prisoner repatriation, differ in substance from the later letters. Sukchong's letter of 1711 to congratulate the sixth shogun, Ienobu (r. 1709-1712), is a special case, on which, see my "Korean-Japanese Diplomacy in 1711."

[29] This insistence on peer-to-peer correspondence is apparent throughout the one hundred twenty volumes of diplomatic correspondence preserved by the bakufu-appointed monks of the Iteian hermitage in *Honpō Chōsen ōfuku sho*.

[30] On the significance of this point see *supra*, Chapter III, pp. 90-97.

Thus, the style, content, and terminology of the official letters exchanged between Edo and Seoul clearly suggest that the king and the shogun regarded each other as peers, sharing the same level of precedence in protocol. The replication of peer-to-peer correspondence at all levels of Japanese-Korean relations reinforced this image of parity between states. This peer status had been expressed in the Chinese classics since the *Shih-chi* and the *Han-shu* by the term *kang-li* (j. *kō-rei*; k. *hangnye*), meaning "to have a peer relationship."[31] Although I have not seen this term explicitly used in contemporary Japanese discussions, it was the term that Korean policymakers used to characterize the relationship between the Yi state and Tokugawa Japan.[32] And indeed this image of the relationship between Japan and Korea as of one between peers was replicated at all levels of state. Whether it was the shogun, the senior council, or the daimyo of Tsushima, each corresponded only with an opposite number who was at least putatively a status peer, and each used language of respect for the other and deprecation for himself that mirrored the usage of the opposite number. From top to bottom, the isomorphism was preserved, reinforcing the image of parity between the two states.

Correspondence on the occasion of the Ryukyuan mission earlier that same year contrasts sharply with that exchanged with Korea. First, and most starkly different, was the fact that the king, Shō Tei, did not qualify to send a letter directly to the shogun. Rather, he addressed the senior council, the shogun's ministers of state, and, humbly "offering up" (*hōtei*; *teijō*), the letter expressed his delight that "your revered Great Prince" (*kitaikun*) had succeeded to office.[33] That is, whether because, by contrast with Korea, Ryukyu was a vassal state of Japan, or simply because the king was deemed

---

[31] Morohashi, *Daikanwa jiten*, 5:142, no. 11889.12.

[32] For example, *Sŭngjŏngwŏn ilgi*, 25:11-12.

[33] Shō Tei to Inaba Mino no kami, Enpō 9/5/16; Shō Tei to Ōkubo Kaga no kami, Doi Noto no kami, Hotta Bitchū no kami and Itakura Naizen no shō, Enpō 9/5/16, in *TKIR*, 1:72-73.

to be of insufficient status to correspond directly with the shogun, Shō Tei was required to imply in his letter to the shogun's ministers that he was presenting tribute to the shogun. He did this by employing the verb *shinjō* ("to offer up"), a term with clear tributary connotations.

In the world of pre-modern East Asia—especially among those peoples who regarded the classical Chinese literature as one of the canons of their norms—the adoption of one state's calendar by another was a mode of public acknowledgment by the adopting country of its status as subordinate to the calendar-giver. Indeed, in the more highly systematized, and hence more readily readable, system of foreign relations which the Ch'ing empire constructed for itself, one of the required obeisances of the vassal state was an annual embassy to Peking to "receive the calendar," and the Chinese term for this, *feng-shuo*, could also be translated, "receiving the commands of the son of heaven."[34]

Ryukyuan usage of the Japanese era name, therefore, in Ryukyuan King Shō Tei's letters to the shogunal ministers was a clear acknowledgment of Ryukyu's status as subordinate to Japan. This was fitting for a monarch whose country had been conquered by Japan in 1609, and remained under Satsuma's domination until the end of the Tokugawa period. As if to reemphasize this hierarchical relationship of Japan and Ryukyu, Shō Tei, in his letter to the roju felicitating the shogunal heir-apparent, the ill-fated Tokumatsu (1679-1683), referred to Japan as the country of "Civilization" (j. *ka*, lit. "flowery") and to his own realm as an "isolated barbarian dependent state" (*ei'i no zokkoku*), or "my small province." In closing, the "barbarian" monarch expressed his great respect for the bakufu, the shogun, and the roju by allowing that, "I prostrate myself to beg that Your Reverences the Great Elders will direct [my message] to the August Hearing. . . "[35]

[34] John K. Fairbank, "A Preliminary Framework," in Fairbank, ed., *The Chinese World Order*, p. 10.

[35] *TKIR*, 1:73.

The contrast between the tone of these letters and that of the replies sent by the shogunal councillors is stark. They are anything but self-deprecatory; in fact, they border on the arrogant and overbearing. Hotta Masatoshi, the *tairō*,[36] spoke of "the August Visage [showing] pleasure," and in a phrase that, taken at face value, suggests that Masatoshi regarded the shogun to be the Son of Heaven, reminded the Ryukyuan king that, ". . . the *benefices* you have been granted are as per the appended catalog."[37]

In contrast to the correspondence between Seoul and Edo, Korean king and Japanese shogun, then, in which all parties strove to maintain the appearance of peer status through protocol—and all the diplomatic traffic between Korea and Japan from the 1630s on was conducted on this assumption of parity—the Ryukyuan king was required repeatedly to indicate in word and deed his subordination to the shogun. If his recognition of Japanese superordination was apparent in the letters that Shō Tei sent to congratulate Tsunayoshi on his succession to the shogunal office, this was merely a restatement of a relationship that was also expressed at the accession of each new Ryukyuan king. For each new king, while he expressed his fealty to China, and received investiture from the Chinese emperor,[38] also owed his installation in office to Japanese benefice, from both the shogun and the daimyo of Satsuma.[39] In recognition of this, each newly installed king was required to send to Edo an embassy of gratitude, as Shō Tei had done in 1671. In his letters that year to the tairo, then Sakai Tadakiyo, and to the four other members of the

---

[36] "Great Elder," an extraordinary office, senior to the roju, appointed in exceptional circumstances, or as an honor to an especially favored member of the roju. During the 260 years of the Tokugawa period there were thirteen appointments (compare 175 appointments as roju). On the special significance of Hotta Masatoshi's years as tairo, see Conrad Totman, *Politics in the Tokugawa Bakufu*, pp. 211-214.

[37] *Onrai*, "A Gift from the Son of Heaven," Morohashi, *Daikanwa jiten*, 4:1038, no. 10591.152.

[38] See Ta-tuan Chen, "Investiture."

[39] *Kagoshima kenshi*, 2:668.

roju, Shō Tei gratefully acknowledged that, "Last year the Governor of Satsuma Province, Mitsuhisa, on receipt of the August [shogunal] order, permitted me to succeed to the rank of King of the Country of Ryukyu . . ." in recognition of which he was sending Prince Kin, in the company of Mitsuhisa, as his ambassador, along with "some local products of my rustic country, which I offer you" as tribute.[40]

The bakufu did not exchange diplomatic correspondence with either China or Holland after the first decades of the seventeenth century. While there seems to have been no statutory prohibition on this, it did become the perceived "regular practice" which would be codified in the last decade of the 1700s by Matsudaira Sadanobu. Thus, for example, when King Willem II of Holland attempted to send the shogun a letter advising him on the international situation in the mid-1840s, the bakufu after much debate rejected the letter as without precedent and declined to reply.[41]

The language of diplomatic correspondence is but one mirror of a perceived "reality," one of those "symbolic systems [which] in essence *create* objects for the senses . by creating distinctions between them."[42] Protocol, too, may serve as a symbolic language expressing the perceived or agreed-upon relationships among the parties to any exchange, as well as being a set of rules to enable the parties to engage in the substance of their exchange in the first place.[43]

---

[40] *TKIR*, 1:63; *Shimazu kokushi*, 27:20-23.

[41] This affair is documented extensively in *Tsūkō ichiran zokushū*, 5 vols. (Osaka: Seibundō Shuppan, 1973), 2:401-530. The correspondence between Abe Masahiro, roju, and Tokugawa Nariaki, daimyo of Mito, on the proper disposition of this affair is preserved in "Shin Ise monogatari."

[42] Janet L. Dolgin, David S. Kemnitzer, and David M. Schneider, eds., *Symbolic Anthropology: A Reader in the Study of Symbols and Meanings* (Columbia University Press, 1977), "Introduction: 'As People Express Their Lives, So They Are . . . ,' " p. 15.

[43] William Roosen, "Early Modern Diplomatic Ceremonial: A Systems Approach," in *Journal of Modern History*, 52:3 (September 1980): 452-476, offers a stimulating argument on the functional value of diplomatic protocol.

In all its aspects, the protocol for the reception of the Korean and Ryukyuan ambassadors at the shogunal castle of Edo was differentiated to reflect the sharp status distinctions between Korea and Ryukyu, on the one hand, and therefore also to help to fix the status of the shogunal state in the world at large. The same might also be said for the treatment of Dutch visitors to the shogunal court—who as mere commercial agents were not regarded to have diplomatic status, and were treated with correspondingly low regard—and to the Chinese, who were not permitted even to come to Edo to pay their respects. In this regard, it will be helpful to examine the treatment of the Korean and Ryukyuan embassies of 1682 when they were received in the castle, and also to compare these with the reception of the Dutch, as noted by Englebert Kaempfer, who was in two Dutch parties from Nagasaki that called on Tsunayoshi about a decade later, in 1691 and 1692.

When Tsunayoshi received Ambassador Yun Chiwan, and his two vice-ambassadors, the so-called "Three Ambassadors" (j. *sanshi*, k. *samsa*) in audience on 29 August 1682, the audience was not limited to the three ambassadors alone, but included several aides and pages, over ten men all told, who were received with great ceremony in the Great Hall (*Ōhiroma*) of Edo Castle.[44] When Tsunayoshi granted audience to Prince Nago three months earlier, on 18 May, only the prince had the honor of an audience.[45]

The bakufu ordered the daimyos to be present to witness both audiences, as it would do for any major state occasion, but the status distinction between who was ordered to participate in the former and the latter events provides an indication of the relative status of each in the world according to Tokugawa eyes. When Tsunayoshi received Korean Ambassador Yun and his entourage in August, the shogun ordered the tairo, the members of the roju, and "all daimyos pos-

---

[44] *Tenna jinjutsu shinshi kiroku*, MS, 68 vols. (Sō Collection, Keio University Library), vol. 63.

[45] *TKIR*, 1:70.

sessed of entire provinces, of the fourth court rank or above"[46] to pay court in the Great Hall, thus making of the audience an exclusive affair for the elite of daimyo society. Such an audience would include only about two dozen of the most exalted tozama and collateral daimyo—fewer than a tenth of all the daimyo, assuming that they were all in Edo at the time, but the most important of them—and the four fudai who comprised the roju and tairo.[47]

Prince Nago must have felt humbled, by contrast, when he entered the Great Hall in May, for although the status of the daimyo in attendance was lower, their numbers were far greater. The fourth court rank was still the cutoff point, but this time it was the "fudai and daimyo *below* the fourth rank" who were obliged to attend.[48]

In both ambassadorial audiences the central ceremony was the ambassadors' presentation of greetings from their respective kings, and on their own behalf, and the presentation of gifts to the shogun. When Ambassador Yun appeared at Edo in August, the Three Ambassadors were called as a group, and, advancing "as far as the second mat below the Middle Stage," they made four-and-one-half obeisances as greeting from their king, then withdrew to a point of less proximity to the shogunal dais, and made four-and-one-half obeisances as their own greeting.[49] The Ryukyuan ambassador, Prince Nago, the preceding May, had likewise been received in the Great Hall, but when he presented greetings "from the Chū-

[46] *TKIR*, 2:484.

[47] Estimate of the number of daimyo involved based on the table of daimyo in 1853, as given in Toshio G. Tsukahira, *Feudal Control in Tokugawa Japan: The Sankin Kōtai System* (East Asian Research Center, Harvard University, 1966), pp. 139-173.

[48] Hitomi Chikudō, *Jinjutsu Ryūkyū haichō ki*, in *Shiryō kōhon*, 203.4, under the date of Tenna 2/4/11. Cf. *Chikudō zenshū*, 3 vols., MS copy (collection Historiographical Institute, Tokyo), vol. 3, entry for Tenna 2/4/11.

[49] *Tenna jinjutsu shinshi kiroku*, vol. 63. Compare the seating diagram for this audience, "Tenna jinjutsu hachigatsu nijūshichinichi Chōsenjin tojō no setsu," MS, 1682, in the collection of the Tokyo Institute of Korean Studies (Kankoku Kenkyūin), reproduced here as Plate 6.

zan King of Ryukyu . . . he made nine obeisances on the fourth mat below the Lower Stage withdrew,'' and then "presented obeisances on his own behalf from the Verandah.''[50]

Whenever persons of radically different status addressed the shogun, it was the custom to have status-qualified intermediaries transmit their words to him, for they would be too base directly to enter the "August Hearing.'' In the case of the Korean ambassadors' greetings on behalf of their king, and on their own behalf, this awesome task was entrusted to one of the *kōke* ("high families"), houses not of daimyo rank but of especially exalted lineage, entrusted with particularly important shogunal ceremonials, thus marking the Korean greetings as especially important. When the Ryukyuan ambassador-prince presented the king's greeting, this mediation was performed by the *sōshaban*, a shogunal master of ceremonies of greater wealth but less important ceremonial status than the *kōke*.[51]

The status distinctions evident in these receptions are sharp, and yet in the eyes of some even these did not accurately reflect the relative inferiority of Ryukyu in the hierarchy. Ogyū Sorai describes receptions for the two Ryukyuan ambassadors in 1711 (one to thank Ienobu for investing Shō Eki as king, one to congratulate Ienobu on his succession as sho-

---

[50] Hitomi Chikudō, *Jinjutsu Ryūkyū haichō ki*, in *Shiryō kōhon*, 203:4; cf. *TKIR*, 1:72. However, Chikudō's own collected works, *Hitomi Chikudō zenshū*, vol. 3, disagrees, and records Prince Nago as having made "six obeisances at the fourth mat of the Lower Stage.'' Chikudō was a prominent Confucian scholar in the employ of the bakufu, second in status only to the Hayashi family. He was in regular correspondence with Tsunayoshi's cousin Tokugawa Mitsukuni, daimyo of the collateral domain of Mito, and himself a devoted Neoconfucianist. Chikudō's family temple, Unryūji, in Tomita, Tochigi Prefecture, preserves several MS signature letters from Mitsukuni to Chikudō.

[51] The *kōke* functioned as shogunal ritualists in relations with the imperial court, the Grand Shrines at Ise, and the shogunal shrines at Nikko. See Sasama Yoshihiko, *Edo bakufu yakushoku shūsei*, p. 165. The most famous *kōke* was certainly Kira Yoshinaka (1641-1702), the "villain'' of the great vendetta of the Akō warriors in 1702.

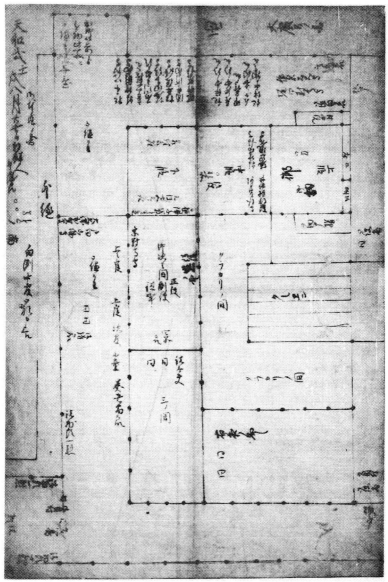

6. Seating diagram for the shogunal reception of the 1682 Korean embassy at Edo Castle

gun) virtually identical to the 1682 reception described by
Hitomi Chikudō. Sorai notes that the Ryukyuan king's subordination to Satsuma meant that the Okinawan envoys were
really only peers of the Satsuma clan elders: "It is only because of His Majesty's desire to bring tranquillity to foreign
peoples that he grants them special treatment,"[52] in the form
of direct shogunal audiences.

The ceremonial distinctions outlined above, delineating a
hierarchical ordering of Japan, Korea, and Ryukyu, were
replicated in virtually all the other aspects of their respective
receptions at Edo. For example, the Korean ambassador and
his retinue were regularly lodged at the Honseiji temple in
the Bakurōchō section of Edo, kept there at shogunal expense. The Ryukyuan missions, by contrast, were lodged in
an Edo residence of the daimyo of Satsuma. Sixty-five members of the Korean ambassador's entourage were entertained
with a fifteen-course banquet occupying five large halls in
Edo Castle. Tsunayoshi did not dine with the ambassadors
himself; rather, his cousins, Tokugawa Mitsusada of Kii,
Tokugawa Tsunatoyo of Kōfu (who would succeed Tsunayoshi in 1709), and Tokugawa Mitsukuni of Mito, were dinner companions of the ambassador, vice-ambassador, and third
ambassador, respectively. Each was presumed to be of the
same rank as his dinner companion, and so they sat facing
each other, the Koreans on the east side, the Japanese on the
west, in the Great Hall. The ambassadors were led in by
tairo, roju, and chamberlains, and served by the sons of several daimyos of rank.[53] In this banquet, and in the simulta-
neous banquets in the Hall of Pines, the Tiger Hall, the Wil-
low Hall, and the Maple Leaf Hall, the service was performed
with punctilio, and, throughout, "distinctions of ranks were
observed in the service."[54] For the ambassador from the
Ryukyuan king, there had been no such banquet. Nor, when

[52] Ogyū Sorai, *Ryūkyū heishi ki*, MS copy (collection Nanki Bunko, Tokyo University Library).
[53] *TKIR*, 2:486-496.
[54] *TKIR*, 2:486.

Prince Nago departed for home, was he bid farewell at his lodgings by members of the roju, on behalf of the shogun, as were Yun Chiwan and his retinue.

What has been outlined here looks like a two-tiered system of foreign relations, in which the bakufu recognized a peer in Korea, while recognizing Ryukyu as an inferior vassal state. That is, both countries sent ambassadors to Edo, both exchanged letters of greeting with the bakufu, and both consummated state-to-state relations with ambassadorial audiences with the shogun. In all of these matters, hierarchical distinctions were maintained in protocol and in terminology which mirrored the hierarchy immanent in the world as ordered by the Confucian values which informed Tokugawa ideology, and by the historical self-image that Japan sought to maintain.[55]

But below this two-tiered hierarchy was a further hierarchy of opposite numbers in external relations, principally comprising Holland and China. Both countries were permitted to participate in trade at Nagasaki as private entities—the Netherlands East India Company, on the one hand, individual Chinese traders, on the other—but were not recognized as foreign states. For this reason, they did not engage in state-to-state correspondence with the bakufu; their rulers did not exchange letters or official greetings with the shogun.

Of these, only the representatives of the Dutch East India Company were permitted even to come to Edo and to present greetings to the shogun, something required of the opperhoofd, generally on an annual basis in the seventeenth century.[56] Bakufu documents speak of the Dutch party, usually the "Oranda Kapitan" (opperhoofd), the physician of the Dutch factory, and two others, along with interpreters,

[55] Uete Michiari, *Nihon kindai shisō no keisei*, pp. 235-245.

[56] For a brief outline history of the Dutch missions to Edo, see Itazawa Takeo, *Nihon to Oranda* (Shibundō, 1955), pp. 128-132. The most thorough and fascinating account of Dutch missions to Edo is Engelbert Kaempfer's participant account of journeys in 1691 and 1692, *The History of Japan*, 3:1-214.

as coming to Edo to present tribute to the shogun. The privilege of coming to Edo, and of being received in audience by the shogun, placed the Dutch on a level somewhat higher than that occupied by the Chinese merchants to Nagasaki, who were not permitted to the capital, much less granted audience. In this way, the protocol distinction between the Dutch and the Chinese mirrored the domestic status distinction so important in grading the hierarchy of samurai classes: those who had the right of audience with the shogun, or with their domain lords (*omemie*), were thereby acknowledged to have higher status than retainers who lacked the privilege.[57] As will be discussed in greater detail below, in 1715 Arai Hakuseki would attempt to underscore even more starkly the inferiority of the Chinese by imposing on their trading ships the requirement of using trading tallies imprinted with the Japanese era name.

The reception of the Dutch emissaries at Edo was even more simple, and certainly to European eyes more degrading, then the treatment accorded the Koreans or the Ryukyuans. Of critical importance, of course, is the fact that the Dutch were not perceived to represent a king or a country as such and that there was in consequence no exchange of diplomatic letters complimenting the shogun. Indeed, the shogun was recorded, not as "receiving the Hollanders in audience" (*inken*, or *nyūetsu*), as he did for the Korean and Ryukyuan embassies, but as "viewing" the Hollanders (*goran*, *joran*), much as he had "viewed" *entertainments* offered by the Korean equestrian troop or the Ryukyuan musicians.[58] But

---

[57] Uete, *Nihon kindai shisō no keisei*, pp. 235-245, discusses the presumption in Tokugawa Neoconfucian thought that there was a normative homology between the hierarchy within Japan, and the hierarchy ordering the external society of countries and peoples. We will return to this point below. On the significance of *omemie*, see Totman, *Politics in the Tokugawa Bakufu*, pp. 131-132; Fujino Tamotsu, *Shintei bakuhan taisei shi no kenkyū*, pp. 330-332.

[58] E.g., *Tokugawa jikki* 5:438, "After the Royal Viewing (*goran*), the Hollanders performed music of their country in the Shiroki no shoin," *ibid.*, p. 473. "There was a Royal Viewing of the Hollanders who had brought trib-

the protocol of the reception, too, reflected the lesser status of the Dutch. The protocols for the reception of the Oranda Kapitan for 5 April 1665, for example:

> His Majesty emerged (*shutsugyo*) into the Great Hall, and went to the Upper Stage. At this time the Oranda Kapitan offered his greeting, which was announced by Matsudaira Bizen no kami [the *gosōshaban*]. His Majesty withdrew (*nyūgyo*) immediately. Then the [Dutch] were guided along the sunken verandah of the Goshoin by Hōjō Awa no kami and Hoda Wakasa no kami [both commissioners for the control of Christianity] and an interpreter. [The Dutch] presented their obeisances from the verandah furthest from the Upper Stage, and withdrew by the same route. Their tribute articles were laid out prior to the Royal Appearance, arrayed on the sunken verandah, in the Royal Line of Sight.[59]

After this brief obeisance it was common for the Dutch to be placed on view for the shogun and his personal court: "7 April 1690. After the public obeisance of the Kapitan, there was a brief Royal Viewing (*jōran*) of the four Hollanders in the Sitting Room (*gozanoma*)."[60] The following year as well, on "29 March 1691 . . . the four Hollanders were summoned to the Sitting Room, and there was a Royal Viewing."[61]

One of those four "Hollanders" was Engelbert Kaempfer,

ute (*nyūkō*). Their tribute articles were (list). They also presented a performance of the musical arts of their country for the Royal Viewing." Compare *ibid.*, p. 457, "The Korean Ambassador was received in Audience" (*inken*), but p. 460, "On the fifth there was to be a Royal Viewing (*goran*) of Korean equestrian arts."

[59] *TKIR*, 6:213, from the *Ryūei hinamiki*. Note that the terms *shutsugyo* and *nyūgyo* are both associated with the movements of the Son of Heaven: *shutsugyo* (Morohashi, 2:177, no. 811.65), "the Son of Heaven's emergence from the inner palace to the public hall," and *nyūgyo* (Morohashi, 1:1038, no. 1415.38), "the Son of Heaven's withdrawal to the inner palace."

[60] *Ryūei hinamiki* for Genroku 3/2/28, in *TKIR*, 6:216.

[61] *Ryūei hinamiki* for Genroku 4/2/30, in *TKIR*, 6:216.

actually a German, and physician to the Dutch factory in Japan. He has left an account of the shogunal "viewing" of 1691 and 1692:

On . the day appointed for our audience, the presents design'd for his Imperial Majesty were sent to court, attended by the Deputies of Sino Cami [Kawaguchi Munetsune, Nagasaki *bugyō*], and of the Commissioners for inspecting foreign affairs, to be there laid in due order, on wooden tables, in the hall of hundred mats, as they call it, where the Emperor was to view them. . . . We were commanded to wait in this guard room, till we could be introduc'd to an audience, which we were told, should be done, assoon as the great Council of State was met in the Palace. We were civilly receiv'd by the two Captains of the Guard, who treated us with tea and tobacco. Soon after Sino Cami and the two Commissioners came to compliment us, along with some Gentlemen of the Emperor's court, who were strangers to us. Having waited about an hour, during which time most of the Imperial Counsellors of State, old and young, went into the palace, some walking on foot, others being carried in Norimons, we were conducted thro' two stately gates, over a large square place, to the palace, to which there is an ascent of a few steps leading from the second gate. The place between the second gate, and the front of the palace, is but a few paced broad, and was then excessively crowded with throngs of courtiers, and troops of guards. From thence we were conducted up two other stair-cases to the palace itself, the first into a spacious room, next to the entry on the right, being the place where all persons, that are to be admitted to an audience, either of the Emperor himself, or of the Counsellors of State, wait till they are call'd in. It is a large and lofty room, but when all the skreens are put on, pretty dark, receiving but a sparing light from the upper windows of an adjoining room, wherein is kept some furniture for the Imperial apartments. It is otherwise richly furnish'd, according to the country fashion, and its gilt posts, walls and skreens, are very pleasing to behold. Having waited here upwards of an hour, and the Emperor having in the mean while seated himself in the hall of audience, Sino Cami and the two Commissioners came in and conducted our Resident into the Emperor's presence, leaving us behind. Assoon as he came thither, they cry'd out aloud Hollanda Captain, which was the signal for him to draw near, and make his obeisances. Accordingly he crawl'd on his hands and knees, to a place shew'd to him, between the presents rang'd in due order on one side, and the place, where the Emperor sat, on the other and then kneeling, he bow'd his forehead quite down to the ground, and so crawl'd backwards like a crab, without uttering one single word. So mean and short a thing is the audience we have of this mighty Monarch.[62]

Some few days after the "audience" described by Kaempfer, which had been "[f]ormerly all we had to do at the Emperor's court," the Dutch party were required, as they had been for "about these twenty years last past," to be "conducted deeper into the palace, to give the Empress and the Ladies of her court, and the Princesses of the blood, the diversion of seeing us."[63] Then in the Sitting Room (goza-no-

[62] Kaempfer, *The History of Japan*, 3:85–88. Kaempfer's "Sino Cami" is Kawaguchi Munetsune (1630–1706), styled Settsu-no-kami, who was Nagasaki magistrate from 1680 to 1693, and was on rotation to Edo at the time of Kaempfer's visit. Settsu-no-kami, or "Governor of the Province of Settsu," was a courtesy title; Settsu, often abbreviated to Tsu, became "Si" in Kaempfer's unsystematic recasting. Kaempfer, *Geschichte und Beschreibung von Japan*, 2:281; I have relied on Kure Shūzō's annotated translation of Kaempfer, *Kenperu Edo sanpu kikō*, 2 vols. (*Ikoku sōsho* series, vols. 7, 8, Yūshōdō, 1928–1929, repr. 1966), 1:457, n. 7a for this identification. "Norimons," or norimono, literally "things to ride in," were the palanquins or sedan chairs in which persons of rank rode. The elaborateness of norimono one was permitted to ride, and whether one was allowed to ride it up to, or beyond, and then how far beyond, the castle gates, were carefully graded to rank and status.

[63] Kaempfer, *History*, p. 89.

ma), "There was a Royal Viewing (*jōran*) of the four Hollanders,"[64] at which the Europeans were required, "to walk, to stand still, to compliment each other, to dance, to jump, to play the drunkard, to speak broken Japanese, to read Dutch, to paint, to sing, to put our cloaks on and off.   " Kaempfer "joined to [his] dance a love song in High German. In this manner, and with innumberable such other apish tricks, we must suffer ourselves to contribute to the Emperor's and the Court's diversion."[65]

Now, it is true that the reception of both Korean and Ryukyuan embassies included entertainments, but in both these instances the ambassadorial retinues were staffed with performing artists, equestrianists in the Korean case, and musicians from the Ryukyus, rather than general members of the entourage being made sport of for the shogunal pleasure.[66] Unlike the Korean embassy, however, who were recompensed with Japanese entertainments, either performances of Nō plays or, in 1711, of *gagaku* (classical court music),[67] neither the Ryukyuans nor the Dutch were entertained with shogunally sponsored performances. Just as with the enter-

[64] *TKIR*, 6:216.

[65] Kaempfer, *History*, 3:93-94. The Dutch captain, however, was not forced to amuse the shogun thus: "The Ambassador, however, is free from these and the like commands, for as he represents the authority of his masters, some care is taken that nothing should be done to injure or prejudice the same. Besides that he shew's so much gravity in his countenance and whole behavior, as was sufficient to convince the Japanese, that he was not at all a fit person to have such ridiculous and comical commands laid upon him" (p. 94).

[66] *Kyokuba jōran no oboegaki* (MS, *Tenna ni jinjutsu no toshi shinshi kiroku*, vol. 42) on the Korean equestrian performance of 1682; also, *TKIR*, 3:55-58; *Tokugawa jikki*, 5:460-461. *TKIR*, kan 91, 92, at 6:51-82, contains documents on the Korean equestrian performances of 1635, 1643, 1655, 1682, 1711, 1719, 1748, and 1764. The Ryukyuan musical performance of Tenna 2/4/14 was recorded in the log of shogunal activities at the Castle, Nikki, kan 18, collection Naikaku Bunko, Box 257, no. 4, vol. 3, which also contains an MS seating chart for the concert, "Ryūkyū shisetsu sōgaku haiza no zu." Compare the notice for that day in *Tokugawa jikki*, 5:444.

[67] E.g., *TKIR*, 2:414.

taining spectacle of the four "Hollanders" in 1691, the Korean equestrians were presented for "Royal Viewing" (*jōran*) before a specially constructed viewing stand outside the castle walls.

Finally, the annual visit to Edo was the occasion on which the "Hollanda Captain" received from the bakufu any revision of the articles of obligation spelling out the duties of the Dutch to the shogunate, and the restrictions under which they were permitted to remain in Nagasaki and trade. As Kaempfer put it, "A few days after [the initial presentation of the Dutch before the shogun], some laws concerning our trade and behavior were read to him, which, in the name of the Dutch, he promis'd to keep. . ."[68] In the year of Kaempfer's first journey to Edo, this ceremony took place on 2 April, two days before the Dutch party departed to return to Nagasaki: "Soon . . . the Ambassador was call'd out himself, and was conducted to a great hall to the left [the Great Hall] where with the usual obeysances he took his audiences of leave, and had the commands of the Emperor read to him, consisting in five articles, relating among other things chiefly to the Portuguese trade."[69]

---

[68] Kaempfer, *History*, 3:89.

[69] *Ibid.*, p. 100. According to *Tokugawa jikki*, 6:202, "On the 4th [of the 3rd month] the Hollanders were granted leave, and were read the Articles of Stipulation as per precedent, and granted seasonal clothing," which consisted, according to Kaempfer, of "30 gowns laid on three tables." In 1682 their farewell had been the same, except that "the young Prince [Tokumatsu, Tsunayoshi's son, d. 1684] gave them 20 [gowns]." *Tokugawa jikki*, 5:439, Tenna 2/3/4. The Articles of Stipulation (*Jōyaku*) of 1681 read as follows: "Whereas the Dutch have been permitted to trade throughout the dynasty, and are suffered to land annually at Nagasaki, they are to have no traffic with followers of the doctrine of the heavenly master of the southern barbarians [Christianity], as has heretofore been decreed. Should there be word from a third country that [the Dutch] are in close relations with [the Catholics], they shall be barred from coming to our country. They shall bear no tidings from that gaggle hither. They shall not bear followers of that sect hither on their ships. If they desire to continue trading with our country as at present, they shall report to the bakufu any news they hear of the doings of the Base Doctrine. If there be any territories newly subjugated

Upon receiving these instructions, which the Dutch did not, of course, obey in any strict sense, the Dutch returned to Nagasaki, and to their commercial duties until the following year. In Nagasaki, they were restricted to residence on the man-made island of Deshima, a few yards off the shore in Nagasaki harbor. Not far from them in Nagasaki were the temples and residences of the Chinese community of that town, a community whose movement within Japan was even more restricted than that of the Dutch. The Chinese lacked even the privilege or journeying to Edo, there to be "viewed" by the shogun. While the Chinese, too, were subject to Japanese regulation, they received their annual "reading" of the "honorable laws and edicts," not directly from the mouth of the Nagasaki magistrate, who was, after all, a direct retainer of the shogun, nor in Edo Castle, but from the mouth of one of the staff interpreters in Nagasaki. This reading was performed upon the arrival of each Chinese ship in port, and, moreover, upon both arrival and departure, the Dutch were required to provide written pledges that they would comply.[70]

Having rejected direct government-to-government relations with China in 1621, the bakufu had demoted China to the lowest rung of its hierarchy of partners, keeping them at arm's length in Kyushu, where they dealt with the Nagasaki magistrate's office. This had been the case since the last years of Ieyasu's life, and according to Hayashi Razan it is a mark

---

by the religion of the barbarians, or if they learn of their plans to make a voyage, whatever they have seen or heard they should report to the Nagasaki magistrate. They are not to prey on Chinese ships bound for our country. In the travels of the Hollanders to various countries, there are bound to be countries where they will meet up with southern barbarians. Even so, the [Hollanders] are to have no traffic with the southern barbarians. Each year they are to make a detailed list of the countries of call, and the captain is to present same to the Nagasaki magistrate upon arrival. Appendix: Ryukyu is a vassal state of our country, and therefore, no matter where you may come upon them, you are not to prey upon their ships." (*Tokugawa jikki*, 5:403–404.)

[70] *TKIR*, 5:239.

of the low status accorded Chinese. "Dealing with barbarians," Razan wrote in an explanation of letters passed to Chinese through the Nagasaki magistracy, "is like dealing with slaves, which is the reason why these matters [of correspondence with China] were handled by low-ranking vassals like [Hasegawa] Fujihiro and [Gotō] Mitsutsugu."[71]

It had been bakufu practice, then, since the last years of Ieyasu's lifetime to deal with Chinese through the Nagasaki magistracy, even though it was not until 1635 that all Chinese commerce was confined to that port. When Chinese attempted to correspond with the bakufu, or to come to Edo to deal with the bakufu, as had happened in 1619-1621, when the Chekiang governor had offered trading terms, or in 1645-1647, when Cheng Chih-lung had sought shogunal aid in restoring the Ming dynasty, these attempts had been thwarted. Just as China dealt with "barbarian" approaches through low-level agents in the port cities, the bakufu, in Razan's words, "dealt with barbarians" like the Chinese in Nagasaki. Even when, as in the case of the spate of letters that Razan composed here, they were "written in accordance with the August Order" of Ieyasu, they were signed by "low-ranking vassals," fit to deal with barbarians and slaves. Similarly, the bakufu had found the letters of Tsui Chih and Cheng Chih-lung, unworthy of presentation to the shogun, and even unworthy of formal reply from the roju, leaving the "barbarians" to the Inspector General and the Nagasaki magistrate.[72]

The relegation of Chinese traders, and China, to the lowest, the "barbarian," level of the international hierarchy was finally completed in the second decade of the eighteenth century. In 1715 the bakufu adopted proposals of the shogun's chief Confucian adviser, Arai Hakuseki, for the regulation of the trade at Nagasaki, known as the "New Regulations of the Shōtoku Era."[73] Among the many provisions of these

[71] *Hayashi Razan bunshū,* p. 136.
[72] See *supra,* Chapter IV, pp. 120-122.
[73] The initial regulations, dated 18 February 1715 (Shōtoku 5/1/15) are in *Tokugawa kinrei kō zenshū,* 6:417-422 (docs. 4117, 4118), and were followed

regulations was one requiring Chinese merchants coming to Nagasaki to carry "credentials" (*shinpai*), or passports, issued them on behalf of the bakufu by the Nagasaki Office of the Chinese Interpreters. These credentials, employing language certain to be regarded as demeaning by Chinese officials, were dated in the Japanese calendar, and bore a "split seal,"[74] very much like the trading tallies that Ming China had required of Japanese vessels wishing to trade on the China coast in the fifteenth and sixteenth centuries.

The regulations drafted by Hakuseki in the spring of 1715, and read to the Chinese trading community in Nagasaki in April, announced that henceforth the bakufu would, ". . . grant credentials to those [Chinese] who say that they will accept (*tatematsuru*) the laws of our country, and permit them henceforth to come hither and engage in trade, while not permitting those who will not accept the laws of our country to pursue their trade, but immediately send them back . . ." to China.[75]

---

in the second month by further regulations, containing the promulgation of the credentials to be required of Chinese merchant vessels (*shinpai*), *ibid.*, pp. 423–431 (doc. 4119). The former two documents are translated by Yosaburo Takekoshi, *The Economic Aspects of the History of the Civilization of Japan*, 3 vols. (The Macmillan Company, 1930), 2:149–153. The regulations, and extensive supporting material are also in *TKIR*, 2:356–436.

[74] In order to prevent forgeries the Interpreters' Office kept a "Register of Split Seal Licenses" (*Wappu-dome chō*), in which each *shinpai* issued was registered, with extensive relevant information. After both the *shinpai* itself, and the information in the *Wappu-dome chō* were completed, the upper right corner of the *shinpai* was laid over the page in the register, and both were stamped with the seal of the Interpreters' Office, the seal overlapping both the *shinpai* and the register page. Yano Jin'ichi, *Nagasaki shishi tsūkō bōeki hen, Tōyō shokoku bu*, gives photo-reproductions of a *shinpai* of 1857, and the corresponding page of the register, clearly showing the split seal, following p. 384. Yamawaki Teijirō, *Nagasaki no Tōjin bōeki* (Yoshikawa Kōbunkan, 1966), p. 145, shows a *shinpai* of 1733, but not the page from the register. The instructions to the Interpreters' Office for drafting *shinpai*, dated 1715/third month, are in *TKIR*, 4:375–376, including a draft form for the interpreters to use as a model.

[75] This is Arai Hakuseki's recollection of the event, from his autobiography, *Teihon Oritaku shiba no ki shakugi*, ed., Miyazaki Michio (Shibundō,

The "New Regulations" had several purposes, among them limiting the number of vessels trading at Nagasaki, the volume of trade, and the export of Japanese specie carried through that port.[76] The issuance of credentials or passports modelled on the Chinese trade tallies of the Ming dynasty gave concrete expression in foreign policy to Hayashi Razan's vision that the reason that Chinese merchants were kept at arm's length in Nagasaki, and there dealt only with "low-ranking officers"—who lower than the Interpreters' Office?—was because the Chinese were barbarians: the credentials were dated in the Japanese calendar; they called China "T'ang," the vulgar Japanese name for that country, rather than "ta-Ch'ing," the formal name usually used in diplomatic discourse; they used a system of split seals; and they were conditioned upon Chinese acceptance of Japanese law. If Chinese merchants accepted the use of the Japanese calendar, were they not also signalling Chinese acknowledgment of Japan's central role in the world, yielding the center to Japan?

Since one of the principal goals of the *shinpai* system was to reduce the number of Chinese ships calling at Nagasaki, it was inevitable that of the fifty-one ships in port at the time that the New Regulations were announced, some would be forced out of the trade for want of credentials. In any event, only forty-seven were allowed to continue: those from Ningpo, Nanking, Canton, Taiwan, and Amoy were able to continue trading, while those from Fukien were excluded. Upon their return to China—empty-handed, of course—the outraged Fukien merchants actually complained to the government, not that they were being excluded from the trade, but that, "For the merchants of Chekiang and Kiangsu to

---

1964), p. 514; cf. Joyce Ackroyd's translation of this passage in *Told Round a Brushwood Fire: The Autobiography of Arai Hakuseki* (University of Tokyo Press and Princeton University Press, 1979), p. 249.

[76] The economic significance of these regulations is analyzed by Robert Leroy Innes, "The Door Ajar," pp. 346-355; Yamawaki, *Nagasaki no Tōjin bōeki*, pp. 140-155; Yano, *Nagasaki shishi*, Ch. 5, "Shōtoku shinrei mae no Nagasaki no Shina bōeki to Shōtoku shinrei."

accept credentials bearing the Japanese era-name (calendar) is to accept as correct the calendar of foreign barbarians, and therefore is tantamount to betraying the [Chinese] imperial court and subordinating themselves to Japan."[77] These merchants, that is, attacked their exclusion from the Japan trade by complaining that Japan was attempting to demote China within the international hierarchy. Since this is exactly what was happening, arguing their economic distress with the authorities in Nagasaki would be to little avail.

Indeed, at just that time, Chinese merchantmen who had not been in Nagasaki when the first round of credentials were distributed, and were therefore excluded from the trade, arrived at Nagasaki to trade, ignorant of the New Regulations.[78] Within two days of their arrival, they were ordered home without the opportunity for trading. They were told by the Interpreters' Office that illegal activity (i.e., smuggling) by Chinese had increased in recent years, along with the increase in the number of Chinese vessels to Nagasaki, and the bakufu had found it necessary to issue new regulations to control them and to limit their numbers. "[The bakufu] had granted a fixed number of split tickets . . . and although His Majesty feels pity for them, those ships which come without a split ticket are to be turned back, for otherwise that would mean that His Majesty's laws are not strict. . . ."[79]

Chinese protests against the new system continued for several years, both as complaints at Nagasaki and as appeals to the Chinese government, and for a time Chinese merchants frequently found their *shinpai* confiscated by Chinese

---

[77] Quoted in Yamawaki Teijirō, *Kinsei Nitchū bōeki shi no kenkyū* (Yoshikawa Kōbunkan, 1960), p. 32.

[78] *Tō tsūji kaisho nichiroku*, 7 vols. (Tōkyō Daigaku Shuppankai, 1955-1968), *Dainihon kinsei shiryō* series, part 3, 7:92.

[79] *Ibid.*, p. 95. On smuggling in this period see Fred G. Notehelfer, "Notes on Kyōhō Smuggling," in *Princeton Papers in East Asian Studies*, I, Japan (1) (August 1972), pp. 1-32.

port officials on their return home.[80] But as the crew of the No. 18 Nanking junk reported to the Nagasaki interpreters when they were interrogated on 22 September 1717, the K'ang-hsi emperor had relented, after an extensive court debate the previous fall. He ordered the *shinpai* returned to the merchants, because "there is nothing in their texts which in the least infringes on the laws of the state," and ordered that the merchants be allowed to ply their trade.[81] What is more remarkable is that at the same time the K'ang-hsi emperor was reported to have ordered the cessation of all of China's maritime trade *except* the trade to Japan.[82]

The *shinpai* system had been implemented successfully, and had been accepted by Chinese imperial decision. It would remain in effect until the end of the Tokugawa period as the licensing system controlling China's access to the Nagasaki trade.

By gaining Chinese acceptance of the credentials system, Arai Hakuseki and the shogunate had succeeded in depriving China of the diplomatic symbols of her claims to superiority and centrality: they had rejected the national title Great Ch'ing, and the use of the Chinese calendar, and had substituted the Japanese calendar in its stead. This acceptance implied, and the implication was strengthened by the emperor's acquiescence, Chinese recognition of Japanese superiority and centrality. Hakuseki had succeeded indeed in demoting China to the lowest level of the Japanese hierarchy, to the "barbarian" status that Hayashi Razan had earlier envisioned.

In order for a symbolic ordering of the countries of the world to be useful, it need not necessarily be consistent with all other beliefs held by the "operators" of the system or by the perceivers of the system. On the contrary, it may be precisely *because* certain "facts" or data of "objective reality" are uncomfortable or inconvenient to the maintenance of a desired or needed self-image and self-perception that peoples

---

[80] *Ka'i hentai*, 3:2692-2742, *passim*, is filled with reports of such incidents.

[81] *Ibid.*, p. 2743.

[82] *Ibid.*, pp. 2743-2744.

construct alternate realities in the symbolic systems of their world, of the world that they can control. Certain aspects of that reality can then be masked, others highlighted, to create and preserve a desired image.

If such a system of protocol and symbols is to be convincing, it need not so much be universally accepted, or populated with some large number of participants, as it must serve the needs of an observer for the sustaining of some deeply felt emotional self-perception. Nor is it necessary that the other participants in the system either share the observer's beliefs about himself, or share his interpretation of the meanings of the symbols involved. Indeed, as Mark Mancall and others have shown, many of the participants in the "Chinese world order" were at best cynical about their acceptance of the Chinese reading of its meaning.[83] Some even rejected it outright, or proposed alternative readings which placed themselves at the center. What was critical for the maintenance of the Chinese self-image, the perception of Chinese centrality, was merely the *appearance* of acceptance by foreign states. Whether they enthusiastically embraced the ideology, like Korea, and therefore eagerly followed the forms, or followed the forms for gain, like Siam, while rejecting the ideology once out of China, nothing they did caused the Chinese any doubt that the universe accepted their position of centrality and paramountcy, and this was sufficient. In the challenge to this perception and in China's inability to blunt that challenge by forcing European states and their representatives in China to conform to these norms in the nineteenth century, the system of mirrors collapsed and the Central Kingdom rampant soon followed suit.

Given the power of the bakufu to order the elements of Japanese external relations which took place within Japan proper, it was not too difficult a matter to organize the symbol system in a manner which enhanced the perceived primacy of Japan in the world and, within Japan, the perceived

---

[83] Mark Mancall, "The Ch'ing Tribute System: An Interpretive Essay," esp. pp. 63-72, "The Chinese Idea of Tribute and its Acceptance Abroad."

primacy of the shogun. But in order for such symbol systems to be effective as a matter of national policy, they must be shared beyond the immediate circle of government executives and policy planners: they must be transformed into public ceremonies of state in which a large part of the country can participate, if only as observers. In part this function was fulfilled during the Edo period by the mere passage of envoys and their entourage to and from Edo. When the Korean embassy of 1682 sailed up the Yodo River from Osaka to Yodo on 28 August, Hong Ujae, an interpreter for the embassy, wrote that the crowds were huge: "A million onlookers milled like ants on the riverbanks. [When] we arrived below the walls of the castle, [there was] a pontoon bridge stretched across the water, and countless thousands were lined up on it to watch us."[84]

In the middle third of the seventeenth century, starting with the Korean embassy of 1636-1637, this public spectacle was reinforced by Korean and Ryukyuan ambassadorial "pilgrimages" to the shogunal shrines at Nikko, where Ieyasu was enshrined as the "Great Avatar who Illumines the East." When the third shogun, Iemitsu, proposed the first such pilgrimage to Ambassador Im Kwang, Sō Yoshinari told him: "The Great Prince wishes to have the embassy make a sightseeing trip [to Nikko], for the glory of the entire country." Four days later the shogun pressed the idea himself during the embassy's audience: "If you Three Ambassadors were to make a sightseeing trip [to Nikko] We would consider it a glory for the entire nation. We should be unable to restrain our joy."[85] Im resisted for several days, but finally consented. He resisted because, he said, a journey to Nikko was

---

[84] Hong Ujae, *Tongsarok*, in *KKS*, 4:30.

[85] Im Kwang, *Pyŏngja Ilbon ilgi*, in *KKS*, 2:339-342. An interesting recent study of the Korean visits to the Nikko shrines is Ōtaki Haruko, "Nikkō to Chōsen tsūshinshi," in *Edo jidai no Chōsen tsūshinshi*, ed. Eizō Bunka Kyōkai (Mainichi Shinbun Sha, 1979), pp. 155-182. See also earlier studies by Matsuda Kinoe, "Nikkō Tōshōgū no hengaku to kane," and Nakamura Hidetaka, "Nikkōzan Tokugawa hengaku no mohòn ni tsuite," (October, 1968), pp. 241-257.

not part of his charge from his king.[86] But Im surely knew
that this would be perceived, not as mere tourism (kankō),
but as a pilgrimage (sankei). Indeed, some shogunal records
suggest that it was not Iemitsu but Im who requested permission to make the pilgrimage, and that he and 217 members of his entourage "were permitted to make a pilgrimage
to Nikko, just as they had requested."[87]

Tokugawa Iemitsu is noted for his reverence for his grandfather, Ieyasu, and for the great efforts that he took to exalt
Ieyasu's memory by promoting the cult of the "Great Avatar
Who Illumines the East," centered on the Nikko shrine.[88]
Iemitsu, not only succeeded in making of this reverence a
national cult, at least among the upper stratum of the bushi
class, with small-scale replications of the Tōshōgū shrine in
Kyoto and in the capitals of many daimyo domains across
the length of Japan; more than that, he now required Korean
and Ryukyuan embassies to make pilgrimages to Nikko to
pay their respects to his grandfather's spirit, now both a Shinto
deity and a Buddhist avatar. By giving the appearance that
it was the spontaneous desire of these envoys from abroad
to pay homage to "Gongen Sama," by obtaining gifts and
"articles of tribute," such as the Korean bell sent in 1643 or
the Dutch chandelier which faces the bell before the Yōmei
Gate, to decorate the shrine and further exalt Ieyasu's sanc-
tity, such foreign pilgrimages could not fail to serve as a
mechanism for extending the numinous range of the cult of
Ieyasu beyond the immediate geographic boundaries of Japan. They gave an aura of universality to the sacral effect of
the "Great Avatar Who Illumines the East." Such had surely
been the understanding of Hayashi Gahō, who wrote: "When

---

[86] Im Kwang, Pyŏngja Ilbon ilgi; cf. TKIR, 3:23-25.

[87] Tokugawa jikki, 3:44.

[88] For a brief overview of Iemitsu's reverence for Ieyasu, his reconstruc-
tion of the shrine at Nikko, and his promotion of the cult of Tōshō Dai
Gongen, see Hayashi Sukekatsu, "Dai sandai Tokugawa Iemitsu," in Tokugawa shōgun retsuden, ed. Kitajima Masamoto (Akita Shoten, 1974), pp.
106-109; Asao Naohiro, Sakoku, pp. 271-278.

the Great Divine Prince who Illumines the East unified the country [the barbarians] were all civilized by his virtue (*tōka*), and since then they have not ceased to come for trade, and they frequently present letters."[89] He also argued that diplomatic documents which survived from the period 1616-1644 demonstrated that the "transformative powers of our country's virtue had reached abroad to foreign lands."[90]

This function of publicizing the illusion of Japanese centrality and primacy, of the submission of foreign lands to Japan and to the shogunate, was also shared by less highly placed members of the Tokugawa state and society: artists and writers regularly celebrated the comings and goings of foreign embassies in both high art and low, and in popularly circulated illustrated booklets turned out after each embassy by the booksellers of Edo, and of the Osaka-Kyoto region.

One such high art depiction, the "Edo zu byōbu," is a celebration of the glory of the shogunate, and particularly of the third shogun, Iemitsu. It was commissioned around 1637 by Sakai Tadakatsu, whom Iemitsu called his "right hand."[91] As is typical of such expansive artworks, the scenes depicted in this pair of six-panel screens take place at multiple times throughout the year, and Iemitsu himself appears in several locations in the twelve panels. But the focal scene in the painting, the "action" taking place in the over-scale Edo Castle that occupies two of the central panels of the screen, and that dominates all of Edo, is the arrival of the Korean embassy of 1636 at the gates of Edo Castle. The chosen moment is the arrival of Ambassador Im Kwang, his sedan chair being

---

[89] "Ikoku ōrai jo," in *Gahō sensei Hayashi gakushi bunshū*, 90:1b. *Tōka*, "to be attracted by the transformative power of virtue, and to submit," Morohashi, *Dai kanwa jiten*, 5:136, no. 11887.48.

[90] "Ikoku raiō honshū jo," leaves 1a-2b.

[91] The screen is reproduced, both in full and in details, in *Edo zu byōbu*, ed. Suzuki Susumu (Heibonsha, 1971), which contains several useful commentaries and analyses. Murai Masuo, "Edo zu byōbu no rekishiteki haikei," in *ibid.*, pp. 22-46, identifies the patron of the screen as Sakai Tadakatsu, and gives the quotation in which Iemitsu calls Tadakatsu, his "right hand," p. 23. See Plate 7.

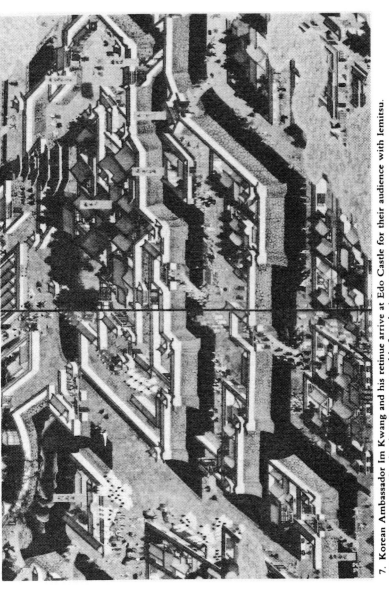

7. Korean Ambassador Im Kwang and his retinue arrive at Edo Castle for their audience with Iemitsu. King Injo's presents for the shogun are arrayed before the inner moat

carried to the first bridge over the outer moat, approaching
the Ōtemon, the main gate to the castle. King Injo's presents
to Iemitsu, tiger skins, leopard skins, falcons, and horses, a
dozen-and-a-half types of "tribute articles," as many considered them, were arrayed for all to see on the plaza between
the Ōtemon and Sannomon gates, while dozens of members
of Im's entourage lined the way to the castle, both along the
public streets of Edo, and within the gates of the castle.[92]

The arrival at Nikko of Ambassador Im and a retinue of
217 was similarly celebrated by a prominent artist of the day,
just as Im's arrival at Edo Castle had been preserved in picture. In 1640, Kanō Tan'yū (1602-1674) was commissioned
by the bakufu to paint a narrative scroll of the history of the
shrine of the Avatar, for presentation to the shrine. The scroll,
with text by the monk Tenkai, prominently includes a representation of Im's pilgrimage to the shrine of Ieyasu, showing his arrival, still seated in his sedan chair, before the *torii*
(ceremonial gate) that marks the entrance of Ieyasu's sep-
ulcher.[93] As a caption, Tenkai wrote of the Korean visit:

[92] A list of the presents Injo sent to Iemitsu in 1636 appears in *TKIR*,
3:102:

10 rolls of damask	30 rolls colored paper
10 rolls of satin	50 golden-bristle writing
30 rolls of white ramie	brushes
30 rolls of black linen	50 boxes writing ink
30 rolls of gold-brocaded	30 blue mink skins
white linen	100 sharkskins
50 catties ginseng	100 catties golden honey
15 tiger skins	10 urns of clear honey
15 leopard skins	20 brace young falcons
20 floral-patterned cushions	2 swift horses, with saddles
	and bridles

Not all the articles listed in the catalog appended to Injo's letter can be
distinguished in the screen painting: the horses and falcons are not readily
seen.

[93] *Tōshōsha engi, kan* 4, reproduced here as Plate 1. The text, under the
title *Tōshōgū Daigongen engi*, is in *Zokuzoku gunsho ruijū*, vol. 1 (Zoku Gunsho Ruijū Kanseikai, 1970), pp. 691-705. Iemitsu was so pleased with Tan'yū's
scroll illustrations that on 19 January 1640 (Kan'ei 16/i11/26) the shogun
presented the artist ten pieces of gold (*Tokugawa jikki*, 3:164), and on 30

"Recently the Korean ambassador and vice-ambassador came to the Province of Musashi and made obeisances before His Majesty. Thereupon, they made a pilgrimage to Nikko Mountain and prayed before the altar of the shrine. The faith with which they revered the sacred precincts was manifest." Tenkai included celebratory poems left by the Three Ambassadors, and concluded that this all bespoke the "correct government [enjoyed by] this country, which will be manifest as the moon in the sky, both in this generation and unto the final generation."[94] Tenkai, it would seem, was convinced that the numinous power of Gongen Sama had spread beyond the seas.

For popular consumption as well, there were inexpensive books and prints that circulated widely among the masses, so that they, too, might share in the glory of foreign "tribute" embassies. Just as Kanō Eikei (1662-1702) celebrated the Korean embassy of 1682 in a scroll painting, probably commissioned by the bakufu or a daimyo,[95] the equestrian performance that embassy presented for Tsunayoshi outside Edo Castle was the subject of a woodblock illustration in an inexpensive pamphlet of scenes of the capital, published in the first decade of the eighteenth century, on the eve of the next Korean embassy.[96] The ukiyo-e artist Hanegawa Tōei celebrated the entry of an idealized Korean embassy into Edo, Mount Fuji resplendent in the background, in a famous mid-eighteenth century polychrome painting,[97] while two of the most famous exponents of the popular arts of the last

---

June (Kan'ei 17/5/11) further granted him 100 pieces of silver, two seasonal kimonos (jifuku), and one haori (a jacket worn over the kimono) (ibid., p. 188).

[94] Tōshōgū Daigongen engi, p. 700.

[95] Kanō Eikei, Chōsenjin gyōretsu zu. Spencer Collection, New York Public Library. Reproduced here as Plates 8 and 9.

[96] Hōei Karaku saiken, plate 10, reproduced in Yi Wŏn-sik, "Tennado (1682) Chōsen shinshi hishō Kō Seitai to Nihon bunshi no hitsudan shōshū ni tsuite," in Chōsen gakuhō, 98 (January 1981): 3.

[97] Hanegawa Tōei, Chōsenjin raichō zu, polychrome painting in the collection Kobe Museum of Nanban Art, reproduced in Kōbe Shiritsu Nanhan Bijutsukan zuroku, 5 vols., vol. 4, p. 17, plate 3. See Plate 10.

third of the Tokugawa period, Jippensha Ikku and Kitagawa Utamaro, are credited with an illustrated booklet commemorating what was to be the last Korean embassy to Japan before the fall of the shogunate, the embassy of 1811.[98] The embassy came, according to Ikku, "solely because of the merit of the Sacred Reign [of Tokugawa Ienari, the eleventh shogun]. . . " The pamphleteers' intention, therefore, was "to distribute this [book] to people who were unable to see the splendid parade of the Korean guests, even to untalented children ignorant of the unmistakable debt we owe for living in the land of the Great Peace."[99]

Ryukyuan embassies were also not exempt from what we today would call "media attention." Inexpensive booklets like *Ryūkyūjin gyōretsu ki* (A Record of the Ryukyuan Procession),[100] for example, circulated more widely, certainly, than did Kanō Tan'yū's depiction of the Korean arrival at Nikko. And, as the anonymous prefacer of this pamphlet understood it, the significance of these Ryukyuan embassies lay in the fact that, "Ryukyu was originally descended from the Heavenly Clan [i.e., Japanese] and is now a vassal of the August Country [Japan], *as is Korea* [emphasis added]. . . Ryukyu has been sending embassies to Japan since antiquity, and these embassies have come regularly since 1649. This time the king of that country sent his ambassadors in gratitude for the benefice of his enthronement."[101]

---

[98] Jippensha Ikku (text) and Kitagawa Utamaro II (illustrations) *Chōsenjin raichō gyōretsu ki* (Edo: Nishimuraya Genroku; Taishū Ōmachi: Mikiya Kizaemon, 1811). The illustrations are reproduced as front matter in *Chōsen shinshi raichō kihan kanroku*, ed. Ishizaka Kōjirō (Kobe: Hyōgo Okagata Komonjo Kankō Iin, 1969).

[99] Jippensha and Kitagawa, *Chōsenjin raichō gyōretsu ki*. The "Great Peace" *(taihei)* was an Edo period epithet for the great era of national peace achieved by the victory of Tokugawa Ieyasu and maintained by the governance of his successors. As such, it was quite specifically a celebration of the glories of Tokugawa rule.

[100] *Ryūkyūjin raichō gyōretsu ki*, anonymous (Fushimi: Tanbaya Shinzaemon, 1832). Reproduced here as Plates 11 and 12.

[101] *Ibid.*

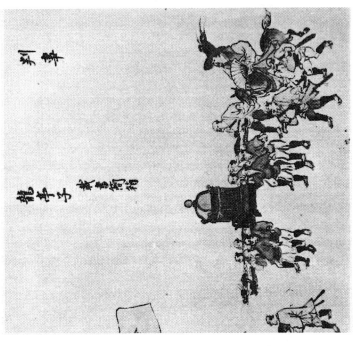

9. Tsushima retainers carry the state letter from Korea's King Sukchong to Tsunayoshi on a palanquin. A member of the ambassador's retinue rides behind

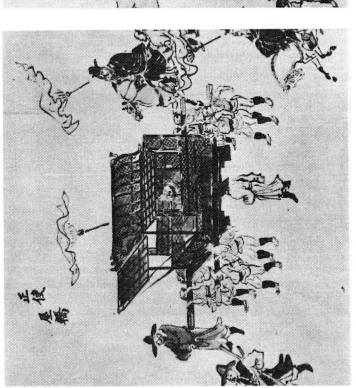

8. Korean Ambassador Yun Chiwan being borne to Edo Castle, 1682, for his audience with Tsunayoshi

THE VIEW FROM THE CENTER

The Japanese view of the external world, and of Japan's external relations, in the Edo period was predicated, as Uete Michiari has observed, on the same ideological dichotomy between the "civilized" (j. *ka*; ch. *hua*) and the "barbarian" (j. *i*; ch. *i*) of Neoconfucianism as was that of China.[102] The distinctions which were at the root of the Chinese self-perception, and which informed the ordering of China's relations with the outside world in the pre-modern period,[103] did not "map" entirely comfortably onto the realities of Tokugawa Japan. Still, Edo-period Japanese, whether of Neoconfucian or Nativist persuasion, to a greater or lesser extent accepted the idea of a normative hierarchy of peoples, and applied this normative mapping to a Japan-centered perception of the world.[104]

It would be fatuous to suggest that all, or perhaps even any, Japanese of the Edo period seriously and unambivalently believed it possible fully to sustain a one-to-one mapping of the Chinese conception of the centrality of China onto a cosmology based on the centrality of Japan. Yet there were elements in the "indigenous" Japanese intellectual and religious tradition which could and did encourage the belief in just such a homology, asserting the numinous or ethical superiority and the centrality of Japan. These beliefs were reinforced, and given a firmer vocabulary of expression, by the spread of Neoconfucianism, and its mapping of moral order onto political and diplomatic order. It will be argued below, after setting forth briefly the background and development of this *weltanschauung* in pre-Edo and Edo-period Ja-

---

[102] Uete Michiari, *Nihon kindai shisō no tenkai*, p. 235.

[103] See John K. Fairbank, "A Preliminary Framework," and Benjamin I. Schwartz, "The Chinese Perception of World Order, Past and Present," in Fairbank, ed., *The Chinese World Order*, for discussion on this point.

[104] Kate Wildman Nakai, "The Naturalization of Confucianism in Tokugawa Japan," and Harry D. Harootunian, "The Function of China in Tokugawa Thought," in *The Chinese and the Japanese: Essays in Political and Cultural Interaction* (Princeton University Press, 1980), pp. 9-36.

10. The townspeople of Edo turn out to watch a Korean embassy enter the city, as depicted in this idealized eighteenth-century woodblock print

pan, that a major ideological function of the foreign relations of the Tokugawa bakufu was to foster and support this conceit of Japanese centrality.

Japanese have long asserted the divinity of Japan. In it best-known usage, the assertion that "Japan is the land of the gods" is the predicate of the entire *Jinnō shōtō ki*, an important fourteenth-century chronicle of Japanese history centered on the imperial line.[105] But the earliest instance of this assertion of Japanese divinity occurs in the context of Japanese foreign relations, in the legendary account of third-century relations with the Korean state of Silla, wherein the king of Silla is reported to have said that he had heard that, ". in the east there is a land of the gods, named Yamato [Japan]. "[106]

Thereafter, the assertion that Japan was the land of the gods appeared frequently in Japanese political discourse, and particularly in times of diplomatic crisis. The rejection in 1270 of Khubilai Khan's demand that Japan submit to Mongol overlordship, for example, was predicated on the fact that

[105] *Jinnō shōtōki, Masukagami*, ed., Iwasa Tadashi, et al. (Iwanami Shoten, 1965 [*Nihon Koten Bungaku Taikei*, vol. 87]), p. 41; cf. H. Paul Varley, tr., *A Chronicle of Gods and Sovereigns: The Jinnō Shōtōki of Kitabatake Chikafusa* (Columbia University Press, 1980), p. 49: "Great Japan is the divine land."

[106] *Nihon shoki*, ed. Sakamoto Tarō et al., 2 vols. (Iwanami Shoten, 1965-1967 [*Nihon Koten Bungaku Taikei*, vols. 67, 68]), vol. 1, p. 339); cf. W. G. Aston, tr., *Nihongi, Chronicles of Japan from the Earliest Times to A.D. 697*, 2 vols. (Allen & Unwin, 1956), 1:230. At issue here is the development of a Japanese national self-image at about the time that the *Nihon shoki* was compiled, i.e., the turn of the eighth century, rather than the veracity of the account itself. On the former problem of the development of national consciousness as it relates to the diplomatic question, see Ishimoda Shō, "Nihon kodai ni okeru kokusai ishiki ni tsuite: kodai kizoku no baai," in *Shisō*, 454 (April, 1962): 2-9. On the latter point, and the entire issue of reading the *Nihon shoki* as a source, see Gari K. Ledyard, "Galloping Along with the Horseriders, Looking for the Founders of Japan," in *Journal of Japanese Studies*, 1.2 (Spring 1975), especially pp. 241-242. On the general question of the historiography of the *Nihon shoki*, which bears directly on the issue of the growth of early Japanese national consciousness, see G. W. Robinson, "Early Japanese Chronicles: The Six National Histories," in W. G. Beasley and E. G. Pulleyblank, ed., *Historians of China and Japan* (Oxford University Press, 1961), pp. 213-228.

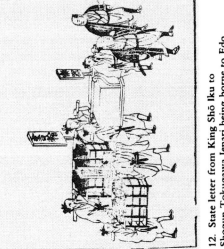

12. State letter from King Shō Iku to Shogun Tokugawa Ienari being borne to Edo with the Ryukyuan embassy of 1832 escorted by Satsuma samurai

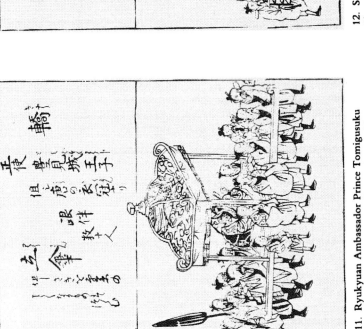

11. Ryukyuan Ambassador Prince Tomigusuku being carried by members of his retinue to his audience with Tokugawa Ienari, 1832

Japan "is the land of the gods." This was certainly the reason that the Japanese believed that the two subsequent Mongol attempts to invade Japan were repelled with the aid of the "winds of the gods" (*kamikaze*).[107] Similarly, in 1419, when Korean forces attacked Tsushima in retaliation for Japanese pirate raids on Korea, members of the Japanese court were appalled that such things might happen in "the land of the gods," and wondered at the audacity of "China, the Southern Barbarians, and Korea," to think of attacking Japan.[108]

This sense of Japan's divinity undergirded a sense of Japanese superiority that was most often expressed in relation to Japan's nearest neighbor, Korea. The *Nihon shoki*, for example, abounds with accounts of kings of the three ancient Korean states sending "tribute" to Japan,[109] and even in the seventeenth century and later Japanese would assert, as Hayashi Razan had in 1611, that Korea called herself a vassal of Japan.[110] In the discourse of the Tokugawa period, one even has the sense that the term "Kan" (k. *Han*), which was the collective name for the states of Korea in the age of the *Nihon shoki*, continued to have the connotation of "Japan's subordinate state, which brings tribute," while the term "Chōsen" (k. *Chosŏn*), the official name of Korea in the Yi dynasty, had connotations of greater equality with Japan.

Particularly in eras when Japan felt culturally self-assertive, however, it became possible for Japan to claim parity with, or even superiority to, China itself, which had defined the idea of a "central kingdom" superior to all surrounding states in the world. As early as the beginning of the seventh century, the Japanese Emperor Suiko claimed to be a peer of the Chinese emperor, addressing herself thus: "The offspring of

---

[107] *Koji ruien*, 26:903-904, "Nihon-koku Dajōkan Mōko-koku Chūshoshō ni chōsu, Kōrai-koku shijin ni fu shite chōsō su," drafted by Fujiwara Nagashige.

[108] *Kanmon gyoki*, entry for Ōei 26/6/23, in *Zoku Gunsho ruijū hoi*, rev. ed. (Zoku Gunsho Ruijū Kanseikai, 1958-1959, 1:87.

[109] *Nihon shoki*, 1:339, 371, etc., for example.

[110] *Hayashi Razan bunshū*, p. 136.

heaven in the land where the sun rises offers a letter to the offspring of heaven in the land where the sun sets."[111] One hundred years later, in the formulation of the new Japanese administrative codes, all foreigners, not only Korean but Chinese as well, were classified as *iteki* (barbarians), which suggests that the self-image of Japan as a "central kingdom" has very deep roots indeed.[112] In fact, Hirano Kunio argues that Suiko's letter to the Sui emperor was a clear rejection of Japan's former acknowledgment of Chinese paramountcy, and a refusal further to participate in a sinocentric system of diplomacy,[113] an action analogous to that of the Tokugawa bakufu in its refusal to enter into relations with Ming China in 1621.

In the late sixteenth century, as in the late thirteenth, Japan faced a potential invasion from abroad, this time from the "southern barbarians" of Portugal and Spain. In confronting this danger, Toyotomi Hideyoshi had recourse to the divinity of Japan, just as Sugawara Nagashige had done in 1270 and Prince Fushiminomiya Sadafusa in 1419. In ordering the expulsion of Jesuit missionaries from Japan in 1587, Hideyoshi argued from the premise that, "Since Japan is the land of the gods, it is manifestly improper that the base doctines of the lands of the Christians be propagated [here]."[114] Four

[111] *Koji ruien*, 26:835. This is usually translated, "The Son of Heaven in the land where the sun rises   ," but, in light of Suiko's gender, I have seen fit to translate here appropriately.

[112] This is the observation of Ishimoda Shō, "Nihon kodai ni okeru kokusai ishiki," p. 8, based on his understanding of the Personnel Code ("Shokuinryō") section of the ancient administrative codes. For the original text on which he bases this interpretation, see *Ritsuryō*, ed., Inoue Mitsusada et al., *Nihon Shisō Taikei*, vol. 3 (Iwanami Shoten, 1976), pp. 190–191; see also the Household Code ("Koryō") section, at p. 229 for similar and corroborative usages.

[113] Hirano Kunio, "Yamato ōken to Chōsen," in *Iwanami kōza Nihon rekishi*, 1 (1975): 241.

[114] "Sadame," dated 24 July 1587 (Tenshō 15/6/19), MS, Matsuura Collection, Hirado, Nagasaki Prefecture, Japan. The version printed in *Shiryō ni yoru Nihon no ayumi, kinsei hen*, ed. Ōkubo Toshikane et al. (Yoshikawa Kōbunkan, 1955), p. 51, differs in minor details from the Matsuura MS.

years later, when telling the governor of Portuguese Goa of his plans to conquer China, Hideyoshi again had recourse to the premise that "our country is the land of the gods."[115]

Nagura Tetsuzō has recently argued that Hideyoshi's conception of Japan as "the land of the gods" was based, not on Japan's possession of an imperial line descended from the gods, and unbroken for all ages, but on a reverence for the war god Hachiman, and that this vision divided the world between the countries of Christendom, on the one hand, and the "three countries of Asia," viz., Japan, China, and India, on the other. This latter "world," according to Nagura, Hideyoshi conceived of as constructed along the lines of a Japan-centered *ka-i* order, where Japanese centrality was predicated on Japanese divinity.[116] Indeed, a closer reading of Hideyoshi's letter to the governor of Portugese India suggests that Hideyoshi also based his assertion of Japanese centrality equally on a belief that Japan embodied the virtues which, in Confucian terms, identified *ka*, "civilization": "In human governance of the world, [the virtue of] humanity (*jin*) is the foundation. Without humanity and duty (*gi*) the ruler is not a proper ruler, the subject not a proper subject. But when people follow humanity and duty, then is established the Way of the great ethical norms of [the fundamental human relationships]."[117]

Now the *ka-i* model of interstate relations, and the *ka-i* model of self-perception, had certainly been available for emulation not only by Japan but by others as well, for millennia. As Nakamura Hidetaka has observed, there were many peoples among the *i* who began to identify themselves as *ka*

See C. R. Boxer, *The Christian Century in Japan*, p. 148, or George Elison, *Deus Destroyed*, pp. 115-116, for full translations of this document.

[115] *Kanpaku* (Toyotomi Hideyoshi) to governor of Portuguese India, dated 12 September 1591 (Tenshō 19/7/25), in *Ikoku ōfuku shokan shū, Zōtei Ikoku nikki shō* (vol. 11 of *Ikoku sōsho*, Komiyama Shoten, 1966), pp. 26-28.

[116] Nagura Tetsuzō, "Hideyoshi no Chōsen shinryaku to 'shinkoku,' " in *Rekishi hyōron*, 314 (June 1976): 29-35.

[117] *Ikoku ōfuku shokan shū*, pp. 26-28.

under the influence of Chinese thought, to whom the *ka-i* dichotomy served as a stimulus to national consciousness. As they developed domestic institutions derived from the Chinese model, and as they absorbed Chinese thought, they also appropriated the distinctions between "inner" and "outer," between *ka* and *i*, and in some cases built for themselves self-centered culture spheres in which they arrogated to themselves the terminology and the role of *ka*.[118] We have already seen that this model was operating in the development of early Japanese national consciousness, especially vis-à-vis Korea, but even in relationship to China, and that these attitudes were beginning to reassert themselves on the eve of the Tokugawa period.

This model also informed the consciousness of the men who formulated the Tokugawa bakufu's foreign policy in its early decades, and worked to determine the diplomatic language and the diplomatic protocol that would be its mirror. Mark Engel has observed that, ". . . we create the world that we perceive, not because there is no reality outside our heads . , but because we select and edit the reality we see to conform to our beliefs about what sort of world we live in,"[119] or perhaps the world that we would like to believe we live in. Lest this sound tantamount to a form of national autism, it is important to recall that, in Fairbank's words, ". . . the Chinese world order was a unified concept only at the Chinese end and only on the normative level, as an ideal pattern."[120] So, too, for the early Tokugawa bakufu, as Tanaka Takeo has observed in the context of seventeenth-century relations with Korea, the goal was "neither books, nor technology, nor profit," in shogunal diplomacy, "but

[118] Nakamura, *NKSK*, 3:469; cf. Tanaka Takeo, *Chūsei taigai kankei shi*, p. 19.

[119] Mark Engel, "Preface," in Gregory Bateson, *Steps to an Ecology of Mind* (Ballantine Books, 1972), p. 7. This is Engel's summation of Bateson's thesis.

[120] Fairbank, "A Preliminary Framework," p. 9.

the establishment of international order."[121] From the Japanese end, that order would be constructed on the premise of Japanese centrality, of complete Japanese autonomy to control Japan's external affairs.[122]

Under the stimulus of widespread Neoconfucianism, a philosophy which became thoroughly "naturalized" in Japan in the seventeenth-century,[123] there was resurgent force behind the historical vision of Japanese centrality in Tokugawa thought. It has been noted that this conceit was already well formed in the minds of some Japanese before the Tokugawa period. This pretense had a close and indeed functional relationship to development of external policy, and, in particular, Toyotomi Hideyoshi had brought ideas of Japanese divinity and centrality once more into the conduct of Japanese diplomacy on the very eve of the Tokugawa era and had even begun to clothe them in Confucian terminology.

After the establishment of the Tokugawa shogunate, the interaction of ideas and foreign policy continued to foster the conceit of centrality. Hayashi Razan wrote to the military governor of Fukien in 1610, for example, that several Ming tributaries, led by Korea, had been affected by the "transformative power" of the Tokugawa kingly virtue,[124] and in early 1611 that the restoration of relations between China and Japan would surely bring "happiness to the two heavens."[125]

To be sure, these early letters also relied on traditional terms

[121] Tanaka Takeo, "Sakoku seiritsu-ki Nissen kankei no seikaku," in *Chōsen gakuhō*, 34 (January 1965): 59.

[122] Manfred Jonas, *Isolationism in America, 1935-1941* (Cornell University Press, 1966), p. 275, makes the point that, "To act independently and exclusively on one's own behalf satisfies national aspirations and demonstrates national aims."

[123] The idea of Confucianism as a "naturalized" creed I take from Kate Wildman Nakai, "The Naturalization of Confucianism."

[124] Honda Masazumi to governor of Fukien, 10 November 1610 ([Keichō 15] kōjutsu/10/6), drafted by Razan, in *Ikoku nikki*, vol. 1; *TKIR*, 5:342.

[125] Nagasaki Magistrate Hasegawa Fujihiro to Ch'en Tzu-chen, 29 January 1611 (Keichō 15/12/16), drafted by Razan, in *Hayashi Razan bunshū*, p. 132; *TKIR*, 5:343.

of respect for China's presumptive primacy in East Asia, but this merely reflects the ongoing ambivalence and cognitive dissonance which characterized the national self-perception of Tokugawa Japan. With elegant wit, Kate Wildman Nakai has suggested that the focus of this cognitive dissonance appeared most powerfully ". . in the Tokugawa Confucian's confrontation with the Sinocentric qualities of Confucianism. "[126] "Lacking," moreover, "the opportunity to work out in face-to-face encounter with contemporary Chinese what may perhaps not too facetiously be termed their oedipal feelings about Chinese civilization, Tokugawa Confucians tended to become involved in a game of one-upmanship played with an invisible opponent . [so that] a certain quality of shadowboxing is endemic to Tokugawa Confucianism."[127]

One important method of winning this "shadowboxing" competition was to detach the attributes of "centrality" and "civilization" from the historical, geographical "China," and to convert them into abstract, universal norms, which might be found as well in contemporary Japan as in China, or perhaps even better in Japan. The problem of reconciling a satisfactory Japanese national image with the normative position of China, and the related question which concerns us here, of the tendency in Tokugawa thought to "centralize" Japan, have been traced in some detail by scholars as diverse as Maruyama Masao, Bitō Masahide, and Uete Michiari; Harry Harootunian, Marius B. Jansen, I. J. McMullen, and Kate Nakai.[128] It will be necessary here, therefore, only to

---

[126] Nakai, "The Naturalization of Confucianism," p. 165.

[127] Nakai, "The Naturalization of Confucianism," p. 173.

[128] Maruyama Masao, "Kindai Nihon shisōshi ni okeru kokka risei no mondai (1)," in Tenbō (January 1949), pp. 4–15; Bitō Masahide, "Sonnō jōi shisō," Iwanami kōza Nihon rekishi, 13 (1977): 41–86; Uete Michiari, Nihon kindai shisō keisei, pp. 233–282; Harry D. Harootunian, "The Function of China in Tokugawa Thought," Marius B. Jansen, Japan and Its World: Two Centuries of Change (Princeton University Press, 1980); I. J. McMullen, "Non-Agnatic Adoption: A Confucian Controversy in Seventeenth- and Eighteenth-Century Japan," in Harvard Journal of Asiatic Studies, 35 (1975): 133–189; Nakai, "The Naturalization of Confucianism," for example.

note some of the most important developments in this trend before returning to the starting point: the interaction of this ideological stream with Tokugawa diplomatic history in the production and maintenance of a national self-image.

Perhaps the first line of defense, certainly the earliest in the Tokugawa period, was the attempt by Fujiwara Seika (1561-1619) to demote China from the center by asserting a nearly Jeffersonian conception of the equality of states: "As long as there is Principle (j. ri; ch. li) there is nowhere that is not under Heaven, that is not upborne by Earth. Our country is so; Korea is so; Annam is so; China is so. . ."[129] Seika's disciple, Hayashi Razan, a leading architect of the bakufu's diplomacy, by contrast reaffirmed an essential Confucian belief in the hierarchical nature of phenomenal existence.[130] And while acknowledging the position of China in some of his diplomatic correspondence with China, he still insisted on asserting, as has been repeatedly apparent, a competing, equivalent center in Japan. In this attempt, furthermore, Razan preferred reliance on the dynastic claims of the Tokugawa house, i.e., the criteria of national unification and dynastic survival for three or more generations, and on the "transformative power" of Tokugawa virtue, rather than recourse to any Tokugawa claims to authority derivative from the emperor. This is the basis of his claims that the various countries of East Asia have "called themselves subject," or "come to pay tribute," and his assertion that there were now "two heavens." Razan was speaking in an explicitly diplomatic context, and in relation to China. His son and successor as shogunal Confucianist, Hayashi Gahō, extended the imagery of Japanese centrality in the several prefaces that he wrote to collections of diplomatic documents and, as has been noted, related the imagery directly to the conduct of sho-

[129] *Fujiwara Seika shū*, 2 vols. (Kokumin Seishin Bunka Kenkyūjo, 1930), 2:394. See the discussion of this point by Minamoto Ryōen, *Tokugawa shisō shōshi* (Chūō Kōron Sha, 1973), p. 18, pointing out the implications of international egalitarianism in Seika's position.

[130] Minamoto, *Tokugawa shishō shōshi*, p. 18.

gunal diplomacy, and to the structure of shogunal diplomatic protocol.[131]

Several contemporaries of Razan and Gahō also, although not reasoning so much from diplomatic as from ethical and Shinto evidence, began to amplify upon the conception of Japan as "central," and to articulate it more thoroughly than had been the case before Neoconfucianism had become "naturalized." Bitō Masahide credits Yamazaki Ansai (1618-1682), Yamaga Sokō (1622-1685), and Asami Keisai (1652-1711) with the transvaluation which converted Japan into *Chūka*, the Central Kingdom, and regards the period 1661-1680 as the critical period in this transformation.[132] These three uniformly opposed granting to Ch'ing China the legitimate use of the vocabulary of exclusive occupation of the "Center" (terms like *chūka*, *chūgoku*, and *kaka*). They argued for the management of Japanese external affairs in a manner calculated to enhance Japanese national self-respect and emphasized a unique Japanese tradition, which for these philosophers included reverence for the emperor.

In order to deny China its special position, of course, China had to be stripped of those value-laden terms which made it difficult to speak of "China" without speaking of China's "centrality." This was accomplished by denying China those formal terms of address that China would herself have chosen, terms which implied superiority and centrality. In much of the discourse of Tokugawa Japan, therefore, China was not "Great Ming," "Great Ch'ing," *Chūka*, or *Chūgoku*, names which implied a normative superiority. Rather, China was simply *Tō* (T'ang), which had become a generic, and hence neutral, name for China. This, indeed, was the term for China that dominated Japanese diplomatic discourse, and it was the name that appeared on the trade credentials issued to Chinese merchants from 1715 to the end of the Tokugawa period.

For Yamaga Sokō in particular, China had lost its claim

---

[131] *Supra*, nn. 16, 89, 90.
[132] Bitō, "Sonnō jōi shisō," pp. 50-51.

to ethical superiority, and hence to centrality. Unlike Japan, China had frequently been conquered by barbarians, Sokō noted in *Takkyō dōmon*, and had accepted barbarians as their sovereign. Thus, not only were Chinese ignorant of the greater duty, but "unlike this country, it has no integrity."[133] As for Japan, "The prestige of her martial prowess has spread to the limits of the four seas, so that even foreign countries fear it, and leaving aside the idea of Japan being conquered by a foreign country, not a single piece of territory has been lost."[134] Japan, which had realized the Way by achieving political stability and by maintaining territorial integrity, he proclaimed as the centerpiece of a Japan-centered *ka-i* ideology, while China was merely a "foreign country (*ikoku*)."[135]

As for Sokō, so for many others, the shock of China's falling to barbarian (i.e., Ch'ing) control was great, and helped to undermine whatever claims to inherent, normative centrality China might hope to retain. For Hayashi Gahō, writing in the late 1670s, it was possible to observe that it had been "nearly forty years since the Tatar barbarians had snatched the flower [meaning China]   but since our country is at peace, the waves of the ocean are gentle, and the winds of virtue blow broadly, summoning merchant ships to Nagasaki from [China]."[136] The repeated attempts of Ming loyalist pretenders to secure Japanese assistance in reestablishing the dynasty and retaking China from the "Tatars," the arrival in Japan of numerous Ming loyalist literati who preferred to "live among the eastern barbarians," as Confu-

---

[133] "Takkyō dōmon," quoted in Bitō Masahide, "Yamaga Sokō no shisō teki tenkai," part 2, in *Shisō*, 561 (March 1971): p. 92. Sokō is speaking here of the ability to maintain the territorial, rather than the ethical, integrity of the country.

[134] "Haisho zanpitsu," in *Yamaga Sokō*, ed. Tahara Tsuguo and Morimoto Jun'ichirō, *Nihon Shisō Taikei* series, vol. 32 (Iwanami Shoten, 1970), p. 333.

[135] Bitō, "Yamaga Sokō," part 2, p. 92, arguing from Sokō's *Chūchō jijitsu*.

[136] "Go Tei ron," in *Gahō Sensei Hayashi gakushi bunshū*, 48:22a.

cius had longed to do,[137] rather than to serve an alien dynasty, could only serve to strenthen the conceit that now Japan was the true "center."[138]

The impact of the Manchu conquest on Japanese images of China was not confined to the intelligentsia, however. On the popular level as well, the effect was profound. One of the greatest box-office successes of the Tokugawa theater was Chikamatsu Monzaemon's *Battles of Coxinga*, which ran for seventeen months at Osaka's Takemoto Theater from 1715 until mid-1717. The focus of the plot is on the attempts of the Ming loyalist movement, led by Coxinga (Cheng Ch'eng-kung), whose mother was Japanese, to turn back the Manchu conquerors and to restore the Ming dynasty to the throne. In Act One, the "loyal" General Go Sankei (the Wu San-kuei who led the Revolt of the Three Feudatories in the 1670s) proclaims to the Ming emperor the barbarizing prospect of

[137] *Analects*, Bk. 9, Ch. 13: "The Master wished to live among the nine eastern barbarian [tribes]." Cf. James Legge, tr., *Confucius: Confucian Analects, The Great Learning, The Doctrine of the Mean* (The Clarendon Press, 1893; Dover reprint, 1971), p. 221. On the larger problem of the concept of *i* (eastern barbarian) in Tokugawa thought see Tsukamoto Manabu, "Edo jidai ni okeru 'i' kannen ni tsuite," in *Nihon rekishi*, 371 (April 1979): 1-18; for his discussion of this passage from the *Analects*, see at p. 3.

[138] Korea also took the fall of China to the hated Manchu conquerors as the sign that the "flower" had passed, if only temporarily, from China to Korean custodianship. Kang Chaeŏn has written that, "When China fell under the control of the Manchus, then in a world of 'northern barbarians,' Korea had herself to shoulder alone the mantle of the small central kingdom, and this idea formed the intellectual foundations of the solitary isolationism that Korea maintained toward the outside world. It was also a powerful intellectual current in the Confucian world obstructing the development of an enlightenment, or internationalist (*kaikoku*) position, which would have been essential for Korea to modernize autonomously." (*Kidai Chōsen no henkaku shisō* [Nihon Hyōronsha, 1973], p. 17.) Kang would seem at first glance to be arguing that a "Korea-centered *ka-i* ideology" functioned in precisely the reverse way that a Japan-centered *ka-i* ideology did for Japan, as argued by Maruyama, "Kindai Nihon shisōshi ni okeru kokka risei no mondai," but Korea continued to hold to a normative historical China—a Ming ideal—for which Korea was a custodian, rather than arguing that Korea was *per se* a "central kingdom."

a Tatar conquest: if the emperor's treacherous minister Ri Tōten's advice is followed, "this land, that has given birth to the sages, will fall under the yoke of the Mongols, and we shall become their slaves, differing from the animals only in that we do not wag tails or have bodies covered with fur."[139]

As Marius B. Jansen has cautioned of this and similar passages in *The Battles of Coxinga*, "It would be foolish to read too much into this extravaganza of stage entertainment."[140] And yet, Japanese intellectuals, government officials, and popular writers all identified the Manchus as the "Tatars," and considered them to be the same people who had tried to invade Japan in the thirteenth century and had failed in the attempt. The fall of China to an alien, "barbarian" dynasty certainly contributed to the demotion of China in the estimation of Japanese, and tarnished the once burnished image of a cultural ideal, even suggested that it had feet of clay. Japan, after all, had had the moral fiber to resist conquest by those self-same "Tatars," though they had twice tried to invade, while China had now twice succumbed. *Coxinga* shows how far, by the early eighteenth century, "this consciousness had permeated down to popular culture as well, and that it proved an attractive theme there."[141]

It was not a simple matter to divorce the geographical, the historical, China from the normative China of textual Confucianism, and Tokugawa Confucianists therefore dealt with the problem in a wide variety of ways. Some, particularly those of the Kimon (Yamazaki Ansai) school, moved toward a position approximating a modern nationalism. Ansai himself, for example, in a passage reminiscent of Fujiwara Seika's view, argued that, "As far as the name 'Chūgoku' is concerned, from each country's own point of view, it is itself

---

[139] Donald Keene, tr., *The Battles of Coxinga*, p. 107. "Go Sankei" is the Japanese pronunciation of the name of Wu Sankuei, the leader of the Revolt of the Three Feudatories in the 1670s.

[140] Marius B. Jansen, *Japan and Its World*, p. 24.

[141] *Ibid.*, p. 22.

the center (*chū*), and the four quarters (*shigai*) are barbarians (*i*)."[142] Therefore, even if a Chinese army were to attack Japan, led by Confucius and Mencius themselves, Ansai told his disciples in a famous anecdote, "I would put on armor and take up a spear to fight and capture them alive in the service of my country. That is what Confucius and Mencius would teach us to do."[143] Others, like Yamaga Sokō, argued for the positive superiority of Japan over China because it epitomized the virtues of Confucianism better than China, because it had never been conquered by a "barbarian" dynasty, and because it was ruled over by an imperial dynasty coeval with heaven.

For others, the argument that worked best was to transform *ka* and *i* into terms of functional, rather than moral, value, as Dazai Shundai (1680-1747) proposed: to call foreigners "barbarians," he suggested, "is to lack propriety, and without propriety, even a person from *Chūka* is the same as a barbarian; if one has propriety, then even though a foreigner (*i*), one is no different from a person from *Chūka*."[144] The criterion upon which one determined whether a person, or a country, was civilized (*ka*) or barbaric (*i*), that is, was whether that country knew proper ethics and observed proper ritual (i.e., forms of government).

An excellent way to determine whether a country knew the proper ethics and was properly governed, of course, was to observe how that country behaved in its relations with other countries. It was here, I would suggest, that the structures of protocol and diplomatic language designed and maintained by the Tokugawa bakufu proved their value. By maintaining what appeared to be a fully autonomous, self-determined relationship to the other countries of the region and to the world, and by excluding those countries which would not abide by the rules of that diplomatic order, the

[142] *Bunkai hitsuroku*, quoted in Bitō, "Sonnō jōi shiso-," p. 51.

[143] *Sentetsu sōdan*, translated in Ryusaku Tsunoda et al., comp. *Sources of Japanese Tradition*, pp. 360-361.

[144] Dazai Shundai, *Keizai roku*, quoted in Uete, *Nihon kindai shisō*, p. 242.

Tokugawa bakufu provided a *climate* which could nurture
conceits of Japanese centrality, the *atmosphere* in which an
intellectual photosynthesis could transform the elements of
indigenous ideas of national divinity and the difficult Confucian dichotomy of *ka* and *i* into an order in which Japan
was *ka* and others, even the historical (if not the normative)
China, were *i*. Other countries, either lacking the traditions
of divinity, or bearing the burdens attendant upon having
recognized the suzerainty of China, were unable to foster
these illusions of self-sustained centrality. In the Korean case,
for example, the onslaught of Western pressures in the nineteenth century would be met with protestations that, while
Korea was independent, it was also subordinate to China,
and in matters of diplomacy would defer to China, as Korea
sought to turn her traditional tributary relationship with China
into a bulwark of national defense.[145]

Japan, however, rejected subordination to China in 1621.
The bakufu proceeded to construct a system of diplomatic
relations which fostered illusions that Japan was the central
ka, surrounded by a few *i* who recognized this, and who
bore tribute to the shogun, increasingly clothed in the vocabulary of universal numinous kingship. Japan had not only
rejected subordination to China, but had claimed parity with
China, even superiority over China. After all, China had
succumbed to foreign barbarian invaders, while Japan remained intact, beholden to none. And in 1715 Arai Hakuseki
had even succeeded in extracting from Chinese merchants
the same sorts of acknowledgment of Japanese superiority
that Ming China had required of Japanese traders three
hundred years before. Why, even the Chinese emperor himself had acquiesced to Chinese use of Japanese trading credentials! It mattered little that no foreigners sincerely believed in the implications of this diplomatic charade, for, as
Fairbank has noted of the Chinese tribute system, it was the

[145] See M. Frederick Nelson, *Korea and the Old Orders in East Asia*, p. 112.

view from the Chinese end that mattered to China[146] and, equally, the view from the Japanese end that mattered to Japan.

Maruyama Masao has argued that the maintenance of Japanese independence, sovereignty, and territorial integrity in the mid-nineteenth century was dependent in part on the catalytic effects of the earlier transvaluation of *ka* into an identifier of Japan, and the construction of a perceived, a *believed*, Japan-centered order of *ka* and *i*. For it was, in Maruyama's view, only through the catalysis of a Japan-centered vision of *ka* and *i* that the Japanese were able to transform late-Tokugawa isolationism and xenophobia (*jō'i*) into the thesis that Japan's survival depended on the autonomous opening of the country to full foreign intercourse (*kaikoku*).[147] For this intellectual atmosphere to be sustained, however, it required, as Nakamura Hidetaka has observed, that Japanese withdrawal from the sinocentric world order which had regulated international intercourse in East Asia prior to the Tokugawa era, and which continued to do so for Korea, in part for Ryukyu, and partially also for other countries on the Chinese periphery. The establishment of *Nihon-koku taikun* diplomacy, that is, established an autonomous place for Japan, an Archimedian "place to stand," and from that place the shogunate could transform the appearance of the world. While other countries in East Asia, which had relied, both intellectually and diplomatically, on the illusion of Chinese centrality, were losing their independence and falling to Western— or even later to Japanese—domination, Japan, which had rejected Chinese centrality and had constructed an alternative, a Japan-centered ideology and diplomacy, remained more free to act, able to retain independence, autonomy, and national integrity.

[146] Fairbank, "A Preliminary Framework," p. 9.

[147] Maruyama, "Kokka risei no mondai." Conrad Totman has recently offered a similar argument, "From *Sakoku* to *Kaikoku*: The Transformation of Foreign-Policy Attitudes, 1853-1868," in *Monumenta Nipponica*, 35.1 (Spring 1980):1-20.

Thus, while Korea in the mid- and late-nineteenth century turned frequently to China for either advice about, or protection from, her diplomatic problems, Japan "played China," and granted permission for Ryukyu, her own "vassal state," to enter into foreign treaties—little matter that Japan could not have prevented France from forcing a treaty of the king of Ryukyu in 1847.[148]

And, further, when Japan began to turn outward once more in the 1850s and 1860s, she had a ready-made canon of protocol and diplomatic behavior to which she turned. When Perry's ships loomed off Uraga in 1853, the bakufu ordered the compilation of Tokugawa diplomatic precedents and procedures.[149] When Harris was to come to Edo for the signing of the Treaty of Trade and Amity in July of 1858, the shogunate looked to those precedents to determine whether Harris deserved the protocol and the status accorded to Korean ambassadors, or whether he ought merely to be granted the lower status and concomitant protocol of a Ryukyuan ambassador.[150] And, a year later, when the shogunate was about to dispatch its first embassy to the United States, to leave in 1860, the Commissioner for Foreign Affairs recommended to the roju that the ambassadors prepare for their meeting with the President on the basis of the precedents from the 1811 reception of the Korean embassy to Japan.[151]

By choosing to have relations only with those countries that would accept ground rules for international intercourse determined solely (at least in appearance) by Japan, by structuring those relationships in a protocol hierarchy crowned by the bakufu, by refusing relations with China that might sacrifice that appearance of primacy, by even achieving a hi-

---

[148] Nakamura, *NKSK*, 3:551-555.

[149] Konishi Shirō, *Kaikoku to jōi* (Chūō Kōron Sha, 1966), pp. 12-15; Kerr, *Okinawa*, pp. 277-278.

[150] *Dainihon komonjo bakumatsu gaikō monjo*, 17:37-44.

[151] Oguri Mataichi (Tadamasa) et al., to (Manabe) Shimōsa no kami (Akikatsu), Ansei 6/10/21 (3 November 1859), in *Ishin shiryō kōhon*, MS, collection Historiographical Institute, Tokyo University, vol. 1092.

erarchy which appeared to devolve from Japan, to Korea, and thence through Ryukyu and Holland to China, the bakufu had created the environment in which the Japan-centered *ka'i* order appeared to exist. This order was a necessary condition for the growth of a Japan-centered *ka'i* ideology, though by no means the only necessary condition. And, while it was by itself certainly insufficient to sustain the ideology and the conceits that it fostered, equally certainly it was one of the essential supports for the ideological mirror that reflected Japan's ideal world.

CHAPTER SIX

Epilogue

DIPLOMACY can help to establish a state, intelligence services can help to defend it, and the skillful construction and manipulation of relations with neighbors abroad can be molded into a language which transcends and transforms reality into a mechanism for the maintenance of some desired world view. Hence it can serve to perpetuate the illusions and ideologies which support the state. The danger, of course, is that such illusions and ideologies may survive beyond comfort to the point of peril, when they become too far removed from their context, so atavistic that they prevent the state from responding effectively to the new truths and new environments.

The diplomacy which helped to legitimate the Tokugawa regime in the early seventeenth century, the avenues of intelligence which kept the shogunate adequately informed of the fluid strategic and economic situations in East Asia in the crisis of the middle and late seventeenth century, the protocols and language which helped to foster the maturation of national traditions of divinity into an emergent ideology of national centrality and ethnic superiority that would ultimately propel Japan into the twentieth century—all of these continued to operate through the eighteenth century and into the nineteenth. They formed a corpus of experience for the state and for the nation, a corpus that came to have the force of normative rules for the ordering of Japan's relationship to the external world.

Some of these norms were part of the conscious design of leaders and planners from the early years of the dynasty, some, accretions of practice over the centuries; some, even, appear to have been reinterpretations by the leaders of late Tokugawa Japan of the actions or intentions of their forebears. Yet, whether intentional or accidental, whether accurate or erroneous, it was this agglomeration of practice, perception, and ideology by which leaders attempted to guide their decisions, and by which the "public"—at least the intellectually aware and politically conscious "public"—attempted to interpret and to evaluate the experience of state, people, and country in the waning years, the final decades of challenge, through which Tokugawa Japan would pass.

To say that this corpus of practice and ideas was out of date, inconsistent with the times, or for that matter inconsistent with objective reality at any time in the Japanese past, is not to negate, however, the power that it had for Japanese of the Tokugawa period. In the daily ordering of international existence, in the choices that Japanese political leaders and thinkers made in response to the challenges of the world around them, it was to this corpus of practices, language, and ideas that they turned, first to comprehend the situation that they faced, and then in the attempt to respond to it.

When, in the summer of 1853, Commodore Matthew Calbreath Perry led his small fleet of "black ships" into Edo Bay and demanded that Japan join the society of nations on terms that had been defined by centuries of Western experience, therefore, or even earlier, when Adam Laxman presented the appeals of Catherinian Russia for trade and intercourse, they were not merely confronting a *tabula rasa* of diplomatic ignorance and inexperience. Rather, they were juxtaposing to the inherited "simplified and intelligible picture of the world," and the corpus of behavior and practice that supported that picture, a new, an insistent and challenging "picture of the world" greatly at variance with, in fact mutually incompatible with, the received vision.[1]

[1] The phrases in quotation marks are from Albert Einstein's remarks on the sixtieth birthday of Max Planck, in Einstein, *The World as I See It* (Covici, Friede, Publishers, 1934), pp. 20-21, which I first encountered in Robert M. Pirsig, *Zen and the Art of Motorcycle Maintenance* (William Morrow, 1974;

So long as the received vision had not been too vigorously challenged from within or without, so long as the picture of a divinely descended Japan, or of a Japan that was the center of the world, a Japan which was "civilized" in the midst of barbarians, was not crushed by the overwhelming weight of undeniable experience, that vision survived, and helped to sustain the system that had devised it and relied upon it.

When Edo ordered an end to the Portuguese trade in 1639, and the last galiot left Nagasaki for Macao, it was not thereby sounding the death knell of Japanese foreign relations for the next two centuries. At the same time that Edo acted to restrict those aspects of external affairs deemed inimical to Japan and to the interests of the bakufu, it also strove to build a diplomatic structure which would enhance bakufu legitimacy, assure Japan a sense of security in an East Asia still troubled by war and piracy, and maintain Japanese access to a secure and expanding foreign trade. If Japanese were denied free travel overseas, and cut off from much that the West had to offer, something was indeed lost, but the bakufu compensated for some of these losses, by ordering the promotion and expansion of trade elsewhere, for example. And the bakufu gained greatly in areas of political and ideological importance as well.

For it was the task of Tokugawa Ieyasu and his successors to resolve a national ambivalence toward their international environment into a workable set of foreign policies that could serve dynasty, state, and nation in the realms of politics and ideology, security and commerce, and be existentially acceptable to the Japanese, consonant with their sense of identity. These imperatives were equally relevant to Asian relationships and to European relationships. The political and ideological implications of early Tokugawa foreign policy have been analyzed here in terms of their effect on the legitimation of the bakufu in the seventeenth century and, in succeeding

repr. Bantam Books, 1975), pp. 106-107. The original text is in Einstein, *Mein Weltbild* (Amsterdam: Auflage Erstdruck, 1934; repr. Frankfurt/M: Ullstein Materialen, 1979), pp. 107-110.

centuries, their influence on the development of Japan's sense of national identity and place in the order of the world.

The place that the bakufu built for itself in East Asia was not, however, one prefabricated by the traditional sinocentric world order of Ming. To be sure, many of the norms of protocol, and even the language of diplomatic correspondence, were of Chinese derivation. But by asserting the shogun's identity as *Nihon-koku taikun*, an unprecedented title, by asserting the primacy of Japanese era names, by bringing foreign embassies to Edo or Kyoto, and by carefully constructing protocol so that in no diplomatic exchange did the bakufu recognize a superior—in all these ways the bakufu was able to create the illusion of an East Asian world order that was Japanese in design and Japanese in focus. The discovery in the 1640s that Japan was a magnet for Ming loyalist armies seeking military aid, and for loyalist literati seeking refuge from the conquering barbarians in China, served only to heighten that illusion. Japan appeared the mover, not the moved.

In the seventeenth century, at the dawn of the Tokugawa dynasty, diplomacy with the other states of Asia, and even with the Europeans in Japan, was manipulated to maximum effect in creating for the dynasty the aura of legitimate claims to national power and authority, and specifically the claims of Ieyasu's line to represent the Japanese state (*Nihon-koku*) in its dealings with the external world.

From the middle of the seventeenth century, first with the increasingly urgent restrictions on the movement of Catholics into and out of Japan, and the movement of Japanese abroad, later, with the development of arm's-length methods of intelligence-gathering, Tokugawa Asian diplomacy served the security interests of the state, served to perpetuate and to maintain the state.

But, most important, the institutions, the behaviors, the modes of thought about the way in which Japan ordered her relations with other states and peoples, and the way in which Japan *ought* to order those relations, resonated deeply with the development of the "national self-image" of Tokugawa Japan. Tokugawa diplomacy and Tokugawa ideology developed a symbiotic, a synergistic, relationship, embodied institutionally in the protocols and language of Tokugawa foreign relations, and intellectually in the writings of Tokugawa intellectuals. These two embodiments of the Tokugawa ideal stressed national autonomy (non-participation in the Chinese world order; the right to make arbitrary decisions in diplomatic affairs), and a hierarchy of nations in which Japan was either *par primi*, i.e., second to none, but a peer of China, or *primus omnorum*, with China, by virtue of barbarian conquest or ethical failure, demoted to the lowest levels of barbarism.

Examining these developments in early Tokugawa foreign relations also reveals some of the inner workings and institutional growth of the bakufu itself. As was the case in domestic policy and administration, the bakufu at the time of Ieyasu did not have any institution with clearly delineated responsibility for making or carrying out foreign policy. As with domestic policy, many of the early foreign policy advisers and functionaries were, like Honda Masazumi, loyal retainers from Ieyasu's days as a local baron in the province of Mikawa. Ieyasu also utilized Zen priests, first Saishō Shōtai, who had served Hideyoshi in a similar capacity, and then Ishin Sūden, who contined to serve under Hidetada and Iemitsu until his death in early 1633. In this, Ieyasu was continuing the diplomatic role which had developed for Zen monks in the medieval period, a role in which they had flourished under the Ashikaga shoguns. Hayashi Razan represents a transition from the Zen monks of the earlier period to the Confucian scholar-official of the Tokugawa period. Just as Neoconfucianism emerged from its refuge in the temples and academies of medieval Zen to take on an independent existence in seventeenth-century Japan, so Razan, who was required by the shogun to dress as a Zen monk, emerged to establish the position of the bakufu's official Confucian scholar as a diplomatic adviser to the shogun.

By the mid-1630s, in concert with the general trend toward more regular institutions within the bakufu, a measure of regularity was introduced into the control of foreign affairs. By 1634 new bakufu regulations placed foreign affairs in the purview of the newly redefined senior council. With Sūden dead, the role of Zen monks within bakufu policy councils declined, and monks in Edo were reduced to the level of document drafters. The bakufu did, however, continue to use monks in their traditional role in a more limited fashion, with the placement of residents in the Iteian hermitage in Tsushima to oversee the daimyo of Tsushima and to give the bakufu some control over the correspondence between Japan and Korea, and to guarantee that Edo's position was not compromised. The former role of Shōtai and Sūden was increasingly concentrated in the hands of Hayashi Razan, and become institutionalized as part of the Hayashi family's role as official bakufu scholars.[2]

With limited exceptions, the senior council and the Hayashis functioned—as envisioned in the senior council's charter in 1634 and restated in 1662—as the nerve center of the bakufu's foreign policy system. The Nagasaki magistrate, the daimyo of Tsushima, and the daimyo of Satsuma all reported to the senior council in matters of diplomatic significance, while directives to those agencies issued from the council. On occasion, as with Sō Yoshinari in 1647, these agents might consult directly with the shogun himself. Only in the handling of the petitions of Ming loyalists for Japanese military aid does it appear that the Tokugawa collateral houses and the senior *fudai* house (who could, of course, be called on to join the council as *tairō* in crises) had what seem to have been the deciding voices. Yet even here the discussion was conducted as a discussion of the council.

In simple matters, such as the repatriation of distressed

[2] The only exception to this was during the years 1709-1716, when Arai Hakuseki usurped the Hayashi family's role, and made major changes in foreign policy. See my "Korean Japanese Diplomacy in 1711." The Hayashis were quickly restored to their traditional role by Yoshimune in 1716, and nearly all the changes instituted by Hakuseki were reversed.

seamen, the Nagasaki magistrate functioned as a clearing-house, and all incoming and outgoing repatriations were processed between the magistrate and the lords of Tsushima and Satsuma.[3] But, even here, there are copious references in the records of the Edo residence of Tsushima to show that each repatriation was reported to, and authorized by, the senior council. Similarly, whenever a foreign embassy was expected, or a diplomatic event of similar consequence arose, one of the members of the senior council was placed in charge, with a temporary title like, "Special Commissioner for Korean Affairs" (*Chōsen goyō gakari*).

The failure of the shogunate in the seventeenth century to establish a full-fledged ministry of foreign affairs has been noted by some to suggest a relatively low level of bakufu interest in the establishment, maintenance, and operation of foreign affairs. There can be no question that the institutions of the bakufu lacked a specialized foreign ministry at any time in its history. Even in the waning decades the *Gaikoku bugyō* (Magistrate for Foreign Countries), established in 1858,

[3] Strictly speaking, Tsushima dealt directly with Korea when repatriating Koreans shipwrecked on Tsushima, or Tsushima mariners cast up in Korea, merely reporting these incidents to the senior council. The Nagasaki magistrate became involved only when the castaways were from somewhere other than Tsushima, in the case of Korea. Similar caveats probably apply to the Satsuma case. For an interesting case where the castaways were neither Japanese nor Korean, but Dutch, illustrative of the functioning of the machinery for the aid of distressed seamen, see Gari Ledyard, *The Dutch Come to Korea* (Seoul: Royal Asiatic Society, Korea Branch, 1971), pp. 75-97. Okada Nobuko, "Kinsei ikoku hyōchakusen," discusses the operations of this apparatus in some detail. She overlooks the question of the handling of Koreans cast up on Tsushima, so that her tabulation of Korean castaways includes cases as far from Korea as Hitachi, on Japan's eastern coast, but none in Tsushima, a highly unlikely situation, contradicted by Tsushima's office logbooks from the Edo residence, the domain capital, and Japan House in Pusan. The regulations for Tsushima's handling of Chinese castaways on the island comprise a 100-leaf manual, *Tōsen hyōchaku teishiki* (MS, ca. 1688, in the Sō Collection, National History Compilation Committee, Seoul). The manual contains detailed procedures for delivery of castaways to Nagasaki, formulae for reports to the roju, etc.

functioned as an appendage of the roju. But in this instance it is important to recall both the domestic record and the comparative context. As noted above, the charter of the roju in 1634 quite clearly included the governance of foreign affairs; this charter was renewed some thirty years later, and was observed in operation throughout the Tokugawa period. Moreover, independent foreign ministries, as opposed to ministers of state whose duties included foreign affairs, were as yet uncommon, if not unknown, even in the multi-state atmosphere of Europe. The Ottoman Empire had not established a true foreign office as late as 1839,[4] and the Ch'ing Empire never established a true foreign office until the twentieth century.[5] The existence or absence of a foreign ministry offers little insight into the existence or absence, or even the relative importance, of foreign affairs in any particular premodern state.

These institutional arrangements were not simply limited to the seventeenth century, nor did they atrophy and wither away in the eighteenth. We have noted, for example, that the intelligence system continued to operate in the mid-nineteenth century, as did the institution of especially appointed senior councillors in charge of a particular diplomatic event. Numerous other officers of the bakufu, the inspectors, the

[4] Carter V. Findley, "The Foundations of the Ottoman Foreign Ministry: The Beginnings of Bureaucratic Reform under Selîm III and Maḥmud II," in *International Journal of Middle Eastern Studies*, 3.4 (October 1972): 408.

[5] The Tsungli Yamen, established in 1861, although often equated with a foreign ministry, had only "powers [that] were very restricted, vague and inadequate . . [and were] neither . . monopolistic executive powers nor extensive foreign policy making powers over China's foreign affairs. . . It was simply one of the various offices which conducted China's foreign affairs." S. M. Meng, *The Tsungli Yamen: Its Organization and Functions* (The East Asian Research Center, Harvard University, distr. by Harvard University Press, 1962). It was not until 24 July 1901, in response to Western demands after the Boxer Rebellion, that the Tsungli Yamen was replaced by a Ministry of Foreign Affairs (*Wai-wu-pu*), *ibid.*, pp. 79-81. For an English text of the edict "reforming" the Tsungli Yamen to create the Ministry, see H. S. Brunnert and V. V. Hagelstrom, *Present Day Political Organization of China*, tr. A. Beltchenko and S. S. Moran (n.p.d.), pp. 106-107.

finance officers, and the like, were involved from time to time, but their roles in foreign policy were not regularized until the 1850s.[6]

When the Russian envoy Adam Laxman appeared at Nemuro in 1792, it was the senior council that determined the response, and to this end the subordinate officers directed the flow of information and negotiation to the roju in Edo. Similarly, when the king of Holland sent a letter to the shogun in 1844—unprecedented, since Holland was a country now defined as a "trading" (tsūshō) partner, not a diplomatic (tsūshin) partner—the Nagasaki magistrate, the daimyo of Hizen, and other locally responsible officers channeled the problem to the senior council, where ultimate disposition of the issue was determined.[7]

Japan's foreign relations in the seventeenth century were complex and dynamic. The dynamism was generated in part by the political needs of a new and rapidly maturing governmental order, in part by the highly fluid political and strategic situation which prevailed on the East Asian continent until the 1680s, in part by changing and expanding trade. During the following period, from Genroku through Shōtoku (1688-1716), however, as the Ch'ing dynasty took firm control of all of China, as Japanese recoinage policies made Japanese currency a less attractive commodity to foreign merchants, as domestic industries began to compete successfully with imports—and even, as Tokugawa culture became more self-assured—Tokugawa foreign relations appear to have entered a period of greater stasis in the eighteenth century.

Diplomacy became less intense; two-thirds of the embassies from Korea, for example, came in the first third of the Tokugawa period. Trade declined as well, and diplomatic issues became less frequent, and less strongly felt. Over the

[6] W. G. Beasley, *Select Documents on Japanese Foreign Policy*, pp. 18-21, briefly discusses this process.

[7] *Tsūkō ichiran zokushū*, 2:401-530. The correspondence of senior councillor Abe Masahiro and the lord of Mito, Tokugawa Nariaki, on this matter is contained in "Shin Ise monogatari."

course of the eighteenth century this atrophied state of foreign relations came to be viewed as the norm, to be interpreted as ancestral law, attributed to the decisions of the first three shoguns, when, in fact, as we have seen, this situation was neither the intention, nor the result, of the policy changes of the 1630s. Rather, it was the unintended result of other policies and developments in the economy, in politics and foreign relations, and in the very nature of the international environment.

Thus, despite the relatively lower level of activity on the international plane, the institutions and norms of foreign relations observed in the seventeenth century continued quietly to function through the eighteenth century, and into the nineteenth. When Commodore Perry challenged Japan in 1853, then, he confronted Japan with a choice, not between international community or none, but between two alternative systems of foreign relations, one newly and forcefully offered, the other developed by the bakufu in the seventeenth century.

It has become common to assume that when Adam Laxman appeared at Nemuro in 1792, or Nicolai Petrovich Rezanov at Nagasaki in 1804—indeed any of the parade of Europeans seeking a new relationship with Japan in the late eighteenth and early nineteenth centuries—until the arrival of Commodore Perry at Uraga in the summer of 1853, the crisis they precipitated in the Tokugawa state arose in large part because Japan was a diplomatic *tabula rasa*. It appeared, that is, that Japan, having seceded from the society of nations in the 1630s, had neither the experience nor the concepts that it needed adequately to respond to the challenge. It is as if a Gulliver had been cast up in the land and, finding no one who spoke English, no one who responded to his verbal pleas, had concluded that the Japanese were a people without a language. It was not that the Japanese spoke no "diplomatic" language, merely that they spoke a "diplomatic" language not understood by their petitioners.

So when the shogunate, or for that matter, the people of Japan, tried to come to grips with the petitions of Laxman or Rezanov or, later, with the exhortation of Willem II, the pleas of Commodore James Biddle, and the demands of Perry, it should not be surprising that they had recourse to the "language" of diplomacy, the "vocabulary" of institutions, behaviors, and ideologies that had carried them through the centuries since Ieyasu. If anything is surprising, it is that we have failed until this late date to recognize that they were speaking a language at all. It may even be suggested that the "language" had at least two dialects: the dialect of the government, which was based on the accumulated institutes and precedents of two hundred years and more of Tokugawa diplomatic practice, and the language of critics in "the field," heirs to over two centuries of religious, scholarly, and ideological discourse and debate.

When the bakufu and its officials first attempted to respond to these new demands on Japan, after over a century of benign neglect from the West, therefore, it was but natural that they had recourse to their own "dialect" of Japanese diplomatic language. Matsudaira Sadanobu did not need, nor did he seek to know, the norms of inter-state behavior in Europe, in 1792, in order to respond to Laxman's mission. Rather, he analyzed the accumulated experience of Japan, his sole referent for the understanding of proper diplomatic practice, categorized it, and decided how Laxman fit in. Sadanobu determined that the entire corpus of Tokugawa diplomacy since the founding fathers could be comprehended under the two rubrics "trading partners" (tsūshō) and "diplomatic partners" (tsūshin). By the time of Rezanov, Sadanobu had determined that these were *closed* categories, and that they comprised *only* those countries with whom Japan had active relations of one type or the other in his day. Moreover, Sadanobu concluded that these catagories were not merely analytical categories, but normative categories, fixed by the dynastic founders as "ancestral law" (sohō), and that they could not be altered.[8]

---

[8] It is noteworthy that Shizuki Tadao's translation of Kaempfer came in the midst of the decade in which Sadanobu was wrestling with policy for

Prior to 1825, the rising Western pressure, though dealt with by intellectuals in refined, if heated, debate, was a relatively minor issue in the shogunal politics of the day. When the debate became more heated than refined, as it did in the writings of Hayashi Shihei, the debate was suppressed.[9] But, after 1825, after the bakufu's edict that foreign ships were to be fired upon if they appeared off Japan's shores, and after the appearance that same year of Aizawa Seishisai's *Shinron*, the terms of debate, the tenor of the discourse, changed. After Aizawa's *Shinron*, perhaps for the first time in nearly two centuries, the legitimacy of the shogunal institution was specifically tied to its performance in foreign policy.

In a very real sense the triumph of Tokugawa foreign policy in the seventeenth century, indeed the triumph which sustained Tokugawa foreign policy, and hence the state, into the nineteenth century, was the bakufu's successful ability "to act," or at least to *appear* to act, "independently and exclusively in [its] own behalf," in diplomatic—foreign—affairs.[10] The ability autonomously to manipulate foreign states and foreign monarchs in the formative years of the dynasty served both to assure the physical security of the Japanese homeland and to prevent the subversion of the state from abroad, on the one hand, and to legitimate the new Tokugawa order, on the other. The current study has shown the legitimating power of the conduct of foreign relations in the early years of the dynasty. Harold Bolitho, moreover, has suggested that the bakufu's development of a "monopoly" on the *conduct* of external relations, being one in a panoply or portfolio of powers that the early shogunate was able to remove from the purview of the several daimyo and arrogate

the northern frontier. There is evidence to suggest that Sadanobu was personally in favor of a more liberal response, at least to Rezanov, but, retired from shogunal office at the time, supported the more conservative views of the roju. On this point see Uchida Ginzō, *Kinsei no Nihon/Nihon kinsei shi*, Tōyō Bunko series, no. 279 (Heibonsha, 1975), pp. 95-100.

[9] On the fate of Hayashi Shihei see G. B. Sansom, *The Western World and Japan*, pp. 213-214.

[10] Manfred Jonas, *Isolationism in America*, p. 275.

exclusively to itself, was an element, in a different way, in the early legitimation of the dynasty. It was important, that is, not only to control what foreign relations there were, with whom, and on what protocol terms, but also who conducted foreign affairs. Marius Jansen, also, has suggested that the very "closing of the country" was itself a legitimating act.[11]

Yet as the ability of the bakufu "to act independently and exclusively in [its] own behalf" in diplomatic affairs declined, the urge to appear to do so increased proportionately. As Europeans became more insistent, as American whalers were more and more frequently sighted off the coast, as "barbarian" castaways became more of a problem, and clearly beyond the ability of the bakufu to control, increasingly the bakufu turned to the looking-glass world. They tried to shore up the failing image of shogunal authority by turning to Ryukyuan, to Korean diplomacy, to give the *appearance* that the world still recognized the claims of the Tokugawas, and that the Tokugawas could still cause the world—or at least the part of it that had traditionally counted for the most—to do its bidding. As noted earlier, it had been common bakufu practice to appoint one or more members of the roju as Special Commissioners for Korean (or Ryukyuan) Affairs anywhere from six to eighteen months prior to the arrival of any anticipated embassy. Although the last Korean embassy, in 1811, had been received in Tsushima, as an economy measure, because the bakufu had decided that the benefits were now minimal, by the 1830s and 1840s the benefits appeared greater, and so frequently the bakufu attempted to promote Korean and Ryukyuan embassies, to refurbish the mirror of Tokugawa glory.[12] What is important here is not that the embassies never materialized, but that the bakufu

---

[11] *Japan and Its World*, p. 16.

[12] Members of the Mizuno family, for example, were repeatedly named Special Commissioners for the "forthcoming Korean embassies" in the 1830s and 1840s, although no embassy came to fruition after 1811. See *Hiyōroku*, *passim*.

expected them to restore the luster on the dynasty's claims to legitimacy, authority, and control over external relations, and that they sought to do so by resorting to the vocabulary of "Tokugawa diplomatic," which constituted their only familiar language.

The vitality of this language, this medium of discourse, is evident in *Shinron*, a critique of shogunal diplomacy intended to affirm shogunal prerogatives in foreign affairs. Aizawa looked to the same mirror fashioned by Tokugawa diplomacy, the native tradition, and the naturalized Neoconfucianism to find that it was Japan that was the "central kingdom," and castigated Japanese who, "perhaps unenlightened about Names and Duties, call Ming and Ch'ing *kaka* (Civilized Hsia) or *Chūgoku* (the Central Kingdom), and thereby sully the national prestige [of Japan]. Or else they follow the times and pander to power, confusing Names and forgetting Duty, regard the heavenly court above as if they were themselves expatriates here, and thus injure the transformations of the Sages [of Japan], while below they harm the Duty of the bakufu."[13] That Aizawa was also reintroducing the em-

---

[13] Aizawa Seishisai, *Shinron*, in *Mitogaku*, ed. Imai Usaburō, Nihon Shisō Taikei, vol. 53 (Iwanami Shoten, 1973), pp. 288 (Chinese text), 67 (Japanese text). "Shikaruni aruiwa meigi ni kuraku, Min Shin o shō shite Kaka Chūka to nashite, motte kokutai o ojoku suru mono, aruiwa toki o ooi, ikioi ni shitagai, mei o midari, gi o wasurete, Tenchō o miru koto gūkō no gotoku, ue wa ressei no ka o yaburi, shita wa bakufu no gi o gai suru mono. . ." My understanding of this passage differs substantially from that of Harry D. Harootunian, "The Functions of China in Tokugawa Thought," pp. 32-33. Still, I agree with Harootunian that, for Aizawa, Japan represented the true "central kingdom." I believe also that Shinron represents a turning point in the development of the meaning of the term *kokutai*. I have translated it here in the sense in which it was used generally in earlier Japanese diplomatic discourse, as "national prestige," but in fact I think Aizawa is using it in both its traditional meaning and in the sense it was to convey thereafter, that of "Japan's unique national polity." Perhaps Harootunian's decision to leave the term untranslated would have been wisest, but we are here engaged "in the analysis of intellectual ambivalences about the present [at least Aizawa's present] and of the expanding range of conceptual vocabulary that expresses them." (Tetsuo Najita, "Method and Analysis in the

peror ("heavenly court") into the discourse does not alter the fact that his perception of *Japan's* proper locus in the worldly scheme was formed by the mix of Tokugawa diplomacy and Tokugawa period ideology. Aizawa was concerned, after all, not to challenge Edo's monopoly on the conduct of external relations, but to shore it up by reference to the shogun's sources of authority.

If Aizawa referred to the corpus of Tokugawa diplomacy, to the language born of practice, to shore up the dynasty and its claims to supremacy in foreign affairs, Yoshida Shōin, a revolutionary intellectual executed in 1859, turned the same vocabulary against Edo in the 1850s. Shōin's devastating critique of Tokugawa foreign policy was based primarily on his reading of Kondō Morishige's compilation of shogunal diplomatic documents, *Gaiban tsūsho*. Shōin's absolute reverence for the emperor, and his consequent conviction that, "The Way of ancient times does not [admit of] diplomacy by mortal subjects,"[14] disposed him not only to condemn Ashikaga Yoshimitsu's admission of an overseas suzerain, but to charge that conduct of foreign affairs by any bakufu, the Ashikaga or the Tokugawa, was inherently illegitimate. Yet, even for Shōin, the vocabulary to which he referred in pressing his indictment of Edo was that of the language articulated by two and a half centuries of Tokugawa diplomatic dominance.

Thus, while early Tokugawa manipulation of terminology, era names, and the like were, to the bakufu, phrases in a declaration of independence removing Japan from the China-centered frame of reference in international affairs, for Shōin

Conceptual Portrayal of Tokugawa Intellectual History," in Najita and Irwin Scheiner, eds., *Japanese Thought in the Tokugawa Period: Methods and Metaphors* [University of Chicago Press, 1978], p. 8).

[14] Yoshida Shōin, "Gaiban tsūryaku," in *Yoshida Shōin zenshū*, 10 vols. (Iwanami Shoten, 1935), 8:221. For discussions of the life and thought of Yoshida Shōin, see David Margary Earl, *Emperor and Nation in Japan*, pp. 109-210, and Thomas M. Huber, *The Revolutionary Origins of Modern Japan* (Stanford University Press, 1981), pp. 7-91. Earl briefly discusses "Gaiban tsūryaku," pp. 168-169, 197-198.

the failure to specify the Japanese era name in a letter to China was as much an act of *lèse majesté* as the employment of the Chinese era name would have been. Shōin was particularly unforgiving of references in some of the earliest diplomatic correspondence to China as the "Central Civilization" (*Chūka*), but he was hard-pressed to find anything at all redeeming in Tokugawa diplomacy, for, he "reverentially observed," that for Tokugawa Ieyasu to represent himself as the "Lord of the country" of Japan, "and privately to conduct relations with foreign countries, his crime was great from the start."[15] The only thing that Shōin found to affirm in Tokugawa diplomacy was the isolationist policy "praised highly by Kaempfer in the Genroku period," and he wondered why Ieyasu sought to expand relations with the "various barbarians."[16]

But if the diplomatic crimes of Edo, real or imagined, were a "stick to beat the bakufu," they remained accessible only through the vocabulary of a discourse constructed by the very conduct of Tokugawa foreign policy, by its media and its purposes. The discourse of the post-Perry years was the product, not just of the relative isolation of Tokugawa Japan from the European "mainstream" of world affairs for decades, but of the nature, the active content, and the conduct of foreign relations by the Tokugawas for over two and a half centuries. In order to confront the challenge of the Western onslaught in the 1850s, therefore, Edo ordered its chief academician, Hayashi Akira, to compile the diplomatic precedents of Tokugawa rule, even before Perry's arrival. These six-hundred-thirty-one fascicles of reference materials, gathered from shogunal archives and from the archives of several domains, constitute in a real sense the official lexicon of the language that we have labelled "Tokugawa diplomatic."

[15] "Gaiban tsūryaku," 8:226.
[16] *Ibid.*, 1:226.

Abe Masahiro	阿部正弘
Abe Shigetsugu	阿部重次
Abe Tadaaki	阿部忠秋
Akō	赤穂
Amenomori Hōshū	雨森芳洲
Amoy	廈門
Andō Shigenaga	安藤重長
Andō Shigenobu	安藤重信
andojō	安堵状
anka	晏駕
Ansei	安政
Arai Hakuseki	新井白石
Arita Mokubei	在田杢兵衛
Asami Keisai	淺見絅齋
Ashikaga Yoshimitsu	足利義滿
Baba Saburōzaemon	馬場三郎左衛門
bakuhan	幕藩
bakumatsu	幕末
Bakurōchō	馬喰町
buke densō	武家傳奏
bushi	武士
Chekiang	浙江
Ch'en Tzu-chen	陳子貞
Cheng Ch'eng-kung	鄭成功
Cheng Chih-lung	鄭芝龍
Cheng Ching	鄭經
Chikamatsu Monzaemon	近松門左衛門
Ch'ing	清
Ching-chou	荊州
Ch'ing T'ai-tsung	清太宗
Chiyoda	千代田
Cho Hyŏng	趙珩
Cho Ŏm	趙曮
Cho T'aeŏk	趙泰億

chōkō	朝貢
Chŏn Kyesin	全繼信
Chŏng Ip	鄭岦
Chŏng Yun	鄭錀
chŏnha	殿下
Chōsen	朝鮮
Chōsen goyō gakari	朝鮮御用係
Chosŏn	朝鮮
chū	中
Chu Shun-shui	朱舜水
Chūgoku	中國
Chūka	中華
Chungjong	中宗
Chung-yüan	中元
Chūshingura	忠臣藏
Chūzan	中山
Coxinga (Kuo-hsing-yeh)	國姓爺
Daiyūin	大猷院
Date Masamune	伊達政宗
Dazai Shundai	太宰春臺
Denbōrin Kintomi	轉法輪公臣
denka	殿下
Deshima	出島
Doi Toshikatsu	土井利勝
ei'i no zokkoku	裔夷之屬國
Enpekiken zuihitsu	遠碧軒隨筆
Enpō	延寶
Fan Ch'eng-mo	范承謨
feng-shuo	奉朔
Foochow	福州
fudai	譜代
Fujiwara Seika	藤原惺窩
Fuji [wara] Toshitsuna	藤[原]智縄
Fukien	福建
fūsetsugaki	風説書
Fushimi	伏見
Fushiminomiya Sadafusa	伏見宮貞成
Fu-wang	福王
gagaku	雅樂
gakei shisetsu	賀慶使節

Genna	元和
gi	義
Gien	義演
Ginowan	宜野灣
go tairō	五大老
Goeku	越來
Gongen Sama	權現樣
goran	御覽
Gosho	御所
Goyōzei-in	後陽成院
Gozan	五山
gozanoma	御座之間
Gushikawa	具志川
Gyokuhō Kōrin	玉峰光璘
haedapsa	回答使
Hakata	博多
Hamada Yahei	濱田彌兵衛
Han ("Korea;" K. surname)	韓
Han ("China")	漢
Hanegawa Tōei	羽川藤永
hangnye	抗禮
Han-shu	漢書
haori	羽織
Hasegawa Fujihiro	長谷川藤廣
hatamoto	旗本
Hayashi Akira	林煒
Hayashi Eiki	林永喜
Hayashi Fukusai	林復齋
Hayashi Gahō	林鵞峰
Hayashi Razan	林羅山
Hayashi Shihei	林子平
Hikone	彥根
Hikozaka Shigetsugu	彥坂重紹
Hino Sukekatsu	日野資勝
Hitachi	常陸
Hirado	平戶
Hitomi Chikudō	人見竹洞
hō	奉
Hō Ch'ŏk	許積
hō'i	寶位

Hōkōji	豊光寺
Honan	河南
Honda Masanobu	本多正信
Honda Masazumi	本多正純
Honda Toshiaki	本多利明
Hong Ch'ijung	洪致中
Hong Hŭinam	洪喜男
Hong Kyehŭi	洪啓禧
Honseiji	本誓寺
hōsho	奉書
Hōshōin	寶勝院
Hosokawa Mitsunobu	細川光信
Hosokawa Tadatoshi	細川忠利
hōtei	奉呈
Hotta Masayoshi	堀田正睦
hua	華
Huang Cheng-ming	黃徵明
Hyojong	孝宗
i	夷
Ii Naosuke	井伊直弼
Ii Naotaka	井伊直孝
Ikkan	一官
ikoku	異國
Im Kwang	壬絖
"Ima no Nihonjin wa zenkoku o tozashite kokumin o shite koku-chū kokugai ni kagirazu aete iiki no hito to tsūshō sezara-shimuru jijitsu ni shoeki naru ni ataureri ya ina ya no ron"	今の日本人は全國を鎖て國民をして國中國外に限らず敢えて異域の人と通商せざらしむる事實に所益なるに與ふれりや否やの論
imsul	壬戌
inken	引見
Inoue Chikugo no kami Masashige	井上筑後守政重
Ishin Sūden	以心崇傳
Inaba Hikobei	稲葉彦兵衛
Inaba Masanori	稲葉正則
Injo	仁祖
Itakura Katsushige	板倉勝重

Itakura Shigemune	板倉重宗
Itakura Shigenori	板倉重矩
Iteian	以酊庵
iteki	夷狄
jifuku	時服
jin	仁
Jingū	神功
Jinjutsu Ryūkyū haichō ki	壬戌琉球拜朝記
jisha bugyō	寺社奉行
jō'i	攘夷
jōran	上覧
jōyaku	条約
ka	華
Kagoshima	鹿児島
ka'i	華夷
kaibōgakari	海防係
Kamio Motokatsu	神尾元勝
kaikoku	開國
Kaka	華夏
kamikaze	神風
kan	貫
Kan'ei	寛永
Kang Taesu	姜大遂
K'ang-hsi	康熙
Kanghwa	江華
kang-li	抗禮
kangō	勘合
k'an-ho	勘合
kankō	觀光
Kanō Eikei	鹿野永敬
Kanō Tan'yū	鹿野探幽
kanshu	館守
Kanshu nikki	館守日記
kashindan	家臣団
Katō Kiyomasa	加藤清正
Kawaguchi Munetsune	川口宗恒
Keian	慶安
Keichō	慶長
keifuku	啓復

Keitetsu Genso	景徹玄蘇
Keng Ching-chung	耿精忠
Kihaku Genpō	規伯玄方
Kii	紀伊
Kim Igyo	金履喬
Kim Kwang	金光
Kim Sajun	金士俊
Kim T'aehŏ	金太虚
Kimongaku	崎門學
Kin	金武
Kira Yoshinaka	吉良義央
kitaikun	貴大君
kiyu	己酉
Kiyu yakcho	己酉約條
Kiyū yakujō	己酉約條
kō bōeki	公貿易
Kōfu	甲府
kōjutsu	庚戌
kōke	高家
kokkō	国交
koku	石
kokudaka	石高
Kokusenya kassen	國姓爺合戰
kokutai	國體
Konchiin	金地院
kong muyŏk	公貿易
kŏngsin	庚申
Konishi Yukinaga	小西行長
kōrei	抗禮
Koryō	戸令
kuge	公家
Kujō Michifusa	九条道房
Kumamoto	熊本
Kumazawa Banzan	熊澤蕃山
Kunigami	國頭
kunimi	國見
Kunōzan	久能山
Kurokawa Dōyū	黒川道祐
Kuze Hiroyuki	久世弘之
Kwanghaegun	光海君

Kwanghsi	廣西
Kwangtung	廣東
kyech'uk	亥丑
Kyorinji	交隣志
Kyōto *shoshidai*	京都所司代
li	禮
Li Tzu-ch'eng	李自成
Lin Kao	林高
lung-chi	龍集[輯]
Lung-wu	隆武
makeiro ni aimiesōrō	敗色ニ相見ヘ候
Makino Takumi no kami	牧野内匠頭
Manji	萬治
Matsudaira Nobutsuna	松平信綱
Matsudaira Sadanobu	松平定信
Matsumae	松前
Matsuura Takanobu	松浦隆信
Mibu Takasuke	壬生孝亮
Min Yŏnghyŏp	閔應協
Ming	明
Ming-shih	明史
Misato	美里
Mito	水戸
miya	宮
Mizuno Tadaharu	水野忠春
Mukden	奉天
Nabeshima Shinano no kami Katsushige	鍋嶋信濃守勝重
Nagasaki *bugyō*	長崎奉行
Nagasaki *Oranda tsūji*	長崎和蘭陀通詞
Nagasaki *Tō tsūji*	長崎唐通詞
Nago	名護
Naha	那霸
Naidaijin	内大臣
Nakijin	今歸人
Nam Ch'ŏnhan	南天漢
Nanking	南京
Nemuro	根室
nengō	年號
nien-hao	年號

Nihon shōgun sama	日本將軍樣
Nihon-koku Taikun	日本國大君
Nihon no gohatto	日本之御法度
Nijō	二條
Nikkō	日光
Niwa Nagashige	丹羽長重
Nobunaga	信長
norimono	乘物
nyūetsu	入謁
nyūgyo	入御
nyūkō	入貢
ō	王
Ōbiroma	大廣間
O Ŏngnyŏng	吳億齡
O Yun'gyŏm	吳允謙
Odōguchō	御道具帳
Ōei	應永
Ōgimi	大宜見
Ōgosho	大御所
Ogosho samma	大御所樣
Ogyū Sorai	荻生徂徠
Okano Magokurō	岡野孫九郎
Ōkōchi (Matsudaira) Masanobu	大河内(松平)正信
omemie	御目見
ometsuke	御目付
ōmetsuke	大目付
Ōmura Suminobu	大村純信
onrai	恩賚
Ōoka Kiyoshige	大岡清重
Oranda kapitan	阿蘭陀加慜丹
Ōtemon	大手門
Ōuchi	大内
Ou-yang Hsiu	歐陽修
Owari	尾張
Pak Myŏngbu	朴明榑
Pak Taegŭn	朴大根
Pekin no taishō	北京之大將
piao	表
Pibyŏnsa	備邊司
Pimiko	卑彌呼

pong	奉
pongsō	奉書
Pusan	釜山
raichō	來朝
raikō	來貢
rei	禮
Rekidai hōan	歷代寶案
Rinzai	臨濟
rōjū	老中
roku o tori	錄ヲ秉リ
Rokuon'in	鹿苑院
rusuigarō	留守居家老
Ryakunin	曆仁
ryō uesama	兩上樣
Ryūei hinamiki	柳營日並記
Saikaku Genryō	最岳玄良
Saishō Shōtai	西笑承兌
Sakai Tadakatsu	酒井忠勝
Sakai Tadakiyo	酒井忠清
Sakakibara Tsunenao	榊原職直
sakoku	鎖國
sakoku no go-hō	鎖國之御法
Sakoku rei	鎖國令
Sakon-no-shōgen	左近將監
sakuhō	冊封
samsa	三使
Sanbōin	三寶院
sankei	參詣
sankin kōtai	參勤交代
sanshi	三使
Sashiki	佐敷
Satsuma	薩摩
Sekigahara	關原
sesshō	攝政
Settsu-no-kami	攝津守
Shanhaikuan	山海關
Shensi	陜西
Shenyang	瀋陽
shigai	四外
Shih-chi	史記

"Shikaruni aruiwa meigi ni
  kuraku, Min Shin o shōshite
  Kaka Chūka to nashite, motte
  kokutai o ojoku suru mono,
  aruiwa toki o ooi, ikioi ni
  shitagai, mei o midari, gi o
  wasurete, tenchō o miru koto
  gūkō no gotoku, ue wa ressei
  no ka o yaburi, shita wa
  bakufu no gi o gai suru
  mono...."

しかるに或は名義に昧く，明清
を稱して華夏中華となして以て
國體を汚辱するもの或は時を逐
ひ勢に狥ひ名を亂り義を遺れて
天朝を視ること寓公のごとく上
は列聖の化を傷り下は幕府の義
を害するもの

Shimabara	島原
Shimazu Mitsuhisa	嶋津光久
Shimazu Yoshihiro	嶋津義弘
shinjō	進上
shinkoku	神國
shinpai	信牌
Shiroki no shoin	白木の書院
Shizuoka	静岡
Shizuki Tadao	志筑忠夫
Shō Boku	尚穆
Shō Eki	尚益
Shō Hō	尚豊
Shō Iku	尚育
Shō Kei	尚敬
Shō Ken	尚賢
Shō Kō	尚灝
Shō Nei	尚寧
Shō On	尚温
Shō Shitsu	尚質
Shō Tai	尚泰
Shō Tei	尚貞
shōgun	将軍
Shōhō	正保
shōka	升遐
Shokuinryō	職員令
shomotsu bugyō	書物奉行
shoshidai	所司代
shugo	守護
shutsugyo	出御

Sō Yoshikazu	宗義和
Sō Yoshinari	宗義成
Sō Yoshitoshi	宗義智
Sō Yoshizane	宗義眞
soehwansa	刷還使
Soga Matazaemon	曽我又左衛門
sohō	祖法
Son Munik	孫文彧
Song Imun	成以文
Sŏngjong	成宗
Song'un	松雲
Sŏnjo	宣祖
sōshaban	奏者番
Suetsugu Heizō	末次平藏
Sugawara Nagashige	菅原長成
Sugimura Uneme Toshihiro	杉村采女智廣
Suiko	推古
Sukchong	肅宗
Sŭngjŏngjŏn	承政殿
Sunjo	純祖
Sunpu	駿府
Szechuan	四川
Tachibana Muneshige	立花宗茂
Tachibana Tadashige	立花忠茂
Ta-Ch'ing	大清
Taihei	太平
taikun	大君
Taira Toshimasa	平智政
tairō	大老
Takkyō Dōmon	卓教童問
Tamagusuku	玉城
Ta-Ming	大明
Tan Feng-hsiang	單鳳翔
T'ang	唐
T'ang-wang	唐王
Tanuma Okitsugu	田沼意次
tatematsuru	奉
teijō	呈上
Tendai	天台
Tenkai	天海

Tenna	天和
Terasawa Hirotaka	寺澤廣高
Tōfukuji	東福寺
Tōdō Takatora	藤堂高虎
"Tōgatsu yokka no shojō Nagasaki yori raichaku, Fukushū otoseshime ori, Tō-ō narabini Ikkan gi taijō-chū no yoshi chūshin sōrō, shikaru ue wa go-sensaku ni oyobazu sōrō"	當月四日之書狀從長崎來着，福州令落居唐王幷一官儀退城中之由注進候然上は不及御穿鑿候
tōka	投化
Tokugawa Hidetada	德川秀忠
Tokugawa Ieharu	德川家治
Tokugawa Iemitsu	德川家光
Tokugawa Ienari	德川家齊
Tokugawa Ienobu	德川家宣
Tokugawa Ieshige	德川家重
Tokugawa Ietsuna	德川家綱
Tokugawa Ieyasu	德川家康
Tokugawa Mitsukuni	德川光圀
Tokugawa Mitsusada	德川光貞
Tokugawa Nariaki	德川齊昭
Tokugawa Tsunatoyo	德川綱豐
Tokugawa Tsunayoshi	德川綱吉
Tokugawa Yorinobu	德川頼信
Tokugawa Yoshimune	德川吉宗
Tokugawa Yoshinao	德川義直
Tokumatsu	德松
Tomigusuku	豊見城
T'ongmun'gwanji	通文館志
Tongnae	東萊
torii	鳥井
Tōshō Dai Gongen	東照大權現
Tōshōgū	東照宮
Toyotomi Hideyori	豊臣秀頼
Toyotomi Hideyoshi	豊臣秀吉
tozama	外樣
ts'e-feng	冊封
Tsu	津

Tsuchiya Kazunao	土屋數直
Ts'ui Chih	崔芝
Tsushima	對馬
tsūshin	通信
tsūshō	通商
Tung-ning	東寧
Ŭiju	義州
ukiyo-e	浮世繪
ŭlmo	乙卯
Uraga	浦賀
Urasoe	浦添
Wa	倭
Waegwan	倭館
Wakabayashi Kyōsai	若林強齋
Wakan	倭館
Wakayama	和歌山
wakō	倭寇
Wan Shih-te	萬世德
wang	王
Wan-li	萬曆
Wappu dome chō	割符留帳
Wei	魏
Wei-chih	魏志
Wen-chou	溫州
Wen-ti	文帝
Wu San-kuei	吳三桂
Yamaga Sokō	山鹿素行
Yamazaki Ansai	山崎闇齋
Yamazaki Gonpachirō	山崎權八郎
Yanagawa	柳川
Yanagawa Kagenao	柳川景直
Yanagawa Shigenobu	柳川調信
Yanagawa Shigeoki	柳川調興
Yi	李
Yi Hyŏngnam	李享男
Yi Hwang (T'oegye)	李晃(退溪)
Yi Ik	李瀷
Yi Kong	李昖
Yi Kwal	李适
Yi Sun	李焞

Yi Tŏkhyŏng	李德馨
Yŏ Ugil	呂祐吉
Yodogawa	淀川
Yōmei	陽明
Yomitanzan	讀谷山
Yŏn	吶
Yonagusuku	與那城
Yŏngjo	英祖
Yŏngsin	靈慎
Yu Sŏngjŭng	俞省曾
Yu T'aehwa	柳太華
Yu Yŏgak	柳汝恪
"yudan arumajiku sōrō"	油斷有間敷候
Yüan-ho	元和
Yun Chiwan	尹趾完
Yun Sunji	尹順之
Yunnan	雲南

ARCHIVES AND MANUSCRIPT/COLLECTIONS CONSULTED

Daiyūin 大猷院. Rinnōji 輪王寺, Nikko, Tochigi Prefecture, Japan.

Kankoku Kenkyūin 韓国研究院 Collection. Tokyo, Japan.

Kawai Bunko 河合文庫. Kyoto University Library. Kyoto, Japan.

Kōbe Shiritsu Bijutsukan 神戸市立美術館. Kōbe, Japan.

Kokuritsu Kokkai Toshokan 国立国会図書館 (National Diet Library). Tokyo, Japan.

Matsumura Yasutake 松村泰岳 Collection. Izuhara, Tsushima, Nagasaki Prefecture, Japan.

Matsuura Shiryō Hakubutsukan 松浦史料博物館. Hirado, Nagasaki Prefecture, Japan.

Nagasaki Ken Kenritsu Toshokan 長崎県県立図書館. Nagasaki City, Japan.

Naikaku Bunko 内閣文庫. Kokuritsu Kōbunshokan 国立公文書館. Tokyo, Japan.

Nanki Bunko 南葵文庫. Tokyo University Library, Japan.

Nomura [Kanetarō] Hakase Shūzō Monjo 野村[兼太郎]博士蒐蔵文書. Komonjoshitsu 古文書室. Keio University Library. Tokyo, Japan.

Ōsaka Furitsu Daigaku Toshokan 大阪府立大学図書館. Osaka Municipal University, Osaka, Japan.

Seikenji 清見寺 Collection. Okitsu, Shizuoka Prefecture, Japan.

Shiryō Hensanjo 史料編纂所 (Historiographical Institute). Tokyo University. Tokyo, Japan.

Sō-ke Kiroku* 宗家記録. National Diet Library. Tokyo, Japan.

Sō-ke Kiroku* 宗家記録. Keio University Library, Tokyo, Japan.

*These are collections of archival materials left by the Sō family and the Tsushima domain administration, now held in six different archives or collections. They represent remnants of the archives and office files of the Tsushima trading post in Pusan (National Diet Library), of the domain offices in Edo (Keio and Tokyo Universities), and the domain capital of Fuchū, the former name of Izuhara (Kenritsu Shiryōkan, Banshōin, and National History Compilation Committee). For convenience, all have been referred to as "Sō Archives," or "Sō Collection" in the notes. Tashiro Kazui, *Kinsei Nitchō tsūkō bōeki shi no kenkyū*, pp. 17–27, gives a more thorough history of these archives and their current status.

Sō-ke Shiryō* 宗家史料. Historiographical Institute, Tokyo University. Tokyo, Japan.

Sō-shi Bunko*† 宗氏文庫. Banshōin 萬松院. Izuhara, Tsushima, Nagasaki Prefecture, Japan.

Sō-ke Bunko*† 宗家文庫. Kenritsu Tsushima Rekishi Minzoku Shiryōkan 県立対馬歴史民族資料館. Izuhara, Tsushima, Nagasaki Prefecture, Japan.

Spencer Collection. New York Public Library. New York, New York.

Suminokura 角倉 Collection. Kyōto Shishi Hensansho 京都市央編さん所 Kyoto, Japan.

Taemado Munsō* 對馬島文書. Kuksa Pyŏnch'an Wiwŏnhoe 國史編纂委員會 (National History Compilation Committee). Seoul, Korea.

Tōshōgū 東照宮 Collection. Nikko, Tochigi Prefecture, Japan.

Unryūji 雲龍寺 Collection. Tomita, Tochigi Prefacture, Japan.

---

† These archives are part of the same collection, which is gradually being transferred from its old quarters in the Sō family temple, Banshōin, to a new, climate-controlled archive in the Kenritsu Tsushima Rekishi Minzoku Shiryōkan (Prefectural Archives for the History and Folklore of Tsushima) recently constructed in Izuhara. Citations give the location of documents as of August 1980, wherever possible. Those cited as "Banshōin" were in the temple storehouse as of the date consulted. Eventually all materials will be in the new collection. All logbooks have been transferred, and are catalogued in *Sōke Bunko shiryō mokuroku (nikkirui)*, comp. Sō-ke Bunko Chōsa Iinkai, (Izuhara: Izuhara-chō Kyōiku Iinkai, 1978).

Abe Yoshio 阿部吉雄. *Nihon Shushigaku to Chōsen* 日本朱子学と朝鮮. Tōkyō Daigaku Shuppankai 東京大學出版會, 1965.

Aimé-Martin, de M. L., comp. *Lettres Édifiantes et Curieuses, concernant l'Asie, l'Afrique, et l'Amérique.* 18 vols. Paris: Société du Panthéon Litteraire, 1863.

Aizawa Seishisai 会沢正志斎. *Shinron* 新論. in Imai Usaburō 今井宇三郎, *et al.*, ed., *Mitogaku* 水戸学. Iwanami Shoten 岩波書店, 1973. (*Nihon Shisō Taikei* 日本思想大系, vol. 53).

Arai Hakuseki zenshū 新井白石全集. 6 vols. Kokusho Kankōkai 國書刊行會, 1905–1907.

Arano Yasunori 荒野泰典, "Bakuhansei kokka to gaikō-Tsushima han o sozai to shite" 幕藩制国家と外交一対馬藩を素材として, in *1978 nendo Rekishigaku Kenkyūkai Taikai hōkoku* 1978年度歴史学研究会大会報告 (*Rekishigaku kenkyū, beppen* 別編), (November 1978), pp. 95–105.

———. "Chōsen tsūshinshi no shūmatsu—Shin Ikan 'Kaiyūroku' ni yosete" 朝鮮通信使の終末一申維翰「海游録」によせて, in *Rekishi hyōron* 歴史評論, no. 355 (November 1979), pp. 63–74.

Asahi shinbun 朝日新聞, 23 November 1980.

Asami Keisai 浅見絅斎, "Chūgoku ben" 中国辨, in *Yamazaki Ansai gakuha* 山崎闇齋学派. Comp. Nishi Junzō 西順蔵, Abe Kōichi 阿部隆一, Maruyama Masao 丸山真男. *Nihon Shisō Taikei*, vol. 31. Iwanami Shoten, 1980. pp. 416–419.

Asao Naohiro 朝尾直弘. *Sakoku* 鎖国. Shōgakkan 小学館, 1975.

———, "Sakoku," in *Kōza Nihon rekishi* 講座日本歴史, 10 vols., Tōkyō Daigaku Shuppankai 東京大学出版会, 1969–1970. 4:59–94.

———, "Shogun and Tennō," in *Japan before Tokugawa*, ed. John W. Hall, et al., pp. 248–270.

———, "Shōgun kenryoku no sōshutsu" 将軍権力の創出, in *Rekishi hyōron* 歴史評論, nos. 241, 266, 293 (1970–1974).

———, "Shōgun seiji no kenryoku kōzō," 将軍政治の権力構造, in *Iwanami kōza Nihon rekishi* 岩波講座日本歴史. 26 vols., Iwanami Shoten, 1975–1977, 10:1–56.

Aston, W. G., tr. *Nihongi*. London: George Allen & Unwin, Ltd., 1956.

Atobe Kōkai 跡部光海. *Nakatsukuni no setsu* (or *Chūgoku no setsu*) 中國之説. MS copy, signed Gūji Munetsugu 宮司宗次, dated Meiwa 明和 1/8/*gejun* (1764/9/16–25). Collection, Ōsaka Furitsu Daigaku Toshokan 大阪府立大学図書館.

Banzan zenshū 蕃山全集. 6 vols., Banzan Zenshū Kankōkai 蕃山全集刊行會, 1940–1943.

Bateson, Gregory. *Steps to an Ecology of Mind.* New York: Ballantine Books, 1972.

Beasley, W. G. *The Modern History of Japan.* New York: Frederick A. Praeger, Inc., Publishers, 1963.

———. *Select Documents on Japanese Foreign Policy, 1853–1868.* New York and London: Oxford University Press, 1955.

Bitō Masahide 尾藤正英, "Sonnō jōi shisō" 尊王攘夷思想, in *Iwanami kōza Nihon rekishi*, 13 (1977), pp. 41–86.

———, "Yamaga Sokō no shisōteki tenkai" 山鹿素行の思想的転回, pt. 1, *Shisō* 思想 no. 560 (February 1971), pp. 22–37; pt. 2, *Shisō*, no. 561 (March 1971), pp. 82–97.

Blussé, Leonard, "Japanese Historiography and European Sources," in *Reappraisals in Overseas History*, ed. P. C. Emmer and H. L. Wesseling. Leyden University Press, 1979, by Martinus Nijhoff Publishers, pp. 193–221.

Bolitho, Harold. *Treasures among Men: The Fudai Daimyo in Tokugawa Japan.* New Haven: Yale University Press, 1974.

Bouwsma, William J., "From History of Ideas to History of Meaning," in *Journal of Interdisciplinary History*, XII:2 (Autumn 1981), pp. 279–291.

Boxer, C. R. *The Christian Century in Japan, 1549–1650.* Berkeley and Los Angeles: University of California Press, 1951.

———. *Jan Compagnie in Japan.* 2nd rev. ed., The Hague: Martinus Nijhoff, 1950; reprinted, Tokyo: Oxford University Press, 1968.

———, "The Rise and Fall of Nicholas Iquan," in *T'ien Hsia Monthly*, vol. XI, No. 5 (April–May, 1941), pp. 401–439.

Brunnert, H. S., and Hagelstrom, V. V. *Present Day Political Organization of China.* rev. ed., tr. A. Beltchenko and E. E. Moran. n.p.d.

Chang Ts'un-wu 張存武. *Ch'ing-Han tsung-fan mao-i 1637–1894* 清韓宗藩貿易. Taipei: Chung-ying Yen-chiu-yuan Chin-tai-shih Yen-chiu-so 中央研究院近代史研究所, 1978.

Chen, Ta-tuan, "Investiture of Liu-ch'iu Kings in the Ch'ing Period," in Fairbank, ed., *The Chinese World Order*, pp. 135–164.

Chōsen ōfuku sho 朝鮮往復書. MS, 72 volumes, 1645–1870. Sō Collection,

Keio University Library. The copy of *Honpō Chōsen ōfuku sho*, q.v., kept in the Tsushima office in Edo.

Chōsen shinshi raichō kihan kanroku 朝鮮信使来朝帰帆官録. ed., Ishizaka Kōjirō 石阪孝二郎. Kobe: Hyōgo Okagata Komonjo Kankō Iin 兵庫岡方古文書刊行委員, 1969.

Chōsen tsūkō taiki 朝鮮通交大紀. comp. Matsuura Masatada 松浦允任. MS, 10 *kan* 巻. Sō Archives, Banshōin, Izuhara, Tsushima.

Chōsen tsūkō taiki. ed. Tanaka Takeo and Tashiro Kazui. Meicho Shuppan, 1978.

Chōsenjin raihei gyōretsu tsuketari 朝鮮人來聘行列附 Woodblock printed scroll, n.d. Collection Kankoku Kenkyūin, 韓国研究院 Tokyo.

Chōsenjin raichō ni tsuki muramura atemono kakiage chō 朝鮮人來朝二付村々宛物書上帳. MS, 1710. Collection of the author.

Chōsenshi 朝鮮史. 36 vols. and index. Keijo: Chōsen Sōtokufu 朝鮮總督府, 1933.

Choson wangjo sillok 朝鮮王朝實録. 48 vols. + index. Seoul: Kuksa P'yŏnch'an Wiwŏnhoe 國史編纂委員會, 1955–1963.

Chun, Hae-jong, "Sino-Korean Tributary Relations in the Ch'ing Period," in Fairbank, ed., *The Chinese World Order*, pp. 90–111.

Chŭngjŏng kyorinji 增正交隣志. Seoul: Asea Munhwasa 亞細亞文化社, 1974.

Cocks, Richard. *Diary Kept by the Head of the English Factory in Japan: Diary of Richard Cocks, 1615–1622*. 3 vols., published under the title *Igirisu Shōkanchō nikki, Genbun-hen* イギリス商館長日記, 原文編, in the series *Nihon kankei kaigai shiryō* 日本關係海外史料, of the Historiographical Institute, University of Tokyo. Tōkyō Daigaku Shuppankai 東京大學出版會, 1978–1980.

———. *Diary of Richard Cocks, Cape Merchant in the English Factory in Japan, 1615–1622*. 2 vols., ed. N. Murakami. Tokyo: Sankosha, 1899.

Dai Nihon kinsei shiryō, Hosokawa-ke shiryō 大日本近世史料, 細川家史料. 7 vols. to date. Tōkyō Daigaku Shuppankai, 1969–

Dai Nihon komonjo bakumatsu gaikoku kankei monjo 大日本古文書幕末外國關係文書. 44 vols. Shiryō Hensanjo 史料編纂所, 1910–

Dai Nihon komonjo iewake dai jūroku Shimazu ke monjo 大日本古文書家わけ第十六嶋津家文書. 3 vols., Tōkyō Teikoku Daigaku 東京帝國大學, 1942–1966.

Dai Nihon komonjo iewake dai ni Asano ke monjo 大日本古文書家わけ第二淺野家文書. Tōkyō Teikoku Daigaku, 1906.

Dai Nihon shiryō 大日本史料. comp., Shiryō Hensanjo. 293 vols., Shiryō Hensanjo, 1901–

Dennerline, Jerry, "Hsü Tu and the Lessons of Nanking: Political Integration and Local Defense in Chiangnan, 1634–1645," in Spence and Wills, ed. *From Ming to Ch'ing*, pp. 89–132.

Deuchler, Martina. *Confucian Gentlemen and Barbarian Envoys: The Opening of Korea, 1875–1885*. Seattle and London: The University of Washington Press, 1977.

Dokai kōshū ki 土芥冠雠記. ed. Kanai Madoka 金井圓. Jinbutsu Ōrai Sha 人物往来社, 1967.

Dolgin, Janet L., David S. Kemnitzer, and David M. Schneider, "Introduction: 'As People Express Their Lives, So They Are ...,'" in Dolgin, Kemnitzer, and Schneider, ed., *Symbolic Anthropology: A Reader in the Study of Symbolic Action*. New York: Columbia University Press, 1977.

Dulles, Allen. *The Craft of Intelligence*. New York: Harper & Row, Publishers, 1963.

Duus, Peter. *Feudalism in Japan*. New York: Alfred A. Knopf, 1969.

Earl, David Margarey. *Emperor and Nation in Japan, Political Thinkers of the Tokugawa Period*. Seattle: University of Washington Press, 1964.

Edo jidai no Chōsen tsūshinshi 江戸時代の朝鮮通信使. comp. Eizō Bunka Kyōkai 映像文化協会. Mainichi Shinbunsha 毎日新聞社, 1979.

Edo zu byōbu 江戸図屏風. ed. Suzuki Susumu 鈴木進. Heibonsha 平凡社, 1971.

Einstein, Albert. *Mein Weldbild*. Amsterdam: Auflage Erstdruck, 1934, repr. Frankfurt/M: Ullstein Materialen, 1979.

———. *The World as I See It*. New York: Covici, Friede, Publishers, 1934.

Elison, George. *Deus Destroyed, The Image of Christianity in Early Modern Japan*. Cambridge, Mass.: Harvard University Press, 1973.

Engel, Mark, "Preface," in Gregory Bateson, *Steps to an Ecology of Mind*, New York: Ballantine Books, 1972, pp. vii–viii.

Fairbank, John K., "A Preliminary Framework," in Fairbank, ed., *The Chinese World Order*, pp. 1–19.

———, ed. *The Chinese World Order*. Cambridge, Mass.: Harvard University Press, 1968.

Fang, Chao-ying "A Technique for Estimating the Numerical Strength of the Early Manchu Forces," in *Harvard Journal of Asiatic Studies*, vol. XIII (June 1950), pp. 192–215.

Farmer, Edward L. *Early Ming Government: The Evolution of Dual Capitals*. Cambridge, Massachusetts: Harvard University Press, 1976.

Findley, Carter V., "The Foundations of the Ottoman Foreign Ministry: The Beginnings of Bureaucratic Reform under Selim III and

Maḥmud II," in *International Journal of Middle Eastern Studies*, vol. 3, no. 4 (October 1972), pp. 388–416.

Fujiki Hisashi, "The Political Posture of Ōda Nobunaga," in *Japan before Tokugawa*, ed., John W. Hall, et. al., pp. 149–193.

Fujino Tamotsu 藤野保. *Bakusei to hansei* 幕政と藩政. Yoshikawa Kōbunkan 吉川弘文館, 1979.

———. *Kaitei zōho bakuhan taiseishi no kenkyū* 改訂増補幕藩体制史 の研究. Yoshikawa Kōbunkan, 1976.

Fujiwara Seika shū 藤原惺窩集. 2 vols. Kokumin Seishin Bunka Kenkyūjo 國民精神文化研究所, 1938–1939.

Fushiminomiya Sadafusa Shinnō 伏見宮貞成親王. *Kanmon gyoki* 看聞 御記. in *Zoku gunsho ruijū hoi* 續群書類從補遺, vol. 2, parts 1, 2. rev. ed. Zoku Gunsho Ruijū Kanseikai 續群書類從完成會, 1958–1959.

Goffman, Erving. *Interaction Ritual: Essays in Face-to-Face Behavior*. Chicago: Aldine Publishing Company, 1967.

Goodrich, L. Carrington, ed., and Ryusaku Tsunoda. tr. *Japan in the Chinese Dynastic Histories, Later Han through Ming*. Pasadena: Perkins Oriental Books, 1968.

Goody, Jack, "Introduction," in Goody, ed., *Succession to High Office* (*Cambridge Papers in Social Anthropology*, no. 4). Cambridge, England: Cambridge University Press, 1966, pp. 1–56.

Grossberg, Kenneth A., "From Feudal Chieftan to Secular Monarch: The Development of Shogunal Power in Early Muromachi Japan," in *Monumenta Nipponica*, vol. XXXI, no. 1 (Spring 1976), pp. 29–49.

Haboush, JaHyun Kim, "A Heritage of Kings: One Man's Monarchy in the Confucian World," Unpublished Ph.D. dissertation, Columbia University, 1978.

Hall, John Whitney. *Government and Local Power in Japan, 500 to 700. A Study Based on Bizen Province*. Princeton: Princeton University Press, 1966.

———, "Hideyoshi's Domestic Policies," in *Japan before Tokugawa*, pp. 194–223.

———. "Notes on the Early Ch'ing Copper Trade with Japan," in *Harvard Journal of Asiatic Studies*, vol. XII, nos. 3–4 (December 1949), pp. 444–461.

———. *Tanuma Okitsugu (1719–1788): Forerunner of Modern Japan*. Cambridge, Mass.: Harvard University Press, 1955.

———. "Tokugawa Japan: 1800–1853," in James B. Crowley, ed., *Modern East Asia: Essays in Interpretation*. New York: Harcourt, Brace & World, Inc., 1970, pp. 62–94.

————, Nagahara Keiji, and Kozo Yamamura, eds., *Japan before Tokugawa: Political Consolidation and Economic Growth, 1500 to 1650*. Princeton: Princeton University Press, 1981.

Harootunian, Harry D., "The Functions of China in Tokugawa Thought," in *The Chinese and the Japanese: Essays in Political and Cultural Interactions*, ed. Akira Iriye. Princeton: Princeton University Press, 1980, pp. 9–36.

Hayashi Akira 林煒. *Tsūkō ichiran* 通航一覧. 8 vols., Kokusho Kankōkai 國書刊行會, 1913; reprint, Osaka: Seibundō Shuppan, 清文堂出版, 1967.

Hayashi Gahō 林鵞峯. *Gahō Sensei Hayashi Gakushi bunshū* 鵞峯先生林學士文集. Contents, prefaces 1 and 2, plus 120 kan, in 51 fascicles; prefaces dated 1689.

———— and Hayashi Hōkō 林鳳岡, comp. *Ka'i hentai* 華夷變態. 3 vols., Tōyō Bunko 東洋文庫, 1958.

Hayashi Nobuatsu 林信篤. *Kan'ei shōsetsu* 寛永小説, in *Zoku shiseki shūran* 續史籍集覽. 10 vols. Kondō Shuppanbu 近藤出版部, 1930, vol. 6.

Hayashi Razan 林羅山. *Hayashi Razan bunshū* 林羅山文集. Osaka: Kōbunsha 弘文社, 1930.

Hayashi Sukekatsu 林亮勝, "Dai sandai Tokugawa Iemitsu" 第三代德川家光, in *Tokugawa shōgun retsuden* 德川将軍列伝. ed., Kitajima Masamoto 北島正元. Akita Shoten 秋田書店, 1974, pp. 88–127.

Henthorn, William. *A History of Korea*. New York: The Free Press, 1971.

Hibbett, Howard. *The Floating World in Japanese Fiction*. Rutland, Vermont & Tokyo, Japan: Charles E. Tuttle Company, 1975.

Hirano Kunio 平野邦雄, "Yamato ōken to Chōsen" ヤマト王権と朝鮮, in *Iwanami kōza Nihon rekishi*, vol. 1 (1975), pp. 227–272.

Hitomi Chikudō 人見竹洞. *Chikudō zenshū* 竹洞全集. 3 vols., abridged MS copy, collection Historiographical Institute, Tokyo University.

Hiyōroku, Kōtoku ben, Han hiroku 丕揚録, 公德辨, 藩秘録. ed. Kitajima Masamoto, Murakami Tadashi, Kanai Madoka 北島正元, 村上直, 金井圓. Kondō Shuppansha 近藤出版社, 1971.

"Hō Chōrō Chōsen monogatari tsuketari Yanagawa shimatsu" 方長老朝鮮物語附柳川始末, in *Shintei zōho Shiseki shūran* 新訂增補史籍集覽. 41 vols. Kyoto: Rinsen Shoten 臨川書店, 1967, vol. 28.

Hofstadter, Douglas R. *Gödel, Escher, Bach: An Eternal Golden Braid*. New York: Basic Books, 1979.

Honda Tadakatsu 本多忠勝, "Honda Heihachirō kikigaki" 本多平八郎聞書, in Naramoto Tatsuya 奈良本辰也, ed., *Kinsei seidō ron* 近世

政道論. (*Nihon shisō taikei*, v. 38). Iwanami Shoten, 1976, pp. 22–29.

Hong Ujae 洪禹載. *Tongsarok* 東槎録, in *Kaikō sōsai*, 4:1–67.

Honjo, Eijiro. *Economic Theory and History of Japan in the Tokugawa Period.* New York: Russell & Russell, Inc., 1965.

Honpō Chōsen ōfukusho 本邦朝鮮往復書. Compiled by the resident monks of the Iteian hermitage, MS copy, 120 vols., collection Historiographical Institute, Tokyo University. Originals in Sō Collection, National History Compilation Committee, Seoul.

Hori, Kyotsu, "The Economic and Political Effects of the Mongol Wars," in John W. Hall and Jeffrey P. Mass, eds., *Medieval Japan, Essays in Institutional History*. New Haven: Yale University Press, 1974, pp. 184–198.

———, "The Mongol Invasions and the Kamakura Bakufu." Unpublished Ph.D. dissertation, Columbia University, 1967.

Hsü, Immanuel C. Y. *The Rise of Modern China*. New York: Oxford University Press, 1970.

Huber, Thomas M. *The Revolutionary Origins of Modern Japan*. Stanford: Stanford University Press, 1981.

Hummel, Arthur W. *Eminent Chinese of the Ch'ing Period (1644–1912)*. Washington, D.C.: United States Government Printing Office, 1943; reprint, Taipei: Ch'eng Wen Publishing Company, 1975.

Hwang Ch'up'o 黄秋浦. *Tongsarok: Mallyōk pyōngsin chutung t'ongsinsa ilhaeng Ilbon wanghwan illok* 東槎録萬暦丙申通信使一行日本往還日録. MS, 1596, in Kawai Bunko 河合文庫, Kyoto University Library.

Hwang Ho 黄㞍. *Tongsarok* 東槎録, in *Kaikō sōsai*, 3:49–115.

Hyojong taewang sillok 孝宗大王實録. 28 kwŏn, in *Chosŏn wangjo sillok*, vols. 36–37.

Ikoku ōfuku shokan shū/Zōtei Ikoku nikki shō 異國往復書翰集・増訂異國日記抄. *Ikoku sōsho* 異國叢書, vol. 11. Komiyama Shoten 小宮山書店, 1966.

Im Kwang 任絖. *Pyŏngja Ilbon ilgi* 丙子日本日記, in *Kaikō sōsai*, 2:312–382.

Inaba Iwakichi 稲葉岩吉. *Shina kinseishi kōwa* 支那近世史講話. Nihon Hyōronsha 日本評論社, 1938.

———. *Kōkaikun jidai no Mansen kankei* 光海君時代の滿鮮關係. Keijo: Ōsakayagō Shoten 大阪屋號書店, 1933.

Injo cho sillok 仁祖朝實録. 50 kwŏn, in *Chosŏn wangjo sillok*, vols. 33–35.

Inobe Shigeo 井野邊茂雄. *Ishin zenshi no kenkyū* 維新前史の研究. Chūbunkan Shoten 中文館書店, 1935.

Inoue Mitsusada, "The *Ritsuryō* System in Japan," in *Acta Asiatica*, no. 31 (1977), pp. 83-112.

Irie Keishirō 入江啓四郎, "Nigen teki genshusei to Meiji ishin" 二元的 元首制と明治維新, in *Nihon gaikōshi kenkyū* 日本外交史研究 (Fall 1957), pp. 22-39.

Ishihara Michihiro 石原道博, "Chōsen gawa yori mita Minmatsu no Nihon kisshi ni tsuite" 朝鮮側よりみた明末の日本乞師につ いて, in *Chōsen gakuhō*, 4 (March 1953): 117-130.

Ishihara Michihiro 石原道博. *Minmatsu Shinsho Nihon kisshi no kenkyū* 明末清初日本乞師の研究. Fuzanbō 富山房, 1945.

Ishii Ryōsuke 石井良助, ed. *Go-tōke reijō; ritsuryō yōryaku* 御當家令條 ・律令要略. Sōbunsha 創文社, 1959. (*Kinsei hōsei shiryō sōsho* 近世 法制史料叢書, vol. 2).

———, ed. *Tokugawa kinrei kō zenshū* 徳川禁令考前集. 6 vols. Sōbunsha, 1959.

Ishimoda Shō 石母田正, "Nihon kodai ni okeru kokusai ishiki ni tsuite: kodai kizoku no baai" 日本古代における国際意識について― 古代貴族の場合, in *Shisō* 思想, no. 454 (April 1962), pp. 2-9.

Ishin shiryō kōhon 維新史料稿本. MS, Collection Historiographical Institute, Tokyo University.

Ishin Sūden 以心崇傳. *Honkō kokushi nikki* 本光國師日記. 7 vols., Zoku Gunsho Ruijū Kanseikai 續群書類従完成会, 1970.

———. *Ikoku goshuin chō* 異國御朱印帳. MS copy, collection Historiographical Institute, Tokyo University.

———. *Ikoku nikki* 異國日記. 4 vols., MS copy, collection Historiographical Institute, Tokyo University.

Itazawa Takeo 板澤武雄. *Mukashi no nanyō to Nihon* 昔の南洋と日本. Nihon Hōsō Shuppan Kyōkai 日本放送出版協會, 1940.

———. *Nihon to Oranda* 日本とオランダ. Shibundō, 1955.

———. *Oranda fūsetsugaki no kenkyū* 阿蘭陀風説書の研究. Yoshikawa Kōbunkan, 1974. (reprint of Nihon Kobunka Kenkyūsho 日本 古文化研究所 ed., 1937).

Itō Tasaburō 伊東多三郎, "Edo bakufu no seiritsu to buke seijikan" 江戸幕府の成立と武家政治觀, in *Rekishigaku kenkyū* 歴史學 研究, 131 (Jan. 1948): 1-10; 132 (March 1948): 29-44.

———, "Shugō mondai to shōgun ken'i" 殊号問題と将軍権威; in *Nihon rekishi* 日本歴史, 67 (December 1953): 2-13.

Iwao, Seiichi, "Li Tan 李旦, Chief of the Chinese Residents at Hirado, Japan in the Last Days of the Ming Dynasty," in *Memoirs of the Research Department of the Toyo Bunko*, no. 17, 1958. pp. 27-83.

————. "Reopening of the Diplomatic Relations Between Japan and Siam During Tokugawa Days," in *Acta Asiatica*, 4 (1963): 1–31.

———— 岩生成一. *Sakoku* 鎖国. Chūō Kōronsha 中央公論社, 1966.

————. *Shuinsen bōeki shi no kenkyū* 朱印船貿易史の研究. Kōbundō 弘文堂, 1958.

Jansen, Marius B. *Japan and Its World*. Princeton: Princeton University Press, 1980.

Japan before Tokugawa: Political Consolidation and Economic Growth, 1500 to 1650. ed. John W. Hall, et al. Princeton: Princeton University Press, 1981.

Japan in the Muromachi Age. ed. John Whitney Hall and Toyoda Takeshi. Berkeley: University of California Press, 1977.

Jinmei daijiten 人名大辞典. 10 vols. Heibonsha 平凡社, 1953–1955.

Jinnō shōtōki, Masukagami 神皇正統記, 増鏡. ed. Iwasa Tadashi 岩佐正, Tokie Akinori 時枝誠記, Kidō Saizō 木藤才藏. Iwanami Shoten, 1965. (*Nihon Koten Bungaku Taikei*. 日本古典文学大系, vol. 87).

Jippensha Ikku (text) 十返舎一九 and Kitagawa Utamaro (illustrations) 喜多川歌麿. *Chōsenjin raichō gyōretsu ki* 朝鮮人來朝行列記. Edo 江戸: Nishimuraya Genroku 西村屋源六, and Ōmachi (Tsushima) 大町 (對州): Mikiya Kizaemon 三木屋喜左衛門, 1811. Photographically reproduced as front matter in *Chōsen shinshi raichō kihanroku*, q.v.

Jonas, Manfred. *Isolationism in America, 1935–1941*. Ithaca: Cornell University Press, 1966.

Jūkyūkō jitsuroku; Sōshi kafu 十九公実録宗氏家譜. ed. Suzuki Shōzō 鈴木棠三. *Tsushima sōsho* 對馬叢書, vol. 3. Murata Shoten 村田書店, 1974.

Kaempfer, Engelbert. *Geschichte und Beschreibung von Japan*. 2 vols. Stuttgart: F.A. Brockhaus, 1964.

————. *The History of Japan Together with a Description of the Kingdom of Siam, 1690–92*. tr. J. G. Scheuchzer. 3 vols. Glasgow: James MacLehose and Sons, 1906.

————. *Kenperu Edo sanpu kikō* ケンペル江戸参府紀行. tr. from Kaempfer, *Geshcichte und Beschreibung von Japan*, by Kure Shūzō 呉秀三. 2 vols. *Ikoku sōsho* 異國叢書, vols. 7, 8. Yūshōdō 雄松堂, 1928, 1929; reprint, 1966.

Kagoshima kenshi 鹿児島縣史. 5 vols. Kagoshima: Kagoshima Ken, 1940–1943.

Kagoshima kenshiryō Kyūki zatsuroku tsuiki 鹿児島縣史料旧記雑録追記. Comp., Kagoshima Ken Ishin Shiryō Hensanjo 鹿児県維新史料編纂所. Kagoshima: Kagoshima Ken, 1971.

Kaikō sōsai 海行惣載. 4 vols. Keijo: Chōsen Kosho Kankōkai 朝鮮古書刊行會, 1914.

Kanda Nobuo 神田信夫. *Heizei Ō Go Sankei no kenkyū* 平西王呉三桂の研究. Meiji Daigaku 明治大学, 1952.

————, "Sanpan no ran to Chōsen" 三藩の亂と朝鮮, in *Shundai shigaku* 駿臺史學, 1 (March 1951): 60–75.

Kan'ei jūsan heishi nen Chōsen shinshi kiroku 寛永十三丙子年朝鮮信使記録. 3 vols. MS copy, collection Historiographical Institute, Tokyo University.

"Kan'ei 6 nen 'go-jōkyō no toki mainikki'" 寛永6年「御上京の時毎日記」, ed. Tashiro Kazui 田代和生, in *Chōsen gakuhō* 朝鮮学報, 95 (April 1980), pp. 73–116.

Kan'ei Shōhō no tabi Yaso shūmon go-genkin ni tsuki Chōsen-koku go-ōfuku go-shokan utsushi. 寛永正保之度邪蘇宗門御嚴禁ニ付朝鮮國御往復書翰寫. Sō Collection, Historiographical Institute, Tokyo University.

Kanezashi Shōzō 金指正三. *Kinsei kainan kyūjo seido no kenkyū* 近世海灘救助制度の研究. Yoshikawa Kōbunkan, 1968.

Kang Chae'ŏn 姜在彦. *Chōsen kindai shi kenkyū* 朝鮮近代史研究. Nihon Hyōron Sha 日本評論社, 1970.

————. *Kindai Chōsen no henkaku shisō* 近代朝鮮の変革思想. Nihon Hyōron Sha, 1973.

Kang Hongjung 姜弘重. *Tongsarok* 東槎録, in *Kaikō sōsai*, 2:205–311.

Kanō Eikei 狩野永敬. *Chōsenjin gyōretsu zu* 朝鮮人行列圖. Spencer Collection, New York Public Library.

Kansei chōshū shokafu 寛政重修諸家譜. 22 vols. and 4 index vols. Zoku Gunsho Ruijū Kanseikai 続群書類従完成会, 1964–1968.

Kanshu nikki 館守日記, or *Mainikki* 毎日記. (logbooks of the overseers of the Tsushima trading factory in Pusan). MS, 860 vols. 1687–1870. Sō Collection, National Diet Library, Tokyo.

Kansō dokugen 閑窓獨言. Variously attributed to Suyama Totsuan 陶山訥庵, Nakagawa Nobuyoshi 中川延良, and Kotō Bun'an 古藤文庵. *Tsushima Sōsho*, vol. 6. Murata Shoten, 1979.

Katagiri Kazuo 片桐一男. "Sakoku jidai ni motarasareta kaigai jōhō" 鎖国時代にもたらされた海外情報, in *Nihon rekishi*, 249 (February 1969): 83–98.

Katō Hidetoshi, "The Significance of the Period of National Seclusion Reconsidered," in *Journal of Japanese Studies*, vol. 7, no. 1 (Winter 1981), pp. 85–109.

Katsumata Shizuo, "The Development of Sengoku Law," in *Japan before Tokugawa*, ed. John W. Hall, et al., pp. 101–124.

Kawashima Masao 川嶋将生, "Sakokugo no shuinsen bōeki-ka" 鎖国後の朱印船貿易家, in *Kyōto Shishi Hensansho tsūshin* 京都市史編さん所通信, no. 143 (April 1981), pp. 1-2.

Keene, Donald. *The Battles of Coxinga*. London: Taylor's Foreign Press, 1951.

————. *The Japanese Discovery of Europe, 1720-1830*. Revised edition. Stanford: Stanford University Press, 1969.

Kerr, George H. *Okinawa, the History of an Island People*. Tokyo: Charles E. Tuttle Company, 1958.

Kessler, Lawrence D. *K'ang-hsi and the Consolidation of Ch'ing Rule, 1661-1684*. Chicago: University of Chicago Press, 1976.

Kim, Key-Hiuk. *The Last Phase of the East Asian World Order: Korea, Japan, and the Chinese Empire, 1860-1882*. Berkeley: University of California Press, 1980.

Kim Seryŏn 金世濂. *Sasangnok* 槎上録, in *Kaikō sōsai*, 2:383-494.

Kimiya Yasuhiko 木宮泰彦. *Nisshi kōtsūshi* 日支交通史. 2 vols., Kinshi Hōryūdō 金刺芳流堂, 1926-1928.

Kitajima Masamoto 北島正元. *Edo bakufu no kenryoku kōzō* 江戸幕府の権力構造. Iwanami Shoten, 1964.

Kobayashi Shigeru 小林茂, "Tokugawa jidai ni okeru Chōsen tsūshinshi no sukegō mondai—Yodo han o chūshin to shite" 徳川時代における朝鮮通信使の助郷問題―淀藩を中心として in *Chōsen gakuhō* 朝鮮学報, 43 (1967): 49-82.

Kōbe Shiritsu Nanban Bijutsukan zuroku 神戸市立南蛮美術館図録. ed., Kōbe Shiritsu Nanban Bijutsukan Zuroku Hensan Iinkai 編纂委員会. 5 vols. Kobe: Kōbe Shiritsu Nanban Bijutsukan, 1968-1972.

Kobori Keiichi 小堀桂一. *Sakoku no shisō* 鎖国の思想. Chūō Kōron Sha, 1974.

Kōda Shigetomo chosakushū 幸田成友著作集. 7 vols. + index. Chūō Kōron Sha, 1971-1974.

Koji ruien 古事類苑. 56 vols., Yoshikawa Kōbunkan, 1969.

Kokusho sōmokuroku 国書総目録. 8 vols. + index, Iwanami Shoten, 1963-76.

Kondō Morishige 近藤守重. *Gaiban tsūsho* 外藩通書, in *Kondō Seisai zenshū*, 近藤正齋全集, 3 vols. Kokusho Kankōkai 國書刊行會, 1906. vol. 3, separate pagination. Also in *Kaitei shiseki shūran* 改訂史籍集覧, 33 vols., Sumiya Shobō すみや書房, 1968, 21:191-454.

Konishi Shiro 小西四郎. *Kaikoku to jōi* 開国と攘夷. Chūō Kōron Sha, 1966.

Korr, Charles P. *Cromwell and the New Model Foreign Policy*. Berkeley: University of California Press, 1975.

Kosa ch'waryo 攷事撮要. comp. Ŏ Sukkwŏn 魚叔權. Keijo: Keijō Teikoku Daigaku Hōbungakka 京城帝國大學法文學科, 1941. (Keishōkaku sōsho [Kyujanggak ch'ongsŏ], 奎章閣叢書, vol. 7).

Kŏun zuihitsu 江雲隨筆. MS copy, coll. Historiographical Institute, Tokyo University. Original in coll. Kenninji 建仁寺 Temple, Kyoto. Copy dated 1887.

"Kuji taiketsu goza-kubari ezu" 公事對決御座配繪圖. MS, 1635, Sō Collection, Historiographical Institute, Tokyo University.

Kujō Michifusa 九條道房. *Michifusa kō ki* 道房公記. 10 vols., MS copy, collection Historiographical Institute, Tokyo University.

Kumazawa Banzan 熊澤蕃山. Gotō Yōichi 後藤陽一 and Tomoeda Ryūtarō 友枝龍太郎, eds. Iwanami Shoten, 1971. (*Nihon Shisō Taikei*, vol. 30).

Kurita Motoji 栗田元次. *Edo jidaishi jō* 江戸時代史上. Naigai Shoseki 内外書籍, 1928.

Kwanghaegun ilgi. 光海君日記. 185 *kwŏn* 巻. In *Chosŏn wangjo sillok*, vols. 26–33. Includes both the T'aebaeksan 太白山, and the Chŏngjoksan 鼎足山 manuscripts.

Kyemi tongsa ilgi 癸未東槎日記. (anon.), in *Kaikō sōsai*, 3 : 194–249.

Kyokuba jōran no oboegaki 曲馬上覽之覺書. MS, 1682. Sō Collection, Keio University Library.

Kyŏng Sŏn 慶暹. *Kyŏng ch'ilsŏng haesarok* 慶七星海槎録, in *Kaikō sōsai*, 2 : 1–71.

Kyŏngguk taejŏn 經國大典. Gakushūin Tōyō Bunka Kenkyūsho 学習院東洋文化研究所, 1974.

Leach, Edmund, "Ritual," in *International Encyclopedia of the Social Sciences*. New York: The Free Press, 1968. vol. 13, pp. 520–526.

Lebensztejn, Jean-Claude, "57 Steps to Hyena Stomp," in *Art News*, vol. 71, no. 5 (September 1972), pp. 60–75.

Ledyard, Gari. *The Dutch Come to Korea*. Seoul: Royal Asiatic Society, Korea Branch, 1971.

———, "Galloping Along with the Horseriders: Looking for the Founders of Japan," in *Journal of Japanese Studies*, vol. 1, no. 2 (Spring 1975), pp. 217–254.

Legge, James, tr. *Confucius: Confucian Analects, The Great Learning & The Doctrine of the Mean*. Oxford: The Clarendon Press, 1893 (Dover Press reprint, 1971).

Lewis, Andrew W., "Anticipatory Association of the Heir in Early

Capetian France," in *American Historical Review*, vol. 83, no. 4 (October 1978), pp. 906–927.

Liang Ch'i-Ch'ao 梁啓超. *Yin-ping-shih ch'üan-chi* 飲冰室全集. Taipei: Wen-Hua T'u-shu Kung-szu 文化圖書公司, 1968.

Mainikki (Edo) 毎日記. (Daily logbooks of the Tsushima domain residence in Edo; volume titles vary, e.g., *Nichinichiki* 日日記, *Hinamiki* 日並記, etc. Grouped together here for convenience as *Mainikki*.) 1077 MS volumes. Sō Collection, Historiographical Institute, Tokyo University.

Mainikki (Izuhara) 毎日記(厳原). (Daily logbooks of the *Omoteshosatsukata* 表書札方 in the Tsushima domain headquarters in Izuhara. Titles vary from volume to volume, and are grouped here for convenience under *Mainikki* (Izuhara). MS, 2053 volumes. Sō Collection, Banshoin Temple, Izuhara, Tsushima.

Mainikki issatsu Edo go-rōjū narabini katagata e tsukawasu gojō hikae issatsu nisatsu gatchō 毎日記一冊江戸御老中并ニ方々ニ遣ス御状控一冊二冊合帳. MS, 1646. Sō Archives, Banshōin Temple, Izuhara, Tsushima.

Mancall, Mark, "The Ch'ing Tribute System: An Interpretive Essay," in Fairbank, ed., *The Chinese World Order*, pp. 63–89.

Manzai 満済. *Manzai Jugō nikki* 満済准后日記. 2 vols. *Zoku gunsho ruijū hoi* 續群書類從補遺, vol. 1, parts 1, 2. Zoku Gunsho Ruijū Kanseikai 完成会, 1958.

Maruyama Masao 丸山眞男, "Kindai Nihon shisōshi ni okeru kokka risei no mondai (1)" 近代日本思想史における國家理性の問題," in *Tenbō* 展望. (January 1949): 4–15.

Masui Tsuneo 増井経夫. *Shin teikoku* 清帝国. Kōdansha 講談社, 1974.

Matsuda Kinoe 松田甲, "Richō Jinso yori kizō seru Nikkō Tōshōgū no hengaku to kane, tsuketari, Daiyūbyō no Chōsen tōrō" 李朝仁祖より寄贈せる日光東照宮の扁額と鐘附大猷廟の朝鮮燈籠 in *Nissen shiwa* 日鮮史話, 2 (1926): 48–77.

Matsuda, Mitsugu, "The Ryukyuan Government Scholarship Students to China, 1392–1868, based on a short essay by Nakahara Zenchu, 1962," in *Monumenta Nipponica*, 21.3–4 (1966): 273–304.

———, "The Government of the Kingdom of Ryukyu, 1609–1872." Unpublished Ph.D. dissertation, University of Hawaii, 1967.

Matsudaira Sadanobu 松平定信. *Uge no hitokoto, Shugyōroku* 宇下の人言, 修行録. Iwanami Shoten, 1942.

Matsudaira Tarō 松平太郎. *Edo jidai seido no kenkyū (1)* 江戸時代制度の研究上巻. Buke Seido Kenkyūkai 武家制度研究會, 1919.

Matsumoto Sannosuke 松本三之介, "Kinsei ni okeru rekishi jojutsu to sono shisō" 近世における歴史叙述とその思想, in Matsumoto Sannosuke and Ogura Yoshihiko 小倉芳彦, ed., *Kinsei shiron shū* 近世史論集. Iwanami Shoten, 1974, pp. 578–615. (*Nihon Shisō Taikei*, vol. 48)

Matsushita Kenrin 松下見林 comp. *Ishō Nihon den* 異稱日本傳. In *Kaitei shiseki shūran*. vol. 20. Sumiya Shobō, 1968.

Matsuura Akira 松浦章, "Kōshū shikizō U-rin-tatsu Bo-ji-shin no Nagasaki raikō to sono shokumei ni tsuite—Kōki jidai no Nisshin kōshō no ichi sokumen" 杭州織造烏林達莫爾森の長崎来航とその職名について—康煕時代の日清交渉の一側面, in *Tōhōgaku* 東方學, no. 55 (January 1978), pp. 62–75.

Mattingly, Garrett. *Renaissance Diplomacy*. Sentry Edition. Boston: Houghton-Mifflin Company, 1971.

McClain, James L., "Castle Towns and Daimyo Authority: Kanazawa in the Years 1583–1630," in *Journal of Japanese Studies*, vol. 6, no. 2 (Summer 1980), pp. 267–299.

McCune, George McAfee, "Korean Relations with China and Japan, 1800–1864," Unpublished Ph.D. dissertation, University of California, Berkeley, 1941.

———, and E. O. Reischauer, "The Romanization of the Korean Language, Based on its Phonetic Structure," in *Transactions of the Korea Branch of the Royal Asiatic Society*, vol. XXXIX (1939).

McMullen, Ian James, "Kumazawa Banzan and 'Jitsugaku': Toward Pragmatic Action," in *Principle and Practicality: Essays in Neo-Confucianism and Practical Learning*, ed. Wm. Theodore de Bary and Irene Bloom. New York: Columbia University Press, 1979, pp. 337–374.

———, "Non-Agnatic Adoption: A Confucian Controversy in Seventeenth- and Eighteenth-Century Japan," in *Harvard Journal of Asiatic Studies*, vol. 35 (1975), pp. 133–189.

McMorran, Ian, "The Patriot and the Partisans: Wang Fu-chih's Involvement in the Politics of the Yung-li Court," in Spence and Wills, ed., *From Ming to Ch'ing: Conquest, Region, and Continuity in Seventeenth-Century China*, pp. 133–166.

Medieval Japan: Essays in Institutional History. ed. John W. Hall and Jeffrey P. Mass. New Haven: Yale University Press, 1974.

Meng, S. M. *The Tsungli Yamen: Its Organization and Functions*. Cambridge, Massachusetts: The East Asian Research Center, Harvard University, distr. by Harvard University Press, 1962.

Miki Seiichirō 三鬼清一郎, "Chōsen eki ni okeru kokusai jōken ni tsuite"

朝鮮役における国際条件について, in *Nagoya Daigaku Bungakubu kenkyū kiyō* 名古屋大学文学部研究紀要, 62 (1974): 1–16.

Minamoto Ryōen 源了円. *Tokugawa shisō shōshi* 徳川思想小史. Chūō Kōron Sha, 1973.

Ming-shih 明史. 6 vols. Taipei: Kuo-fang Yen-chiu Yuan 國防研究院, 1962.

Mitogaku 水戸学. Ed., Imai Usaburō 今井宇三郎, et al. Iwanami Shoten, 1973. (*Nihon Shisō Taikei*, vol. 53).

Miyake Hidetoshi 三宅英利, "Genna Chōsen shinshi raihei riyū e no gimon" 元和朝鮮信使来聘理由への疑問, in *Kyūshū shigaku* 九州史学, 52 (1973): 31–42.

———, "Kan'ei jūsannen Chōsen shinshi kō" 寛永十三年朝鮮信使考, in *Kitakyūshū Daigaku Bungakubu kiyō* 北九州大学文学部紀要, 6 (1970): 1–20.

———, "Kan'ei shokai no Chōsen shinshi," 寛永初回の朝鮮信使, *Kyūshū shigaku* 九州史学, 53–54 (1974): 63–78.

———, "Rishi Kōsō-chō Nihon tsūshinshi kō" 李氏孝宗朝日本通信使考, in *Kitakyūshū Daigaku Bungakubu kiyō B keiretsu* 北九州大学文学部紀要 B 系列, 3.1 (1969): 1–32.

———, "Sakoku chokugo no Chōsen tsūshinshi" 鎖国直後の朝鮮通信使, in *Kitakyūshū Daigaku Bungakubu kiyō* 北九州大学文学部紀要, 5.1–2 (1961): 23–52.

———, "Tenna Chōsen shinshi kō" 天和朝鮮信使考, in *Shigaku ronshū—taigai kankei to seiji bunka* 史学論集対外関係と政治文化. 2 vols. Yoshikawa Kōbunkan, 1974. 1: 163–192.

———, "Tokugawa seiken shokai no Chōsen shinshi" 徳川政権初回の朝鮮信使, in *Chōsen gakuhō* 朝鮮学報, 82 (January 1977): 101–132.

Miyata Toshihiko 宮田俊彦, "Kinsei shoki no Ryūmin bōeki" 近世初期の琉明貿易, in *Nihon rekishi* 日本歴史, no. 340 (September 1976): 1–19.

Morgenthau, Hans J. *Politics among Nations*. (third edition) New York: Alfred A. Knopf, Inc., 1960.

Morohashi Tetsuji 諸橋哲次, comp. *Daikanwa jiten* 大漢和辞典. 13 vols., Taishūkan 大衆館, 1955–1960.

Murai Masuo 村井益男, "Edo zu byōbu no rekishiteki haikei" 江戸図屏風の歴史的背景, in *Edo zu byōbu*, q.v., pp. 22–46.

Murakami Naojirō 村上直次郎, tr. *Dejima Rankan nisshi* 出島蘭館日志. 3 vols., Bunmei Kyōkai 文明協會, 1938–1939.

———, ed. *Ikoku ōfuku shokan shū/Zōtei Ikaku nikki shō* 異国往復

書翰集・増訂異国日記抄. Yūshōdō Shoten 雄松堂書店, 1966. (*Ikoku sōsho* 異国叢書, vol. 11).

———, tr. *Nagasaki Oranda Shōkan no nikki* 長崎オランダ商館の日記. 3 vols. Iwanami Shoten, 1956–1958.

Nagasaki kenshi, hansei hen 長崎県史藩政編. Yoshikawa Kōbunkan, 1973.

Nagazumi Yōko 永積洋子, tr. *Hirado Oranda shōkan no nikki* 平戸オランダ商館の日記. 4 vols. Iwanami Shoten, 1969–1970.

———, "Japan's Isolationist Policy as Seen through Dutch Source Materials," *Acta Asiatica*, 22 (1972), pp. 18–35.

———, "Orandajin no hogosha to shite no Inoue Chikugo no kami Masashige" オランダ人の保護者としての井上筑後守政重, in *Nihon rekishi*, no. 327 (1975): 1–17.

Nagura Tetsuzō 奈倉哲三, "Hideyoshi no Chōsen shinryaku to 'shin-koku'" 秀吉の朝鮮侵略と「神国」, in *Rekishi hyōron* 歴史評論, no. 314 (June 1976), pp. 29–35.

Naitō Shunpo 内藤雋輔. *Bunroku Keichō no eki ni okeru hiryonin no kenkyū* 文禄慶長の役における被擄人の研究. Tōkyō Daigaku Shuppankai, 1976.

Najita, Tetsuo, "Method and Analysis in the Conceptual Portrayal of Tokugawa Intellectual History," in Najita and Irwin Scheiner, eds., *Japanese Thought in the Tokugawa Period*. University of Chicago Press, 1978. pp. 3–38.

Nakada Yasunao 中田易直, "Shuin seido sōsetsu ni kansuru shomondai" 朱印制度創設に関する諸問題, in *Chūō Daigaku Bungakubu kiyō* 中央大学文学部紀要, no. 55 (1969): 1–42; no. 61 (1971): 18–62.

Nakai Chikuzan to sōbō kigen 中井竹山と草茅危言. Taishō Yōkō 大正洋行, 1943.

Nakai, Kate Wildman. *Arai Hakuseki and Confucian Governance in Tokugawa Japan*. Forthcoming. Harvard University Press.

———. "The Naturalization of Confucianism in Tokugawa Japan: The Problem of Sinocentrism," in *Harvard Journal of Asiatic Studies*, 40, 1 (June 1980), pp. 157–199.

Nakamura Hidetaka 中村栄孝, "Kiyū yakujō saikō" 己酉約条再考, in *Chōsen gakuhō*, 101 (October 1981): 39–50.

———. "Nikkōzan Tokugawa Ieyasu byōshadō hengaku no mohon ni tuite" 日光山徳川家康廟社堂扁額の模本について, in *Chōsen gakuhō* 朝鮮学報, 49 (1968): 241–257.

———. *Nissen kankei shi no kenkyū* 日鮮関係史の研究. 3 vols. Yoshikawa Kōbunkan, 1965–1969.

Nakamura Kōya 中村孝也. *Edo bakufu sakoku shiron* 江戸幕府鎖國史論. Hōkōkai 奉公會, 1914.

————, comp., *Tokugawa Ieyasu monjo no kenkyū* 徳川家康文書の研究. 4 vols. Gakujutsu Shinkōkai 学術振興会, 1958–1961.

Nakamura (Nakayama) Kyūshirō 中村(中山)久四郎, "Minmatsu no Nihon kisshi oyobi kisshi" 明末の日本乞師及び乞資. in *Shigaku zasshi* 史學雜誌, 26.5–6 (1915).

Nakamura Tadashi 中村質, "Shimabara no ran to sakoku" 島原の乱と鎖国, in *Iwanami kōza Nihon rekishi* 岩波講座日本歴史, 26 vols., Iwanami Shoten, 1975–1977, 9:227–262.

Nam Kon'gok 南壺谷. *Pusangnok* 扶桑録. in *Kaikō sōsai*, vol. 3, pp. 250–413.

Nihon shoki 日本書紀. ed. Sakamoto Tarō 坂本太郎, Ienaga Saburō 家永三郎, Inoue Mitsusada 井上光貞, Ōno Susumu 大野普. 2 vols. Iwanami Shoten, 1965–1967. (*Nihon Koten Bungaku Taikei*, vols. 67, 68).

Nikki 日記. MS. Daily logbooks of Edo Castle; titles vary, also known as *Onikki* 御日記, *Ryūei hinamiki* 柳營日並記, etc. Collection Naikaku Bunko 内閣文庫, Tokyo.

Nikkan shokei 日韓書契. comp. Ungai Dōtai 雲涯道岱. 8 vols., MS copy, pref. dated 1726, collection Historiographical Institute, Tokyo University.

Notehelfer, Fred G., "Notes on Kyōhō Smuggling," in *Princeton Papers in East Asian Studies, I. Japan* no. 1 (August 1972), pp. 1–32.

Ŏ Sukkwŏn 魚叔權, comp., *Kosa ch'waryo* 攷事撮要. Keijo: Keijō Teikoku Daigaku Hōbungakubu 京城帝國大學法文學部, 1941.

O Yun'gyŏm 吳允謙. *Tongsasang illok* 東槎上日録, in *Kaikō sōsai*, 2:78–110.

Ofuregaki Kanpō shūsei 御觸書寛保集成. Iwanami Shoten, 1934.

Ogyū Sorai 荻生徂徠. *Ryūkyū heishi ki* 琉球聘使記. MS copy in Nanki Bunko 南葵文庫, Tokyo University Library.

Ogyū Sorai 荻生徂徠. ed., Yoshikawa Kōjirō 吉川幸次郎, Maruyama Masao 丸山真男, Nishida Tai ichirō 西田太一郎, Tsuji Tatsuya 辻達也. *Nihon Shisō Taikei*, vol. 36. Iwanami Shoten, 1973.

Ojima Sukema 小島祐馬. *Chūgoku no kakumei shisō* 中国の革命思想. Chikuma Shobō 築摩書房, 1967.

Okada Nobuko 岡田信子, "Kinsei ikoku hyōchakusen ni tsuite—toku ni Tō Chōsen sen no shogū" 近世異国漂着船について特に唐朝鮮船の処遇, *Hōsei shigaku* 法政史学, 26 (March 1974): 39–49.

Ōkubo Toshikane 大久保利謙, et. al., ed. *Shiryō ni yoru Nihon no ayumi, kinsei hen* 史料による日本の歩み, 近世編. Yoshikawa Kōbunkan, 1955.

Ooms, Herman. *Charismatic Bureaucrat: A Political Biography of Matsudaira Sadanobu, 1758–1829.* Chicago: University of Chicago Press, 1975.

Osa Masanori 長止統, "Keitetsu Genso ni tsuite—ichi gaikō sō no shutsuji to hōkei" 景徹玄蘇について— 一外交僧の出自と法系, in *Chōsen gakuhō*, 29 (1963): 135–147.

———, "Nissen kankei ni okeru kiroku no jidai" 日鮮関係における記録の時代, in *Tōyō gakuhō*, 50.4 (March 1968): 70–124.

Ōshima Nobujirō 大島延次郎, "Ryūkyū shisetsu no Edo sanrei," 琉球使節の江戸参禮, in *Rekishi chiri* 歴史地理, 61.3 (March 1933): 48–56; 61.4 (April 1933): 35–42.

Ostrower, Alexander. *Language, Law, and Diplomacy: A Study of Linguistic Diversity in Official International Relations and International Law.* 2 vols. University of Pennsylvania Press, 1965.

Ōtaki Haruko 大瀧晴子, "Nikkō to Chōsen tsūshinshi" 日光と朝鮮通信使, in *Edo jidai no Chōsen tsūshinshi*, q.v., pp. 155–182.

Ou-yang Hsiu 歐陽修. *Ou-yang Wen-chung-kung chi* 歐陽文忠公集. (Ssu-pu ts'ung-k'an 四部叢刊 ed.). Shanghai, 1920.

Pak Ch'ungsŏk 朴忠錫, "Richō kōki ni okeru seiji shisō no tenkai—toku ni kinsei jitsugakuha no shi'i hōhō o chūshin ni" 李朝後期における政治思想の展開一特に近世実学派の思惟方法を中心に, in *Kokka Gakkai zasshi* 国家学会雑誌, vol. 88, nos. 9–10 (September 1975), pp. 1–49; 88.11–12 (November 1975): 1–65; 89.1–2 (January 1976): 1–55.

Palais, James B., "Korea on the Eve of the Kanghwa Treaty, 1873–1876." Unpublished Ph.D. dissertation, Harvard University, 1967.

———. *Politics and Policy in Traditional Korea.* Cambridge, Massachusetts: Harvard University Press, 1975.

Pibyŏnsa tŭngnok 備邊司謄録, 28 vols. Seoul: National History Compilation Committee, 1959–1960.

Pirsig, Robert M. *Zen and the Art of Motorcycle Maintenance, An Inquiry into Values.* New York: William Morrow, 1974; repr. Bantam Books, 1975.

Pyŏllye chibyo 邊例集要. 2 vols. Seoul: Tamgudang 探求堂, 1973.

Rakuchū rakugai zu 洛中洛外図. ed. Kyōto Kokuritsu Hakubutsukan 京都国立博物館. Kadokawa Shoten 角川書店, 1966.

Ri Jinhi (Yi Chinhŭi) 李進熙. *Richō no tsūshinshi* 李朝の通信使. Kōdansha 講談社, 1976.

Ritsuryō 律令. ed. Inoue Mitusada 井上光貞, *et al.* Iwanami Shoten, 1976. (*Nihon shisō taikei* 日本思想大系, vol. 3).

Roosen, William, "Early Modern Diplomatic Ceremonial: A Systems Approach," in *Journal of Modern History*, vol. 52, no. 3 (September 1980), pp. 452–476.

————. *The Age of Louis XIV: The Rise of Modern Diplomacy*. Cambridge, Massachussetts: Schenkman Publishing Company, 1976.

Rosen, Stephen Peter, "Alexander Hamilton and the Domestic Uses of International Law," in *Diplomatic History*, vol. 5, no. 3 (Summer 1981), pp. 183–202.

Ryūkyūjin gyōretsu ki 琉球人行列記. Fushimi: Tanbaya Shinzaemon 丹波屋新左衛門, *et al.*, 1832.

Sakai, Robert K., "The Ryukyu (Liu-ch'iu) Islands as a Fief of Satsuma," in John K. Fairbank, ed., *The Chinese World Order*, pp. 112–134.

————, "The Satsuma-Ryukyu Trade and the Tokugawa Seclusion Policy," in *Journal of Asian Studies*, vol. 23, no. 3 (May 1964), pp. 391–403.

Sakamaki, Shunzo, ed. *Ryukyuan Names: Monographs on and Lists of Personal and Place Names in the Ryukyus*. Honolulu: East-West Center Press, 1964.

————. *Ryukyu: A Bibliographic Guide to Okinawan Studies*. Honolulu: University of Hawaii Press, 1963.

Sakihara, Mitsugu, "The Significance of Ryukyu in Satsuma Finances during the Tokugawa Period." Unpublished Ph.D. dissertation, University of Hawaii, 1971.

San-kuo-chih 三國志. Ch'en Shou 陳壽, ed., 5 vols. Peking: Chung-hua Shu-chü 中華書局, 1971.

Sansom, G. B. *The Western World and Japan, A Study of European and Asiatic Culture*. New York: Alfred A. Knopf, 1950.

Sasaki Junnosuke 佐々木潤之介, "Sakoku to Sakokusei" 鎖国と鎖国制, in *Rekishi kōron* 歴史公論 (Spring 1976), pp. 34–44.

Sasama Yoshihiko 笹間良彦. *Edo bakufu yakushoku shūsei (zōho ban)* 江戸幕府役職集成（増補版）. Yūzankaku 雄山閣, 1974.

Satō Shin'ichi 佐藤進一, "Muromachi bakufu ron" 室町幕府論, in *Iwanami kōza Nihon rekishi* 岩波講座日本歴史. 23 vols. Iwanami Shoten, 1962–1964, 7:1–48.

Satow, Sir Ernest. *A Guide to Diplomatic Practice*. 2 vols. London: Longmans, Green and Co., 1917.

Schwartz, Benjamin I., "The Chinese Perception of World Order, Past and

Present," in John K. Fairbank, ed., *The Chinese World Order*, pp. 276–288.

Sejong taewang sillok 世宗大王實錄. 163 *kwŏn*, in *Chosŏn wangjo sillok*, vols. 2–5.

Seno Bayū, 瀬野馬熊, "Seitō kigai jōyaku ni tsuite" 正統癸亥條約 に就いて, in *Shigaku zasshi* 史學雜誌, vol. 26, no. 9 (September 1915): 103–123.

Shigeno Yasutsugu 重野安繹, Kume Kunitake 久米邦武, and Hoshino Hisashi 星野恒. *Kōhon kokushigan* 稿本國史眼. Shigakkai 史學會, 1980, rev. ed., 1908.

Shimazu kokushi 島津國史. comp. Yamamoto Masayoshi 山本正誼. prefaces and 25 *satsu* 冊. 1800. MS copy, collection Historiographical Institute, Tokyo University.

Shimizu Hirokazu 清水紘一, "Nagasaki bugyō ichiranhyō no saikentō" 長崎奉行一覧表の再検討, in [*Kyōto Gaikokugo Daigaku*] *Kenkyū ronsō* [京都外国語大学] 研究論叢, 15 (1974): 1–24.

"Shin Ise monogatari" 新伊勢物語, in *Kyū bakufu* 舊幕府, 4.6, 7 (1900).

Shinpojiumu Nihon rekishi 11 bakuhan taisei ron シンポジウム日本歴史 11 幕藩体制論. Gakuseisha 学生社, 1974.

Shinshi kiroku 信使記録. MS, 425 vols. Sō Collection, Keio University Library.

Shintei zōho Sansei sōran 新訂増補三正綜覧. Kamakura: Geirinsha 藝林舎, 1973.

Shin'yashiki Yukishige 新屋敷幸繁. *Shinkō Okinawa issennen shi* 新講 沖縄一千年史. 2 vols. Yūzankaku 雄山閣, 1961.

Shiryō kōhon 史料稿本 (also called *Hennen shiryō* 編年史料). MS drafts of published and unpublished portions of the *Dai Nihon shiryō*, q.v., prepared by, and held in the archives of the Historiographical Institute, Tokyo University.

Shizuki Tadao 志筑忠雄, tr., "Sakoku ron" 鎖國論 (by Engelbert Kaempfer), in *Shōnen hitsudoku Nihon bunko* 少年必讀日本文庫. 12 vols. Hakubunsha 博文社, 1891–1892. vol. 5.

Shōtoku Chōsen shinshi tojō gyōretsu zu 正徳朝鮮信使行列圖. Collection National History Compilation Committee, Seoul. Facsimile edition, *Chōsen shiryō sōkan* 朝鮮史料叢刊, vol. 20. Keijo: Chōsen Sōtokufu 朝鮮總督府, 1938.

Smith, Thomas C., "Pre-modern Economic Growth: Japan and the West," *Past and Present*, 60 (August 1973): 128–160.

So, Kwan-wai. *Japanese Piracy in Ming China During the Sixteenth Century*. East Lansing: Michigan State University Press, 1975.

Sō-ke Bunko shiryō mokuroku (nikkirui) 宗家文庫史料目録（日記類）. comp. Sō-ke Bunko Chōsa Iinkai 宗家文庫調査委員会. Izuhara 厳原: Izuhara-chō Kyōiku Iinkai 厳原町教育委員会, 1978.

Sŏnjong taewang sillok 宣宗大王實録. 221 kwŏn, in *Chosŏn wangjo sillok*, vols. 21–25.

Spence, Jonathan D. *Ts'ao Yin and the K'ang-hsi Emperor, Bondservant and Master*. New Haven: Yale University Press, 1966.

———, and John E. Wills, Jr., eds. *From Ming to Ch'ing: Conquest, Region, and Continuity in Seventeenth-Century China*. New Haven: Yale University Press, 1979.

Ssu-ma Kuang 司馬光. *Tzu-chih t'ung-chien* 資治通鑑. 10 vols. Peking: Hsin-hua Shu-tien 新華書店, 1956.

Statler, Oliver. *Shimoda Story*. New York: Random House, 1969.

Sternberger, Dolf, "Legitimacy," in *International Encyclopedia of the Social Sciences* (1968), 9:244ff.

Strayer, Joseph R. *On the Medieval Origins of the Modern State*. Princeton: Princeton University Press, 1970.

———, "The Tokugawa Period and Japanese Feudalism," in John W. Hall and Marius B. Jansen, eds., *Studies in the Institutional History of Early Modern Japan*. Princeton: Princeton University Press, 1968, pp. 3–14.

Su Shih (Tung-p'o) 蘇軾（東坡）. *Ching-chin Tung-p'o wen-chi shih-lüeh* 經進東坡文集事略. 60 *chüan* in 5 *ts'e* 冊, (Ssu-pu ts'ung-k'an 四部總刊 ed.), Shanghai, 1920.

Sugimoto, Masayoshi, and David L. Swain. *Science and Culture in Traditional Japan, 600–1854*. Cambridge, Massachusetts: The MIT Press, 1978.

Sukchong taewang sillok 肅宗大王實録. 65 kwŏn, in *Chosŏn wangjo sillok*, vols. 31–33.

Sŭngjŏngwŏn ilgi 承政院日記. 141 vols. Seoul: National History Compilation Committee, 1961–1977.

Tabohashi Kiyoshi 田保橋潔. *Kindai Nissen kankei no kenkyū* 近代日鮮關係の研究. 2 vols. Keijo: Chōsen Sōtōkufu Chūsūin 朝鮮總督府中樞院, 1940. Reprint, Munetaka Shobō 宗高書房, 1972.

Taishū hennen ryaku 對州編年略. Tōkyōdō Shuppan 東京堂出版, 1974.

Takekoshi, Yosaburo. *The Economic Aspects of the History of Japan*. 3 vols. New York: The Macmillan Company, 1930.

Takeno Yōko 武野要子. *Han bōeki shi no kenkyū* 藩貿易史の研究. Mineruva Shobō ミネルヴァ書房, 1979.

———, "Satsuma han no Ryūkyū bōeki to bōeki shōnin Ishimotoke no kankei" 薩摩藩の琉球貿易と貿易商人石本家の関係, in Hidemura Senzō 秀村選三, ed. *Satsuma han no kiso kōzō* 薩摩藩の基礎構造. Ochanomizu Shobō お茶の水書房, 1970, pp. 465–491.

Tanaka Takeo 田中健夫, "*Chōsen tsūkō taiki zakkō*" 『朝鮮通交大紀』雑考, in *Chōsen gakuhō* 朝鮮学報, 79 (1976): 47–76.

———. *Chūsei kaigai kōshōshi no kenkyū* 中世海外交渉史の研究. Tōkyō Daigaku Shuppankai, 1959.

———. *Chūsei taigai kankei shi* 中世対外関係史. Tōkyō Daigaku Shuppankai, 1975.

———, "Kangō-fu, kangō-in, kangō bōeki" 勘合符・勘合印・勘合貿易, in *Nihon rekishi*, no. 392 (January 1981), pp. 1–21.

———. "Sakoku seiritsu ki Nissen kankei no seikaku" 鎖国成立期日鮮関係の性格, in *Chōsen gakuhō*, no. 34 (January 1965), pp. 29–62.

———. *Wakō to kangō bōeki* 倭寇と勘合貿易. Shibundō 至文堂, 1961.

Tashiro Kazui 田代和生, "Jūshichi jūhachi seiki Nissen bōeki no suii to Chōsen tokō sen" 十七・十八世紀日鮮貿易の推移と朝鮮渡航船, in *Chōsen gakuhō* 朝鮮学報, 79 (April 1976): 13–46.

———. "Kan'ei 6 nen (Jinso 7; 1629) Tsushima shisetsu no Chōsen-koku 'Go-jōkyō no toki mainikki' to sono haikei" 寛永6年(仁祖7;1629)対馬使節の朝鮮国「御上京之時毎日記」とその背景, in *Chōsen gakuhō* 朝鮮学報, nos. 96 (July 1980), 98 (January 1981), 101 (October 1981).

———. *Kinsei Nitchō tsūkō bōeki shi no kenkyū* 近世日朝通交貿易史の研究. Sōbunsha 創文社, 1981.

———. "Kinsei Tsushima han ni okeru Nissen bōeki no ichi kōsatsu" 近世対馬藩における日鮮貿易の一考察, in *Nihon rekishi*, 268 (1970): 88–114.

———. "Tsushima han's Korean Trade, 1684–1710," in *Acta Asiatica*, 30 (1970): 85–105.

Teihon Oritaku shiba no ki shakugi 定本折りたく柴の記釈義, ed., Miyazaki Michio 宮崎道生. Shibundō 至文堂, 1964.

Tenkai 天海. *Tōshōgū Daigongen engi* 東照宮大権現縁起. in *Zokuzoku Gunsho ruijū* 続々群書類従, vol. 1, pp. 691–705. Zoku Gunsho Ruijū Kanseikai, 1971.

"Tenna jinjutsu hachigatsu nijūshichinichi Chōsenjin tojō no setsu" 天和壬戌八月廿七日朝鮮人登城之節 MS chart, 1682. Collection Kankoku Kenkyūin 韓国研究院, Tokyo.

Tenna jinjutsu shinshi kiroku 天和壬戌信使記録. 68 vols., MS, 1682. Sō Collection, Keio University Library.

Tenryūin kō jitsuroku 天龍院公實録. comp. Amenomori Hōshū 雨森芳洲. 2 vols., MS, 1675. Sō Collection, Banshōin, Tsushima.

Tō sen hyōchaku teishiki 唐船漂着定式. MS, ca. 1688. Sō Collection, National History Compilation Committee, Seoul.

Tō tsūji kaisho nichiroku 唐通事會所日録. comp. Tōkyō Daigaku Shiryō Hensanjo 東京大学史料編纂所. 7 vols. (*Dainihon kinsei shiryō* 大日本近世史料 series, part 3). Tōkyō Daigaku Shuppankai, 1955-1968.

Toby, Ronald, "Korean-Japanese Diplomacy in 1711: Sukchong's Court and the Shogun's Title," in *Chōsen gakuhō* 朝鮮学報, 74 (1975): 1-26.

Toguchi Masakiyo 渡口真清. *Kinsei no Ryūkyū* 近世の琉球. Hōsei Daigaku Shuppankyoku 法政大学出版局, 1975.

Tōheiran fūsetsu kōgi e ōseagerare sōrō hikae narabini Chōsen koku sanzoku totō goannai ōseagerare sorō hikae 唐兵亂風説公儀に被仰上候控幷朝鮮國山賊徒黨御案内被仰上候控. MS, ca. 1734. Sō Collection, Keio University Library.

Tokugawa jikki 徳川實記. 10 vols., Yoshikawa Kōbunkan, 1964. (vols. 38-47 in *Shintei zōho kokushi taikei* 新訂増補國史大系).

Told Round a Brushwood Fire: The Autobiography of Arai Hakuseki. tr., Joyce Ackroyd. Princeton and Tokyo: Princeton University Press and The University of Tokyo Press, 1979.

T'ongmun'gwanji 通文館志. Chōsen Sōtokufu 朝鮮總督府, 1944; reprint, Kyŏng'in Munhwasa 景仁文化社, 1973.

Totman, Conrad, "From *Sakoku* to *Kaikoku*: The Transformation of Foreign Policy Attitudes, 1853-1868," in *Monumenta Nipponica*, vol. XXXV, no. 1 (Spring 1980), pp. 1-19.

―――. *Politics in the Tokugawa Bakufu, 1600-1843*. Cambridge, Mass.: Harvard University Press, 1967.

Trachtenberg, Marc, "The Social Interpretation of Foreign Policy," in *Review of Politics*, vol. 40, no. 3 (July 1978), pp. 328-350.

Tsao, Kai-fu, "The Rebellion of the Three Feudatories against the Manchu Throne in China, 1673-1681: Its Setting and Significance." Unpublished Ph.D. dissertation, Columbia University, 1965.

Tsuji Tatsuya 辻達也. *Edo kaifu* 江戸開府. Chūō Kōron Sha, 1966.

―――, "Kan'ei-ki no bakufu seiji ni kan suru jakkan no kōsatsu" 寛永期の幕府政治に関する若干の考察, in *Yokohama Shiritsu Daigaku ronsō* 横浜市立大学論叢, 24.2-3 (1973): 31-60.

Tsuji Zennosuke 辻善之助. *Zōtei kaigai kōtsū shiwa* 増訂海外交通史話. Naigai Shoseki 内外書籍, 1930.

Tsukahira, Toshio G. *Feudal Control in Tokugawa Japan: The Sankin Kōtai System*. Cambridge, Massachusetts: The East Asian Research Center, Harvard University, 1966.

Tsukamoto Manabu 塚本学, "Edo jidai ni okeru 'i' kannen ni tsuite" 江戸時代における「夷」観念について, in *Nihon rekishi*, no. 371 (April 1979), pp. 1–18.

Tsūkō ichiran zokushū 通航一覧續輯. Yanai Kenji 箭内健次, ed., 5 vols. Osaka: Seibundō Shuppan 清文堂出版, 1967–1973.

Tsunoda, Ryusaku, et al., comp. *Sources of Japanese Tradition*. New York: Columbia University Press, 1958.

Uchida Ginzō 内田銀藏. *Kinsei no Nihon; Nihon kinseishi* 近世の日本・日本近世史 ed. Miyazaki Michio 宮崎道生. Tōyō Bunko 東洋文庫 series, no. 279. Heibonsha, 1975.

————. *Kokushi sōron oyobi Nihon kinseishi* 國史總論及日本近世史. Dōbunkan 同文館, 1921. (*Uchida Ginzō ikō zenshū* 内田銀藏遺稿 全集, v. 3).

Uete Michiari 植手通有. *Nihon kindai shisō no keisei* 日本近代思想の形成. Iwanami Shoten, 1974.

————, "Taigai-kan no tenkai" 対外観の展開, in Hashikawa Bunsō 橋川文三 and Matsumoto Sannosuke 松本三之介, eds., *Kindai Nihon seiji shisō shi* 近代日本政治思想史 2 vols., Yūhikaku 有斐閣, 1971, 1:33–74.

Ura Yasukazu 浦簾一, "Minmatsu Shinsho Senman kankei shijō ni okeru Nihon no chi'i" 明末清初鮮滿關係に於ける日本の地位, in *Shirin* 史林, vol. 19, no. 2 (April 1934), pp. 24–48; vol. 19, no. 3 (July 1934), pp. 122–146.

————, "Tōsen fusetsugaki no kenkyū" 唐船風説書の研究, in *Ka'i hentai*, (q.v.), pp. 1–78.

Varley, H. Paul, tr. *A Chronicle of God and Sovereigns: Jinno Shotoki of Kitabatake Chikafusa*. New York: Columbia University Press, 1980.

Wagner, Edward Willett. *The Literati Purges: Political Conflict in Early Yi Korea*. Cambridge, Massachusetts: East Asian Research Center, Harvard University, 1974.

Walker, Hugh Dyson, "The Yi-Ming *Rapprochement*: Sino-Korean Foreign Relations, 1392–1592." Unpublished Ph.D. dissertation, University of California, Los Angeles, 1971.

Wang Yi-t'ung. *Official Relations between China and Japan, 1368–1549*. Cambridge, Massachusetts: Harvard University Press, 1953. (Harvard-Yenching Institute Studies, IX).

Webb, Herschel. *The Japanese Imperial Institution in the Tokugawa Period.* New York: Columbia University Press, 1968.

——, and Ryan, Marleigh. *Research in Japanese Sources: A Guide.* New York: Columbia University Press, 1965.

Webster, C. K. *The Congress of Vienna, 1814–1815.* London: Oxford University Press, n.d.

Wen-hsien t'sung-pien 文獻叢編. 2 vols. Taipei: Kuo-feng Ch'u-pan-she 國風出版社, 1964.

Williams, William A., "The Legend of Isolationism in the 1920s," in *Science & Society,* XVIII (Winter 1954), pp. 1–20; reprinted in *Essays in American Diplomacy,* ed., Armin Rappaport, London: The Macmillan Company, 1967, pp. 215–228.

Wills, John E., Jr., "Maritime China from Wang Chih to Shih Lang—Themes in Peripheral History," in Jonathan D. Spence and John E. Wills, Jr., eds., *From Ming to Ch'ing: Conquest, Region, and Continuity in Seventeenth-Century China.* New Haven: Yale University Press, 1979. pp. 201–238.

——. *Pepper, Guns and Parleys: The Dutch East India Company and China, 1622–1681.* Cambridge, Massachusetts: Harvard University Press, 1974.

Wright, Mary C., "What's in a Reign Name: The Uses of History and Philology," in *Journal of Asian Studies,* 18.1 (November 1958): 103–106.

Wu, Silas. *Passage to Power: K'ang-hsi and His Heir Apparent, 1661–1722.* Cambridge, Massachusetts: Harvard University Press, 1979.

Yamaga Sokō 山鹿素行. ed., Tahara Tsuguo 田原嗣郎 and Morimoto Jun'ichirō 守本順一郎. *Nihon Shisō Taikei,* vol. 32. Iwanami Shoten, 1970.

Yamaguchi Keiji 山口啓二. *Bakuhansei seiritsuy shi no kenkyū* 幕藩制成立史の研究. Azekura Shobō 校倉書房, 1974.

Yamamoto Mieno 山本美越乃, "Ayamareru shokumin seisaku no kikeiji: Ryūkyū" 誤まれる殖民政策の奇形兒一琉球, in *Keizai-gaku ronsō* 經濟學論叢. 23 (1926), 24 (1927), 25 (1927), 26 (1928).

Yamawaki Teijirō 山脇悌二郎. *Kinsei Nitchū bōeki shi no kenkyū* 近世日中貿易史の研究. Yoshikawa Kōbunkan, 1960.

——. *Nagasaki no Tōjin bōeki* 長崎の唐人貿易. Yoshikawa Kōbunkan, 1964.

Yamazaki Ansai gakuha 山崎闇齋學派. Comp. Nishi Junzō 西順蔵, Abe Kōichi 阿部隆一, and Maruyama Masao 丸山真男. *Nihon Shisō Taikei,* vol. 31. Iwanami Shoten, 1980.

Yanagawa kuji kiroku 柳川公事記録. 3 vols. MS copy, collection Historiographical Institute, Tokyo University.

Yanagawa kuji kiroku. MS, 1 packet of letters, diagrams. Collection Historiographical Institute, Tokyo University.

Yanagawa Shigeoki kuji no toki Hō Chōrō narabini Matsuo Shichiemon e otazune nararu seitō no chō 柳川調興公事之時方長老幷松尾七右衛門に被成御尋請答の帳 MS, n.d., 1634 or 1635?, in Sō Collection, Historiographical Institute, Tokyo University.

Yano Jin'ichi 矢野仁一 *Nagasaki shishi Tsūkō bōeki hen Tōyō shokoku* 長崎市史通交貿易編東洋諸國 Nagasaki: Nagasaki Shiyakusho 長崎市役所, 1938.

Yi Hyŏnjong 李鉉淙. *Chosŏn chŏn'gi tae'Il kyosŏp-sa yŏn'gu* 朝鮮前期對日交渉史研究. Seoul: Han'guk Yŏn'guwŏn 韓國研究院, 1964.

———, "Kiyu choyak naeyong ŭi sasŏ-byŏl ch'ongnam kŏmt'o" 己酉條約内容의史書別綜覽檢討, in *Taegu sahak* 大丘史學, 7–8 (December 1973): 281–300.

———, "Kiyu choyak sŏngnip simal kwa segyŏnsŏnsu e taehayŏ" 己酉條約成立始末과歲遣船數에對하여, in *Hangdo Pusan* 港都釜山, 4 (1964): 229–312.

Yi Ik 李瀷. *Sŏngho saesŏl* 星湖僿説. ʾ vols., Seoul: Kyŏng'in Sŏrim 景仁書林, 1967.

Yi Kyŏngjik 李景稷. *Pusangnok* 扶桑録, in *Kaikō sōsai*, 2: 111–205.

Yi Pyŏngdo 李丙燾, *et al. Han'guksa* 韓國史. 7 vols. Seoul: Ŭryu Munhwasa 乙酉文化社, 1959–1965.

Yi Wŏnsik 李元植, "Chōsen Shunso shinmi Tsushima no hōnichi ni tsuite—Tsushima ni okeru Nikkan bunka kōryū o chūshin ni" 朝鮮純祖辛未対馬の訪日について─対馬における日韓文化交流を中心に in *Chōsen gakuhō*, 72 (1974): 1–50.

———. "Jinran sōshō Shōun Taishi bokuseki no hakken ni yosete—Katō Kiyomasa jin'ei e no ōhen o chūshin ni" 壬乱僧将松雲大師墨跡の発見に寄せて─加藤清正陣営への往返を中心に, in *Kan* 韓 (*The Han*), 5.5–6 (May 1976): 218–224.

———, "Tennado (1682) Chōsen shinshi hishō Kō Seitai to Nihon bunshi no hitsudan shōshū ni tsuite" 天和度(1682)朝鮮信使裨将洪世泰と日本文士の筆談唱酬について, in *Chōsen gakuhō*, no. 98 (January 1981), pp. 1–62.

Yokoi Shōnan 横井小楠. comp. Yamazaki Seitō 山崎正董. 2 vols. Meiji Shoin 明治書院, 1938.

Yoshida Shōin zenshū 吉田松陰全集. comp., Yamaguchiken Kyōiku Kai

山口縣教育會 10 vols., Iwanami Shoten, 1935, repr. 12 vols., Iwanami Shoten, 1938–1940.

Yoshizane-kō go-kafu 義眞公御家譜. anon. MS, n.d. Sō Collection, Banshōin, Tsushima.

Zuikei Shūhō 瑞溪周鳳. *Zenrin Kokuhō ki* 善隣國寶記 in *Kaitei shiseki shūran*, 33 vols. Sumiya Shobō, 1968, 21 : 3–82.